T0328795

ESSAYS IN ECONOMICS

ESSAYS IN ECONOMICS
Theories, Theorizing, Facts, and Policies

Wassily Leontief

With a New Introduction by the Author

Routledge
Taylor & Francis Group

LONDON AND NEW YORK

First published 1985 by Transaction Publishers

Published 2019 by Routledge
2 Park Square, Milton Park, Abingdon, Oxon OX14 4RN
52 Vanderbilt Avenue, New York, NY 10017

Routledge is an imprint of the Taylor & Francis Group, an informa business

This Transaction paperback edition is published by arrangement
with M.E. Sharpe, Inc.

Library of Congress Catalog Number: 84-28090

Library of Congress Cataloging in Publication Data

Loentief, Wassily W., 1906-
      Essays in economics.

      Reprint. Originally published: White Plains, N.Y.:
International Arts and Sciences Press, c1966-1977.
With new introd.
      Includes bibliographical references and indexes.
      1.   Economics—Addresses, essays, lectures.
I.   Title.
HB171.L617   1985   330.1   84-28090
ISBN 0-87855-993-0 (pbk.)

The author gratefully acknowledges permission to reprint from the following publishers:
Indiana University for translation of Chapter 1 in *Foundations of Soviet Strategy for
Economic Growth—Selected Short Soviet Essays, 1924-1930,* ed. N. Spulber, copyright
© 1964 by Indiana University Press; *The American Economic Review* for Chapters 3 and 8;
The Review of Economics and Statistics for Chapters 4 and 6; North-Holland Publishing
Company for Chapters 5 and 9; and New York University Press for Chapter 11, originally
published in Charles C. Moskowitz Memorial Lectures of the College of Business and
Public Administration at New York University, *The Economic System in an Age of Discon-
tinuity: Long-Range Planning or Market Reliance?* By Wassily Leonief and Herbert Stein,
Copyright© 1976 by New York University.

ISBN 13: 978-0-87855-993-0 (pbk)

Contents

Preface

One of the secondary themes that comes up again and again, and with ever stronger emphasis in the essays collected in this volume, is neglect by academic economics of hard, systematic, empirical analysis in favor of elegant but vacuous formal, mainly mathematical, theoretical exercise.

In the course of the fifteen years elapsed since I spoke about this in my presidential address at the 1972 annual meeting of the American Economic Association ("Theoretical Assumptions and Nonobserved Facts") included in part 4 of this volume, this shift from factual inquiry into abstract speculation became even more pronounced. This prompts me to reproduce below, instead of writing a new foreword, a letter to the editor, published under the title "Academic Economics" in the July 9, 1982 issue of *Science* magazine.

Wassily Leontief
1984

To
My Parents
and
Estelle

Introduction to the Transaction edition

Wassily Leontief

Academic Economics

"A dismal performance. . . .What economists revealed most clearly was the extent to which their profession lags intellectually."[1] This editorial comment by the leading economic weekly (on the 1981 annual proceedings of the American Economic Association) says, essentially, that the "emperor is naked." But no one taking part in the elaborate and solemn procession of contemporary U.S. academic economics seems to know it, and those who do, do not dare speak up.

Two hundred years ago the founders of modern economic science—Adam Smith, Ricardo, Malthus, and John Stuart Mill—erected an imposing conceptual edifice based on the notion of the national economy as a self-regulating system of a great many different but interrelated, interdependent activities; a concept so powerful and fruitful that it gave impetus to Charles Darwin's pathbreaking work in his theory of evolution.

The central idea of what is now being referred to as classical economics attracted the attention of two mathematically trained engineers, Léon Walras and Vilfredo Pareto, who translated it with considerable refinement and elaboration into a concise language of algebra and calculus and called it the General Equilibrium Theory. Under the same neoclassical economics, this theory now constitutes the core of undergraduate and graduate instruction in this country.

As an empirical science, economics dealt from the outset with phenomena of common experience. Producing and consuming goods, buying and selling, and receiving income and spending it are activities engaging everyone's attention practically all the time. Even the application of the

[1] *Business Week,* 18 January 1982, p. 124.

scientific principle of quantification did not have to be initiated by the analyst himself—measuring and pricing constitute an integral part of the phenomena that he sets out to explain. Herein lies, however, the initial source of the trouble in which academic economics finds itself today.

By the time the facts of everyday experience were used up, economists were able to turn for bits and pieces of less accessible, more specialized information to government statistics. However, these statistics—compiled for administrative or business, but not scientific, purposes—fall short of what would have been required for concrete, more detailed understanding of the structure and functioning of a modern economic system.

Not having been subjected from the outset to the harsh discipline of systematic fact-finding, traditionally imposed on and accepted by their colleagues in the natural and historical sciences, economists developed a nearly irresistible predilection for deductive reasoning. Many entered the field after specializing in pure or applied mathematics. Page after page of professional economic journals are filled with mathematical formulas leading the reader from sets of more or less plausible but entirely arbitrary assumptions to precisely stated but irrelevant theoretical conclusions.

Nothing reveals the aversion of the great majority of today's academic economists for systematic empirical inquiry more than the methodological devices they employ to avoid or cut short the use of factual information. Instead of constructing theoretical models capable of preserving the identity of hundreds, even thousands, of variables needed for the concrete description and analysis of a modern economy, they first resort to "aggregation." The primary information, however detailed, is packaged in a relatively small number of bundles labeled "capital," "labor," "raw materials," "intermediate goods," "general price level," and so on. These bundles are then usually fitted into a model—a small system of equations describing the entire economy in terms of a small number of corresponding aggregative variables. The fitting, as a rule, is accomplished by means of least squares or another similar curve-fitting procedure.

A typical example of a theoretical production function intended to describe the relationship between, say, the amount of steel produced, y_1, and the quantities of the four different inputs, y_2, y_3, y_4, and y_5 needed to produce it is, for instance, described as follows:[2]

$$y_1^{\rho_1} = a_1 |G^2|^{\rho_1} + (1 - a_1) |G^3|^{\rho_1}$$

where:

[2] L.R. Christensen, D.W. Jorgenson, and L.J. Lau, "Transcendental logarithmic production functions," *Review of Economic Statistics* 55, no. 28, 1972.

$$-G^2 = [a_2|y_2|^{\rho_2} + (1 - a_2)\ |y_3|^{\rho_2}]^{\frac{1}{\rho_2}}$$
$$-G^3 = [a_3|y_4|^{\rho_3} + (1 - a_3)\ |y_5|^{\rho_3}]^{\frac{1}{\rho_3}}$$

or, alternatively:

$$\ln |G^2| = \tfrac{1}{2}\ln |y_2| + \tfrac{1}{2}\ln |y_3|$$
$$\ln |G^3| = \tfrac{1}{2}\ln |y_4| + \tfrac{1}{2}\ln |y_5|$$

or, finally:

$$\ln y_1 = a_1 \ln |G^2| + (1 - a_1) \ln |G^3|$$

To ask a manager of a steel plant or a metallurgical expert for information on the magnitude of the six parameters appearing in these six equations would make no sense. Hence, while the labels attached to symbolic variables and parameters of the theoretical equations tend to suggest that they could be identified with those directly observable in the real world, any attempt to do so is bound to fail: the problem of identification of aggregative equations after they have been reduced—that is, transformed, as they often are—for purposes of the curve-fitting process, was raised many years ago but still has not found a satisfactory solution. In the meantime, the procedure described above was standardized to such an extent that, to carry out a respectable econometric study, one simply had to construct a plausible and easily computable theoretical model and then secure—mostly from secondary or tertiary sources—a set of time series or cross-section data related in some direct or indirect way to its particular subject, insert these figures with a program of an appropriate statistical routine taken from the shelf into the computer, and finally publish the computer printouts with a more or less plausible interpretation of the numbers.

While the quality and coverage of official statistics have recently been permitted to deteriorate without eliciting determined protest on the part of their potential scientific users, masses of concrete, detailed information contained in technical journals, reports of engineering firms, and private marketing organizations are neglected.

A perusal of the contents of the *American Economic Review,* the flagship of academic economic periodicals over the last ten years, yields the picture in Table 1. These figures speak for themselves. In a prophetic statement of editorial policy, the managing editor of the *American Economic Review* observed ten years ago that "articles of mathematical economics and the finer points of economic theory occupy a more and more prominent place than ever before, while articles of a more empirical,

xi

Table 1
Percentages of Different Types of Articles Published in the
American Economic Review

Type of article	March 1972 to December 1976	March 1977 to December 1981
Mathematical models without any data	50.1	54.0
Analysis without mathematical formulation and data	21.2	11.6
Statistical methodology	0.6	0.5
Empirical analysis based on data generated by the author's initiative	0.8	1.4
Empirical analysis using indirect statistical inference based on data published or generated elsewhere	21.4	22.7
Empirical analysis not using indirect statistical inference based on data generated by author	0.0	0.5
Empirical analysis not using indirect statistical inference based on data generated or published elsewhere	5.4	7.4
Empirical analysis based on artificial simulations and experiments	0.5	1.9

policy-oriented or problem-solving character seem to appear less frequently."[3]

Year after year economic theorists continue to produce scores of mathematicl models and to explore in great detail their formal properties; and the econometricians fit algebraic functions of all possible shapes to essentially the same sets of data without being able to advance, in any perceptible way, a systematic understanding of the structure and operations of a real economic system.

How long will researchers working in adjoining fields, such as demography, sociology, and political science on the one hand and ecology, biology, health sciences, engineering, and other applied physical sciences on the other, abstain from expressing serious concern about the state of stable, stationary equilibrium and the splendid isolation in which academic economics now finds itself? That state is likely to be maintained as long as tenured members of leading economics departments continue to exercise tight control over the training, promotion, and research activities of their younger faculty members and, by means of peer review, of the senior members as well. The methods used to maintain intellectual discipline in this country's most influential economics departments[4] can occasionally remind one of those employed by the marines to maintain discipline on Parris Island.

[3] G.H. Borts, *American Economic Review* 62, no. 764, 1972.

[4] M.W. Reder, *Journal of Economic Literature* 20, no. 1, 1982.

PART ONE

1

Note on the pluralistic interpretation of history and the problem of interdisciplinary co-operation

The problem of the relationship between various disciplines in general and those belonging to the field of social studies in particular is quite old. In the past it preoccupied mainly philosophers of history and sociologists; now, however, economists and psychologists, political scientists and anthropologists, are being drawn more and more into the controversy and called upon to take a stand. The following few thoughts are advanced in realization of the far-reaching effect which the outcome of this current discussion is bound to have on the development of individual disciplines; they are also formulated in the strong conviction that even a special practitioner must take his stand not on some secondary positions but along the line of fundamental and central issues.

The subject of this note can be approached from a substantive point of view as a question about the nature of the forces operating throughout the process of historical development, or it can be dealt with methodologically as a problem of the role of various disciplines in the explanation of this process. In the last analysis the two formulations come to one and the same. For the purpose of the present discussion the second, with its implied acceptance of a more or less conventional distinction of the separate disciplines, seems to be preferable, since it centers our attention on the problem of interdisciplinary co-operation and competition.

From *The Journal of Philosophy*, Vol. XLV, No. 23, Nov. 4, 1948.

The monistic interpretation of history as compared with the pluralistic offers at first sight a peculiar advantage. It designates a chosen discipline as the principal explanatory instrument. From the point of view of consistent historical materialism, for example, the explanation of economic processes as developed by economic science is at the same time a basic explanation of the historical process in general. A consistent theological explanation would assign the role of such basic science to theology, the anthropological, to anthropology. What is, however, the role of any non-economic discipline, say, anthropology, as considered from the point of view of a historical materialist? He can deny it the separate existence of an autonomous discipline. That is, he can deny the existence of anthropological "laws of development" having their peculiar internal logic (I use this word in a loose Hegelian rather than in its strict formal sense) different from that of the laws of economic development. Or, if he does not ignore their existence entirely, he must adhere to a peculiar theory of correspondence, according to which the autonomous anthropological line of argument must have a rather singular property of leading to exactly the same factual implication, which can be derived from an independent economic argument. Such methodological parallelism would, of course, be compatible with a philosophical belief in the primacy of the economic factor in history. It would, however, be equally compatible with the fundamental belief in the primacy of anthropological laws. Operationally, that is, for purposes of explanation of past not to say possible predictions of future events, the economic and anthropological interpretation of history would be strictly equivalent.

Turning to the actual present-day state of all the established disciplines which have some bearing on the explanation of the historical process, one can observe first, that each one of them, be it economics, anthropology, linguistics, or geography, seems to have established its own analytical pattern and has achieved at least some explanatory successes, and, second, that these separate patterns are entirely autonomous, that is, irreducible into each other. This state of affairs, it must be admitted, does not exclude the possibility that in the course of some future developments perfect reduction formulae will be found leading to the establishment of complete parallelism between all the various lines of argument, which incidentally would mean simultaneous vindication of all the different monistic interpretations of history.

At present, however, we face the choice between obdurate insistence on some monistic interpretation—which means overtaxing the analytical resources of one, chosen discipline and neglecting the capacities of all the others—or, practical pluralism. The nature of the pluralistic interpretation is the main subject of the following remarks.

"To consider all the different aspects of the problem." No other proposition sounds as sensible and even platitudinous when uttered in the form of general methodological advice and hardly any turns out to be as devoid of any concrete meaning in actual application. Stripped of superfluous verbiage, an interpretation which is supposed to take into account the relevant political, economic, and, say, anthropological factors proves to be similar to the decision arrived at by counting the pros and cons. The often repeated comparison with a parallelogram of forces is a wrong analogy since the separate factors are basically incommensurable, each behaving in this case according to its own "law of motion."

Examining various instances of what appears to be a successful explanation, or at least interpretation, of historical development, one notices that in every case the argument has actually been conducted in terms of one peculiar type of "necessity"—economic in some cases, psychological, or even purely physical in other cases. The pluralistic character of any single explanation reveals itself not in simultaneous application of essentially disparate types of considerations but rather in the ready shift from one type of interpretation to another. The justification of such methodological eclecticism lies—and this is the principal point of the argument that follows—in the limited nature of any type of interpretation or causation (I use these two terms interchangeably). Neither the economic, nor the anthropological, or, say, geographical argument can, in the present state of the development of the respective disciplines, lead to statement of uniquely defined necessities. Considering any given sequence of events alternatively in the

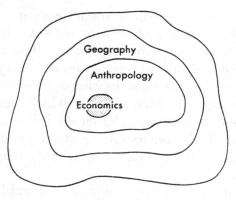

Figure 1

light of each one of such different approaches, one can at best assign it to as many different ranges of "possibilities." Although the internal logics of the respective disciplines are incommensurable, the various ranges of possibilities thus derived are comparable, since all of them are described in terms of alternative developments of the same particular process. Using the familiar illustrative device, one can describe the set of all imaginable developments growing out of a particular situation as a large area enclosed by the approximately circular boundary and the particular ranges of possible developments admissible from the point of view of each of the separate disciplines as contained in smaller areas drawn in within that larger area of "all conceivable developments." The actual course of events must necessarily fall within the range of possibilities which appear to be admissible from the point of view of every one of the individual disciplines. That is, it must necessarily fall within the area enclosed by every one of the smaller circles. Stated in negative terms it means that no development declared to be impossible from the point of view of any one of the separate disciplines can actually take place. This requirement implies, of course, that the size and the position of the smaller "circles" is such that they would overlap each other in some portion of the area of all conceivable developments.

Facing the situation in which such area of common overlap does

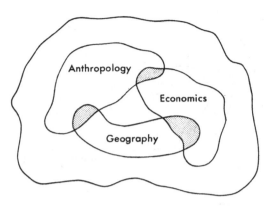

Figure 2

not seem to exist, as, for example, in Figure 2—where the range of anthropological possibilities includes some economic and also some geographic ones but none which are common to both of them —one must come to the inescapable conclusion that at least one of these three kinds of reasoning is definitely wrong.

Considering the non-contradictory situations in which an area of general overlap actually does exist, one can distinguish a number of different cases. Figure 1 describes the simplest one. Here economics applied alone obviously gives the best possible explanation. The shaded area represents the narrowest range of possible developments although it is also compatible with both the anthropological and also the geographical explanation. Taking into account either one of these would in that particular instance not have improved the result obtained on the basis of a purely economic argument alone.

A necessary co-operation between two disciplines is called for, however, in the case described in Figure 3. Here the closest explanation will be obtained by combining the economic and the anthropological line of reasoning. It is important to emphasize that each of the two lines of argument retains in this as in any other case its peculiar character. The co-operation between the sciences consists in superimposition of two sets of results independently obtained. This does not mean, of course, that the se-

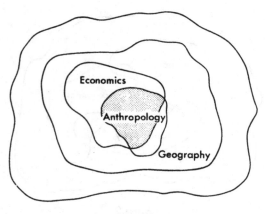

Figure 3

quence in which one proceeds to take up the two lines of argument is entirely irrelevant. On the contrary, insofar as the smallest (shaded) range of possible developments coincides more nearly with the area of anthropological "possibilities," it is advisable to explore this area first and take up the economic aspects of the given process next. In this way one might be able to avoid the exploration of the vast part of the region included in economics but finally eliminated through its superimposition over anthropology. The size of the "surplus area" within anthropology is in this case obviously much smaller than the size of the surplus area of the complete range of economic possibilities.

If the foregoing analysis is correct, the efficiency or, better, the usefulness of one type of approach as compared with any other lies not so much in its ability to interpret the particular sequence of events in terms of its peculiar type of analysis—since any one of the alternative approaches can necessarily do the same—but rather in its power to exclude from the range of all admissible possibilities certain sequences which form the point of view of all the other disciplines seem to be entirely possible.

To emphasize the pragmatic implications of this argument one might say that there exists no logical necessity for the different experts (called in to explain some particular event) to work together. On the contrary, each one of them could be placed in a separate room and asked to work out the largest range of sequences which appear to be admissible from the point of view of his particular discipline. Then an outsider could collect the separate reports, superimpose them, conceptually speaking, over each other, and obtain the best possible solution of the problem at hand. At the end it might be found that some experts have been working in vain since the explanatory regions derived by them prove finally to be superseded by the narrower, that is, more specific, explanations, given by the other members of the team. It is for this reason that an initial consultation among all the participants can be of some use. An approximate, preliminary comparison of their respective ranges might have allowed immediate elimination of those specialists whose final contribution could obviously not have improved the ultimate result.

The advantages of such preliminary conference—not to mention of arrangements enabling the representatives of various disciplines to keep in touch with each other throughout the whole procedure—can occasionally be outweighed by a peculiar practical or, better to say, psychological, disadvantage. Should some of the potentially superfluous experts be desirous of "remaining in the game," they would, after preliminary consultations, be tempted to trim, consciously or unconsciously, the full range of possibilities admissible from their own particular point of view so as to make it appear "at least as good" as the competing approaches. To this end it would be sufficient for them to stress the (obvious) fact that they too can get a plausible interpretation of a given course of events, but fail to mention their unfortunate ability to explain also some alternative developments which can be proven to be impossible in the light of other types of analysis.

Up to this point the discussion was centered on the examination of a single event or a short sequence which could have been treated as a single unit of happening. The long chains of development which typically come up in historical analysis can naturally be subdivided into a larger or smaller number of individual links. Any one of these has to be examined and explained separately, each individual explanation being constructed along the lines described above. The configuration of the explanatory ranges of various disciplines as applied to the analysis of consecutive links in a given chain of events will often vary in the same way as the colored pieces in a kaleidoscope change their position after it has been shaken: the pattern of explanation will very likely change from one link of the chain to another. Purely anthropological interpretation might prove to be the most efficient at one juncture, a purely economic one at the next, and a combination of the two with, say, the geographical approach will possibly give the best results at some later stage. No wonder the proponents of various monistic interpretations of history are nearly always able to point out some specific instances in which their favorite discipline can explain, all by itself, the particular course of events. The error which they commit in generalizing their respective claims is, however, more dangerous than that committed by those non-discriminating pluralists who insist on combining all possible approaches in every case. The latter by the process of systematic elimination that was described above can in the end arrive at the combination of explanatory principles best suited to a particular situation, while the former, in refusing to take account of any other but their pet factors, run a serious risk of contenting themselves with "partial" interpretation which could be markedly improved, that is, narrowed down, by introduction of additional, limiting considerations.

The choice of the most suitable explanatory combination of disciplines depends not only on the nature of the event which has to be explained; it is also determined by the state of development of each of the separate sciences involved. Any advancement in economics would, for example, affect (insofar as it is at all relevant to the issue at hand) our graphs by narrowing down the area of developments admissible from the point of view of economic analysis. The same applies, of course, to all other disciplines. Such change might or might not affect the nature of the best explanatory scheme, depending on whether it does or does not modify the shape of the (shaded) narrowest area of the most restricted possibilities. Without elaborating that line of argument it is sufficient to point out that occasionally a very slight advancement will transform a discipline—which formerly should have been entirely disregarded in the analysis of a particular situation—into a most important, maybe the single element, of the most efficient explanatory scheme.

But what about the ultimate end of scientific progress? Extrapolating *ad infinitum* the process in the course of which each one of the separate areas of "unexcluded possibilities" shrinks more and more, we would arrive at a final state in which every one of them is ultimately reduced to a single point of absolute certainty and more than that: this limiting point must necessarily be the same for all the alternative approaches, since, had it not been the same, this final situation would be similar to that depicted in Figure 2 above: the explanations offered by separate sciences would appear to be mutually exclusive, that is, contradictory. This conclusion is actually not so paradoxical as it appears to be at the first sight. It expresses the often expounded idea of the unity of science. Such unity could, however, actually be realized only if all individual disciplines had already reached the state of ultimate perfection and, thus merging with each other, lost their separate identities.

The well-known merger of certain parts of modern physics and chemistry indicates the general nature of this process of gradual unification. A similar relationship seems to have lately been established, for example, between psychology and certain aspects of anthropology. This is the kind of development envisaged by Auguste Comte in his hierarchical classification of sciences: a systematic absorption of the special by the more general, that is, more "basic," type of analysis. The former loses in such a process its logical sovereignty and becomes at best a conveniently manageable province of the latter.

One of the most serious errors committed by some of the contemporary proponents of the doctrine of unity of science and many promoters of interdisciplinary co-operation is that they forget that the ideal age is not yet here. Far from being members of a well-integrated family of sciences, the individual disciplines still retain for the most part their sovereignty. The interrelationship and collaboration between such essentially independent analytical systems poses a peculiar problem which requires a quite special solution. This note is intended to indicate the general direction in which such solution might be sought.

2

When should history be written backwards?

"Prédire les gros évènements de l'avenir n'est pas . . . un tour de force plus extraordinaire que celui de deviner le passé . . . Si les évènements accomplis ont laissé des traces, il est vraisemblable d'imaginer que les évènements à venir ont leurs racines."

HONORÉ DE BALZAC, *Le Cousin Pons.*

I

At the time when King Francis the First founded this Collège de France, the growth of National Income and the advance of science and the arts were already favored subjects of scholarly discourse. Four hundred years went by and essentially the same problems of economic growth seem to be of primary concern to economic theorists, not to mention economic historians and practical politicians.

Under the cold, neutral light of scientific inquiry the phenomena of development and progress—or of decline, as the case may be—present themselves to the investigator as various aspects of the process of change, that is, of a well-ordered sequence of events forming an infinite chain of causes and effects stretching from the past through the present and into the not yet realized future.

The first successful attempts to combine well-articulated theoretical reasoning with systematic, whenever possible, numerical description of the observed fact was undertaken by students of economic change only some thirty years ago. The mathematical theory of dynamic systems supplied, for obvious reasons, the

This is a translation from the French of a lecture given at the Collège de France in March 1962, published in the *Economic History Review*, Second Series, Vol. XVI, No. 1, 1963.

fundamental notions which continue to make up the formal basis of most analysis of this kind. This explains why in the critical appraisal of new models shown—in the United States, at least—by the well-known econometric designers once or even twice a year, the question of dynamic stability plays such an important, not to say decisive, role. The models adjudged as stable pass muster; those which are found to be unstable are, as a rule, rejected out of hand. But why this predilection for stable systems?

I I

Figures 1a and 1b below depict in graphic terms two very simple dynamic systems. Each represents a typical solution of a set of two linear differential, or difference, equations in two variables, X_1, and X_2. In a schematic description of a developing national economy one of these variables might measure, for example, the output of Consumers' Goods and the other the output of Producers', that is, investment, Goods. The state of such a system at any given time can thus be represented on the graph by a single point; magnitude, X_1, of the corresponding output of Consumers' Goods being measured along the horizontal, and that of Producers' Goods, X_2, along the vertical axis. The changes of both outputs, characterizing the past and the future development of the system, are traced by the curved line passing through that particular point. The time direction of its movement along that path is marked by the little arrows.

All the developmental trajectories of the system described on graph 1a converge (in the direction of the arrows) toward the "long run equilibrium" path, of. This means that with the passage of time the outputs of the two sectors of the particular economy will gradually approach a ratio described by the slope of that long-run equilibrium line. Hence, the system is called stable. The system presented in graph 1b for analogous reasons is called unstable. Starting from any point—not located on the straight line of—that system in its movement along the corresponding path in the direction indicated by the arrow will progressively diverge from that "equilibrium path."

13

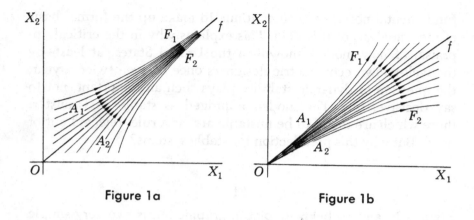

Figure 1a   Figure 1b

Since the notion of stability seems to carry with it the connotation of something good and that of instability of something bad, most builders of economic models show, as I said above, decided preference for systems which are stable and discard those which are not. I suggest instead that the "strategy" of historical inquiry should in each instance be adjusted to the equilibrium properties of the dynamic systems that seem to fit best the particular developmental process we have set out to explain.[1]

By explanation of a developmental process, I simply mean prediction of the state of the corresponding dynamic system at some particular point of time; a prediction based on direct information of the position of the same system as observed in some other point of time. Assuming that its internal structure is known and is described by a set of all possible developmental paths—such as, for example, are represented on graphs 1a or 1b—such "prediction" depends accordingly on our ability to ascertain with sufficient accuracy the position of that system in some base year.

---

[1] The reference is made here to the properties of the theoretical system rather than of the economic process to which it is to be applied because the observed, yet unanalyzed, facts like uncut cloth have no shape. Only when cut up to shape according to a superimposed theoretical pattern do they acquire formal properties such as those which distinguish stable from unstable dynamic systems.

Since direct observation of social and economic phenomena is very difficult, it is particularly important for an economic historian to know in advance what effects the errors, which are bound to creep into his base-year observation, would have on the accuracy of the prediction of the position of the system in the other years.

In a stable system represented in Fig. 1a—whatever its initial position might be, for example, A_1 or A_2—the corresponding developmental paths, when followed in the direction of the flow of time, inevitably lead toward the small region, F, comprising F_1 and F_2. This means that even if the historian makes a considerable error in ascertaining the initial position of the system and takes it to be located, for example, in region A_1—while in fact its true location at that time was in A_2—his prediction, that with the passage of time that system will pass through region F_1 would nevertheless turn out to be nearly correct. From A_2 the current of change will actually carry the system into F_2, that is, which lies in the immediate neighborhood of F_1. If the dynamic process which we have set out to explain happens to be stable, the passage of time will correct, at least so far as the prediction of the future is concerned, the error committed in the observation of the past.

The situation is, however, quite different when the dynamic system confronting the historian is unstable. The divergent layout of time paths in Fig. 1b leads from A_1 to F_2, but from A_2 it leads into F_1. A starting point located in A_1 might be situated in a very close vicinity of another starting point located in A_2; but this small difference, and nothing else, explains why after a sufficiently long interval of time the process of dynamic change would carry the system in one instance into F_1 and in another instance into F_2. A historian who sets out to explain the development of such a system by tracing the sequence of events in time is indeed embarking on a very exacting, not to say practically impossible, enterprise. A small, hardly perceptible mistake in the description of the original base-year position of an unstable dynamic system is bound to bring about a major error in the prediction, that is, explanation of its later states. With the increase in the interval of time that separates the target year of the prediction from its base, the error will become greater and greater.

I V

But is it necessary in analyzing the sequence of events in a developmental process to trace the causal connections between them in following the flow of time? A prophet has, of course, no choice in this respect since the factual information on which he bases his predictions must of necessity be confined to the past. But the historian whose interest is confined to events which have already occurred, can choose to describe and to explain their sequence by moving against time instead of floating downstream with it. Geologists, paleontologists, and cosmologists do it as a matter of course. Why should the student of human history not do the same?

Despite the great advances in documentation and in method of statistical description attained in recent years, our factual knowledge even of the contemporary economy and society is still very incomplete; it becomes more and more fragmentary as the empirical inquiry turns from the present to the past.

In following the paths of historical development—as they are represented, for example, on the two adjoining graphs—in the direction of time, the analyst finds himself, in most instances, engaged in the rather thankless task of trying to derive known from unknown or, at least, better-known from less well-known facts. Would it not be much more efficient to reverse this procedure? By establishing the base of his operations, that is, the principal store of primary factual information in the present or a very recent past, and then moving on backward with the help of theoretical weapons step by step toward the more and more distant past, the analytical historian could make most effective use of the limited amount of direct factual information to which he usually has access.

This method of writing analytical history backwards, that is, from the present into the past, is greatly favored by the configuration of developmental paths which characterize dynamic systems defined as unstable.

16

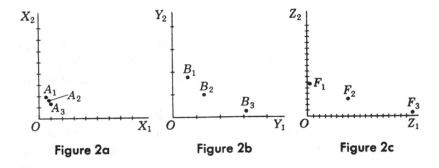

Figure 2a   Figure 2b   Figure 2c

If it were true that a slight difference in the state of the emperor's health—a difference the existence of which could hardly be established by direct observation and even less so by reliable documentation—could have determined the outcome of a crucial battle and thus have had a decisive effect on subsequent political, social, and economic developments in France and Europe, it is very doubtful that an even most painstaking inquiry into the medical history of Napoleon I could yield a firm factual basis for a convincing explanation of the social and economic state of Europe in, say, 1848. On the contrary, if the European system were actually unstable in a way implied by the aforementioned historical hypothesis, even a very approximate familiarity with the state of Europe in 1848 should permit the biographer of Napoleon to conclude, despite the absence of any evidence of a direct kind, that the emperor must have indeed been suffering from a slight head cold on the day of the fateful battle.

The example presented above is admittedly somewhat facetious, but the argument which it serves to illustrate is not. So long as research remains essentially descriptive, the order in which one takes up the study of the successive stages of a developmental process has little importance. However, as soon as more exacting causal analysis comes into play, "backward" explanation (in which the earlier events are derived from those which have occurred later) might prove to be much more effective than the forward-looking, conventional approach. The stability properties of the dynamic system used must influence decisively the choice between the two.

17

V

The question of a possible dependence between the state of an entire country and of the state of health of single men leads naturally to the problem of qualitative change as an object of quantitative analysis.

The construction of long-run statistical series which are supposed to represent a quantitative description of the development of National Income, to measure the growing Productivity of Labor and so on, is now considered to constitute a practically indispensable preliminary stage of every serious analysis of economic change. Although, in many instances, such figures give a good description of prevailing general trends, the methodological position according to which numerical comparison constitutes the very basis of all empirical inquiry does not seem to be justified either in terms of the internal logic of the quantitative method in general, or its application to the study of economic change in particular. When a historical time series shows that the Gross National Product of some particular country is four times as large as it was sixty years ago, or that the productivity of the transportation industry has increased by 300 per cent from 1860 to 1960, the difference between the horse-drawn carriage, the railroad of 1860, the car and the airplane of 1960 seems to be neglected; and when we are told that in the preliminary calculation each type of vehicle has been given its proper weight before being included in the corresponding aggregate, this only means that these long-time series do not describe directly the observed facts, but rather represent results of more or less arbitrary numerical manipulations.

The weakness of aggregative indices is, of course, not an exclusive fault of historical statistics; in other fields of empirical analysis—for example, in interregional comparisons—it always leads us from the nearly unlimited diversity of the immediately observed world into the simplified realm of aggregative magnitudes which can be described and analyzed with greater ease since the number of distinct variables in it is relatively small. The way leading from one into the other world is, however, a one-way route. We cannot pass from the aggregative concept to the economic phenom-

18

ena as they have been directly observed any more that we can turn an omelette into the whole eggs from which it has been made. This is why the economic analysis in its most aggregative, but because of that also most systematic and easily manageable, form carries with it a faint but unmistakable air of unreality.

The unreality of the aggregative approach can be reduced only through the use of less aggregative models. An analytical system which permits us to distinguish horse-carriages from cars and cars from airplanes can obviously maintain a closer, less equivocal relationship to the observed facts than a system that leaves no room for such qualitative distinctions. This means, however, that in shifting from the more summary to more detailed descriptions of economic change we will have to give up the use of long aggregative time series and replace them by a larger number of less aggregative series. Each one of them will of necessity be shorter, but also more definite in its qualitative and consequently in its quantitative content.

Within the framework of a reasonable disaggregated analytical scheme a comparison of the total number of transportation vehicles produced in the years 1860 and 1960 makes little sense. Neither is such a comparison required for an explanation of the developmental process extended over the long period of time comprising both these years.

"Comparativism" as a method of scientific inquiry is greatly overrated. In economic research, particularly of a quantitative kind, it offers convenient refuge to unimaginative minds. If one is at a loss in finding an effective analytical interpretation of a given set of facts, it is always possible to compare, particularly if one is ready to disregard destinations. But after the comparison is completed, what next? Too often one turns to the comparison of something else.

The logic of mathematical analysis permits us to construct and to employ, in describing the observed facts, systems comprising quantitative relationships between objects which possess different dimensions and hence are incommensurable and incomparable. The economist works constantly with these kinds of relationships. Human labor is measured in hours, days, or years; its output, if it consists of cloth, in yards, in pages, or words, if it happens to be the product of a typist. Thus labor and its output are certainly incommensurable. Nevertheless, the economic analysis of production is based to a large extent on the study of the technologically determined quantitative relationships between the amount of labor absorbed by a given plant or industry and the level of its physical output, both quantities being measured in terms of different qualitatively incomparable physical units.

In the analysis of economic change we study the sequential dependence of the successive states of the economic system. If both the quality and the quantity of a particular good happen to remain the same from one year to another, still a significant difference between these two otherwise identical items can and should be registered along the time dimension. A car produced in 1960 and an identical car produced in 1961 must be distinguished since in the study of economic change time itself is certainly a significant dimension.

The interdependence between the quantities of the same good produced or consumed in different periods of time can be described and treated analytically exactly in the same way as the interdependence between two different goods belonging to the same period of time. Once this is admitted, it becomes evident that no fundamental difficulty can arise in describing the interdependence between the quantities of goods which differ from each other not only in respect to their position in time, but also in terms of other so-called qualitative dimensions.

The observation that the U.S. steel output (measured in tons) in 1961 was twice—or half—as large as the labor input (measured in man years) of iron mining in 1960 makes little sense if these two "incommensurable" quantities were to be compared as one compares in conventional time-series analysis the output of steel in 1960 and in 1961. However, within the framework of a (dynamic) analytical system such quantitative relationship between the labor input of one year and the steel output of the next can play a significant explanatory role. If neither of the two goods linked in this kind of "dated" relationship in fact existed at the same time as the other—if the labor and the steel of 1961 were, for example, qualitatively different from the steel and labor of 1960—or even if the commodity called "steel" did not exist at all in 1960—the material contents and the formal structure of the analytical procedure described above would still remain the same.

The three small graphs (p. 17) depict, like successive images on a strip of a cinematographic film, the development of a dynamic system involving qualitative change over three successive periods (or points) of time. Six different goods, each measured in different and essentially incomparable physical units, appear successfully on the screen, two at a time: X_1 and X_2 in the first, Y_1 and Y_2 in the second, and Z_1 and Z_2 in the third year.

Among the infinity of possible developmental paths, only three are traced on our graphs. The first starts at point A_1 in Fig. 2a, passes through B_1 in Fig. 2b and leads to F_1 in Fig. 2c; the second goes from A_2 through B_2 to F_2; and the third from A_3 through B_3 to F_3.

In comparing the relative position of the three points on each graph, we see that a relatively small shift from the starting point A_1 to the starting point A_2 in period one would lead to larger shift —from B_1 to B_2—in the next period represented on Fig. 2b and a still greater displacement—from F_1 to F_2—in Fig. 2c. This means that a small displacement in the original position of the time period one, will result in a relatively larger shift in the time period two, and a still larger in the time period three. The system is unstable. The classical notion of stability that we have discussed in detail before can obviously be applied also to dynamic systems that involve qualitative change. Thus observation on the differences between strategy of empirical research appropriate to stable and unstable systems should be applicable in this case too.

3

Mathematics in economics

1 Gibbs and mathematical economics.

American economists have a good and special reason to honor J. Willard Gibbs. The late Professor Irving Fisher—the author of the earliest monograph on Mathematical Economics published on this side of the Atlantic and one of the truly great economists this country has produced—was a pupil of Gibbs. He was in 1929 the first to represent social sciences in this series of memorial lectures. The second was Professor Edwin B. Wilson, mathematician and economist, also one of Gibbs's immediate disciples, and author of the early treatise on Vector Analysis based on his teacher's original lectures on that subject.

Professor Fisher and Professor Wilson were leading spirits in the organization—twenty-three years ago—of the international Econometric Society which now unites 2500 economic statisticians and economists who claim the ability to speak—or at least to understand when spoken to—the "language of mathematics" which Josiah Gibbs used with such compelling and poetic power.

I did not know Gibbs and I am not a mathematician. I cannot present to you personal reminiscences about this great man nor am I able to develop before you any one particular application of

The twenty-seventh Josiah Willard Gibbs Lecture, delivered at Baltimore, Maryland on December 28, 1953, under the auspices of the American Mathematical Society; published in the *Bulletin of the American Mathematical Society*, Vol. 60, No. 3, May 1954.

mathematics to economics—which could possibly be of technical interest to a professional mathematician. I will try instead to survey the logical structure of the present-day economic theory emphasizing formal aspects of some of the problems which it faces and pointing out the mathematical procedures used for this solution. The views to be presented are, of course, not necessarily shared by other economists. Even leaving out those who feel with Lord Keynes that mathematical economics is "mere concoctions," theoretical disagreements and methodological controversies keep us from sinking into the state of complacent unanimity.

2 The general structure of economic theory.

The object of economic analysis is the observed, or at least the observable, economic process. The typical variables in terms of which an economic system is described are the amounts of various goods and services produced, consumed, added to and subtracted from existing stocks, sold and purchased; also the prices at which these purchases and sales are made.

The available quantities of natural and human resources, the state of technical knowledge, and the nature of consumers' preferences (with those, in our modern much regulated economy, one must mention also the aims and preferences of the regulating governmental authorities)—all described within the setting of a specific institutional framework—constitute what might be called the operating conditions of the particular economic system. These are the "data" which in verbal analysis are used to explain the "unknown" outputs, employment, prices, investments, and so on.

Translated into mathematical language this means that the available quantities of natural and human resources, the state of technical knowledge, and consumers' preferences determine the structure of equations (or inequalities) which in their turn determine the values taken on by what we choose to define as the dependent "variables" of the economic system.

The first systematically formulated mathematical theory of general Economic Equilibrium was constructed just about seventy-five years ago by Léon Walras.[1] He incorporated in it much of the so-called classical theory developed in the writings of the great English and French economists of the late eighteenth and early nineteenth centuries. Some essential pieces of the conceptual apparatus used by Walras—such, for example, as the concepts of supply and demand functions and the notion of diminishing marginal utility—were already cast in mathematical form by such men as Daniel Bernoulli,[2] Augustin Cournot,[3] and E. J. Dupuit.[4]

Elaborated and extended by Vilfredo Pareto[5] and his contemporaries and successors, the general theory of economic interdependence is gradually being combined—into what promises to become a unified logical structure—with two other fields of analytical inquiry, the theory of market mechanism and the analysis of the behavior of an individual firm and of a separate household.

3 Maximizing behavior.

It is in this latter connection, in explanation of the operation of the ultimate decision-making units, that the common notion of "economic behavior" finds its principal analytic application.

Consider the profit maximizing firm. It purchases or hires certain commodities and services and utilizes them for the production of other commodities or services. The production process itself can be described as a transformation of one set of variables —the inputs, into another—the outputs. The quantitative relationships between the inputs and the outputs are determined by the set of all available technological alternatives.

The outlays, the costs, incurred by the firm can obviously be considered as a function of the input combination used, while its gross revenue depends upon the amounts of its outputs. Among all the input-output combinations technically attainable, the firm chooses the one which maximizes the difference between its total costs and revenue.

In a simple case in which all available transformation possibilities are stated in the form of one or more well-behaving "production functions" with continuous derivatives throughout the entire relevant range, a local maximum can be described by a set of simple equations involving its first partial derivatives and parameters entering the profit function such, for example, as the prices of all commodities sold and purchased.

It is not surprising that these conditions were discovered and stated by some economists verbally without any recourse to mathematics. A correct formulation and interpretation of the secondary conditions for a maximum, involving inequalities in higher derivatives, had, however, to wait for the introduction into the argument of formal calculus.

The problem becomes more intricate as soon as the well-behaving continuous production functions are replaced by the more realistic description of technical input-output relationships involving linearities, discontinuities, and inequalities. Then the question concerning the optimization conditions in the small is replaced by their study in the large. Under the name of "linear programming" much advanced work has, for example, been done recently on the problem of determining maxima with the constraining transformation functions stated in the form of a set of positive vectors; the positive and negative components of each vector describe in this case the sets of outputs and, respectively, inputs corresponding to the operation on a unit level of one particular kind of productive activity. Differential calculus and elementary algebra—the two traditional tools of the mathematical economist—are being thus replaced or at least supplemented by those of topology and matrix algebra.

The explanation of consumer's behavior is developed along similar lines. A household like a firm has an income (derived from the sales of the services of persons or property rights) and an outlay; to the transformation functions of the firm there corresponds the utility function of the household. It describes the level of satisfaction corresponding to the amounts of goods and services consumed.

Within the constraints imposed by its budget, the household is supposed to select a combination of goods and services which brings it to the highest level of satisfaction. In early theories, utility was treated as a measurable quantity. On closer examination, its cardinal measurement turned out to be neither necessary for formulation and solution of the maximum problem at hand nor, essentially for that very reason, operational in terms of actual experience.

Consider two individuals facing identical budgetary restrictions. If one of them derives from any combination of commodities consumed, say, twice as much satisfaction as the other, both will obviously find their respective utilities maximized by exactly the same sets of purchases. Insofar as a consumer's observed movements through commodity space constitute the only objective source of information about the shape of his utility function, ordinal comparison of its different levels is all that can be achieved or required for explanatory purposes.

This is where the matter stood till the recently revived interest in the old eighteenth-century problem of choice under conditions of uncertainty led to renewed attempts to rehabilitate the cardinal utility function. The argument hinges on the assertion[6] that from the point of view of "rational" behavior, if,

(a) $U(X_1)$ and $U(X_2)$ are the utility levels associated in the mind of a decision-making consumer with certain but alternative possession of the two specific commodity combinations, X_1 and X_2, and

(b) p is a true positive fraction such that

(c) this consumer, when offered the choice between the "chance with the probability p of possessing X_1" and "the chance with the probability $(1 - p)$ of possessing X_2" will find both these offers to be equally desirable, then,

$$\frac{U(X_1)}{U(X_2)} = \frac{(1-p)}{p}.$$

Once this is admitted, a cardinal comparison of utilities must obviously be accepted as operationally feasible. Whether a particular individual actually behaves in accordance with this assertion or not can be empirically tested—through introduction of a third commodity combination, X_3, with an accompanying probability, q. Two choices, one between the chances involving $U(X_3)$ and $U(X_1)$, and another involving $U(X_3)$ and $U(X_2)$, should lead to measures consistent with the comparison of $U(X_1)$ and $U(X_2)$ as shown above. If they do not, the subject of the experiment is declared to be "irrational." The reference to "rational" or, should I say, "economic" behavior as used in this connection is intended to justify the acceptance of a crucial proposition "ex definitione." Substantively, it denies the phenomenon of the pleasure (the utility) of gambling by disallowing the possibility of using a utility function of the more general form, such, for example, as $U(X_1, p)$.

In this, as in many other similar instances, the economist must be prepared to make up his mind whether he is aiming at a positive explanation of observed facts or at setting up normative rules for, in some sense, "reasonable" behavior and tracing out their logical implications.

In the discussion of public economic policies—in contrast to the analysis of individual choice—the normative character of the problem has been clearly and generally recognized. Here the mathematical approach has crystallized the analysis around the axiomatic formulation of the (desirable or conventional) properties of the "social welfare function." Social utility is usually postulated as a function of the ordinally described personal utility levels attained by each of the individual members of the society in question.

The only other property on which something like a general consensus of opinion seems to exist is that "the social welfare is increased whenever at least one of the individual utilities on which it depends is raised while none is reduced." Without any furthermore stringent limitation on its possible shape, such a social welfare function allows only a partial ordering of all possible combinations of individual utility levels. A much more specific description of its properties would have to be required if the social welfare function were to reflect—in axiomatic formulation—concrete normative judgments pertaining, for example, to the problem of income distribution. The struggle to increase the utility levels of some groups of individuals at the cost of reducing the welfare of others constitutes, no doubt, the core of much of the present-day politico-economic controversy.

The important contribution of the mathematical approach to our thinking on such controversial issues consists in showing how difficult it actually is to formulate in concise operational terms any specific normative attitude toward questions of public welfare in general and the problem of equitable distribution of income in particular.

4 Consistency criteria in the theory of interdependent choices.

The analysis of the behavior of individual firms and households is and—if it has to have explanatory rather than normative significance—should be not more than a direct translation into concise mathematical language of problems of maximizing choice as seen from the actual decision-makers' point of view. The restraining relations and parameters which the economist assumes as "given" must, of course, be precisely those which the household or firm actually considers as being independent of its action, and the set of variables—the optimal combination of which the theorist explains—must indeed include all those, and only those, on which the real economic units actually operate in putting into effect their profit or, respectively, utility maximizing decisions.

So long as one does not radically widen the conventional universe of economic discourse, the invariance of technological transformation functions in respect to changes in specific input combinations can be taken for granted. The same, however, cannot be said about the functions and parameters which—although they are treated as fixed constraints in the explanation of individual maximizing behavior—within the larger framework of the general theory of economic interdependence turn up in the role of dependent variables rather than of "given" data.

Farmer Jones, when he decides on the most profitable number of hogs to grow, takes into account the market price at which they can be sold. In doing so, he most likely considers that price as "given," that is, to be practically independent of the specific outcome of that decision. In explaining farmer Jones's output, the economist accordingly treats the price as one of the parameters entering the solution of the corresponding profit maximization problem.

In his very next step, in presenting the general equilibrium theory (which I will presently take up), the economist lists all prices —including the price of hogs—among the unknowns to be determined through the solution of an appropriate system of equations. In particular, he then proceeds to explain, in terms of that system, why the price of hogs would fall if all farmers, say, for experimental purposes, had produced and thrown on the market 10 per cent more hogs than before. Another argument based on the same general equilibrium equations shows that, within the range of output variations accessible to him, farmer Jones's belief in his own inability to affect the market price of hogs to any appreciable extent is indeed entirely correct. If, however, it had turned out—again within the framework of the general equilibrium theory—that farmer Jones's individual action could have influenced the price of hogs—as indeed would have been the case had he owned half of all the hogs in the country—the entire analysis in both its parts would have been false. The explanation of farmer Jones's maximizing behavior, because it was derived from an assumption that now proved to be inconsistent with the implication of further general equilibrium analysis based on that very explanation, the general equilibrium analysis, obviously would be false for the same reason.

All problems dealt with in the analysis of market behavior lead to such questions of theoretical consistency. Their logical structure is frequently quite subtle and the circular test outlined above is difficult to apply without recourse to mathematical formulation.

The analysis of duopoly and oligopoly, that is, of the relationships between two or few mutually interdependent sellers, also the explanation of bilateral monopoly, a situation in which a single seller faces a sole buyer, each clearly and appreciably affecting by his actions the other's profit, all lead to the same theoretical problem—the explanation of maximizing behavior of two or more mutually interdependent units.

Beginning with Augustin Cournot,[3] that is, for over a century, mathematical economists have wrestled with that question without apparent success. The modern Theory of Games[7] has contributed greatly toward a more concise formulation of the issues involved, but an acceptable theory of interdependent maximizing behavior has yet to be offered. As in the discussion of the cardinal measure of utility, an elaboration of the logical consequences of arbitrary normative assumptions here, too, has occasionally been mistaken for a solution of the positive problem. Possibly, such a solution can be even shown not to exist.

5 The theory of general interdependence.

The Theory of General Equilibrium—the analysis of the mutual interdependence of all the producing and consuming units making up a national economy or—if one wants to take into consideration international trade—the world economy as a whole, makes up the core of modern economic theory.

The simplest standard model of the general equilibrium system —stripped of all optional equipment and adornments—is designed to explain the determination of the (time-) rates of production (sales) and consumption (purchases) of all commodities and services by each of the individual decision-making units as well as the prices at which all these inputs and outputs are traded.

The explanation is presented in the form of a system of simultaneous equations. Their number just suffices to determine the values—unique or multiple—of the unknowns. All sales and purchases of each particular commodity are supposed to be transacted at the same price and the prices of all commodities and services are to be such as to make the combined output (supply) of each commodity by all the units equal to its aggregate input (demand) by all the units.

The quantity of each commodity produced or consumed (it could be both) by any unit has already been shown to depend— through the budgetary restriction—on prices; its own as well as those of the other goods. The "supply" and the "demand" functions, so frequently referred to by the economist, are meant to describe this dependence; their shape is obviously implicitly determined by the equations (or inequalities) which in the description of its maximizing behavior served to determine the optimal position of the individual decision-making unit in the commodity space.

Although some of its constituent equations are thus based on the satisfaction of certain maximizing conditions, the general equilibrium system itself cannot legitimately be thought of in any other but quasi-mechanical terms. This does not mean that an eighteenth-century believer in the Invisible Hand or his present-day counterpart, the modern welfare theorist, could not have legitimate interest in finding out whether the actual economy—as described by the set of the general equilibrium equations—does or does not satisfy the normative social welfare criteria of his particular choice.

Let me add that under certain ideal conditions, the outcome of the automatic operation of the competitive price mechanism, as reflected in the general equilibrium system described above, can be shown—so far as the organization of *production* is concerned —to be identical with that which would be achieved by an omniscient and all-powerful planning committee of efficiency experts. In a state satisfying the Walrasian equilibrium equations, the total output of no commodity can be increased and the input of no scarce primary resource diminished without reduction in the output of at least one other commodity or an increase in the input of at least one other commodity or an increase in the input of at least one other scarce primary resource.

In other words, if outputs are measured as positive and inputs as negative quantities in the many dimensional commodity space, the actual equilibrium position of a competitive economy is represented by a point located on the hull of the compact space comprising all input-output combinations attainable to it on the basis of the given transformation functions; each vector connecting any two points on that hull necessarily contains components of opposite signs.

This obviously applies to any optimal position which an individual profit-maximizing enterprise would choose among all the input-output combinations attainable to it.

The truth of that theorem in the case of the competitively operating economy as a whole follows from the fact that it can be shown to apply to the sum of the optimal input-output vectors of any group of profit-maximizing enterprises simultaneously operating within the same price system.

This makes it possible for the economist, when he studies the quantitative aspects of the input-output relationships within the theoretical framework of a competitive general equilibrium system, to disregard its subdivision among the many individual enterprises and to speak of an "industry," groups of industries, and even of the economy as a whole as if it were a large single enterprise.

6 Dynamics.

The quasi-mechanical nature of the economic system as a whole becomes particularly clear when, as has occurred over the last twenty-five years, the mathematical economists engaged increasingly in exploring its dynamic properties.

The static, essentially timeless system of general equilibrium equations described above is an idealization of limited empirical validity. The technical transformation functions, for example, in order to reflect more closely the conditions of actual production, should contain the values of at least some of the variables as related to different points in time: This year's harvest depends on last year's sowing.

Consider, for instance, the process of economic growth. Insofar as it involves the accumulation of capital, its explanation leads back to the fundamental observation that the output of a finished product—expressed as a rate of flow, per unit of time—cannot be described as depending only on the flow rates of requisite inputs. It requires also the presence of certain specific stocks: stocks of buildings, stocks of machinery, inventories of raw materials and of intermediary semi-finished products. But stocks can mostly be described as flow rates (or differences of flow rates) integrated over time.

The dynamic process of capital accumulation in its simplest form can be described and explained in ordinary language. With the introduction of other kinds of dynamic relationships, the theoretical system becomes unmanageable without the use of mathematics. The theory of the so-called "business-cycle," that is, of the fairly regular succession of ups and downs in output, employment, trade, and prices experienced by all advanced Western economies is a case in point. From the time the first major nineteenth-century depression hit England in 1819, economists have searched for a systematic explanation of that phenomenon. But not before the 1930's when the mathematical economists became interested in the subject was there introduced into its discussion the notion of self-generated periodic fluctuations corresponding to the pairs of complex roots which frequently appear in the solution of difference or differential equations.[8]

No wonder that from that time and up to two or three years ago, when the Theory of Games and problems of linear programming came in vogue, dynamic general equilibrium theory has been the favored hunting ground of mathematically inclined economists. Integral and differential, difference and mixed difference and differential equations, phase graphs of linear and non-linear oscillating systems—all of these and many other tools of applied analysis have found their place in the recent discussion of economic dynamics. Having likened the austere outlines of Walras's original general equilibrium system to a standard, stripped down "model T," I cannot help but compare some of the latest dynamic models with the super-deluxe editions of hard-top convertibles equipped with everything from white-wall tires to a concealed bar.

7 Paucity of operationally significant conclusions.

One has, unfortunately, to admit that neither the simpler type of economic theory nor its most modern dynamic versions have brought us very far along the road toward detailed explanation, not to say prediction, of the specific states of the actually observed economic system.

Seldom, in modern positive science, has so elaborate a theoretical structure been erected on so narrow and shallow a factual foundation. Traditionally—and that tradition still prevails among mathematical and non-mathematical economists alike—"pure" theory has not been implemented with empirical determination of any of the numerical parameters involved. As can be seen even from the sketchy outlines presented above, all empirical assumptions on which such theories are based are qualitative in character and, at that, they are quite vague and general. So are the few operational propositions at which pure economic theory arrives.

Paul Samuelson, who more than anybody else contributed to the systematic codification of modern economic theory and a clarification of its logical structure,[9] pointedly brings out the parallelism between the method used by economists to derive certain meaningful implications of maximizing behavior and the elegantly general modes of reasoning found in J. Willard Gibbs's celebrated treatise *On the Equilibrium of Heterogeneous Substances*. The following simple but typical argument from the theory of consumers' behavior will show what I have in mind.

Let the elements of a non-negative row matrix, X, represent the quantities of commodities which a household, with a dollar income, r, can purchase at prices described by the element of the column matrix, P. Under the budgetary constraint,

$$(1) \qquad\qquad XP_i = r_i,$$

where the subscript, i, is used to identify some specific price income situation, the household will choose to purchase those particular amounts, X_i, which will maximize his utility $U(X)$. About $U(X)$, we only know (a) that it is a non-decreasing function of X and (b) that—since utilities can be compared only in the ordinal sense—it admits transformation by any increasing function, $F(U(X))$.

Let X_1 and X_2 represent the optimal consumption patterns corresponding to two different price-income situations P_1, r_1 and P_2, r_2. If

$$(2) \qquad X_1P_1 = r_1 \geqq X_2P_1, \quad \text{then necessarily} \quad U(X_1) > U(X_2),$$

since otherwise when placed in the price-income situation P_1, r_1, the consumer would purchase X_2 rather than X_1.
For analogous reasons,

$$(3) \qquad U(X_1) > U(X_2) \quad \text{implies} \quad X_2P_2 = r_2 < X_1P_2.$$

It follows that

$$(4) \qquad (X_1 - X_2)P_1 \geqq 0 \quad \text{implies} \quad (X_1 - X_2)P_2 > 0.$$

34

Propositions (2) and (3) make it possible in some, but unfortunately not in all, cases to infer from the change in the observed price-purchase pattern of the consumer to the direction of the corresponding change in his level of welfare. Proposition (4) imposes certain limitations on the shape of individual demand functions.

Analogous arguments make it possible to impose similar empirical limitations on the shape of the behavior equations of profit maximizing firms.

Insofar as the individual demand and supply functions enter into the analysis of the economy as a whole, these limitations carry over into the general equilibrium system as well. This applies, in particular, to the input-output relationships characterizing the operations of the productive sectors of the economy. Whenever the economy operates within the framework of competitive pricing, these relationships are identical with those which would have prevailed within one single large profit maximizing enterprise operating on the basis of the same technological horizon. This is why the "pure" general equilibrium theory seems to yield richer empirical results in respect to production than when it deals with household consumption. It also explains why in studying the quantitative aspects of an economic system one sometimes legitimately disregards the details, or should I say accidents, of its particular institutional organization and conducts the entire analysis in terms of only such basic data as the supply of primary resources and the "state of the arts," that is, the technologically given transformation functions. Reduced to these simplest terms, the same general theoretical propositions apply to the highly advanced American private enterprise economy, the centrally planned Soviet system and, say, the economy of an isolated primitive tribe.

With all that, or rather because of that, the legitimately harvested empirical yield of the general equilibrium theory is very limited. An interesting attempt was made by Abraham Wald[10] to impose further limitation on the admissible shape of the general equilibrium equations by introducing the requirement that all prices and quantities as determined by it have to be positive. On closer examination the operational implications of this argument turn out to be disappointing: Any number of alternative sets of sufficient conditions for such a result can be stated, but they obviously would be of little significance from the economic point of view. The necessary conditions for such a positive solution applying to any particular observed price output situation would, on the other hand, be so special that even if stated explicitly they also would be devoid of empirical interest.

Furthermore, the entire question is misplaced from the point of view of the purpose it is intended to serve. One of the interesting empirical questions which an economist occasionally has to answer is whether with a given combination of (virtual) operating conditions, an economic system would be capable of yielding positive outputs, that is, whether it could exist at all. In posing the question, one obviously must allow for the possibility of a negative answer.

In dynamic analysis, a similar search for additional limitations on the empirically admissible shapes of the basic quantitative relationships has produced the suggestion that only convergent systems leading to stable solutions should be considered. If that proposal were taken seriously, how would we go about explaining the rapid and apparently limitless growth of the modern Western economies?

8 Indirect inference.

Please note that while questioning the validity of such quasi-empirical generalizations, I do not impugn the error of circular reasoning to those who make them. If the invisible, but indirectly inferred structural properties of a theoretical system were used to "explain" only those of its directly observed characteristics from which these properties were derived in the first place, the argument could indeed be rejected as heuristically useless. When, however, the indirectly inferred structural properties of the theoretical system serve to derive new factual propositions, not obviously and immediately related to the first set of empirical statements on which the original inference has been based, the explanatory power of the theory has been clearly increased.

If indirect statistical inference is to be used to obtain the numerical parameters for our system, methods of modern mathematical statistics should obviously supply the tools for such an undertaking. In his 1929 Gibbs Lecture, Irving Fisher refers to "smoothing of statistical time series, correlation and probabilities" as, at that time, newly introduced applications of mathematics to economics. The original systematic attempt to derive a "statistical demand curve" for an individual commodity was made by Henry Moore as early as 1917.[11] Soon it was followed by a whole series of similar studies.

The first, let me call it the "unsophisticated" phase, of econometric work, aimed at an indirect determination of the structural parameters of the economic system through statistical analysis of the behavior of its variables, reached its high point in the works of Henry Schultz,[12] Paul Douglas,[13] and Jan Tinbergen.[14]

It was characterized by rather careful collection and organization of primary statistical material and straightforward—some might say indiscriminate—application of the "least square" curve fitting techniques in calculation of the actual parameters. There was little in it of mathematical interest (except for Tinbergen's use of difference equations for empirical determination of the complex components of fluctuating time series) and the empirical results obtained appeared to be of rather doubtful significance. After fitting a first, second, or third degree parabola to a price-quantity scatter, one did not know whether it represented the supply or the demand curve for the commodity in question or possibly some weighted average of the two.

It was only natural to make the crudity of the statistical procedure used responsible for such disappointing substantive results. The late 'thirties and the 'forties witnessed an unprecedented concentration of intellectual effort on problems of methodology.[15] Far from being satisfied with the simple adaptation of recent advances in mathematical statistics, the new econometric school made a number of original contributions to the theory of stochastic systems and the methodology of indirect statistical inference. Such significant advances as the theory of identification (analyzing the relationship between the statistical parameters of an observed stochastic system, on the one hand, and the constants of the underlying theoretical model, on the other) can rightfully be said to have issued from that series of methodological investigations.

The theory of probability and many other modes of mathematical reasoning found in all these studies a most varied and fertile application. I will not invite you now, however, to consider them; they belong in the field of general statistics rather than that of economics. Moreover, the positive contribution which these advanced methods were able to make toward actual empirical determination of the specific quantitative properties of the observed economic system proved to be quite limited, hardly greater than that made by the primitive methods used in studies belonging to the first, unsophisticated phase of that econometric movement.

The explanation of this disappointing result lies, I think, in the fact that for a study of a set of quantitative interrelationships as complex as those underlying a modern economy indirect statistical inference, however refined methodologically, simply will not do.[16] Statistical reliability measures, if properly applied to even the most favorable situation—so far as primary information is concerned—yield confidence limits so far apart as to negate the empirical usefulness of the numerical parameters obtained.

It is as if we were asked to reproduce the blueprint of a complicated motor on the basis of our knowledge of the general principles of operation of internal combustion engines and no other specific information but that conveyed by the few dials located on the dashboard and possibly the noise coming from under the closed hood. And as if that were not difficult enough, the structural characteristics of the engine the economist is studying are known to change under the impact of its continual operation.

The task as presented can hardly be accomplished. It certainly becomes much easier if we are allowed to look under the hood. It would, of course, be even more convenient if it were possible to stop the motor, take it apart, and subject each of its components to any desired tests and measurements. That is what experimental scientists can do and economists cannot. But look under the hood he can, although in economics as in the garage it is an inconvenient and often a dirty operation. Admittedly, had we been able to reproduce the blueprint of the engine by indirect inference from the behavior of the gauges, such intellectual accomplishment would earn a much higher rating. Nevertheless, some economists rolled up their sleeves and looked under the hood.

9 Direct structural analysis.

Direct observation and detailed description of the various aspects of economic reality are as old as our discipline itself. As statistical information became more and more available, descriptive quantitative economics came to be recognized as one of its important branches. But far from seeking to establish a close—not to say intimate—co-operation with the theorist, many of the empirically minded investigators came to consider direct observation as a separate self-sufficient approach to the explanation of the functioning of the economic system rather than the necessary descriptive complement of its theoretical analysis.

The empiricist school developed even a kind of a quantitative descriptive technique all its own. Its principal or rather only tools are averaging and aggregation (an aggregate of a set of magnitudes is defined as a weighted sum of its elements). While the theorist discovers or, should I say, introduces order into the complex multiplicity of measurable economic phenomena by reducing it to a system of equations, the radical empiricist simplifies the quantitative picture by describing it in terms of a few broad aggregates and averages. A detailed tabulation of the amounts of all the many kinds of goods and services consumed in the course of a given year by households or invested in all the various industries to expand their productive capacity is replaced, for example, by one single figure identified as *the* annual Net National Income. This figure represents the sum total of the dollar values of all the individual commodities and services mentioned above. Similarly, the multidimensional set of the corresponding prices is replaced by a single number—a weighted average of its individual components—called the General Price Level.

As conveniently simplified—but albeit necessarily blurred—descriptions of quantitative phenomena such aggregates and averages proved to be useful, nay, indispensable to economists. Even pure theorists use it—more often probably than they should—as a pedagogical device which lends the appearance of realism to their schematic general equilibrium models. Some of these models purport to depict the operation of the entire economic system in terms of five, four, or even only three aggregative variables. As a substitute for theoretical analysis and generalization, such simplifying devices are obviously valueless. To the extent to which broad aggregates are not directly observable (and few of them are) but have to be compiled from separate measurements of the component variables, in utilization of primary observational data, no economy can be achieved through their use either.

Direct factual study and quantitative descriptions of the structural properties of the economic system, detailed in content, comprehensive in coverage, and systematically designed to fill the specific requirement of an appropriate theoretical scheme, seem to offer the only promising approach to empirically significant understanding of the operational characteristics of the modern economy.

The task thus imposed on the collector of primary factual information exceeds by far anything demanded hitherto from quantitative empirical research in economics or any other social science. It is only reasonable to suggest that the theorist should meet him half way by redesigning his analytical scheme so as to take advantage of the strengths and mitigate the weaknesses of the observational data to which it will have to be applied.

As an example of such mutual accommodation between theoretical formulation and observational capability, let me say a few words about the so-called input-output analysis in which I myself happen to have an interest of long standing.[17, 18]

The difficulty, the challenge which an economist faces in trying to analyze and to describe in concrete numerical terms the specific operational characteristics of a modern national economy is caused by the complexity of the interindustrial or, more generally, intersectoral relationships which it comprises. A reduction in the consumers' purchases of automobiles leads, for example, to a fall in the demand for the electric energy required for production of aluminum which goes into the manufacture of cylinder heads.

Economic theory tells us that in order to trace through such a chain of relationships, one must determine the actual shape of the transformation (production) functions of all the individual sectors of the economy in question, insert them into an appropriate system of general equilibrium equations and finally compute the effect which the assumed increase or decrease in final demand would have on the output in question.

Since a fully detailed description of the actual shapes of all the transformation functions comprised, say, in the structure of the American economy, is obviously impossible, the theory had to be reformulated in terms of linear transformation functions—considered to represent the first approximation to the actual functions. The solution of the general equilibrium problem was accordingly reduced to inversion of the coefficient matrix of a system of linear equations: If a_{ik} represents the input coefficient showing the number of units of the product of industry i absorbed by industry k per unit of its respective output, the relationships between the total gross outputs, $x_1, x_2, \ldots, x_n$, of the n industries constituting the national economy and the so-called final demand comprising consumption and new investment (accumulation), must satisfy the following matrix equation:

$$(I - A)X = Y \quad \text{or} \quad X = (I - A)^{-1}Y$$

in which A is the square non-negative matrix of all input coefficients (with a_{ik} its general element), X a column matrix of the n gross outputs, and Y the corresponding matrix of final demand.

Matrix A represents a concise numerical description of the structural properties of the specific economy; it summarizes the results of painstaking and systematic empirical inquiries. Even a highly aggregated picture of the U. S. economy described in terms of 100×100 matrix required over a year's factual research by 20 trained economists; a more detailed 200×200 matrix—two years' work by 75 persons. The most detailed input-output matrix of the American economy yet compiled is of the order 450×450.

The inversion of such matrices presents a real challenge even to modern large-scale computing machines. A system of so many simultaneous linear equations would—if its coefficients were randomly chosen—be highly unstable; its numerical solution would show hardly more than an accumulation of round-off errors. As an economist, I was not astonished, however, to find the inverses of the empirical input-output matrices to be very stable. The economy of the United States actually operates as a kind of a large-scale calculating machine, continuously working out the solution of problems which it poses itself. Applying the conventional standards of computational accuracy, one must say that these solutions certainly do not prove to be excessively unstable.

This last analogy leads quite naturally to the consideration of a workable empirical approach to dynamic problems. Again, the requirements of factual implementation demand the use of a greatly simplified theoretical framework. The dynamic input-output theory which is now undergoing its first empirical tests is based on the introduction into the original scheme of so-called stock-flow relationships. It leads to the following system of linear differential equations with constant coefficients,

$$(I - A)X(t) - B\dot{X}(t) = Y(t).$$

The general term b_{in} of the square matrix B represents the *stock* of the products of industry i required by industry k per unit of its respective output: $B\dot{X}$ describes the time rate of change of all stocks, that is, the rate of accumulation or decumulation of all kinds of "capital" in their dependence on changes in the rate of output, $\dot{X}$, of all the individual industries.

The determination of the magnitude of the elements of the capital coefficient matrix B involved a series of empirical studies even more exacting than those aimed at the derivation of the flow coefficients a_{ik}.

A 100×100 B (stock) matrix of the American economy is now available. A numerical general solution of a homogeneous system of 20 linear differential equations based on consolidated 20×20 A and B matrices of the American economy was completed a few weeks ago by Kenneth Iverson on the new Harvard Mark IV calculating machine.

Even if I had time—which I do not have—to outline the study of the formal properties of the linear system described above, and had shown how more and better empirical data will permit the use of a more refined analytical scheme, I admittedly could not dispel the sense of intellectual retreat which by now you must have felt. From the heights of general theorems describing the formal properties of broadly defined systems, we have step by step descended into the realm of elaborate factual observation followed by equally laborious computations: From Gibbs to crude numerical analysis. But such a rebound has probably been unavoidable. Economics, mathematical economics, in particular, acquired very early in its development the attitudes and manners of the exact empirical sciences without really having gone through the hard school of direct, detailed factual inquiry. Possibly it will do us good to be sent down in order that we may catch up with the experience we have missed. And when one has put a hand to it, one cannot help but derive a peculiar satisfaction from seeing masses of seemingly amorphous facts do the bidding of the orderly and ordering mathematical thought.

Bibliography

1. Léon Walras, *Éléments d'économie politique pure*, Lausanne, 1874.
2. Daniel Bernoulli, *Specimen theoriae novae de mensura sortis*, Commentarii academiae scientiarum imperialis Petropolitanae, vol. 5 (1738) pp. 175-92, St. Petersburg.
3. Augustin Cournot, *Researches into the Mathematical Principles of the Theory of Wealth* (translated from the original, 1838, French ed.), New York, 1897.
4. Robert Dorfman, *Application of Linear Programming to the Theory of the Firm*, Berkeley, 1951.
5. Vilfredo Pareto, *Manuel d'économie politique*, Paris, 1909.
6. Jacob Marschak, Rational behavior, uncertain prospects, and measurable utility, *Econometrica*, vol. 18 (1950) pp. 111-41.
7. John von Neumann and Oskar Morgenstern, *Theory of Games and Economic Behavior*, 2d ed., Princeton, 1947.
8. Ragnar Frisch, Propagation problems and impulse problems in dynamic economics, in *Economic Essays in Honor of Gustav Cassel*, London, 1933.
9. Paul Samuelson, *Foundations of Economic Analysis*, Cambridge, 1947.
10. Abraham Wald, On some systems of equations of mathematical economics, *Econometrica*, vol. 19 (1951) pp. 368-403.

11. Henry L. Moore, *Forecasting the Yield and Price of Cotton*, New York, 1917.
12. Henry Schultz, *The Theory of Measurement of Demand*, Chicago, 1938.
13. Paul H. Douglas, *Real Wages in the United States, 1890-1926*, Boston, 1930.
14. Jan Tinbergen, *Statistical Testing of Business Cycles Theories*, II: *Business Cycles in the United States of America, 1919-1939*, Geneva, 1939.
15. Tjalling Koopmans, ed., *Statistical Inference in Dynamic Economic Models*, by Cowles Commission research staff members and guests, Wiley, New York, 1950.
16. Warren Weaver, Science and complexity, *American Scientist*, vol. 36 (1948) pp. 536-44.
17. Wassily Leontief, *The Structure of the American Economy, 1919-1939*, 2d ed., New York, 1951.
18. Wassily Leontief *et al.*, *Studies in the Structure of the American Economy*, New York, 1953.

4

The problem of quality and quantity in economics

I

The dialectic juxtaposition of quality and quantity, of uniqueness and repetition, of abstract theory and of concrete description, has from far back been the leitmotiv of the running methodological controversy in social science. The nineteenth-century Continental, particularly the German, philosophic tradition supplied the general background for the first stages of this discussion. In economics the issue was originally raised in the full-dress attack mounted in the third quarter of the last century by the so-called German historical school against the then dominant classical theory. It is not surprising that such antitheoretical orientation found no prominent adherents among economists in England, although among the English historians it was quite recently most eloquently espoused by so prominent a scholar as Collingwood.

The emphasis on the singular as against the common, on the organic as against the mechanical, found on the other hand a receptive soil for its development in the economic thought of the United States. Both Thorstein Veblen and Wesley Mitchell, two of the most eminent representatives of indigenous American economic thought, carried on the *Methodenstreit* against quantitative, analytical economics in the grand style of the German historical school. The fact that at the turn of the century the German academic influence in the United States was as strong as and possibly even stronger than the English might be in part responsible

From *Daedalus*, Vol. 88, No. 4, 1959.

for this. In discussing the issue of quality *vs.* quantity, one must keep in mind that it represents only one facet, one stage, of the wider contest between the proponents of concise analytical methods and the defenders of the descriptive individualizing approach.

Among the social sciences, economics came to be considered—and rightly so—a quantitative science par excellence. Quantification in this instance is more than a methodological device employed by the investigator: it is also an object of the inquiry itself. The modern *Homo economicus* may not be the much maligned predatory hedonist, but he certainly is a consciously calculating animal. It is only natural that in explaining his behavior the economist resorts to mathematics, too. However, lest one draw from this the erroneous conclusion that quantitative analysis is restricted to only those aspects of the economic process which involve directly observed, consciously (or rather self-consciously) quantifying attitudes, let me emphatically state that this is not the case. Some of the most advanced applications of mathematical methods in economics are found in the fields of general equilibrium analysis and business-cycle theory—both recognized as quasi-mechanical, automatic phenomena formed and operating to a large extent beyond the calculations, outside the control of, and mostly against the wills of, the millions of individuals whom they affect.

II

The raw materials from which the economist forms his theory—or if one prefers a more fashionable term, from which he constructs his analytical models—are the millions of various combinations in which specific goods and services are made and used within the economic system he observes. The principal elementary building blocks which he makes up out of his materials are the "production function" and the "utility" or the "consumption function." These he then uses to explain certain manifestations in the behavior of individuals, or of groups of individuals; that is—if one again prefers to use esoteric language—to explain the decisions being taken by the "players" in the vast economic "game."

A "production function" is a description of the quantitative relationship between the inputs absorbed and the outputs emerging from a particular production process. A baking receipt stating that it takes two pounds of flour, two cups of milk, two eggs, and a quarter of a pound of butter to make two loaves of bread is a typical production function; so is the concise listing of all the various combinations of ore, coke, auxiliary materials, and the labor required to produce various amounts of pig iron.

Let x_1, for example, represent the number of tons of ore, x_2, the number of tons of coke, and x_3, the man-hours of labor used to make y tons of pig iron. The corresponding quantitative input-output relationship can be concisely described by an equation of the form:

$$(1) \qquad y = f(x_1, x_2, x_3)$$

the specific shape of the function $f(x_1, x_2, x_3)$ being determined by the given state of technology. The identification of all the variables involved and the definition of the units in which each one of them is measured represent the qualitative side of this concise description of the economically relevant aspects of the iron-making process; without these specifications the mathematical formula has no empirical meaning.

The production function—with the appropriate identification of variables involved—can be viewed as a relationship derived from a much larger, and qualitatively much richer, set of far more complete descriptions of all the known methods of making iron, or —as the case may be—baking bread. Such a description would, for example, dwell in full detail on the role played by the temperature maintained in the blast furnace, and the pressure and the oxygen content of air supplied to its top or base. A complete technological production function would thus contain in the parentheses enclosing the predicate of many such additional variables not included in its abbreviated version used in equation (1). The economist eliminates them and thus reduces the qualitative complexity (the dimensionality) of the material with which he will have to deal from then on. He retains only those variables the magnitudes of which affect *directly* either the costs incurred in, or the revenue received from, the operation of the production process he describes. Since ore, coke, and labor, as well as pig iron itself, have positive prices, the change in the magnitude of any one of these variables will directly affect the costs incurred in (or the revenue received from) the iron-making process. Thus, if any one of these variables were omitted from the production function, the economist would be unable to identify the profit-maximizing input-output combination which he assumes will be in fact maintained by the producer whose actions he sets out to explain.

It is of course true that variations in the amount of air supplied under pressure to the furnace, or changes in its internal operating temperature, would affect the efficiency and consequently the profitability of the entire process as well. Such "non-priced" variables, however, exert their influence on costs or revenue only indirectly, through modifying the quantitative relationships between the "priced" factors: a change in the supply of air or in the furnace temperature would, for example, increase or decrease the pig-iron yield obtained from given fixed amounts of ore, coke, and labor, or affect the amount of coke required to produce a fixed amount of pig iron with given quantities of ore and labor. As a matter of fact, the profit-maximizing producer can be expected to adjust the magnitudes of all the non-priced variables in such a way as to attain an efficient relationship between the quantities of the priced variables. On the assumption that he actually does so, the economist proceeds to explain the producer's action in terms of a reduced production function, that is, a production function which describes not all the possible combinations of all the technologically relevant variables, but only certain preselected efficient relationships between the priced variables.

It is worth noting that no irreparable damage is caused if, by oversight or for some other reason, the economist's condensed production function did contain some of the extra technological variables. It could still be used to explain correctly the producer's profit-maximizing behavior; except that the explanation (that is, the calculations) would have to be carried out in a larger number of dimensions than is absolutely necessary.

Another simpler and fundamentally much more general device which the economist uses to reduce the number of qualitative distinctions required for the explanation of observed facts is the method of formal substitution.

Let us enlarge the scope of the previous example by including in it the ore-mining and the coke-making sectors of the economy along with the blast-furnace industry itself. This can be done by setting up two additional production functions. In the description of mining operations, the variable x_1 representing (as it did before) the quantity of ore will appear on the left-hand side of the equation as the output; on its right-hand side, under the function sign ϕ—representing the appropriate reduced technical relationship—this equation will contain new input variables: say $z_1 =$ the tonnage or the cubic yards of ore bearing deposits, $z_2 =$ the number of kilowatt hours of electric power, and $z_3 =$ man-years of miners' work:

$$(2) \qquad x_1 = \phi\,(z_1, z_2, z_3)$$

Similarly, another equation describing the production of coke shows its quantity, x_2, as related to the quantities of the inputs, coal, v_1, and labor, v_2:

$$(3) \qquad x_2 = \theta\,(v_1, v_2)$$

In widening the scope of the inquiry, we have thus introduced five new qualitatively distinct variables and two additional functional relationships. But having made this step forward, we can now take a half-step back. Let us substitute for the variables x_1 and x_2 as they appear on the right-hand side of equation (1) their production functions presented in equations (2) and (3). Thus we obtain a new, enlarged production function for pig iron:

$$(4) \qquad y = f\,[\phi\,(z_1, z_2, z_3),\, \theta\,(v_1, v_2),\, x_3]$$

This function is more comprehensive than the first insofar as it reaches back behind the iron-smelting process and covers two other sectors of the economy, one engaged in the mining of ore

(x_1), and the other in the making of coke (x_2). These two variables are, however, not entered explicitly on the right-hand side of the enlarged equation. Instead, that side shows the inputs used by the ore-mining and coke-making industries, respectively. Of the nine variables appearing in the first three equations, the two mentioned above have been eliminated in the last, without making our analysis less concise. The purpose of this example is to show that the formal operation of algebraic substitution, when used in analysis of real (that is, observable) phenomena, permits us to describe them with fewer qualitative terms.

I V

Turning to the "utility function," we again meet the substitution method—but used in reverse. In analyzing the behavior of consumers, the economist assigns to this function a role similar to that which he gives to the production function in the description and explanation of the behavior of producers. The inputs consist now, not of ore and coke, but of such consumers' goods as bread and shoes; the output is not pig iron but utility. But what is utility, how can it be measured, does it exist at all? Strangely enough, the economists began to ask themselves these questions only relatively recently. Before that, they spoke of satisfaction or utility as if it were an object with as distinct, immediately observable qualities as steel or bread. However, as soon as the pedantic Edgeworth and the skeptical Pareto expressed their doubts on that score, a lively, not to say violent, discussion ensued which has not subsided yet. Some theorists maintain that utility exists and can indeed be measured like steel or bread, although the yardsticks applied to different persons and the resulting measurements can in no way be compared with one another. Others deny the possibility of any such cardinal measurement, even for a single person; they assert that the amounts of utility from which an individual has opportunity to choose can be compared with one another only ordinarily: as in the case of pain, one does not know how much one has of it, but only feels that it is becoming more or less intense. Finally, there are theorists who do not care whether utility exists and is measurable or not. They say that the behavior of a consumer (for example, the change in the quantities of various goods he buys and in the amount of work he will do to earn the income with which to pay for them) can be explained without recourse to a variable called utility.

There is an obvious analogy between the problem of the existence or non-existence of utility and of its explanatory use, and the question of whether one can or should substitute the intermediate variables, x_1 and x_2, which came up before when we discussed the problem of compounding the interrelated production functions for pig iron, ore, and coke. Imagine a situation in which the inputs and outputs accessible to direct observation by the economist are only those described by the variables shown in the compound production function (4). This means that his empirical data permit him to establish a valid quantitative relationship between the amounts of ore-bearing land (z_1), electric power (z_2), and labor (z_3) absorbed in mining operations; the quantities of coal (v_1) and labor (v_2) used for making coke; and the amount of blast-furnace-tending labor (x_3) on the one hand: and on the other the quantity of pig iron (y) emerging at the end of the entire combined operation. This information will obviously permit him to construct and use for further analytical purposes the integrated over-all production equation (4); such factual information, however, will not be sufficient to enable our economist to reconstruct each one of its component parts, that is, the three production functions describing separately the pig-iron-smelting process and the processes of mining ore and of making coke. Neither his immediate empirical evidence nor his theoretical model will contain any reference whatsoever to either the qualities or quantities of such objects as ore or coke.

This could not, however, prevent our investigator from embarking on what will appear to be an arbitrary theoretical construction of the three interrelated intermediate functions containing two new "artificial" variables, x_1 and x_2. Not only their dimensions (that is, their qualitative properties) but even their very existence would obviously depend in this case only on circumstantial evidence combined with certain essentially arbitrary a priori assumptions. The analytical purpose of introducing these two additional variables would be to provide a means of breaking down one complicated quantitative relationship into three simpler ones. If numerical manipulations are involved, a theoretical reformulation of this kind often leads to considerable simplification of the computational procedure.

Returning to the problem of the existence (if one assumes that it does exist) of alternative measures of utility, we can now see by analogy that it is essentially a question of introduction or omission of an auxiliary variable and of a corresponding reformulation of a given system of theoretical relationships.

V

The delicate interplay between direct observation and analytical construction has been dramatically illuminated by the following curious incident from the recent history of economic thought. Twenty years ago a prominent Soviet Russian mathematician, Professor L. V. Kantorovich, published a paper in which he developed a new approach to production planning. The problem he set out to solve was essentially one of choosing among several technologically possible methods of producing a given goods that which would maximize its output. In particular he considered cases in which each one of the available alternative methods could be described as a specific combination of the amounts of various factors required to produce a unit of the finished goods and in which the total available quantities of all factors were fixed. In our previous example, one method would, for instance, require a ton of ore, three tons of coke, and two man-hours of labor for every ton of pig iron; another, one and a quarter tons of ore, but only two and a half tons of coke and one and three-quarters man-hours of labor; and so on. Given a total supply, say, of 600,000 tons of ore, 15,000 tons of coke, and 11,000 man-hours, what method or what combination of methods would enable us to produce the largest possible amount of pig iron? This was Kantorovich's question.

He found that the calculation of a correct answer—if the number of distinct possible input combinations and the number of inputs involved is fairly large—is greatly facilitated if one introduces certain auxiliary variables which he called "allocation coefficients," represented in his theoretical formulae by the symbols $\lambda_1, \lambda_2, \ldots, \lambda_n$.

At the time of publication, Kantorovich's paper apparently found little response among Russian economists and none among the practical planners. It did not reach the West when published in 1939; the hot war and the subsequent cold war intervened, so that Western economists had the opportunity of acquainting themselves with its contents only a short time ago. They were surprised to find that Kantorovich's "allocation coefficients" were actually the prices of the individual goods and services, which appeared as inputs in his production functions. That is, the quantitative relationship established by Kantorovich between these λ_i's on the one hand and the shapes of his production functions and the given total amounts of the various inputs on the other, was exacty the same as is used in Western economic theory to explain the determination of factor prices in a competitive economy.

This theory in its modern version views the entire national economy as a kind of gigantic computor. Propelled by the profit-maximization motive and other similar forces, it automatically solves the problem of the efficient allocation of all available resources. The computational technique which this natural machine employs to arrive at correct answers is the so-called iterative procedure, that is, the method of step-by-step approximation through trial and error.

For Western economists, prices are elements of the observed reality, as real as are the tangible physical properties of various goods. The objects of Kantorovich's analysis were only these physical quantities and the technical relations between them. There is good reason to believe that in the context of the planning problem which he intended to solve, the actual existence of observable prices was not taken into account by him at all. Facing a well-defined empirical problem, he was led by the internal logic of the theoretical argument, combined with considerations of computational convenience, to the artificial construction of peculiar measurable qualities which under somewhat different conditions actually happen to exist. The Western theory of linear programming, which Kantorovich's original contribution has anticipated in part, uses the term "shadow prices." The relationship between observed and constructed qualities and quantities in modern science, indeed, reminds one of a Pirandello play.

V I

The conceptual apparatus of modern economics described above has a rather fragile but at the same time precisely balanced structure. It contains variables which represent directly observed facts; by this I mean facts were more often observed by someone else rather than the economist himself, and were usually described in ordinary, everyday language or in the technical language, not of economics, but of some other discipline. These variables make up the cutting edge of the analytical tool without which it could have no operational significance. As we have seen, this tool also contains in its inner works auxiliary concepts of a rather artificial kind. Both qualitatively and quantitatively the two types of variables are mutually aligned, like gears in a well-made clock. This does not mean that the qualitative characteristics of the artificial variables are similar to those of the variables belonging to the more realistic group. On the contrary, it is precisely their different qualitative make-up on which the effective analytic combination of the two kinds of variables depends.

The introductory paragraphs of this essay contained a reference to Wesley Mitchell as representative of a major anti-theoretical trend in American economic thought. While criticizing the erection of elaborate theoretical models, he proposed to rely on direct observation not based on any preconceived notions, and in particular advocated massive measurement of the observed facts. To Mitchell, to his pupils, and to his successors, this country owes the large-scale development of descriptive economic statistics, without which not only modern economics but many of the modern economic institutions could not possibly exist.

While they are suspicious of theoretical speculation, the proponents of this self-professed positivistic approach nevertheless make up new scientific concepts or at least adopt some of those already in use. Typical examples are the regularly published figures of the "U.S. national income," of the "U.S. output of consumers' goods," and the "price level of agricultural products." None of these terms refers to a concrete object familiar to the direct participants in daily practical economic transactions. Each one refers, however, to a group of such objects defined in a rather simple, not to say simple-minded, way. The "output of consumers' goods" is obviously meant to be the combined total of the measured outputs of bread, shoes, men's suits, TV sets, and so on; the "average price level of agricultural products," the average price of wheat, cotton, oranges, meat, etc. The objects in each such group have some property in common—that of being used by consumers or being prices of all products of agricultural enterprise—but they differ from one another in many of their qualities, too. In no case does there exist a common unit which can be unambiguously used to measure the magnitude of all the individual members of each group before one proceeds to sum them up or to average them out. The operation of determining the magnitude of such artificial aggregative objects—the economic statistician calls them index numbers—involves, in other words, adding pounds or tons of steel and yards or meters of cloth. The final result thus necessarily depends on the arbitrary choice of units in which one measures the magnitude of each one of the component parts.

If one speaks of the "output of consumers' goods" instead of the outputs of bread, shoes, and books, or of the "price of agricultural commodities" instead of the price of wheat, the entire economic system can indeed be described in fewer words. However, the reduction in qualitative variety is attained at the cost of ever increasing quantitative indeterminacy; as we have seen, the more general the contents of an index number, the more vague and arbitrary will its measure be. This puts strict upper limits on the effectiveness of verbal generalization—and on that of the corresponding quantitative procedure of averaging or of aggregating—as a tool of economic research. On the lower levels of scientific inquiry its use of course cannot possibly be avoided. When one speaks in general of "appliances" instead of "consumers' durables," one excludes automobiles but leaves unspecified whether one has in mind refrigerators, washing machines, or TV sets; and when one speaks of refrigerators, one still omits the distinction between those run by electricity and those operated by gas. Only an ideal theoretical system could take in all observable distinctions and explain them to the last detail. At any given stage of its development, economic analysis—like theoretical analysis in any other empirical discipline—can operate effectively on a certain level of qualitative differentiation, but not further down. However, the cutoff point below which the economist has to ignore qualitative distinctions (since he cannot explain them) can be expected to shift downward.

Both the theoretical analyst and the anti-theoretical empiricist must rely on crude verbal generalization as the only means they can begin with to reduce to manageable proportions the seemingly unfathomable variety of the immediately observed facts. The difference between the two shows up in what they do next. The theorist sets out to develop generalizations of a more complex and systematic kind, with which he expects first of all to master the obvious qualitative distinctions preserved at the first descriptive stage. He furthermore proceeds to recover and to incorporate into his analytical system successive layers of finer differences which were neglected or suppressed in the original verbal purge.

The empiricist, to the extent to which he wants to generalize at all, prefers to follow the first verbal step with a second, third, and so on. The entire sequence involves thus nothing more than omitting details, averaging, and aggregating. In following this apparently simple and safe procedure, the opponent of theoretical speculation soon finds himself facing unexpectedly the highly speculative and—what is worse—essentially unsolvable problems of so-called index-number theory. He winds up either with a system of quantitatively well-defined relationships between qualitatively ill-defined variables or with a set of quantitatively indeterminate—or at least loosely described—relationships between sharply defined variables.

The process of the gradual deepening and expansion of economic inquiry naturally brings it into closer contact with adjoining fields. Modern economics has established with technical-engineering disciplines a close co-operative relationship based on an effective division of labor. However, its borders with other social sciences are still very little explored, and its relations with them are marked not so much by active co-operation as by jurisdictional disputes in which each side raises claims on some outlying territories which with their present analytical resources neither can in fact occupy or hold. Two fields of scientific inquiry can be interconnected effectively only through a clear conceptual overlap. Moreover, the overlapping (that is, the common) concepts must have proven their internal operational effectiveness separately in each one of the adjoining disciplines. If these basic conditions are not satisfied, interdisciplinary committees and interdisciplinary negotiation can yield no more than an exchange of reciprocal propaganda claims.

5

Implicit theorizing: a methodological criticism of the neo-Cambridge school

I

Interest in methodological problems has so often been branded as a sign of theoretical frustration that the subject has practically vanished from the field of economic discussion. The silence which for a number of years surrounds this range of questions is so persistent as to become conspicuous. It is particularly notable in view of the fact that since the advent of the new Cambridge School, the methods of theorizing have undergone fundamental transformation.[1] Yet it would seem to be the form of analysis rather than the material content of his theories which imprint upon so many a prominent member of our scientific community the unmistakable mark of a "Cambridge economist." A show-down between the Cambridge (or rather the neo-Cambridge) and the orthodox type of theory, if it ever comes, must be fought out on methodological grounds. The solution of the fundamental issue cannot be advanced through persistent but dispersed scrimmages concerning such questions as equality of Saving and Investment, the significance of the so-called "Multiplier," and the like.

The difference between the two lines of thought appears to be neither a disagreement in final scientific outlooks, nor a divergence

From the *Quarterly Journal of Economics*, Vol. 51, No. 2B, Feb. 1937.
[1] It is interesting to note that the latest contribution to this field came not from a Cambridge economist, but from the orthodox pen of Professor Lionel Robbins. Not less significant is the fact that no other than Professor Cannan was given the task of reviewing the "Nature and Significance of Economic Science" for the Economic Journal.

in identification of the immediate objects of observation—the economic realities of common experience. With both, the point of departure and the ultimate goal are essentially the same. What is different is the intermediate path.

From the point of view of Laplacian superhuman intelligence, which would be able to see without the least mental friction all the infinite number of logical implications of any given system of assumptions, however large—an intellect for which "logically necessary" is synonymous with "obvious"—the difference between the two paths would be no greater than that between two algebraic equations, one written in Latin script and the other in Greek, otherwise identical. But in the actual process of scientific investigation, which consists in its larger part of more or less successful attempts to overcome our own intellectual inertia, the problem of proper arrangement of formal analytical tools acquires fundamental importance. For a hypothetical person with absolute logical pitch, the choice of one or another type of definition, of one or another method of proof, would be entirely divorced from the analysis of the truth-content of any theoretical statement and for such a person questions concerning any kind of formal set-up in general cease to be of vital methodological importance. But for a limited human intellect the problem of choosing from among the infinite number of logically equivalent procedures that which reduces the chance of a logical mistake (inconsistency) to a minimum becomes *the* methodological science. In course of the following argument, I shall adhere to this specific distinction between logical and methodological aspects of the analytical procedure, bearing in mind that the latter is definitely psychological in its nature.[2]

There exists no generally accepted criterion of the "simplicity" of a logical argument, because the nature of the mental friction which makes a theoretical proposition appear more or less "difficult" is different from one person to another. One economist finds

[2] The older, classical logic had a definite tendency to confuse these two different problems. With the advent of the new formalistic schools, the psychological or methodological, in our sense of the word, questions seem to have been driven into the background.

it easier to understand five lines of algebraic formula than to follow five pages of verbal proof, while another would rather read twenty pages of text than decipher a single equation. And still there exists a definite "statistical" correlation between different (but logically equivalent) patterns of theoretical analysis and the degree of mental resistance which arises in connection with their actual use. Multiplication of CLXXVIII and LXIX with exclusive use of Roman numerals would for a majority of people appear to be much more difficult than an equivalent calculation with the help of an Arabic system of numerals; and for a few exceptional minds the solution $178 \times 119 = 21,182$ is so obvious that they could dispense with any type of mathematical notation.

The degree of mental resistance which accompanies the use of one or another formal pattern is furthermore rather closely (although also only "statistically") and positively correlated with the chance of committing logical mistakes. Mistakes of this kind may manifest themselves either in the inability to perceive the "evidence" of a correct argument or in the practically much more dangerous readiness to be convinced by a false one.

In the following pages, I attempt to indicate the fundamental characteristics which distinguish the logical pattern used by Cambridge economists from the formal set-up of the "orthodox" type of theories, and then try to show how and why the Cambridge pattern is liable to increase the danger of theoretical errors and fallacies. Finally, I shall substantiate my general contentions by discussing a few typical cases of implicit theorizing.

I I

The outstanding characteristic of what for brevity will hereafter be referred to as the Cambridge pattern lies in a peculiar use of definitions.

Within the structure of any theoretical analysis, we can distinguish two elements. The first comprises a set of fundamental statements, which are introduced into the argument from outside and are not supposed to be scrutinized within the body of the given theory to any large extent, only so far as may be necessary to verify their logical compatibility. The source of these fundamental postulates may be direct observation; or they may be derived as the conclusions of some other theory; or they may be inductively unverifiable (that is, normative) postulates. The nature of their origin, however, can in no way affect the position of these initial statements within a theoretical system. The logical implications of the "profit motive," within a system of economics, for example, will be the same whether we interpret it as an observable fact or only as an ideal, normative postulate.

The other part of a theory consists of a larger or smaller number of logical implications *obtained from* the primary set of fundamental propositions. The formal validity of all these different implications is absolutely equal, but their (psychological) evidentness is not at all uniform. Thus we can single out a class of implications which have immediate evidence, then a second class comprising statements which do not appear to be obvious from the point of view of the basic postulates, but are evident in relation to (that is, can be directly derived from) those placed in the first class, and so on. The distinction between these successive classes of theorems (we shall use this term as synonymous with "deductively derived theoretical statement") will not necessarily be indicated with clearness by their distance from the set of fundamental postulates. If—as is mostly the case in the field of empirical sciences, which take many of their propositions from common experience—the number of these basic statements is very large, no *immediate* implications obtained by simultaneous use of *all* the given "data" are possible. In other words, while theorems of the first class can be derived by using only one part of these postulates, those of the second class might be derived from those of the first class plus some additional data and so on. Thus we face very often, not a linear progress from the initial postulates toward implications of greater and greater remoteness, but an intricate network of methodological interconnections. Each particular theorem will frequently be derived from propositions of many different classes. For the purpose of the following discussion, the class (or "type") of a theorem may be defined as being one degree higher than that of the highest class of theorems used in its derivation. The possibility of choosing for the purpose of logical implication only a part of theorems belonging to a given class very often causes a branching of the argument into many different paths. These separate branches for obvious reasons are always logically compatible with each other.

The method of progressing gradually from stage to stage enables us to reach remote conclusions which lie far beyond the normal horizon of immediate logical perception. If, however, the scientist finds himself unable to use any concepts other than those contained in the set of initial fundamental propositions, his progress will be impeded by the increasing bulk of ever more and more complicated theorems. This burden would very soon become absolutely prohibitive, and is made bearable only by use of the powerful device of *intermediate definitions*. Like any other methodological tool, every such definition must first of all pass a test of logical validity. The introduction of an intermediate definition means, from a formal—logical—point of view, adaptation of a new, auxiliary postulate side by side with the initial set of basic propositions. It contains one *new* term (the defined term) and a number (at least two) of concepts already contained among the previously accepted postulates (these are the defining terms[3]). As the only formal test which has to be satisfied by an initial postulate is that of compatibility with the other simultaneously accepted postulates, every intermediate definition obtains its logical license automatically: Containing a new term, hitherto not used, such proposition can never be in contradiction with any of the other previously accepted postulates and definitions. The familiar assertion that no definition can ever be logically wrong is incontestable; but definitions can be methodologically useless and often harmful.

In introducing an intermediate definition whenever his propositions become too cumbersome, the theorist is able to formulate the next stage of the argument with the same simplicity as the previous one. The economy is particularly great if the same theorem

[3] From a purely formal point of view a definition could contain a single defining term. Methodologically, this type of definition, $A \equiv B$, cannot possibly be of any advantage. Hence it is actually never used.

is used in many parallel branches of his argument, so that a new definition introduced at the point of division can be utilized in each of these separate lines of analysis.

So long as no logical mistake has been committed, any theorem expressed this way can be easily traced back to the original postulates. *The elimination of intermediate definitions at each and every stage of the argument can be accomplished by automatic substitution without raising any additional methodological difficulties.*

Skillful use of definitions enables the scientist to extend his deductive analysis to the remotest stages of implication, such as otherwise would be far beyond his mental reach. If not skillfully used, it often confuses his methodological co-ordination, leads him in circles and toward formal inconsistencies, that is, open logical mistakes.

III

A typical methodological mistake of this kind can be characterized as the method of *implicit solutions.* Its logical pattern is simple. Given a number of compatible fundamental postulates expressed in terms of A, B, C . . . we can make, without infringing upon rules of logic, *any* other statement concerning the same elements A, B, C . . . provided we introduce into it at least one new term, X. The reason for this freedom lies in the fact that the new term can subsequently always be defined so as to make our additional statement compatible with the initial set of basic postulates. In other words, the initial postulates taken in conjunction with the new theorem give an *implicit definition* of the term, X.

The profound methodological difference between an explicit and an implicit definition cannot be overemphasized. The second one presents a methodological problem of which the first is a solution. Error arises when it is assumed that the formulation of such an implicit theorem (that is, a theorem containing implicitly defined terms) is methodologically equivalent to a complete solution of a given problem. It is true that the perfect Laplacian intellect could at once supply the necessary explicit definition which, if substituted in our implicit statement, would transform it into a desired explicit theorem. It could indeed go so far as to visualize unlimited series of intermediate substitution, each of which if applied "backward" would return us to the original set of fundamental postulates.

The question is whether an ordinary mind would be able to do the same. If it could, the intellectual effort used to perform the feat would be equal to that demanded by the use of orthodox methods. Most probably it would lose its bearings in the maze of intermediate definitions, and then, the task having been dropped short of its ultimate goal, all the intermediate results must be written off as a complete loss.

An implicit statement if not accompanied by a note describing in which direction it is supposed to be developed, can mean almost anything. The theorem $A = B$ includes, implicitly, the whole of economic theory. Defining A as product of a quantity of money and its velocity of circulation and B as the sum total of transactions, so we obtain the well-known monetary equation of exchange. If one of the two implicit terms, say A, is interpreted to denote the marginal revenue, and the other, B, the marginal costs, the same statement is transformed into the fundamental theorem of the theory of production.[4]

Ironically enough those who most often use the method of implicit solutions very seldom undertake themselves the onerous task of explicit interpretations. They formulate a number of implicit theorems, extend the argument one or two steps forward or backward, and then let the reader find the way home by himself. If an uncautious critic ventures to express some doubts as to the "correctness" of the whole procedure, the short-cut theorist triumphantly points out that his implicit definition necessarily has *some* explicit meaning. If the critic follows a path of his own, makes a serious attempt to find his way out and gets lost, the theorist rightly but uncharitably accuses him of logical inconsistency and of inability to understand the correct meaning of the theorem.

[4] This example might explain why it is comparatively easy to discover similarity between some propositions of economic theory and thermodynamic, electrodynamic, or other types of physical equations.

Scientific discussion degenerates into a comedy of errors and mistaken identities.

At first sight it might appear astounding that a great number of scientists, including the proponents of this procedure themselves, do not seem to notice the dangers and limitations of the described method. On the contrary, every new implicit leap into the theoretical unknown seems to elicit nothing but ever increasing admiration for the miraculously painless method of scientific progress and additional contempt for pedestrian pluggers of the more cautious school. The explanation of this uncritical attitude lies apparently in the fact that the methodological outlook of most theorists is still dominated by habits developed through the use of conservative patterns. Within the framework of an orthodox theory all definitions are explicit definitions and as such they cannot hide any unsolved problems. The superficial likeness which exists between explicit and implicit formulation induces unsuspecting minds to accept the latter with the same uncritical attitude as the former. Within the orthodox pattern, the progress of a theory could be judged, so to speak, by the position of its most advanced foreposts. Applying the same criterion to measure the progress of an implicit theory, we are easily impressed by finding its forces advanced far ahead of the regular army. The fact that these implicit scouting parties have no communication whatever with their own theoretical basis and thus are in the position of prisoners, remains entirely unnoticed. Under these conditions a competitive debasement of theoretical standards becomes unavoidable.

The previous discussion makes it clear that it is the position of a statement within the given theoretical pattern—in particular its relation to the fundamental set of primary assumptions—which gives it the character of an implicit theorem. Specifically, it is the impossibility (without additional analytical efforts) of expressing the meaning of such a theorem in terms of these original assumptions.

Thus a short-cut theorist can always preclude the request for an explicit statement of any of his implicit propositions by expressly elevating the questionable theorem to the status of a fundamental postulate and by interpreting the undefined new term as an independent datum. The controversial issue acquires formally an entirely different aspect. The methodological task of finding the explicit meaning of an implicit proposition is now replaced by that of showing that the explicit theorem could be derived without making use of the additional postulate, that is, of proving that the augmented set of fundamental assumptions has been made larger than is logically necessary. A problem remains unsolved.

The main difficulty in dealing with implicit theorizing is that it is impervious to logical criticism. The weakness of its short-cut methods consists not in formal mistakes but rather in the irrelevance and unconclusiveness of the results obtained. If accused of not being able to find the explicit meaning of his own statements, an implicit theorist usually replies that such a demand is unreasonable. If, on the other hand, on consenting to elucidate a theory, he actually commits a logical mistake, he hardly will be ready to admit that this slip is the consequence of error in the methodological set-up.

One of the most effective devices used by the short-cut theorists consists in restating an explicitly derived proposition in implicit terms. The outward impressiveness of this kind of display is very great; its real significance is obviously nil.

IV

In the following paragraphs a few typical examples of *implicit analysis* are adduced. I do not entertain the hope of settling the methodological controversy: all that I wish to do is to present a few illustrations—circumstantial evidence of this kind of intellectual delinquency. The examples are chosen not on the basis of their material importance, but as typical instances of the Cambridge pattern of short-cut reasoning.

Corrected Units. The case of "corrected units" is particularly interesting for two reasons: first, it contains a perfect example of implicit definition, and second, the methodological futility of the procedure has been finally admitted with most commendable frankness by its author, Mrs. Joan Robinson.

The concept of efficiency unit was devised as a means of "simplifying" the theory of production by making all the physical production functions linear and all the physical marginal returns constant. The new corrected unit is defined as the physical quantity of any factor of production which, if added to any total quantity previously employed, would increase the output by the same fixed amount (measured in its natural, non-adjusted units). So, for example, if some particular production process described in original non-adjusted terms is subject to decreasing returns, each additional adjusted unit of the cost factor will contain more and more unadjusted units, the changing proportion being varied in such a way as to render its marginal productivity constant. The underlying idea is obviously that by some appropriate transformation of coordinates any manifold, however complicated, can be changed into another manifold of a simpler shape.

What Mrs. Robinson did not seem to have noticed while proposing the new concept is that all the mental energy which was saved by using the new simplified production function instead of the old one ought to have been spent in figuring out the appropriate transformation formula. As mentioned above, in this particular instance, she realized her methodological error.[5]

Short-cut solution of theoretical problems with help of implicit transformations of coordinates has been repeatedly used by Cambridge economists when faced with intricacies of quantitative analysis (see, for example, Mr. J. M. Keynes's definition of "labor units" and "wage units" in the General Theory of Employment, pp. 41-4).

Ideal Output. The more intricate an analytical task appears to be, the greater is the temptation to tackle it with the apparatus of implicit analysis. One of the most difficult (very likely unsolvable) theoretical questions an economist has ever to face is the welfare problem.

Mr. R. F. Kahn[6] begins his discussion of *ideal output* by assum-

---

[5] "I should like to take this opportunity of pointing out that the device suggested in my *Economics of Imperfect Competition* (p. 332) for getting over the difficulty by constructing "corrected natural units," is completely worthless, "Euler's Theorem. . . ." *The Economic Journal,* September 1934, p. 402.

[6] "Some Notes on Ideal Output," *Economic Journal,* March 1935.

ing that "the price of any commodity (is) denotes its marginal utility" and that the "differences in the marginal utility of money to different people" do not exist. After having stated curtly that the analysis of these assumptions "belongs to a separate compartment of economics of welfare" he plunges into an elaborate discussion of the remaining problems without giving the discarded issue a second thought. The term which gives Mr. Kahn's theory an implicit character, is his concept of the "marginal utility of money." Mr. Kahn intimates that it presents an unsolvable problem by referring us to the "other department"; and when mentioning in the next passage the "average consumer," he even indicates the typical form in which so many an implicit concept enters economic theory—the form of an index number.[7]

The impasse thus created is not as harmless as in the case of Mrs. Robinson's adjusted units. All the efforts to solve the theoretical index number problem have hitherto been entirely unsuccessful. Very likely the concept can be shown to be fundamentally irrational. Mr. Kahn's implicit assumption would become in this case not only methodologically useless, but also logically false, and the entire structure of his theory of ideal output would have to be razed from top to bottom.

Elasticity of Substitution. The discussion centering around the elasticity of substitution gives an illuminating example of what an unsettling influence such an implicitly defined term is likely to have. Since Mr. Hicks first introduced this concept in his *Theory of Wages*, no less than nine Cambridge and two orthodox economists have tried, in over twenty articles, notes and replies, to clarify and explain to each other its exact meaning. Now (in November 1936) after three years of intensive discussion, Mr. Hicks asks himself, "What sense (if any) is left in our standard proposition[8] . . . ?" and finds the situation so precarious that he is already looking toward a "second line of hypothesis (?) in case the

[7] In tracking down implicit concepts, it is in general very useful to look first of all for "theoretical" index numbers.

[8] The "standard proposition" is this: "an increase in the supply of a factor will increase the factor's share in the social dividend if the elasticity of substitution between it and the other resources employed is greater than unity." *Review of Economic Studies*, October 1936, p. 10.

first gets us into difficulties." Following Mr. Hicks's ingenious attempts to catch the elusive "sense" of his own short-cut definition, it is interesting to note how easily his explanations end up in the emergence of new implicit theorems. Discussing "complication" number two (that of imperfect competition) he solves the difficulty by introducing a new parameter with a new name, the *measure of exploitation*. It is defined with the help of a new formula which indicates that the *elasticity of substitution*, multiplied by the *measure of exploitation*, gives the distribution ratio of the product between the two factors of production. "It seems, therefore, that we shall not get a very (?) wrong impression if we use our theory even under conditions of imperfect competition—provided we remember to ask the supplementary question, have any new opportunities emerged for exploitation— . . . ?" Mr. Hicks does not appear to see that his method of solving the problem consists in replacing one implicit assumption by another. With equal logic he could put down another formula, according to which the distribution ratio would be equated to the ratio of the physical inputs of the two factors multiplied by a new parameter entitled, say, the *coefficient of redistribution*. He could even retain the final sentence as it stands, merely changing the phrasing of the "supplementary question" from "opportunities for exploitation" to "opportunities for redistribution."

I do not doubt that it is logically possible to find a definition of elasticity of substitution which (unlike the narrow technical interpretation) would make Mr. Hicks's standard proposition explicit, consistent, and universally true at the same time. I doubt, however, whether an intellectual *tour de force* of that kind would yield results of greater theoretical significance than those which could be and have been already obtained, with much smaller loss of mental energy on the basis of orthodox methodological pattern.

Aggregate Supply and Aggregate Demand Functions. No list of implicit theories could be complete without mentioning Mr. Keynes's economic writings. It is the embarrassment of plenty in his case which makes the proper choice of an example particularly difficult. The new concept of aggregate supply and demand functions used in the *General Theory of Employment* presents an interesting instance of implicit treatment of the general equilibrium problem.

The classical concept of general equilibrium presupposes the existence of a great number of *independent data* (production functions, indifference functions, etc.) which simultaneously determine the quantities, prices, and all other variables of the system. In putting forward a *specific* set of equations, the orthodox economist first makes an attempt to verify the logical consistency of his fundamental postulates, secondly, he expects to discover in this way some less obvious aspects of the price-quantity mechanism.

Mr. Keynes's equations of aggregate supply and aggregate demand are removed a great number of steps from any basic assumption and data. Even so Mr. Keynes himself would hardly deny the obvious observation that both functions depend upon an identical set of primary data, that is, that they are fundamentally interdependent. Methodologically, these two functions are analogous to the distribution formula devised by Mr. Hicks for analysis of a not perfectly competitive situation (see pp. 68, 69). In one case, the implicit element consists of a *newly introduced term* —the coefficient of exploitation; in the other it is represented by the entirely *indefinite form* of the postulated relations.

Without imperiling the logical consistency or the theoretical usefulness of his statements, Mr. Keynes could interpret the D and C of the two equations not as the aggregate demand and aggregate supply, but as the total chicken food supply and total chicken food demand respectively: there obviously must exist *some* kind of relation between each of these two quantities and the total amount of employment, N. The "equilibrium value" of N could be defined by the point of intersection of these two curves —the point at which the total demand for chicken food would be equal to its total supply.

The methodological danger connected with the use of such implicitly defined concepts of aggregate supply and demand curves reveals itself as soon as an attempt is being made to apply them in the analysis of economic change. Discussing in one of the last chapters of his book the response of total employment to a given change in aggregate demand, Mr. Keynes makes this reaction dependent upon the shape—in particular, the elasticity—of the aggregate supply function. He obviously implies a situation in which one of the two functions "shifts" while the other retains its shape and position unchanged; a situation which is, because of the fundamental interdependence of the two functions, highly improbable not to say impossible. The methodological danger of potential misinterpretation, which is inherent in any implicit statement, here actually leads to an open logical inconsistency.

In choosing these examples from the writings of Cambridge economists, I do not wish to imply that theirs is the only school of economic thought which has indulged in this type of short-cut reasoning. A bare mention of the Austrian concept of the "period of production" or of the Marxian concept of the "socially necessary labor" (used as the measure of value) would suffice to dispel any such impression. It would seem, however, that a procedure which in the work of other authors appears to be an occasional methodological lapse, becomes in the hands of a now conspicuous group of theorists the major analytical weapon.

6

The significance of Marxian economics
for present-day economic theory

The subject of this discussion can be conveniently approached under three separate headings. First, I will say a few words about the significance of Marxian economics for the modern theory of value. Next, I propose to advance toward the frontier line of contemporary theoretical discussion—the problems of business cycles and of progressive economy in general. I shall conclude this survey by raising certain issues connected with the methodological aspect of Marxian economics.

The modern theory of prices does not owe anything to the Marxian version of the classical labor theory of value nor can it, in my opinion, profit from any attempts toward reconciliation or mediation between the two types of approach. A number of economists who consider themselves as belonging to the Marxist school of thought have taken a similar stand, so that in stressing this point further I could be rightfully accused of trying to break into an open door.

There exists, however, in the value controversy one point which apparently did not attract sufficient attention. In the very first pages of the first volume of *Capital*, Marx raised against the "vulgar" (I guess he would call them today "orthodox" or "neo-classical") economists the accusation of "fetishism." Instead of looking for the ultimate deep-lying price-determinants, they operate,

From the *American Economic Review Supplement*, Vol. XXVIII, No. 1, March 1938.

according to Marx, with superficial, imaginary concepts of supply and demand, money costs, etc., all of which refer to purely fictitious relations. Although these subjective concepts acquire in the mind of acting economic individuals the quality of independent, tyrannically dominating forces, actually they are nothing but the products of deliberate actions of the same individuals.

This typically Hegelian observation is strikingly correct. Is, however, the theoretical conclusion which Marx seems to draw from it actually justified? If it were, his criticism would indict modern price theory even in a greater degree than any of the theories of his contemporaries, John Stuart Mill, Senior, or Malthus.

Is it not a pure and simple fetishism to construct a theory of duopoly in terms of evaluation by Mr. Jones of Mr. Smith's expectations concerning Mr. Robinson's probable actions?

The procedure of the modern value theory comprises two clearly separable and fundamentally different types of analysis. First, it considers the behavior of individual entrepreneurs and householders in terms of their own economic motivations and explains this behavior in terms of their own notions—in terms of individual demand schedules as they appear to them, of the monetary cost curves as they appear to them, and so on. Next, the modern theory shows how the actions of these individuals determine independently of their rational will and, using the famous Marxian expression, "behind their consciousness," the shape and position of the very same imaginary demand and cost curve.

In the first stage of his analysis, the modern theorist simply reproduces the rational considerations of entrepreneurs engaged in the business of maximizing their profits, and describes the reactions of consumers seeking the best possible satisfactions of their wants. In principle, at least, each individual knows this part of economic theory and acts accordingly. For the theorist, it would be inadmissible to introduce at this stage of his analysis any other concepts but those which dominate the mind of actual producers and consumers. He explains their actions in terms of their own beliefs and fetishes.

The opposite is true of the second part of economic theory,

which could be called the theory of external interdependence. Here we analyze certain objective repercussions of individual economic activities entirely independently of the subjective attitude of the individual actors. As a matter of fact, and this has been repeatedly pointed out, a large part of theoretical analysis at this stage of argument is based on the assumption that the economic individuals concerned are ignorant of any such objective repercussions of their own activities. If they were to taste the apple of knowledge their behavior would become fundamentally different and our theoretical system would turn false the very moment it became the property of manufacturers, workers, or consumers.

At this level of the argument, the theorist actually removes the veil of subjective appearances and, instead of interpreting actions of economic individuals in terms of subjective motivations and beliefs, he explains these very beliefs and motivations in terms of objective actions and reactions.

What did Marx mean exactly in accusing the bourgeois economist of fetishism? If he simply wanted to intimate that the second stage of theoretical explanation constituted a necessary complement to the first, the modern theorist will heartily agree with him and point to the Walrasian theory of general equilibrium or the recently developed theory of monopolistic competition as two outstanding examples of this type of analysis. It must have been the guardian angel of Marx, the prophet, who made some of the modern theorists introduce expectations, anticipations, and various other *ex ante* concepts, thus justifying *ex post* some of the most vitriolic pages of the first volume of *Capital*. But I prefer to let these modern theorists settle their own account with Marx.

Should, however, the Marxian theory of fetishism be understood as a forthright condemnation of the first stage of our theoretical analysis—the stage which deals with conscious reactions of individual entrepreneurs and householders—his objection must simply be turned down as fundamentally erroneous.

Unlike the modern theory of prices the present-day business cycle analysis is clearly indebted to Marxian economics. Without raising the question of priority it would hardly be an exaggeration to say that the three volumes of *Capital* helped more than any other single work to bring the whole problem into the forefront of economic discussion.

It is rather difficult to say how much Marx actually contributed to the solution of the problem. After years of intensive controversy, there is still no solution. I expect that this statement will not elicit any open contradiction, although I do not remember having read or heard a business cycle theorist admit that he was unable to solve this or that problem; the nearest he comes to such an admission is when he declares that the particular problem is insolvable, which implies that not only he but that also no one else will be able to solve it.

The two principal variants of the Marxian explanation of business cycles, or rather "economic crises," are well known. One is the theory of under-investment based on the famous law of the falling rate of profits, the other is the theory of under-consumption. Both might contain some grain of truth. Which business cycle theory does not?

Scanning the pages of Marxian writings it is easy to find numerous hints and suggestions which can be interpreted as anticipating any and every of the modern theoretical constructions. Here is a curious example of this kind—an excerpt from a letter to Friedrich Engels, dated May 31, 1875:

> I communicated to Moor a story (*Geschichte*) with which I wrangled privately for a long time. He thinks, however, that the problem is insolvable or at least insolvable at the present time because it involves many factors which must be yet determined. The issue is the following one: You know the tables representing prices, discount rates, etc., in the form of zigzags fluctuating up and down. I have tried repeatedly to compute these "ups and downs" [the English expression is used by Marx]—for the purpose of business cycle analysis—as irregular curves and thus to calculate the principal laws of economic crises mathematically. I still believe that the task can be accomplished on the basis of a critically sifted statistical material.

Thus it appears that toward the end of his life Marx actually anticipated the statistical, mathematical approach to the business cycle analysis. An approach which, incidentally, only recently was declared by an authoritative Soviet Russian textbook on mathematical statistics to be nothing else but an insidious invention of the intelligence division of the French general staff.

The significance of Marxian economics for the modern business cycle theory lies, however, not in such indecisive direct attempts toward the final solution of the problem but rather in the preparatory work contained mainly in the second and partly in the third volume of *Capital.* I have in mind the famous Marxian schemes of capital reproduction.

Whatever the ultimate clue to the final theoretical solution might be, an intelligent discussion, not to say explanation, of economic fluctuations must be based on some kind of a theoretical model revealing the fundamental structural characteristic of the existing economic system. In this field the original contributions of post-Marxian economics are rather uncertain. On the one hand, we have the Walrasian scheme of m householders and n individuals, each one buying from and selling to the other. It is pretty certain that in terms of a schematic picture of such extreme generality it would be hardly possible to give an adequate realistic description of the process of economic fluctuations.

On the other hand, there is the well-known Böhm-Bawerkian model of a simple linear flow of commodities and services, originating in some distant point where only land and labor are being applied and emptying itself, after a greater or smaller number of intermediate stages, into the final reservoir of finished consumers goods. The picture certainly does not lack concreteness. Unfortunately its concreteness is utterly misplaced.

The actual structure of the present-day economic system is anything but linear. The mutual interrelation of industries is anything but that of simple vertical succession and—what is particularly important—that initial stage characterized by exclusive application of the "original factors of production" is nonexistent. If Böhm-Bawerk did actually set out in search of this hypothetical first stage, he would find himself now still on the road.

The controversial issue is not of mean importance. It affects even such relatively simple problems as, for example, the question of substitution of machinery for labor. If approached without preconceived notions, the matter is a rather simple one. Should, let us say, the price of "horse labor" increase in relation to the costs connected with the operation of a tractor, the farmer would substitute tractors for horses. The demand for horses would decrease. If horses were able and willing to exist on smaller hay rations the postulated price discrepancy would disappear and they would find complete employment at a lower level of "forage rates." Otherwise serious unemployment appears to be inevitable. Put the word "workers" instead of "horses," "wage rates" instead of "forage rates," and "entrepreneur" instead of "farmer" and you have a fairly accurate statement of the problem and its solution.

Now comes the compensation theorist and objects. According to him, the price of tractors could not fall in relation to the price of horses in the first place. Referring to the vertical structure of the Böhm-Bawerkian scheme he substantiates his objection but points out that "in the last instance"—in the famous first stage—all mechanical instruments are produced by labor and land alone and concludes that an increase in the price of labor would necessarily cause an equivalent rise in the tractor price.

If a faulty structural picture of our economic system can produce confusion even in the discussion of a relatively simple theoretical problem, it is bound to raise havoc with the incomparably more complicated analysis of cyclical business fluctuations.

Marx successfully combated the Böhm-Bawerkian point of view in attacking the contemporary *théorie des débouchés* of Jean Baptiste Say. He also developed the fundamental scheme describing the interrelation between consumer and capital goods industries. Far from being the *ultimo ratio* of this line of analysis, the Marxian scheme still constitutes one of the few propositions concerning which there seems to exist a tolerable agreement among the majority of business cycle theories. It is interesting to note in this connection that even Professor Hayek, as can be seen from his recent articles, is busy reconstructing his own triangular investment diagram. One does not need to be a prophet to predict that sooner or later he will present to us a circular arrangement of the orthodox Marxian type.

The controversy which thus seems to be drawing toward a happy ending has incidentally put both disputing parties into a rather paradoxical situation. The dean of the bourgeois economists insisted on theoretical reduction of all capital goods to pure labor; he was opposed by the formidable proponent of the labor theory of value in the role of a defender of the independent, primary function of fixed capital.

However important these technical contributions to the progress of economic theory, in the present-day appraisal of Marxian achievements they are overshadowed by his brilliant analysis of the long-run tendencies of the capitalistic system. The record is indeed impressive: increasing concentration of wealth, rapid elimination of small and medium sized enterprise, progressive limitation of competition, incessant technological progress accompanied by the ever growing importance of fixed capital, and, last but not least, the undiminishing amplitude of recurrent business cycles—an unsurpassed series of prognostications fulfilled, against which modern economic theory with all its refinements has little to show indeed.

What significance has this list of successful anticipations for modern economic theory? Those who believe that Marx has said the last word on the subject invite us to quit. The attitude of other somewhat less optimistic—or should I say pessimistic—critics is well expressed by Professor Heimann: "Marx's work remains by far the most comprehensive and impressive model of what we have to do." The whole issue of the significance of Marxian economics for modern theory is thus transformed into a methodological question.

I enter this higher plane of discussion with feelings of considerable reluctance and serious apprehension. Not that Marx and his followers were sparse in their contributions to controversial methodological questions; on the contrary, it is rather the overabundance of contradictory and, at the same time, not very specific advice that makes it so difficult to find our way through the maze of divergent interpretations and explanations. It was in the same spirit of despair that Marx himself, in one of his lighter moods, exclaimed, "I am not a Marxist."

Roughly all these methodological prescriptions can be divided into two groups. On the one side the general considerations, which, although highly interesting from the point of view of philosophy and the sociology of knowledge, are entirely non-operational from the point of view of practical scientific work. It might be true, for example, that a bourgeois economist, by the very virtue of his social and economic position, is essentially unable to recognize the driving forces and to discern the fundamental relations which govern the rise and fall of capitalist society. But what can he do about it? Give up teaching and investigating and join the proletarian ranks? This might render him a more useful member of society, but will anybody seriously maintain that such a change could improve his economic theory?

Into the same group of essentially non-operational prescriptions I would also place all references to the efficiency of the dialectical method. It might be true that the concept of unity of opposites inspired Newton in his invention of infinitesimal calculus and helped Marx in his analysis of capital accumulation—at least it would be rather difficult to disprove such contentions—but it is very doubtful whether even a most careful reading of Engel's exposition of this principle could help Mr. Keynes, for example, with his solution of the unemployment problem.

On the other hand, Marxian methodology seems to contain some more concrete principles and concepts which deserve serious and detailed consideration. It is this aspect of the problem which was so ably brought to light by Dr. Lange in his brilliant article "Marxian Economics and Modern Economic Theory."[1] Translating the Marxian slang into the vernacular of modern economics, he defines the issue at stake as the problem of data and variables in economic theory.

Admitting the superiority of the modern equilibrium theory, Dr. Lange tries to explain the marked success of Marxian prognostications by the particular attention which the author of *Capital* gave to the treatment of his data. It is an interesting thesis and it deserves a closer, critical scrutiny.

Data comprise all those elements of a theory which are used in

[1] *Review of Economic Studies,* June 1935.

the explanation of the variables but are not explained themselves within the system of the same theory, that is, they are simply considered as being "given."

Among these there are first of all those general propositions which indicate whether we are going to talk about cabbages or kings and thus describe the general "universe of discourse," as the logician calls it. These data are predominantly qualitative in character. The so-called institutional assumptions of economic theory belong to this first category.

Marx persistently derided contemporary classical economists for their failure to specify explicitly the institutional background of their theories. He was doubtless right and the same criticism applies equally well to some of the modern theorists. Fortunately enough in the process of their actual work the bourgeois economists implicitly and maybe even unconsciously framed their theories in complete accordance with the fundamental, relevant facts of the institutional background of capitalist society. Thus the subjective methodological shortcomings did not impair the objective validity of their theoretical deductions.

The second type of data comprise statements of basic interrelations which constitute the immediate point of departure for derivation and formulation of specific propositions of our theoretical system. Technical production functions, shapes of the demand curves describing the consumers' choice, schedules of liquidity preferences—all these are examples of this second type of data. They are predominantly quantitative in character.

It is this category of data which was meant by Clapham in his famous reference to the "empty boxes of economic theory." The boxes are not much fuller now than they were twenty years ago, but the Marxian theory hardly contains the stuff which could be used to fill the vacuum.

Dr. Lange seems to be of a different opinion. He points out in this connection the concept of technological progress as the mainstay of the Marxian theory of economic evolution of the capitalist society. This progress is being made responsible for the formation of a permanent army of unemployed which in its turn is supposed to prevent the otherwise unavoidable absorption of all profit by an ever increasing national wage bill. Dr. Lange's statement of the problem suffers, however, from serious ambiguity.

As indicated before, substitution of machinery for labor can easily take place without new inventions, simply through movement from one point of a given production function to another. Reduced interest rate due to ever increasing supply of accumulated capital might easily lead to such a result. The technical datum—the technical horizon of the entrepreneur—will remain in this case as stable as for example the cost curve of a monopolist might remain stable while he is changing his position by sliding along his curve in response to some demand variations.

A quite different phenomenon takes place when an entrepreneur reduces his demand for labor not in response to changing interest or wage rates but because a previously unknown new invention makes it profitable to use less labor and more machinery, even if interest as well as wage rates were to remain the same as before. Here we are facing a genuine change in primary technological data.

Both types of adjustment mark the evolution of capitalist economics. Dr. Lange does not seem to make a clear-cut distinction between the two, but the general drift of his argument points toward the second rather than first type of labor displacement. Neither is the position of Marx himself particularly clear. The great stress put upon the process of progressive accumulation, which the author of *Capital* considers to be a necessary condition of the very existence of the present economic system, indicates that it is rather the first type of substitution which he has in mind.

Anyway, the fact that the Marxian theory lends itself on this point to so many different interpretations, shows that insofar as the careful specifications and analysis of basic data are concerned, it is rather the Marxist who can learn from modern economists than vice versa.

Finally we come to the third and last aspect of this methodological conflict. Modern economic theory limits itself to a much narrower set of problems than that which is included in the scope of Marxian economics. Many items treated as data in the first system are considered to be in the group of dependent variables in the second. Insofar as the general methodological principle is concerned any effective extension of a theoretical system beyond its old frontier represents a real scientific progress.

To avoid a misunderstanding it must be kept in mind that such extension cannot possibly result in a complete liquidation of independent data. It simply replaces one set of data by another. So, for example, if we were to include governmental action as a dependent variable within the system of economic theory, the amount of public expenditure of the height of import tariffs had to be considered as a function of some other economic variables in the same way as the output of a firm in competition is considered to be a function of the prevailing market price. It is perfectly obvious, however, that the first type of relationship is much less definite in its character than the second. This, I think, is the reason why the modern economist is reluctant to discuss both types of interrelations on the same plane. And he is right because neither part can profit from such artificial connection, which does not mean that the result of the two types of investigation could not and should not be fruitfully combined in attempts toward some kind of a wider synthesis. Occasional alliances and frequent cooperation are, however, something quite different than radical unification accompanied by complete obliteration of existing border lines.

Neither his analytical accomplishments nor the purported methodological superiority can explain the Marxian record of correct prognostications. His strength lies in realistic, empirical knowledge of the capitalist system.

Repeated experiments have shown that in their attempts to prognosticate individual behavior, professional psychologists systematically fall behind experienced laymen with a knack for "character reading." Marx was the great character reader of the capitalist system. As many individuals of this type, Marx had also his rational theories, but these theories in general do not hold water. Their inherent weakness shows up as soon as other economists not endowed with the exceptionally realistic sense of the master try to proceed on the basis of his blueprints.

The significance of Marx for modern economic theory is that of an inexhaustible source of direct observation. Much of the present-day theorizing is purely derivative, secondhand theorizing. We often theorize not about business enterprises, wages, or business cycles but about other people's theories of profits, other people's theories of wages, and other people's theories of business cycles. If before attempting any explanation one wants to learn what profits and wages and capitalist enterprises actually are, he can obtain in the three volumes of *Capital* more realistic and relevant firsthand information than he could possibly hope to find in ten successive issues of the *United States Census,* a dozen textbooks on contemporary economic institutions, and even, may I dare to say, the collected essays of Thorstein Veblen.

PART TWO

7

The fundamental assumption of Mr. Keynes's monetary theory of unemployment

I

The difference between Mr. Keynes's new theory of economic equilibrium and the "orthodox" classical scheme is fundamentally a difference in assumptions, or rather in one basic assumption. While the two divergent points of view come to a clash more specifically in the discussion concerning the shape of the supply function for labor, the theoretical issue involved is much more general in its scope. In the present note I shall first of all try to redefine the contested principle in precise terms, then interpret its relevant theoretical implications, and finally make an attempt to examine the arguments which Mr. Keynes raises against the "orthodox" solution of the problem and in favor of his own standpoint. I shall confine myself to the strictly theoretical problems.

The theoretical picture underlying the economic analysis of general equilibrium is that of the system of interrelated household and entrepreneurial units engaged in more or less continuous economic transactions. The quantity of each particular kind of commodities and services sold or purchased by each individual enterprise or household is considered to be a function of a number of different prices. On the basis of certain assumptions concerning the forces which are supposed to govern the behavior of business firms and individuals, economic theory is able to derive the general characteristics of these functional interrelations between prices and quantities.

From the *Quarterly Journal of Economics*, Vol. 1, No. LI, November 1936.

One of these fundamental assumptions—that which Mr. Keynes is ready to repudiate—defines an important universal property of all supply and demand functions by stating that the *quantity of any service or any commodity demanded or supplied by a firm or an individual remains unchanged if all the prices upon which it (directly) depends increase or decrease exactly in the same proportion.* In mathematical terms, this means that all supply and demand functions, with prices taken as independent variables and quantity as a dependent one, are homogeneous functions of the zero degree. In course of the following discussion, this theorem will be referred to as the "homogeneity postulate."[1] The term "price" is used here in its general theoretical sense, that is, it includes money wage rates paid for all the different kinds of services as well as commodity prices.

The significance of this theorem for the analysis of monetary influences within the framework of our economic system has been mentioned often enough. It is best expressed by the well-known hypothetical "experiment" of doubling overnight the cash holdings of all business enterprises and households. Ricardo used this device to show that the prices of all commodities and services will undergo under this condition a proportionally equal change, and the quantities produced, traded and consumed by all individual firms and households will remain exactly the same as before. His conclusion is obviously based upon the homogeneity postulate. The practical implications which Ricardo was inclined to draw from this hypothetical case obviously imply also a second assumption, and an unrealistic one—that our economic system is absolutely free from any kind of frictions and time-lag effects; that is, that it adjusts itself to any primary variation (in this case it is a monetary one) instantaneously.

In order to admit the possibility of monetary influences upon the quantitative, material set-up of an economic system it is neces-

[1] The homogeneity postulate applies to the simple Walrasian type as well as to all possible kinds of "dynamic" equations which include among the independent variables "expected prices," derivatives of the given price changes, etc. It hardly needs to be mentioned that this postulate has nothing whatever to do with the controversial issue of homogeneous and non-homogeneous production functions.

sary to sacrifice at least one of these two assumptions. The modern "orthodox" monetary theory definitely dropped the second one, its analytical apparatus being dominated by more or less explicit introduction of time lags and frictions of various kinds. Mr. Keynes is ready to repudiate also the first, the homogeneity postulate. He does not in any way neglect time-lag phenomena; they definitely constitute an important element of his latest as well as his previous system. In analyzing the new theory, it is very important, however, to realize that the abandonment of the homogeneity assumption alone would suffice to make the automatically neutral behavior of the economic system toward monetary influences impossible.

Let us modify the set-up of the frictionless, lagless and "homogeneous" economic system by assuming that one demand or one supply curve of any single household or enterprise is not homogeneous (in the previously defined sense). A proportional price variation with unchanged quantity relations becomes, under this condition, logically impossible; the new non-homogeneous household or enterprise would be induced by an all-round price rise or price fall to demand (or to supply) larger or smaller quantities of one or more particular commodities than before, while the amount demanded and supplied by all the other households and enterprises, still subject to the homogeneity condition, would remain unchanged. A discrepancy would arise incompatible with conditions of general equilibrium. This shows that *in a frictionless system with at least one or more non-homogeneous elements, the quantity of money ceases to be a "neutral" factor*. On the contrary, the equilibrium amount of every commodity or service produced or purchased by *any* household or business unit must be now considered to be a function of this quantity.

The determination of the monetary maximum for the output of any commodity, or of the maximum employment of any kind of service (say labor) becomes a simple mathematical problem. It is, of course, very unlikely that the monetary optima computed for each of the many different kinds of goods and services would be the same. The quantity of money which brings about the maximum output of automobiles might be much smaller or much larger than that which would secure the greatest possible employment to some particular kind of labor. Monetary unemployment of any factor of production as well as the monetary underproduction (=underconsumption) of any and every commodity can be consequently defined as the difference between the theoretically computed monetary maximum and the actual figure of employment or production. On the basis of the non-homogeneity assumption, the interest rate becomes of course a function of the quantity of money (and vice versa) in the same way as are the employment and output figures of all industries. That is, the main point of Mr. Keynes's theory of interest follows as simply and directly from his basic assumption as his interpretation of monetary unemployment.

Summarizing the argument, we conclude that a monetary theory of unemployment, unless it is based on time-lag and friction phenomena, stands and falls with the non-homogeneity condition.

I I

Mr. Keynes assumes that the supply function for labor is non-homogeneous. Unfortunately for the present discussion, he does not commit himself to a precise, clear-cut statement of this basic postulate. In particular, it appears to be practically impossible to say which of his assertions concerning the behavior of labor are supposed to set forth the main thesis and which are used to substantiate its correctness.

If taken literally, all of Mr. Keynes's remarks concerning the behavior of labor in relation to prices and wages are compatible with the "orthodox" homogeneity assumption. The assertion, for example, that "in the event of a small rise in the price of wage-goods relatively to the money-wage . . . the aggregate supply of labor willing to work for the current money-wage . . . would be greater than the existing volume of employment" (p. 15) (the omitted part of sentence deals with the demand for labor) expresses a widely accepted "orthodox" theorem concerning the "negative inclination" of the supply curve for labor. It is perfectly compatible with the classical homogeneity assumption. If we turn to another somewhat more general statement by Mr. Keynes, of the same idea, his view appears to be that the fact that a reduction of money wages might be accompanied by an increase in real wages (that is, proportionally greater decrease in the prices of consumption goods) militates against some basic assumptions of the classical theory (pp. 11-12). By the use of the most "orthodox" analysis it can be shown that within the framework of a classical Walrasian system this particular type of price variation can occur as easily as any other. The nearest Mr. Keynes comes to a precise formulation of the crucial issue is his assertion that the supply of labor depends not upon the "real" but (also?) upon money wages (pp. 8-9).[2]

The homogeneity postulate is not introduced by the classical economists as an axiom; it is derived from a series of fundamental assumptions concerning the economic behavior of individuals and business firms. The most effective way of disputing their theory would be that of discrediting these initial assumptions. Mr. Keynes has not resorted to this method of attack but has attempted to show directly that the contested postulate itself is at variance with facts. In order to be successful in this endeavor, he would have to find a series of empirical situations in which all the prices which might exercise a direct influence upon the size of the labor supply, although constant in their *relative* magnitude, would differ from case to case in absolute height. The non-homogeneity of the labor supply function would be proven if, under these conditions and in absence of friction and time lags, the amount of labor employed would change (in a significant degree) with the variation of the price level, instead of remaining constant as expected by "orthodox" theorists. No demonstration of this kind is given in the pages of the *General Theory of Unemployment*. There is good reason to believe that in view of the scarcity of available statistical information and because of the presence of the great number of frictional phenomena, no direct demonstration could be made. Mr. Keynes's assault upon the

[2] Mr. Keynes's interpretation of the "orthodox" theory is liable to produce the false impression as if the dubious index concept of "real" wages constitutes an essential element of this theory. As a matter of fact, if carefully stated, the "static" "classical" supply function does not include any other variables than the amount of labor, prices of the consumer's goods, the interest rate, and the money wage-rates.

fundamental assumption of the "orthodox" economic theory seems to have missed its target.

These critical remarks are concerned with what appears to be the essentially novel contribution of the *General Theory of Unemployment* to the monetary "theory of total output"—the attempt to modify one of the basic static assumptions of the "orthodox" economists. The static character of the proposed innovation is somewhat obscured by the fact that in his endeavor to give a realistic analysis of economic forces and interrelations, Mr. Keynes has introduced into his theory a number of dynamic considerations, most of them in one form or another already incorporated in the apparatus of the modern monetary and business cycle theory.[3]

The essentially static foundation of the new theory of unemployment becomes quite obvious as soon as we try to visualize a stationary state with constant prices, unvarying output and perfect foresight. If Mr. Keynes's theory were correct, this economic system could and most probably would be subject to involuntary monetary unemployment.

Dynamic considerations are introduced into the *General Theory of Employment* mostly in connection with analysis of deflationary tendencies which are supposed to threaten the expansion of employment opportunities. This latter effect is inseparably tied up with the responsiveness of the economic system to monetary influences, which again leads back to the non-homogeneity of the labor supply. Thus it appears that Mr. Keynes's case has yet to be proven.

[3] The "method of expectations" so ingeniously used by Mr. Keynes and interpreted by Mr. J. R. Hicks (in his review of the *General Theory of Employment, Economic Journal,* June 1936) can be characterized as an attempt to simplify the analysis of dynamic phenomena by application of a static theoretical pattern. Instead of considering, as the "orthodox" mathematical economists do, the expected prices and the expected rate of interest to be a function of the present or rather past price and interest rates, this method interprets them as independent data.

One cannot resist the temptation to cite in this connection, Mr. Keynes's ill-tempered remark directed against the "pseudo-mathematical method" which "assumes strict independence between factors involved" where it should not and "allows the author to lose sight of the complexities and interdependencies of the real world."

8

Postulates: Keynes's *General Theory* and the classicists

"Yet after all there is no harm in being sometimes wrong—especially if one is promptly found out." (Keynes in "Alfred Marshall, 1842-1924," EJ, 1924, p. 345.)

I

In staging his assault against orthodox theory, Keynes did not attack the internal consistency of its logical structure; he rather attempted to demonstrate the unreality of its fundamental empirical assumptions by showing up what he considered to be the obvious falsity of its factual conclusions. The orthodox theory proves that involuntary unemployment cannot exist, but we know that it actually does exist. Since the formal logic of the orthodox proof is essentially correct, the fault must be sought in its choice of the basic empirical premises. This is the general plan of the Keynesian attack.[1] It took the overzealous enthusiasm of numerous neophytes to confuse the elegant outlines of the master's enveloping strategy by opening a non-discriminating sniping at the orthodox adversary all along the line of the argument.

Since it is the question of factual premises on which Keynes chooses to base his criticism of the traditional theory, an examination of these assumptions and of those substituted by him in their place can serve as a convenient starting point for a comparative study of the two systems.

The nature of the supply of labor and that of the demand for money are the two principal points of divergence between the

From *The New Economics*, ed. S. Harris, New York: Knopf, 1948.
[1] Its peculiar indirect nature is clearly revealed in Keynes's willingness to accept the orthodox analysis as a valid, albeit practically unimportant, special case of his own general theory.

basic postulates of the *General Theory* and the teachings of the classical doctrine. The departure from orthodox analysis in the treatment of these two particular issues enables Keynes to lift the traditional theory off its hinges and develop his own peculiar theory of effective demand and involuntary unemployment. The problem of labor supply is technically the less intricate one of the two and we will follow Keynes's own example in taking it up first.

I I

Traditional analysis considers the aggregate quantity of labor supplied, in the case where this supply is a competitive one, to be a function of the *real* wage rates; Keynes on the contrary assumes that up to a certain point—defined by him as the point of full employment—one particular level of *money* wages exists at which the supply of labor is perfectly elastic and below which no labor can be hired at all. The deliberate exclusion of the cost of living as a determinant of labor supply makes the latter independent of the level of *real* wages.[2]

Not only are the two statements describing the nature of the labor supply incompatible, but the positions occupied by them within the theoretical structures to which they respectively belong are also different. The monetary supply curve of labor is a fundamental postulate of the *General Theory* in the true sense of the term. A starting point of a long chain of deductive reasoning, it is itself not theoretically derived within the body of the Keynesian system; if it were, if the salient properties of his labor supply function had been derived from some other, more general, propositions of the Keynesian theory, the statement of these properties itself could not have been considered to constitute a fundamental postulate. It would become one of the many deductively demonstrable theorems. A truly fundamental postulate by its very nature cannot be verified by deductive reasoning, in empirical science it must be accepted or rejected on the basis of

[2] Keynes himself did not consider in any detail the conditions of a labor supply possibly exceeding full employment level. Most of his interpreters assume, however, that beyond that critical point the nature of the supply schedule changes and the quantity of labor offered for hire becomes a function of the real wage rate alone.

direct reference to facts. In keeping with this principle, the author of the *General Theory* justifies his own assumptions concerning the nature of the labor supply curve through direct reference to immediate experience of the mechanism of actual labor markets. Taking up the criticism of the alternative, orthodox approach—which explains the magnitude of labor supply in terms of real rather than money wages—Keynes by analogy refers to it as a fundamental postulate, which it obviously is not. The extreme form of this Keynesian interpretation of the classical position is expressed in the often repeated statement that the orthodox theory assumes the existence of full employment, a statement which obviously reveals confusion between the conclusions to which an argument leads and the assumptions with which it begins.

Far from being directly assumed, the real supply curve of labor is derived by the modern non-Keynesian theory from a set of other much more general propositions. The truly fundamental postulates of the orthodox theory deal with the general nature of economic choice. Without embarking upon a technical discussion of this familiar piece of analysis, it is sufficient to make here two observations on the particular aspect of this theory which has a direct bearing upon the issue at hand: in sinking its foundations deeper in the ground of experience than does the Keynesian analysis, the traditional theory is able to use a smaller number of separate assumptions and thus to achieve a more integrated system of theoretical conclusions. Instead, for example, of making one separate assumption describing the shape of the labor supply schedule, another defining the properties of the demand schedule for consumers' goods, and yet a third stating the nature of the relationship between the income of an individual and his propensity to save, the classical economist derives all three kinds of relationship from the same set of more general assumptions. This, incidentally, enables him also to reveal the mutual interdependence of the three kinds of schedules.

In making the phenomena, which the orthodox theorist thinks himself able to explain in terms of some common principle, objects of separate fundamental postulates, Keynes imparts to his system the freedom to deal with assumed situations which from the point of view of the orthodox approach are clearly logically

impossible and thus theoretically unmanageable. This characteristic double-jointedness of his analytical apparatus gives Keynes
a good reason to claim that his theory is more general than that
of the orthodox economists. If, on the other hand, the ability to
explain a given set of phenomena on the basis of a smallest possible set of independent assumptions were used as the criterion
of generality, the Keynesian approach would clearly appear less
general than the classical.

III

It is only natural that attempts have been made to place under
the Keynesian postulate some kind of theoretical underpinnings
which would bring the foundation of his analytical structure to
the level of orthodox argument. One approach would follow very
closely the line of classical procedure in deriving the monetary
supply curve of labor from a general utility function. In contrast
to the classical, this Keynesian utility function would include,
among the ultimate constituents of an individual's preference
varieties, not only the physical quantities of (future and present)
commodities and services but also the money prices of at least
some of them. In particular the *money* wage rate would be considered as entering directly the worker's utility function: confronted with a choice between two or more situations in both of
which his real income and his real effort are the same, but in one
of which both the money wage rates (and, consequently, also
the prices of consumers' goods) are higher than in the other, he
would show a definite preference for the former. A classical
Homo economicus would find neither of the two alternatives to be
more attractive than the other.

From such a monetary utility function, a monetary supply curve
of labor can be easily derived. In contrast to its classical counterpart, it will show the labor supply as dependent not only on the
relative but also on the absolute prices and wage rates.[3]

The same is true of all the other demand and supply curves

[3] In mathematical language, that means that all the classical supply and demand schedules are homogeneous functions (of all the present and expected
future prices and wage rate) of the zero degree, while the corresponding
Keynesian supply and demand curves are not.

derived from a basic monetary preference function. In particular the propensity to save—which Keynes considers as depending only on the size of the real income—will necessarily vary with even a proportional rise or fall in prices and wages.

Although neat and internally consistent, such "psychological" interpretations of the monetary element of the Keynesian theory of wages are hardly appropriate. They contradict the common sense of economic behavior. The reference to the fact that no worker has ever been seen bargaining for real wages—even if true—is obviously beside the point, since while bargaining in terms of dollars the worker, as any one else, can still be guided in his behavior by the real purchasing power of his income. Moreover, the "psychological" interpretation of the monetary element in consumers' behavior deprives Keynes's unemployment concept of its principal attribute. Why should any given rate of employment or unemployment be called "involuntary," if it is determined through conscious preference for higher money wages as against larger real income?

IV

Much more in keeping with the spirit of the *General Theory* is an interpretation which ascribes the monetary bias of the Keynesian supply curve of labor to the influence of some outside factors, that is, factors clearly distinguishable from the preference system of the workers. A minimum wage law offers a good example of such an outside factor. Whatever the shape of the intrinsic or potential supply curve (curve S_1S_2 in Fig. 1) no workers can be hired in this case at a wage rate which is lower than the legal minimum, OA. In other words, the effective supply curve would be strictly horizontal up to the point, F, in which the potential supply curve S_1S_2 crosses it from below. From that point on, a further addition to the labor supply can be obtained only at a price exceeding the legal minimum, and the effective supply curve thus coincides with the potential. That is precisely the type of a supply curve described by Keynes in the first chapters of the *General Theory*. If the position of the demand curve, say D_1D_2, happened to be such that it intersects the effective supply curve

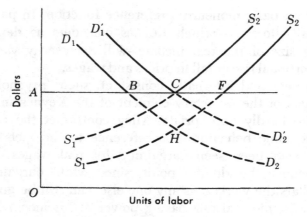

Figure 1

to the left of point F, say at B, the amount of employment, AB, is determined by the level, OA, of the minimum wage rate. The difference, BF, between this actual employment and the maximum amount, AF, which could be achieved without any change in the wage rate, provided the demand curve had shifted so as to cross the effective supply curve at F rather than at B, has been defined by Keynes as involuntary unemployment.

Although Keynes's labor market functions as if it were operating under a strictly enforced minimum wage law, the author of the *General Theory* explicitly refuses to limit the application of his theoretical scheme to obvious instances of such outside influence. The real reason for this obstinate insistence on universal validity of an apparently quite special assumption will become clearer after examination of the monetary determinants of effective demand. Keynes treats this issue as a problem of the demand for money; the orthodox economists describe it as the question of the velocity of circulation of money.

V

The existence of a reservation price for labor would not lead to involuntary unemployment, if the relative position of the classical supply curve of labor and of the corresponding demand curve happened to be such that they intersected on or above the level of the minimum wage rate. So, for example, the supply curve $S_1'S_2'$ intersects the demand curve $D_1'D_2'$ in point C, establishing the equilibrium wage rate OA and employment AC. The corresponding Keynesian supply curve $ABCS_2'$ gives in combination with the demand curve D_1D_2 the same equilibrium position C.

Involuntary unemployment could thus always be eliminated through an upward shift of the classical monetary supply and demand curves, a shift which necessarily would follow a general rise of all prices (excluding the price of labor). Additional employment (BC) created by a reduction in the purchasing power of money which, for example, would have lifted the submerged classical equilibrium point H up to the effective minimum wage level OA, must—as can be easily noted on the diagram—be smaller than the amount of unemployment (BC) defined as being involuntary in the original situation. With a higher cost of living and a positively inclined classical supply curve of labor, the amount of labor seeking employment at the prescribed minimum wage rate will be necessarily reduced.[4]

It hardly needs to be added that any further inflation, raising the classical equilibrium point above this minimum level, can have no additional effect on the amount of employment.

V I

The theory of liquidity preference provides the Keynesian system with a deflationary mechanism which defeats, through the process of automatic hoarding, every tendency toward inflationary reduction of involuntary unemployment. The outstanding characteristic of this particular part of the *General Theory* is its exclusively dynamic character. The speculative motive—which is the very heart of this deflationary mechanism—reacts not to the absolute magnitudes of the relevant variables, which are the rate of

[4] In case of a negatively inclined supply curve of labor, additional employment achieved through a general price rise would on the contrary exceed the original amount of involuntary idleness.

interest and the present and expected prices, but only to the rates of change of these variables.

Keynes does not deny the possibility of maintaining a quantity of money great enough to support any given level of prices, once this quantity is already in circulation and the corresponding price level actually established. In this respect, his theory of liquidity preference does not differ in its assumptions and conclusions, although it does in formulation, from the simple quantity theory of money. In particular it can not and does not refute the classical proposition that with a given money rate of interest a proportional change in all prices will leave the *real* demand for money exactly the same as before.

It is the transition from one price level to another which according to Keynes might prove to be impossible. Without entering into the details of the argument, it is sufficient to indicate that it runs in terms of the effects of a potential change in the price level on the velocity of circulation.

Having centered his attention on the problem of change, Keynes does not, however, treat it in explicitly dynamic terms. True to the Cambridge tradition, he resorts to the Marshallian substitute for dynamic theory—the "short-run" analysis. The short-run analysis is related to a truly dynamic approach in the same way as the, also Marshallian, partial equilibrium theory stands in respect to the Walrasian general equilibrium analysis. In both instances the problem at hand is simplified by selective omission of some of the relevant relationships, on the one hand, and treatment as independent of some of the really dependent variables, on the other. The theory of liquidity preference considers the effects which a deviation of the interest rate from its long-run equilibrium level would have on the short-run demand for money. This relationship is analyzed on the assumption of a given price level. The conclusion that under these conditions the price level cannot be raised through an increase in the supply of money is analogous to the conclusion that one cannot walk up a flight of stairs since, if one considers the position of the left foot at the first step as given, the right foot cannot possibly reach the upper platform of the stairway. For the analytical purpose at hand, this short-run argument is hardly more adequate than a static theory satisfied with description of the two hypothetical long-run equilibria, one preceding and the other succeeding the actual ascent.

Having observed the dynamic element in the Keynesian theory of money, one might turn back to his theory of wages and ask to which extent his assumption of rigid money rates possibly also represents a first awkward move in the direction of dynamic analysis. Indeed, a short-run interpretation of a time lag leads easily to treatment of the lagging variable as if it were a constant. A dynamic relationship between money wages and the cost of living, considered from the point of view of supply of labor, implies the existence of a definite lag between the former and the latter. Hence the short-run assumption that the wage rates are constant. This interpretation of the Keynesian monetary supply curve of labor seems to harmonize with the obvious reluctance of the author of the *General Theory* to commit himself to some specific institutional explanation of this particular assumption. Moreover it points the way to a further generalization of this type of reasoning which, although not advocated by the master himself, found universal acceptance among the great majority of his followers: if the stickiness assumption is a legitimate device in treatment of dynamic relationship, there is no reason why its use should be limited to the analysis of the labor market. Thus in the newer Keynesian literature not only money wage rates but also all the other prices are more often than not assumed to be fixed throughout the argument.

The limited usefulness of this simplified approach to the problem of change is unwittingly demonstrated by those authors who, on top of the typical short-run assumption of sticky money wages and fixed prices, also introduce genuine dynamic relationships into their theoretical models. The incongruity of conclusions, in which the short-run cyclical fluctuations are derived from explicitly stated dynamic relationships and long-run unemployment is explained on the basis of the short-run postulate of universal stickiness, can hardly remain unnoticed.

In the light of the foregoing observations, the principal difference between the Keynesian and the orthodox type of analysis would appear to be procedural rather than substantial. With its set of basic assumptions formulated without reference to the dynamic aspects of the problem, the classical approach suffers from what might be called theoretical farsightedness—the ability to appraise correctly the long-run trends, coupled with a singular inability to explain or even to describe the short-run changes and fluctuations. The Keynesian lenses improve somewhat but do not really correct the analytical vision so far as the short-run phenomena are concerned. However they put entirely out of focus the longer views of economic development. Only a careful reformulation of the basic postulates of the traditional theory in explicitly dynamic terms would make it applicable to the study of short-run changes without subjecting the long-run conclusion to the distorting influence of the artificial conventions of Marshallian short-run analysis.

VIII

Interwoven with short-run and monetary analysis, there runs through the fabric of the *General Theory* the thread of an argument which, although at first it seems to be quite unorthodox, proves on closer inspection to be entirely in line with the basic postulates of traditional doctrine. Its subject is the relationship between the level of employment and the rate of investment, and its conclusion is the proposition that an increased rate of investment means a higher, and a reduced rate of investment a lower, -rate of employment.

The orthodox demonstration of this relationship would in its simplest form run in terms of comparative utility of leisure (or disutility of labor), on the one hand, and of the products of labor —in this instance of investment goods—on the other. Increased demand for housing, machinery or any other new commodity could easily induce the society to redouble its labor efforts in the same way and for the same reason that causes the aborigines to crowd the employment offices of colonial plantation enterprises after they have been acquainted with and acquired a new "need" for imported glass beads and gaily colored cloth squares. A more artificial but not less mandatory need of paying taxes with money which cannot be secured by any other means but longer hours of work can obviously lead to the same result, as does compulsory labor service or, say, a program of planned industrialization.

The second set of examples fits the Keynesian line of thought obviously better than the first; the reason being that it inserts into the argument what might be called the distributive element. In a society as closely integrated and at the same time as greatly differentiated as ours, any particular set of new needs or, say, of new investment opportunities more often than not appears as a problem of free economic choice only to some relatively small section of the community; the rest is confronted with the indirect results of this choice in the form of "changed circumstances," favorable or otherwise. The demand for labor in particular is often expanded and contracted because of some primary change in tastes or opportunities other than those of the worker himself.

The apparent paradox of the situation lies not in the mechanics of economic interdependence—which can readily be described and explained without departure from classical postulates—but rather in its welfare implications. If all members of society were equally situated in respect to all the relevant choices and economic decisions, if each was employee and employer, saver and investor, farmer and city dweller, all at the same time, the distributive problem could not possibly arise: the fall in employment resulting from everybody's reduced demand for housing could (except in some special cases of external economies or diseconomies or of market imperfections) not be called involuntary any more than a morning headache could be called an involuntary result of a late party on the night before.

The liberal economist of the past century was prone to overlook the troublesome distributive aspects of economic change. Keynes, as Karl Marx before him, did well in pointing out this indeed most serious omission. They seemed to press, however, for reconstruction of the whole foundation in order to mend a leaky roof.

9

The consistency of the classical theory
of money and prices

In his recent article "The Indeterminacy of Absolute Prices in Classical Economic Theory,"[1] Don Patinkin arrives at the conclusion that "due to the traditional assumption that the demand for goods depends only on relative prices," the classical system as presented by Cassel is inconsistent. I have the impression that Mr. Patinkin's argument and consequently also his conclusion are erroneous. Since his criticism is aimed at the logical foundations of the non-Keynesian theory of general equilibrium, a further airing of the controversial issues involved can serve a useful purpose.

Patinkin considers a system involving n commodities of which the first $n-1$ represent real goods, the nth being paper money. The price of money p_n equals 1. The system consists of n demand equations:[2]

$$(6.1) \qquad D_i = f_i(p_1, p_2, \ldots, p_{n-1}), \qquad (i = 1, \ldots, n);$$

n supply equations:

$$(6.2) \qquad S_i = g_i(p_1, p_2, \ldots, p_{n-1}), \qquad (i = 1, \ldots, n);$$

and n equilibrium equations stating that the demand for each commodity equals its supply:

$$(6.3) \qquad D_i = S_i, \qquad (i = 1, \ldots, n).$$

All in all there are $3n$ equations and $3n - 1$ unknowns: n quantities supplied, n quantities demanded, and $n-1$ prices of real

From *Econometrica*, Journal of the Econometric Society, Vol. 18, No. 1, January 1950.
[1] *Econometrica*, Vol. 17, January 1949, pp. 1-27.
[2] The numbers identifying various equations correspond to those used in Patinkin's article.

goods. Not all the equations, however, are independent. The demand for money D_n (expressed as a rate of flow per unit of time) is according to the classical theory identical with the total supply of real commodities, each multiplied by its respective price. Similarly, the supply of money S_n equals the aggregate values, that is, quantities times prices, or all real demands. Thus in his equation (6.6) Patinkin shows that if the first $n-1$ equations in (6.3) are satisfied, the last, $D_n = S_n$, also necessarily holds true, that is, it is not independent of the rest of the system and should not be regarded as a separate equilibrium condition. Its elimination reduces the total number of equations to $3n-1$, which can now be solved for the $3n-1$ prices of real commodities, the price of paper money, p_n, having been fixed in advance.

At a later stage of his argument, Patinkin substitutes the supply and demand equations (6.1) and (6.2) in the equilibrium equations (6.3) and thus reduces the original system to n excess-demand functions with $n-1$ unknown prices. If $D_i - S_i \equiv X_i$,

$$(10.8) \qquad X_i(p_1, \ldots, p_{n-1}) = 0, \qquad (i = 1, \ldots, n).$$

The last of these can, according to the foregoing argument, be dropped as redundant.

Having thus presented what he considers to be the core of the classical general equilibrium theory, Patinkin proceeds to demonstrate its inconsistency. First of all he establishes the following mathematical theorem: *"If every equation of a system of K independent equations in K variables is homogeneous of some degree t in the same set of variables, then the system possesses no solution (i.e., it is inconsistent), with the possible exception of the one which sets each of the variables equal to zero"* (page 10).

Then he observes that according to the classical assumptions the $n-1$ supply and the corresponding $n-1$ demand functions for real commodities are homogeneous of degree zero in the $n-1$ prices, $p_1, p_2, \ldots, p_{n-1}$. That means that a simultaneous proportional increase of all these prices would leave all the quantities supplied and demanded unchanged. He furthermore shows that the equations describing the demand and supply for money are also homogeneous in the same prices but of the first degree;

that is, a proportional increase in prices would result in a same relative increase in demand and supply of money.

Having thus established that all the excess demand functions in system (10.8) are (according to the classical assumptions) necessarily homogeneous, Patinkin observes that "no matter what equation of (10.8) we drop (by virtue of their interdependence) we are left with $n - 1$ independent equations in $n - 1$ variables, where each of the equations is homogeneous in all the variables" (page 14). This being exactly a case referred to in the previously cited mathematical theorem, Patinkin concludes that "the Casselian system (6.1)-(6.3) is inconsistent."

Now I will show that Patinkin's argument, notwithstanding the system (6.1)-(6.3), is inconclusive. Having correctly indicated that the last, the monetary, equilibrium equation in (6.3) can be dropped since it is not independent of the other $n - 1$ equations of the same set, he failed to notice that the classical system as presented above must necessarily contain a second redundant relationship: any one of the $2n - 2$ individual supply and demand equations for *real* commodities [included in sets (6.1) and (6.2)] can be derived from the other $2n - 3$ real supply and demand equations.

Since money does not enter in his utility, that is, preference function, an individual according to the classical theory of economic behavior offers real commodities and services for sale only in order to be able to purchase other real goods and services. This means that the shapes of the $2n - 2$ functions describing his demand and supply for each of the real goods (as derived from his preference function) are necessarily interrelated in such a way that the unknown form of any one of them can be directly derived from the given shapes of the other $2n - 3$.

Let us consider, for example, a simple system in which two competitively behaving individuals trade with each other two commodities, using paper money as a medium of exchange. If $D_1 = f_1(p_1/p_2)$ is the first individual's demand equation[3] for com-

---

[3] I write the demand functions as $f_1(p_1/p_2)$ and $f_2(p_1/p_2)$ rather than in the more general form $f_1(p_1, p_2)$ and $f_2(p_1, p_2)$ in order to show that they are homogeneous of the degree zero in prices, p_1 and p_2.

modity 1, his supply equation for commodity 2 must necessarily be of the following shape: $S_2 = (p_1/p_2)f_1(p_1/p_2)$. This is so because *with any given p_1 and p_2* his money receipts from the sale of commodity 2 must be always equal to his expenditures on commodity 1. Similarly, if $D_2 = f_2(p_1/p_2)$ is the other individual's demand for commodity 2, his supply of commodity 1 must be $S_1 = (p_2/p_1)f_2(p_1/p_2)$.

For the aggregate demand and supply of paper money we have

$$(6.4) \qquad D_3 \equiv p_1 S_1 + p_2 S_2 = p_2 f_2(p_1/p_2) + p_1 f_1(p_1/p_2),$$

$$(6.5) \qquad S_3 \equiv p_1 D_1 + p_2 D_2 = p_1 f_1(p_1/p_2) + p_2 f_2(p_1/p_2).$$

The complete set of excess-demand equations corresponding to Patinkin's system (10.8) appears now in the following form:

$$X_1 \equiv D_1 - S_1 = f_1(p_1/p_2) - (p_2/p_1)f_2(p_1/p_2) = 0,$$

$$(10.8) \qquad X_2 \equiv D_2 - S_2 = f_2(p_1/p_2) - (p_1/p_2)f_1(p_1/p_2) = 0,$$

$$X_3 \equiv D_3 - S_3 = [p_2 f_2(p_1/p_2) + p_1 f_1(p_1/p_2)]$$
$$- [p_1 f_1(p_1/p_2) + p_2 f_2(p_1/p_2)] = 0.$$

Patinkin correctly states that the last of these equations is a linear combination of the first two and thus does not represent an independent equilibrium condition. He is also obviously right in observing that the remaining two equations are homogeneous in p_1 and p_2. He erroneously assumes, however, that these two equations are independent of each other, and thus arrives at the conclusion that the system is over-determined, that is, contradictory. Actually the first two equations are linearly interdependent: $X_1 p_1 = - X_2 p_2$. Thus with positive prices, $X_1 = 0$ implies $X_2 = 0$, and vice versa. Far from being contradictory, the classical system can easily be solved for the price ratio p_1/p_2, and this solution as obtained from any one of the three excess-demand equations will necessarily satisfy also the other two.

It is not the purpose of this note to consider the numerous other criticisms of the classical and neoclassical theory contained in Patinkin's article. Insofar as some of them are directly or indirectly based on the argument discussed above, they must obviously stand and fall with it.

10

The pure theory of the guaranteed annual wage contract

The purpose of this note is to show that the so-called guaranteed annual wage contract establishes a market relationship fundamentally different from that which underlies the conventional wage-rate contract and to indicate the implications of this difference in terms of the pure theory of exchange.

To bring out the main line of argument as clearly and as simply as possible we approach the question as a general problem of exchange of two commodities (commodity A and commodity B) between two groups of individuals. Without distorting the central theoretical issue involved, we can further simplify the analysis by assuming that each group consists of essentially identical individuals, that is, individuals with identical preferences in their choice among all the possible combinations of the two commodities and also endowed prior to the establishment of exchange relationships with the other group with the same amount of their particular "stock in trade."

These assumptions make it possible to reduce the discussion to a consideration of exchange between two individuals—one representing the "average" member of the first and the other the "average" member of the second group. The average in this instance is strictly identical with any and every other member of the group which he represents, since, whether competing with each other on equal footing or banded together in a single monopoly, they will act in exactly the same way.

From the *Journal of Political Economy* Vol. LIV, No. 1, February 1946.

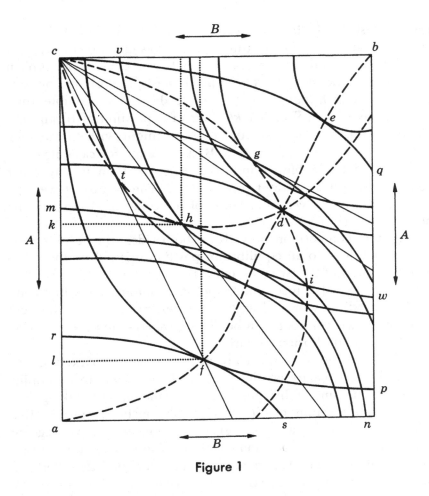

Figure 1

With the help of conventional Edgeworth-Pareto notation, the basic data of our problem can be depicted by two superimposed sets of indifference lines (see Fig. 1). One set with its origin, that is, its zero point, in *a* is represented by the curves conforming in their shapes of *cfp*, while the other with its zero point at *b* consists of lines with opposite curvature similar to that of *ceq*. The two sets are superimposed in such a way that point *c* indicates the original position of both representative individuals, the distance *ac* showing the amount of commodity A in possession of the first and the distance *bc* indicating the amount of commodity B in the hands of the second. Before the exchange has taken place, the first man has no B and the second does not own any A. The broken curve *cthd* is the offer curve of seller (that is, the original owner) of A. The point *h* located on this curve shows, for example, that, facing a given "price" of "*ck/kh* units of A per unit of B" and being free to acquire any amount of B he might wish to buy, the seller of A would buy *kh* units of B in exchange for *ck* units of A: In *h* he reaches a higher indifference curve than in any other point on the given straight price line *ch*. The broken curve *cgdi* is the similarly derived offer curve of the seller of B (that is, the potential buyer of A).

If perfect competition prevails on both sides, the resulting exchange will lead to an equilibrium position marked by the intersection point *d* of the two offer curves.

If the sellers of B form a monopolistic combination while competitive conditions prevail among the sellers of A, two different types of market contracts can be distinguished—each one resulting in a different equilibrium situation.

Under conditions of the conventional type of marketing, the monopolist is able to set the price and the buyer to determine freely the amount of his purchase. The monopolist—taking into account the reaction of the buyers—obviously establishes that price which leads to an equilibrium position more advantageous to him than any other position corresponding to some other price. In terms of our graph that means that the monopolistic seller of B can choose any point located along the offer curve *cthd* of his potential customers. His choice will obviously fall on point *h* situated on his indifference line *mhin;* any alternative position along the offer curve *chd* would place him on a "lower" level of his particular preference ssystem. The monopolist brings about this particular equilibrium position by quoting the price of *ck/kh* units at A per unit of B and letting the buyers (of B) *freely* choose *kh* as the amount the purchase of which places them at point *h*, that is, on the highest indifference curve *vhiw* of their own preference system attainable along the given straight price line *ch*.

The second method of trading is exemplified by the "guaranteed annual wage" contract. The great variety of labor contracts described by this term has one common characteristic: they fix not only the wage rates to be paid but also include a guaranty of a certain minimum total wage bill, that is, they commit the employed to maintenance of a specified minimum labor force, a purchase of a certain minimum aggregate amount of labor-hours or labor-days. In those instances in which the actual amount of labor hired by the entrepreneur (at the contractual wage rates) happens to exceed the stipulated minimum, the guaranty clause of the contract does not represent an effective limitation of his freedom of action. Thus the resulting supply-demand relationship does not differ in this case from that which would be established under a conventional labor contract fixing the same wage rate but leaving the decision concerning the number of workers to be hired entirely in the hands of the employer. The preceding analysis of conventional "price-setting" monopoly with "free" quantity determination by the purchaser obviously applies also to such instances of ineffective employment guaranty.

The market relationship becomes, however, radically different as soon as the guaranty becomes really effective—as soon as the employer finds himself obliged to use a larger number of workers than he would have chosen to hire, at the contractual wage level, in the absence of the aforementioned employment guaranty.

It is this type of market situation—in which the labor contract effectively restricts the freedom of entrepreneurial decision not only in respect to the price but also the amount of labor to be hired—which leads to a new kind of market equilibrium radically different from that explained by the conventional monopoly theory reviewed above.

An effective guaranteed annual wage contract permits the monopolistic seller not only to quote the price but also to force the buyer to purchase a total amount exceeding that which he would have acquired at that price of his own free choice. In our example the buyers of B are faced with the alternative of either taking one particular amount of this commodity at a particular price—both named by the seller—or abstaining from all exchange. Such a "take it or leave it" proposition means for them a choice between two and only two combinations of commodities: that which would result from acceptance of the joined price-quantity offer and that which they have in their possession before any trading has taken place. In terms of our graph it is a choice between location at point c or at one other point in the rectangular field of the diagram (the joint price-quantity offer can obviously be stated in terms of the total amounts of A and B to be exchanged). In general, any price-quantity offer which places the resulting equilibrium position to the right of the indifference line cfp, on which point c is located, will be accepted, while any offer leading to a point situated to the left of this indifference line will be rejected by the prospective buyers of B.

What offer will the monopolistic seller of B actually put forward? Obviously that which among all the offers still acceptable to the other contracting party will place him on the highest possible indifference line of his own preference system, that is, an offer which will locate the equilibrium point to the right of the curve cfp and as near as possible—that is infinitesimally near—to point f at which that curve is tangent to his own indifference line rfs. To attain this result, the monopolist will offer to sell *not less* than lf units of B at the price of cl/lf units of A per unit of B. The fact that both the price and the quantity involved are stated by the seller is of fundamental significance. Had he quoted the price and let the buyer choose freely the amount of the purchase, the latter would have stopped along this particular price line ctf at point t rather than point f.

The comparison of the two equilibrium positions—one at h and the other at f—resulting from the two types of monopolistic marketing demonstrates that, by including in his offer both the price to be paid and the quantity to be purchased,[1] a monopolist can drive a harder and more profitable (from his point of view) bargain than by using the more conventional method of fixing only the price and letting the other contracting party determine freely the volume of the transaction or—as in the case of an auction sale—offering a fixed amount and letting the price be determined

[1] Strictly speaking, it is sufficient for him to stipulate the *minimum* quantity which the purchasers have to take at the given price.

through free and independent bidding of prospective customers.

If, reversing the previous relationship the buyers rather than the sellers of B form a monopolistic combination facing a group of competing sellers, the ordinary price-fixing type of monopolistic action will establish an equilibrium position in g—corresponding to h in the case discussed above. A simultaneous price-quantity method of contracting would enable the combined buyers of B to push the equilibrium point as far as e which corresponds to f in the first case.

It is a well-known proposition of "welfare economics" that a conventional monopoly, while it shifts the market equilibrium in favor of the monopolist at the expense of the other side participating in the exchange, results in inefficient allocation of resources. The competitive equilibrium position in point d marks an efficient distribution of the two commodities between the two groups of individuals involved in the sense that no other exists in which both of them would at the same time be better off (that is, would both be located on higher indifference lines of their respective systems); any and every move away from d will necessarily reduce the utility level of at least one of the two parties involved. The equilibrium position in h resulting from a price-fixing (but not quantity-fixing) policy of the monopolistically organized sellers of B is, on the contrary, inefficient: by redistributing the commodities in such a way as to place the new position somewhere in the cigar-shaped area inclosed by the two indifference lines *mhin* and *vhiw* between the two intersection points h and i, it would be possible to improve the situation of both groups of individuals; both the sellers as well as the purchasers of B would find themselves after such shift on a higher level of their respective systems of indifference lines.

In terms of income distribution the "guaranteed quantity" type of monopolistic action leads to a greater departure from competitive equilibrium than the ordinary price-fixing kind. The shift from the competitive equilibrium position in d to point h—resulting from conventional price-fixing monopolistic action by the sellers of B—means a gain to the latter and a loss to the sellers of A. A further shift to the equilibrium position in f which would be brought about if the monopolist could not only fix the price but also enforce a separate quantity "guaranty," means a new gain for the seller of B and an additional real income loss to its buyer.

Although marking, in terms of income distribution, a greater departure from competitive equilibrium than a conventional price-fixing monopoly, this compounded price-quantity type of monopolistic action leads, however, to establishment of perfectly *efficient* commodities allocation: The equilibrium location in *f* is efficient in the same sense as the competitive equilibrium point in *d* is efficient; no other point exists in the rectangle of our diagram in which *both* groups of individuals would simultaneously be better off than they are in *f*. A monopoly which combines price-fixing with quantity-fixing leads to efficient (which in no way necessarily means desirable) redistribution of income in contrast to conventional price-fixing or *quantity-fixing monopoly which results in inefficient redistribution.*[2]

It is interesting to note that the second, that is, the price-quantity type of monopolistic trading, is equivalent to the theoretically familiar procedure of perfect price discrimination: By selling the first unit at the highest, the second at a lower, the third at a still lower price, etc., the monopolist can and will establish a final equilibrium position identical with that which he can achieve through the device of a combined price-quantity offer. Leaving the formal demonstration of this proposition to the reader, it might be suggested that the graphic picture of the process of successive steps of discriminating exchange would entail a broken exchange path which originates in point *c* and, clinging as closely as possible to the purchasers' "marginal" indifference line *cfp*, would lead him to the final equilibrium point *f*, or, more correctly, to a point located on a somewhat higher indifference line in the infinitesimal neighborhood of *f*.

The bearing of the foregoing theoretical observations upon the problem of guaranteed annual wage contracts is obvious: The

[2] As in all points located on the "contract curve" *afdeb*, the "marginal rate of substitution" between the commodities A and B is in *f* as it is in *d* the same for both contracting parties. In *d* it is also equal to the price ratio of the two commodities, while in *f* this latter equality does not hold.

introduction of this new type of trading in place of the conventional wage agreement signifies replacement of the conventional methods of wage determination by price-quantity type of bargaining. Such change extends appreciably the magnitude of the maximum advantage which the stronger of the two contracting parties can obtain, at the expense of the weaker, through exercise of monopoly power. If the employers constituted the stronger side, this increased gain would be theirs. If the labor unions could secure for themselves a dominant bargaining position, they would definitely increase their distributive share by letting the total amount of labor to be hired as well as the wage rates to be paid become an object of collective bargaining.

It is interesting to observe that the drive for guaranteed annual wages represents only one particular instance of the more general tendency to replace the conventional method of monopolistic marketing—which allows the other party to the transaction to choose freely the amount which it will buy (or sell) at the given price—with a new kind of agreement which fixes both the total volume as well as the price of purchase. Another notable manifestation of this new tendency can be observed in the field of international economic relations, where not only the prices of commodities to be exchanged but also the volume of contemplated transactions becomes a subject of negotiations and bilateral agreements.

11

The use of indifference curves in the analysis of foreign trade

The recent developments in analysis of international trade have made it difficult to handle all the various theoretical cases by the traditional means of numerical examples. The following graphic application of indifference curves may provide a comparatively simple and handy tool of representation and analysis for the problem involved.

The theoretical tools applied are those of Marshall, Edgeworth, Pareto, but they are used in such a way as to enable us to disclose the intimate connection between the "national" and the "international" elements of economic equilibrium.

Figure 1 illustrates the elementary case in which the possessor of the quantity b of commodity B is exchanging a part of it against another commodity, A, the terms of exchange being given. Representing the given rate of exchange (the "terms of trade") of B against A by the slope of the straight line bP_1, we find that the possessor of B will attain an equilibrium position by exchanging a quantity (bC_1) of B for P_1C_1 of A and retaining OC_1 of B; P_1 being the point where the exchange line is touching the "highest" indifference curve and consequently secures him the maximum utility. If there is movement away from this point (P_1) in either direction, by stopping the exchange nearer to b, or by pushing it further along the exchange line in the opposite direction the total utility of both commodities in his possession would be re-

From the *Quarterly Journal of Economics*, Vol. XLVII, May 1933.

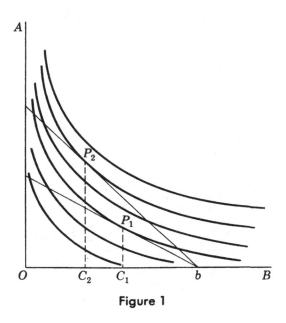

Figure 1

duced. Another—more favorable—exchange line bP_2 will bring about a different equilibrium point, P_2. This new position is marked by a larger quantity of both commodities exchanged and by a "higher" indifference curve; hence a greater total utility is attained.

The response of the quantities to a given change in the terms of trade depends entirely upon the shape of the indifference curves. Figure 2 shows how the equilibrium point of a country shifts when the exchange line changes its slope.[1] The curve bP_1P_2 indicates that from b to P_1 the demand is elastic; an improvement in the terms of trade between the two limits raises both the exports and the imports. After this point is passed the demand becomes inelastic; any further betterment of the terms of trade is still accompanied by increasing import but leads to a reduction of export.

Evidently, under the assumption of constant opportunity costs,

[1] This diagram leads directly to the demand-supply curves of Marshall and Edgeworth.

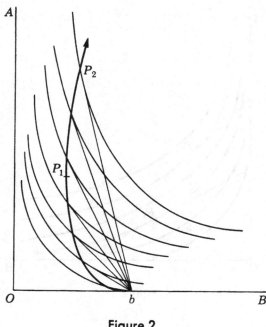

Figure 2

the same diagram can illustrate the distribution of a given amount of productive forces of a country between two alternative branches of industry. The opportunity costs of B in terms of A and vice versa, will remain constant when each of the two commodities concerned is produced at constant cost.[2] In this case, Ob (Fig. 1) represents the possible total output of B if this good only were produced. The slope of the line bP_1 indicates the possible results of diversion of productive forces into the other industry. In complete analogy with the previous case, the equilibrium will be attained in P_1 or P_2 respectively.

If both industries are subject to decreasing returns, the production curve will be concave toward the axes as indicated in Fig. 3.

Given the choice between diverting the production into the B

[2] For the sake of theoretical completeness, the exceptional case may be mentioned in which a combination of increasing costs in one branch of production and decreasing costs in the other may result in a constant opportunity cost relation between the two commodities.

118

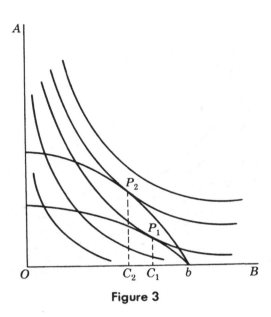

Figure 3

industry along a given (straight) production line and providing the same commodity by trade moving along a given path of exchange (bP_2), the preference will be given to the line of the steeper slope, which in any case will lead to a "higher" indifference curve. However, in most cases the production path will be of a curved type as represented in Fig. 4. In this case some of the B-stuff will be produced and some will be acquired in exchange for A-stuff. The maximum utility will be attained by moving along the production curve to the point K, and then proceeding along the exchange line to P_1. Analytically defined, K is the point at which a line with a given "exchange" slope $\left(\dfrac{P_1R}{RK}\right)$ will touch as a *tangent* the fixed production curve.

In the equilibrium position, Kg ($= RC$) of the total quantity CP_1 of A is produced at home and P_1R is imported from abroad. The total production of B amounts to Og; Og of which is retained at home and Cb sent abroad. Evidently a change in the terms of trade will alter the whole situation, shifting the point K either to the right or to the left. At K_1 (which corresponds to P_1 in Fig. 3)

119

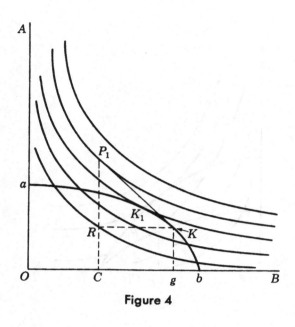

Figure 4

the country will evidently discontinue its foreign trade and reach a state of self-sufficiency. But should the slope of the exchange line, P_1K, decrease even more and move the point of tangency to the left of K_1, an "inverse" trade will start. It will become profitable to export A and to import B. Figure 5 represents this situation. In complete analogy to Fig. 4, the quantity nq of B will be produced, an additional quantity, fP_2, of the same commodity will be exchanged "along" the qP_2 line for a quantity, nm of A. The distance, mO, will represent the amount of A which is retained in the country after the new equilibrium is reached.

Figure 6 combines Figs. 4 and 5 in one system of coordinates, and gives a complete picture of balanced trade relations between two countries. So long as the analysis referred to only one country, the "terms of trade" represented by the slope of the exchange lines were considered as given. Now only the indifference curves and the cost curves of the two countries are considered as "data." In Fig. 6 both countries have the same system of indifference lines; but the following analysis could be equally well applied if two different systems of indifference lines were charted. The terms

120

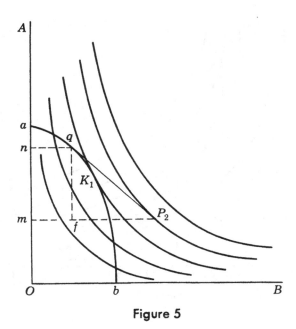

Figure 5

of trade and the quantities produced and exchanged can be deduced. The two conditions of equilibrium are: (1) both countries are dealing on the same terms of trade, that is, the exchange lines are parallel, and their slopes are equal; and (2) the imported and exported quantities of each commodity are equal,

$$qf = P_1R \quad \text{and} \quad fP_2 = RK.$$

The same condition can be expressed more simply by

$$qP_2 = P_1K,$$

that is, both countries have to proceed equal distances along their respective paths of exchange.

Without trying to make a point against the spirit of the theory of comparative costs, it may be interesting to observe that two countries with costs of production which are equal not only comparatively, but even absolutely, will start an exchange of their products if their systems of indifference lines, i.e. their relative demands, are different. In Fig. 7 the case is represented graphi-

121

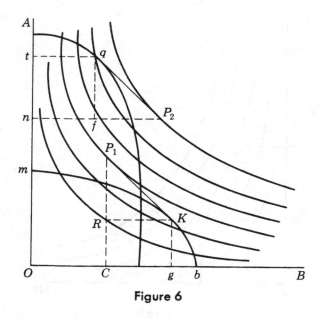

Figure 6

cally. The curve ab is the common opportunity cost line of the two countries. The two sets of indifference lines represent the different utility systems of the two countries. The indifference lines with the steeper slopes apply to country A, those with the lesser slopes apply to country B. In a state of self-sufficiency, country A would reach its equilibrium point in P_1, producing and consuming the quantity P_1C_1 of A-stuff and P_1D_1 of B-stuff. The other country has its point of self-sufficiency in P_2 with P_2C_2 of A and P_2D_2 of B-stuff produced and consumed. Applying our previous reasoning, we find that both countries will profit by exchanging part of their products. Each will produce, after the international equilibrium is reached, NK of B-stuff and MK of A-stuff, respectively. But according to their different needs, they will redistribute their equal products by mutual exchange. Country A will attain its highest utility point P_1' by moving along the exchange line from K to P_1', while country B will proceed an equal distance in the opposite direction, from K to P_2'. The trade between the two countries will consist in exchanging $P_2'R_2(=KR_1)$ of A-stuff against $P_1'R_1(=KR_2)$ of B-stuff. The case is not as artificial as it may ap-

122

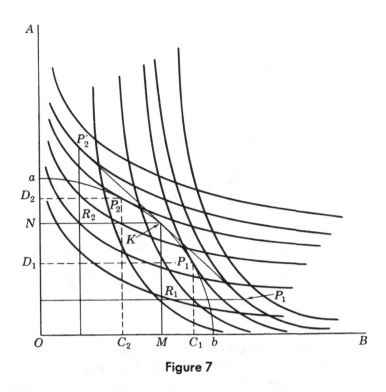

Figure 7

pear at first sight. It may partly explain the highly developed interchange of commodities between countries with similar industrial structure.

The influence of an import duty is illustrated in Fig. 8: the dotted curve MP_1D_2b represents the "demand curve" (the same curve as the demand curve in Fig. 2). Under conditions of free trade, P_1 is the equilibrium point if P_1b represents the path of exchange. Imposition of a duty means that a certain part of imported goods or an equivalent amount of the B-stuff has to be surrendered to the customs officials. If P_1D_1 is the amount of the tax (which is supposed to be *ad valorem*), D_1 represents the new (reduced) utility point of the consumer under the fictitious assumption that the amount of trade is not altered. The net exchange line is bD_2D_1 the slope of which represents the domestic terms of exchange between A-stuff and B-stuff. This utility point can be

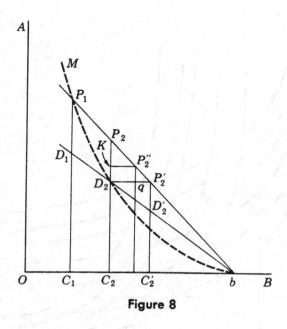

Figure 8

displaced in either direction along the bD_2D_1 line by a corresponding contraction of expansion of foreign trade.

The new maximum utility position is indicated by D_2 which is the cross point of the demand curve MP_1D_2b with the net exchange line bD_2D_1. Should the whole (proportionally reduced) amount of the duty be paid in A-stuff, the external equilibrium point would be P_2; P_2C_2 representing in this case the total imports, P_2D_2 the quantity of A-stuff surrendered to the customs and D_2C_2 the remainder "on hand." The same utility point, D_2 could be attained if the total trade would be reduced to P_2' but the amount of the tax which, estimated in A-stuff, is now equal to $P_2'D_2'$ would be actually paid in an equivalent quantity, D_2P_2' of the home-made B-stuff.

Between these two marginal cases many intermediate ways of discharging the duty are possible. Stopping at P_2'' the movement along the exchange line bP_1, it is possible to discharge the duty by surrendering $P_2''K$ of B-stuff and $P_2''q$ of A-stuff, so that D_2 will still indicate the "net" position of the consumer. In a monetary economy the "distribution" of the duty between the two kinds of

124

goods is equivalent to the question how the government spends the money collected. The effect of the duty evidently depends to a large extent upon the form of the demand curve, MP_1D_2b.

The same method of approach can be directly applied to a case where an opportunity cost curve is introduced.

When speaking about the ultimate utility point attained, we have of course to distinguish D_2 and P_2'' (or P_2, or P_2'). D_2' represents the utility attained directly by the consumer, P_2'' (or P_2 or P_2') indicates the "total" utility position of the country, including the market value of goods collected in payment of the import duties (estimated on consumers indifference curves).

The previous analysis was conducted on the assumption that the slope of the exchange line is fixed.

This limitation can be removed, and a complete picture of all the interrelations obtained, by taking into account the other country. The reduction of imports which results from the new tax will eventually shift the terms of trade. The character of the shift as well as the resulting change in the quantities of imports and exports depend upon the cost curves of the two countries and their respective lines of indifference.

This method of treatment can be readily extended. Another commodity can be introduced by adding a third dimension. More "countries" with their respective indifference lines and cost curves may be included in the same diagrams. Capital movements and the general transfer problem can also be analyzed by the method. The monetary side of the problem can be attacked by the introduction of special "monetary indifference curves"; but these are not treated here because they would call for a fundamental discussion of the theory of money and credit.

12

Composite commodities and
the problem of index numbers

I

1. Modern economic theory is making ever increasing use of index numbers.[1] This is a logical result of the predominant tendency toward quantitative analysis. In a loose qualitative description, such terms as "real wage" and "producer's goods" may simply indicate the totality of commodities which have certain characteristics in common. But this simple interpretation fails to satisfy the theorist when he tries to find definite functional relations, for example, the supply and demand curves of these commodities. The complicated algebraic formulae of modern monetary theory are evidently built on the assumption that composite commodities have exactly the same definitely measurable dimensions of quantity, price, utility, etc., as any of the individual commodities.

Nobody would contest the practical difficulty of measuring composite prices and quantities. This circumstance certainly reduces the practical usefulness of the abstract deductions in which they are introduced; it would, however, hardly imperil their theoretical significance as long as we assume that these composite quantities and prices exist at least as theoretical realities. The

In the fall of 1933 this article was communicated to Professor Schumpeter's Discussion Group at Harvard. On June 24, 1935, it was presented at the meeting of the Econometric Society in Colorado Springs, and published in *Econometrica*, Vol. 4, No. 1, January 1936.
[1] The June 1935 issue of the *Review of Economic Studies* contains a paper on index numbers by Dr. Hans Staehle in which the treatment of several topics is very similar to that given in the present article.

strong belief in their existence certainly constitutes one of the most important items in the credo of some present-day theorists.

The important practical task of measuring these collective prices and quantities is usually left to the statistician. Turning to the statistical literature devoted to the problem of index numbers, we find, however, a development directly antithetical to the increasing optimism of the general theorist. Assigned the task of measuring certain objects, the statistician became doubtful of their very existence. What appeared to be a practical difficulty seems to reveal itself as a logical impossibility.

The theorists readily made certain concessions. Many of them abandoned the notion of a general price level. But this served only to transfer the emphasis to partial price levels. Such an attempt to meet the difficulty halfway cannot solve the problem. The theoretical problem of lumping together several commodities is essentially the same whether their number be 5000, 50, or only 2.

Many misunderstandings in the discussion of index numbers seem to be the result of an insufficient discrimination between statistical and theoretical aspects of the problem. The most often repeated statement to the effect that one or another index formula gives an approximate measurement of "real wages," or "retail prices," and so on, can have two totally different meanings. It may indicate that due to inadequacy of data or imperfect statistical technique the result does not represent the exact measurement of the unknown but nevertheless theoretically existing true value of the "real wage" or "general retail price," or it may mean, in addition, that the unknown ideal value at which the statistical computation is aimed lacks in itself theoretical precision.

2. Keynes's *Treatise on Money* contains an excellent comprehensive survey of established opinion on index numbers and may be used advantageously as a point of reference in the following discussion. The larger part of his presentation is devoted to a specific composite commodity—"consumers' goods"—and he discusses predominantly the reciprocal of its composite price—the "purchasing power of money." But it is evident that the arguments of Chapter 8, Vol. I, of the *Treatise* must apply to composite goods

in general.[2] The theoretical conclusions of this discussion may be stated in the following points:

1. An exact computation of the composite price of consumers' goods is limited to
   a. persons of similar tastes,
   b. and among them only those who receive equal real incomes.

2. Under these conditions the composite prices of consumers' goods for different persons or for the same person at different times is proportional to the total monetary expenditures.

In order to elucidate the exact meaning of this statement and at the same time to provide a precise tool for our further analysis, we may resort to a graphic respresentation. The illustration can be simplified without impairing the generality of the results if we assume first that only two goods, say bread and meat, enter the consumer's budget.

The tastes of a consumer may be represented in a two-dimensional diagram by a series of indifference lines, as in Fig. 1.

Measuring the quantity of meat along OB, the ordinate, and the quantity of bread along the abscissa, OA, we can represent all the possible combinations of these two commodities by corresponding points on the plane AOB. Each of the successive indifference curves (I, II, III, etc.) connects points of equal utility, that is, all the equivalent bread and meat combinations which, in the estimate of the given person, are considered equal in their utility.

The points which are situated on different indifference lines evidently indicate combinations of unequal utility. Although it is impossible to measure the absolute amounts of satisfaction, the relative position of the indifference lines indicates the "more" or "less" of corresponding utilities.

Similarity of tastes, which is the first theoretical condition (1a) for the calculation of a price index, means identity in the systems of indifference lines. A composite price which is calculated for a given system of indifference lines has no significance whatever for

[2] See also H. Staehle, *International Comparison of Food Costs, A Study of Certain Problems Connected with the Making of Index Numbers.* Reprinted from Studies and Reports of The International Labor Office, Series N, No. 20.

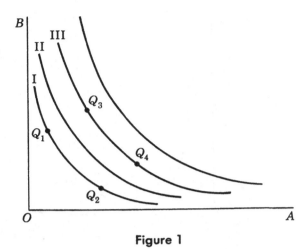

Figure 1

any other differently shaped system. The second condition (1b) concerning equality of real incomes means that only such combinations of meat and bread as are situated on the same indifference lines (for example, Q_1 and Q_2, or Q_3 and Q_4, in Fig. 1) can be lumped together in a single composite commodity.

Following the definition of a price index given above, we can derive the composite price relation between two equivalent combinations of A and B graphically. In Fig. 2 a third dimension, M, is introduced and used for measurement of the total monetary income (= expenditure). The points Q_1 and Q_2, situated on the same indifference line $i - i$, represent the two equivalent combinations of the commodities A and B whose prices are to be compared. The slopes, bo/co and do/ao of the two tangents cb and ad indicate the relative prices, that is, the exchange ratios between the commodities A and B in the two "positions" Q_1 and Q_2, respectively. If the slope (fo/ao) of the line, fa, corresponds to the price of the commodity B in the position Q_2, fo (measured along the monetary coordinate M) will represent the total expenditure of the consumer in this position, that is, the total price of the combination Q_2, or $\Sigma p_2 q_2$ according to the usually accepted notation.[3]

[3] Given the price of B and the exchange value of A in B, we can derive the corresponding price of A, which is given for the position Q_1 by the slope of the line fb, fo/bo.

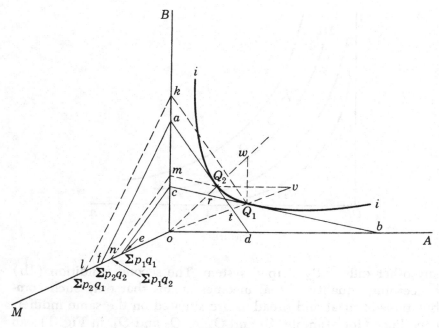

Figure 2

The same line of reasoning shows that if the slope of the line *ce*, (*eo/co*), represents the price of *B* in position Q_1, *eo* gives the total actual expenditure for the combination Q_1 ($\Sigma p_1 q_1$). Finally, according to the foregoing definition of a price index, we find that the relation *fo/eo* or $\Sigma p_2 q_2 / \Sigma p_1 q_1$ measures exactly the change of the composite price between the positions Q_2 and Q_1.

Figure 3 represents a case in which Q_1 and Q_2 are situated in the same indifference system, but on separate indifference curves, Q_1 on $i - i$ and Q_2 on $j - j$. Under this condition two theoretical price comparisons can be made; one on the level of the indifference curve $i - i$ and another on the level of the curve $j - j$. In order to find these indices, two additional points of comparison must be determined: point $\overline{Q}_1$ indicating the quantities of *A* and *B* which would be consumed on the $i - i$ utility level *under the price conditions of Q_2*, and $\overline{Q}_2$ indicating the position to which the consumer would have to shift in order to attain the utility level

130

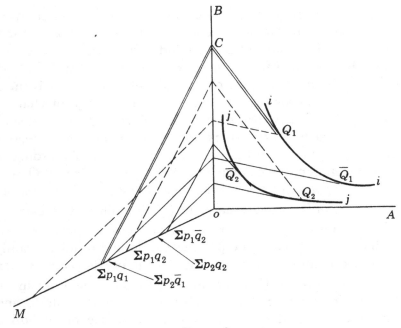

Figure 3

j — j with prices which are prevailing in Q_1. Subsequently, the
price level of $\overline{Q}_1$ can be compared with Q_1, and $\overline{Q}_2$ with Q_2. In
both cases the problem is identical with the previously described
comparison of two equivalent combinations of A and B. The result of this calculation is two different and theoretically independ-
ent price indices, $\Sigma p_1 q_1 / \Sigma p_2 \overline{q}_1$ and $\Sigma p_1 \overline{q}_2 / \Sigma p_2 q_2$. The independence of these two results must be stressed particularly in view of
the frequent misunderstandings it has been subject to. Neither of
the two ratios really gives a comparison of the price levels in Q_1
and Q_2. Such an interpretation would be possible only on the as-
sumption that the price levels in $\overline{Q}_2$ and $\overline{Q}_1$ are equal to the price
levels in Q_1 and Q_2, respectively. This would mean that the price
change between $\overline{Q}_2$ and Q_1 is necessarily equal to the price difference between $\overline{Q}_1$ and Q_2, which evidently is disproved by the
double result of the previous calculation.

131

There seems to remain, however, one possibility to circumvent this objection and to extend the comparability of composite prices beyond the narrow limits of a single indifference curve to the full range of the system. Very often the opinion is expressed that, although an absolutely general comparison of price levels is unattainable, it is still possible to cover the whole range of changes "from the point of view" of a given income level. By means of such a partial approach some authors hope to overcome the objection which was formulated in the preceding paragraph. According to their interpretation, the comparison of composite prices in Q_1 and Q_2 "from the point of view" of the income level $j - j$ can reasonably be made *only* through the point $\overline{Q}_2$. The alternative calculation through $\overline{Q}_1$ is rejected as being made from the point of view of the income $i - i$. Thus, the paradoxical double result is readily avoided, and nothing seems to contradict the previous assumption that the price level in $\overline{Q}_2$ is identical with the price-level in Q_1 With the help of a similar approach it would be possible to find for any other—even the most remote—point of the plane BoA a corresponding point on the curve $j - j$. With the aforementioned qualifications, the comparability of price levels throughout the whole system of indifference curves seems to be proved.

The fundamental weakness of this argument, however, can be easily revealed. If the price of the composite commodity in $\overline{Q}_2$ should really be the same as in Q_1, the ratio of the total expenditures, $\Sigma p_1 q_1 / \Sigma p_2 \overline{q}_2$, would necessarily indicate the relation of the corresponding composite quantities. In Fig. 4, in addition to the points Q_1 and $\overline{Q}_2$ of the previous comparison, we introduce points $\overline{Q}_2$ and Q_3, the second being situated on a third indifference line, $e - e$. The price levels in Q_3 and $\overline{Q}_2$ are "equal" in the same sense as they are equal in $\overline{Q}_2$ and Q_1, the ratio of the total expenditures in Q_3 and $\overline{Q}_2$, $\Sigma p_3 q_3 / \Sigma p_3 \overline{q}_2$ (equal lo/no), represents the relation between the composite quantities in Q_3 and $\overline{Q}_2$.

Comparing the two quantity indices, we see that according to Fig. 4

$$\frac{\Sigma p_1 q_1}{\Sigma p_1 \overline{q}_2} < \frac{\Sigma p_3 q_3}{\Sigma p_3 \overline{q}_2}.$$

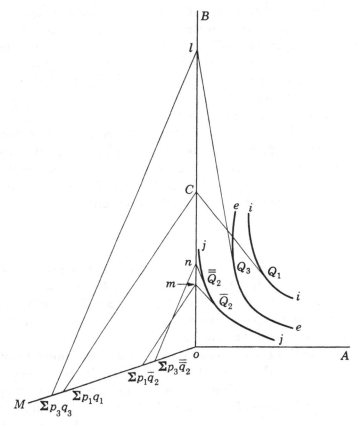

Figure 4

"From the point of view" of the income level $j - j$, the quantity of the composite commodity in $\overline{\overline{Q}}_2$ and $\overline{Q}_2$ is necessarily the same. It follows that the quantity of the composite commodity in Q_3 is larger than in Q_1. Point Q_1 is situated, however, on a "higher" indifference curve than point Q_3, which indicates that the utility in Q_3 is lower than in Q_1. This shows that the previous conclusion is wrong, because in a fixed system of taste a larger quantity can in no case represent a smaller utility. It has been proved that even "from the point of view" of a fixed income level the validity of the usual index numbers is in general strictly limited to comparisons between points which are situated on the same utility level.

In concluding this critical survey, it has to be pointed out that only on rare occasions will the actual index calculations lead to such openly contradictory results. In a vast majority of practical cases these results are quite plausible, which does not prove, of course, that they have a clear theoretical meaning.[4] In such instances one may speak of statistical approximations to a theoretically indeterminate concept. Indeed, a proper compromise between statistical optimism on one hand and theoretical purism on the other seems under these circumstances to be inevitable. But, in view of this necessity, a clear statement of the theoretical side of the case appears to be particularly important.

I I

3. After discussing many different formulae, Keynes (*A Treatise on Money*, Vol. I, Ch. 8) ultimately comes to the conclusion that two of them may be theoretically and practically eligible for use in the measurement of composite prices—the method of "highest common factors" and the "method of limits."

The first method is identical in its theoretical concept with the well-known method of "equal food baskets." Its weaknesses have often been pointed out. Putting it in the language of our diagrams (Fig. 1), the theoretical condition under which the "highest common factor" method could precisely be applied amounts to the requirement that the two points of comparison should be situated not only on the same curve in identical sets of indifference lines, but in addition should occupy exactly the *same point* on this identical curve. All the advantages of its practical simplicity can hardly compensate for the extreme limitations of this method.

The "method of limits" has received the most favorable consideration in theoretical literature on index numbers and its application, seemingly, does not imply any special theoretical assump-

[4] Under special circumstances, for example in case the indifference curves are "degenerated" in a system of parallel straight lines or at least can be approximated by such a system, these results will even have a definite theoretical meaning. But in such symmetrical cases any index calculation becomes rather superfluous.

tions. The usually accepted interpretation of its results is, however, somewhat misleading.

The first step in application of the method of limits consists in the calculation of the hypothetical expenditure which the person situated in Q_1 (see Fig. 2) would incur if he had to buy goods according to the prices which actually existed in position Q_2, and, analogously, the expenditure which would result if the combination of goods in point Q_2 had to be paid for according to the prices of position Q_1.

In order to find the hypothetical expenditure in point Q_1 we draw Q_1k parallel to Q_2a and kl parallel to af; lo is then the total expenditure for Q_1 evaluated according to Q_2 prices. Similarly, we draw Q_2mn parallel to Q_1ce and find that no is the expenditure for Q_2 according to the prices in Q_1. Following the generally accepted algebraic notation, lo can be replaced by $\Sigma p_2 q_1$, fo by $\Sigma p_2 q_2$, no by $\Sigma p_1 q_2$, and eo by $\Sigma p_1 q_1$.

Now it is possible to show that the ratio between the hypothetical and actual price of Q_1 $\Sigma p_2 q_1/\Sigma p_1 q_1$, cannot be smaller than the "true" index ratio $\Sigma p_2 q_2/\Sigma p_1 q_1$ and, on the other hand, that the ratio $\Sigma p_2 q_2/\Sigma p_1 q_2$ in no case can be larger than $\Sigma p_2 q_2/\Sigma p_1 q_1$. In other words, under the given assumptions, $\Sigma p_2 q_1/\Sigma p_1 q_1$ indicates the upper, and $\Sigma p_2 q_2/\Sigma p_1 q_2$ the lower limit of the "true" price change, $\Sigma p_2 q_2/\Sigma p_1 q_1$.

The practical significance of this result appears, however, to be rather small if we realize that under the given assumptions the available data on total monetary expenditures in the two positions of comparison enable us to derive directly and exactly the true relation, $\Sigma p_2 q_2/\Sigma p_1 q_1$, without the calculation of any limits. The importance of this consideration is enhanced by the fact that when these assumptions are not fulfilled, the method of limits ceases to function properly. It has been demonstrated previously that, if two income points are situated on different income levels, a theoretical computation leads to two different ratios. It is evident that the double result which is yielded by the method of limits cannot coincide with the two true theoretical ratios. But there still remains the hypothetical possibility that the statistical calculation indicates the limits between which both theoretical indices are located. The following consideration shows, however, that this is not the case:

The theoretical comparison of Q_2 and Q_1 (Fig. 3) leads, as was previously mentioned, to the double result $\Sigma p_2 q_2 / \Sigma p_1 \bar{q}_2$ and $\Sigma p_2 \bar{q}_1 / \Sigma p_1 q_1$. Applying the method of limits to the given positions Q_2 and Q_1 in the same way as was demonstrated in Fig. 2, we get (Fig. 3) the supposed lower and upper "limits" $\Sigma p_2 q_2 / \Sigma p_1 q_2$ and $\Sigma p_2 q_1 / \Sigma p_1 q_1$.

From the relative positions of all points involved in the argument, we derive the following inequalities:

$$\frac{\Sigma p_2 q_2}{\Sigma p_1 \bar{q}_2} > \frac{\Sigma p_2 \bar{q}_1}{\Sigma p_1 q_1} \quad \text{and} \quad \frac{\Sigma p_2 q_2}{\Sigma p_1 q_2} < \frac{\Sigma p_2 q_1}{\Sigma p_1 q_1},$$

$$\frac{\Sigma p_2 q_2}{\Sigma p_1 q_2} < \frac{\Sigma p_2 q_2}{\Sigma p_1 \bar{q}_2} \quad \text{and} \quad \frac{\Sigma p_2 q_1}{\Sigma p_1 q_1} > \frac{\Sigma p_2 \bar{q}_1}{\Sigma p_1 q_1}$$

This means that the upper "limit" of the empirical calculation is higher than the lower value of the theoretical relation and that the lower empirical "limit" is smaller than the higher theoretical. Consequently, the theoretical values may with equal probability be situated outside or within the empirical "limits." In other words, the two additional points $\Sigma p_1 q_2$ and $\Sigma p_2 q_1$ are of no help in the determination of the position of the true theoretical values.

Summarizing this preliminary analysis of the method of limits, we may say that, in cases in which it is theoretically correct, it appears to be useless practically, and in the other cases in which its application seems to be desirable, its results are faulty or, at least, inconclusive.

Unlike Keynes, Dr. Haberler (*Der Sinn der Index-Zahlen,* Tübingen 1927, pp. 94-6) has noticed the possibility of such an apparent contradiction, but in discussing this question he misses the real clue to the problem and, instead of tracing the difficulty to the incompatibility of unequal utility levels (real incomes), he holds the difference in monetary (nominal) incomes of the two positions responsible for this failure.

It is easy to see that Fig. 3 can be modified in such a way that point $\Sigma p_1 q_1$ will be coincident with point $\Sigma p_2 q_2$ (which means equality of monetary income of the two positions) without affecting any of the inequalities stated above, that is, without eliminating the fundamental difficulty.

4. What is the source of all these contradictions?

According to its fundamental set-up, the "method of limits" (and with it also all the other methods of index calculation which are mentioned in Dr. Keynes's survey) is based on the assumption that the price as well as the amount of a composite commodity is a *non-measurable magnitude.*

Such magnitude cannot be measured, that is, described as multiple of some appropriately chosen units (dollars, pounds, yards, etc.). Given two magnitudes of this kind, it is, however, possible to tell whether they are equal or not and, in the latter case, which is the larger and which the smaller one. The ratio of two non-measurable magnitudes equals 1 if they are identical, otherwise no definite numerical value can be attached to it. In general, such quotients can be described only as being larger or smaller than one ($\gtrless 1$). A series of indifference lines is a typical example of this kind of interrelation. The order of their increasing or decreasing magnitudes (higher or lower utility levels) is well established, but there is no sense in asking *how much* one of them is higher or lower than another one. A method of index number calculation based solely on a given "system of tastes" as represented by a succesion of indifference lines cannot possibly lead to any other result than a series of non-measurable magnitudes.[5] If, notwithstanding, these results are given in the form of definite numbers, we have to discard their numerical meaning entirely and take into account only the respective order of magnitudes. Insofar as such an index number represents a *ratio* between two composite prices or quantities, its economic significance, if it exists at all, can be represented in terms of one of the three signs: > 1, < 1 or $= 1$ (or, using percentages: > 100 per cent, < 100 per cent, $= 100$ per cent). Any further numerical definiteness which an index number seems to convey is devoid of economic meaning. No wonder that

---

[5] It is interesting to note that Pareto called his indifference lines "*indices* of utility," stressing through the use of the word "index" their non-measurability.

every attempt toward a numerical interpretation will, in the given circumstances, produce nothing but confusion.

Applying these considerations to the interpretation of the numerical results obtained through application of the "method of limits," we see that the alleged "limits" are not limits at all. They do not indicate the numerical margins between which a "true" value is situated. All they can do is to show whether the magnitude of the "true" composite price or quality ratio is larger, equal to, or smaller than, one ($\gtrless 1$).[6]

The following table indicates all the possible combinations of the magnitudes of the "upper" and "lower limits" and the corresponding magnitudes of the true *quantity index*.

Table 1

	"UPPER LIMIT" $\dfrac{\Sigma p_2 q_1}{\Sigma p_2 q_2}$	"LOWER LIMIT" $\dfrac{\Sigma p_1 q_1}{\Sigma p_1 q_2}$	THE MAGNITUDES OF THE "TRUE" QUANTITY INDEX
I	1	1	1
II	1	>1	>1
III	1	<1	<1
IV	>1	1	>1
V	>1	>1	>1
VI	>1	<1	$\gtrless 1$ (indeterminate)
VII	<1	1	<1
VIII	<1	>1	$\gtrless 1$ (indeterminate)
IX	<1	<1	<1

This survey shows that the result obtained has an economic mean-

[6] Given a series of *non-measurable magnitudes*, $a_1 < a_2 < a_3 < a_4 < a_5$, etc., it is, indeed, possible to indicate that one of them, say a_3, is located between some other two, say a_1 and a_4. But these limits must necessarily be expressed in terms of two magnitudes belonging to the same series. Dividing all the members of the original series, for example, by a_2, another succession of relative numbers can be obtained, $a/a_2 < 1 < a_3/a_2 < a_4/a_2 < a_5/a_2$ etc. This new series is more determined than the first one insofar as it is possible to tell whether any given element is larger than, smaller than, or equal to, 1. The statement that a_3/a_2 has as its limits the numbers 5/4 and 9/8 has no more meaning and conveys no more information than an indication that $a_3/a_2 < 1$.

ing only if both "limits" are larger or smaller than 1 and also in the singular cases where one or both of them equal 1: It signifies that the first point, as compared with the second, is situated on a higher, lower, or on the same indifference curve, respectively. In all other cases the result is purely negative; the magnitude of the true quality index remains entirely indeterminate.

In application to *price comparison*, the economic significance of the result obtained by application of the method of limits is even more restricted than in the case of quantity indices. The "limits" of a price index, $\Sigma p_1 q_1 / \Sigma p_2 q_1$ and $\Sigma p_1 q_2 / \Sigma p_2 q_2$, are obtained by dividing the quotient of the total expenditures $\Sigma p_1 q_1$ and $\Sigma p_2 q_2$ in two positions by the two "limiting" quantity indices, $\Sigma p_1 q_1 / \Sigma p_1 q_2$ and $\Sigma p_2 q_1 / \Sigma p_2 q_2$:

$$\text{"lower limit" of the price index: } \frac{\Sigma p_1 q_1}{\Sigma p_2 q_2} : \frac{\Sigma p_1 q_1}{\Sigma p_1 q_2} = \frac{\Sigma p_1 q_2}{\Sigma p_2 q_2};$$

$$\text{"upper limit" of the price index: } \frac{\Sigma p_1 q_1}{\Sigma p_2 q_2} : \frac{\Sigma p_2 q_1}{\Sigma p_2 q_2} = \frac{\Sigma p_1 q_1}{\Sigma p_2 q_1}.$$

The total expenditures are *measurable* economic quantities and so is their quotient, $\Sigma p_1 q_1 / \Sigma p_2 q_2$. The two "limits" of the *quantity* index, although expressed in numbers, have (with the exception of case 1 of Table 1) no definite numerical meaning. As shown above, in a number of cases they are void of any economic significance at all. It follows that we have to discard at the outset all the price indices calculated on the basis of such meaningless numbers. It stands to reason that any attempt to achieve a price comparison in the case where the composite quantities are entirely indeterminate would necessarily violate the very foundation of the whole procedure and led to contradictory results. But the logical limits of possible price comparison, at least so long as it is based upon the "method of limits," are even much narrower than that.

The "true" quantity index, even if successfully obtained, in generneral has still no definite numerical meaning. It is a magnitude defined solely in its relation to unity.

The ratio of the numerical quotient of the expenditures and of the non-measurable magnitude of the quantity index cannot, in

139

general, be anything else but a numerically indefinite magnitude itself, defined only through the sign $\gtreqless \Sigma p_1 q_1 / \Sigma p_2 q_2$:

$$\Sigma p_1 q_1 / \Sigma p_2 q_2 : \gtreqless 1 = \gtreqless \Sigma p_1 q_1 / \Sigma p_2 q_2.$$

The following table covers all possible combinations of the sizes of the magnitudes involved in a price index computation.

The price index obviously remains entirely indeterminate if the magnitude of the corresponding quantity index is unknown (Case I) and, on the other hand, it acquires a definite numerical value in the singular situation in which the quantity index equals 1 (Case II). Otherwise, the expenditure ratio, $\Sigma p_1 q_1 / \Sigma p_2 q_2$, indicates the lower (Case III) or the upper (Case IV) limit of the "true" price index (in the same way as unity can be called the limiting value of the "true" quantity index. See Table 1).

The economic significance of the latter result depends on the numerical value of the given expenditure ratio, $\Sigma p_1 q_1 / \Sigma q_2 p_2$. If the magnitude of the price index is defined as in Case III $(> \Sigma p_1 q_1 / \Sigma p_2 q_2)$ and the expenditure ratio is at the same time larger than 1, say 1.5 (150 per cent), the price level in the first point of comparison is proved to be definitely higher than it is in the second point. However, should the expenditure ratio be smaller than 1, say 0.5 (50 per cent), the answer to the fundamental question concerning the *direction of the price level change remains entirely indeterminate,* because a magnitude defined through the sign > 0.5 may be smaller, as well as larger, than 1. A similar indeterminateness must inevitably appear in Case IV if the expenditure ratio happens to be larger than 1.

Table 2 does not contain any reference to the previously mentioned "upper" and "lower limits" ($\Sigma p_1 q_2 / \Sigma p_2 q_2$ and $\Sigma p_1 q_1 / \Sigma p_2 q_1$) of the price index. The reason for this omission is the fact that the knowledge of these two numerical values cannot convey any information at all concerning the magnitude of the "true" price ratio. The preceding discussion makes it obvious that the indeterminate situation in Case I of Table 2 may coincide with every possible combination of magnitudes of the alleged "limit" of the price index. This means that, whatever their numerical values are, they not only do not convey any information concerning the direction of the "true" price change, but can not even indicate whether it is at all determinable on the basis of given statistical information.[7]

Summing up the economic analysis of the "method of limits," it is interesting to note that the often mentioned symmetry between any given price-index and the corresponding quantity index is rather superficial. So far as the fundamental statistical set-up is concerned, there exists, so to speak, a definite priority of the quantity index. The price magnitude of the composite commodity may be derived only if the magnitude of its "quantity"[8] can be also determined. In all the cases, however, in which the size of the total expenditures moves in the same direction as the magnitude of the composite quantities, the direction of the corresponding composite price change is fundamentally indeterminate.

The foregoing analysis is not intended to be a criticism of the use of conventional index numbers in general; many theoretical

---

[7] A good example of such a difficulty in the interpretation of statistical data may be found on p. 46 (Table VII) of Dr. Staehle's book (op. cit.). A comparison of German (Berlin) and Danish (Copenhagen) family budgets gives a following series of values:

$$\Sigma p_1 q_1 = \text{R.M. } 369.83, \qquad \Sigma p_1 q_2 = \text{R.M. } 379.52,$$
$$\Sigma p_2 q_2 = \text{R.M. } 334.77, \qquad \Sigma p_2 q_1 = \text{R.M. } 337.94.$$

Deriving the two "limits" of the quantity index, we obtain:

$$\frac{\Sigma p_1 q_1}{\Sigma p_1 q_2} = \frac{369.83}{379.52} > 1,$$

$$\frac{\Sigma p_2 q_1}{\Sigma p_2 q_2} = \frac{337.94}{334.77} < 1.$$

According to Table I, this result shows that the "true" quantity index is entirely indeterminate and that, consequently, no price level comparison between the two countries is possible. And still the alleged "upper" and "lower" limits of the conventional price index give a definite indication that the price level in Copenhagen is higher than in Berlin:

$$\frac{\Sigma p_1 q_1}{\Sigma p_2 q_1} = \frac{337.94}{369.83} = 0.9138,$$

$$\frac{\Sigma p_1 q_2}{\Sigma p_2 q_2} = \frac{337.94}{379.52} = 0.8820.$$

In terms of the given theoretical assumptions, the result has obviously no economic meaning.

[8] Strictly speaking, this magnitude should not be called "quantity" because it is essentially non-measurable. For want of a better expression, this obviously contradictory use of terms seems to be unavoidable.

Table 2

	EXPENDITURE RATIO	MAGNITUDE OF THE QUANTITY INDEX	MAGNITUDE OF THE "TRUE" PRICE INDEX
I	$\dfrac{\Sigma p_1 q_1}{\Sigma p_2 q_2}$	$\gtrless 1$	$\lessgtr \dfrac{\Sigma p_1 q_1}{\Sigma p_2 q_2}$
II	$\dfrac{\Sigma p_1 q_1}{\Sigma p_2 q_2}$	1	$\dfrac{\Sigma p_1 q_1}{\Sigma p_2 q_2}$
III	$\dfrac{\Sigma p_1 q_1}{\Sigma p_2 q_2}$	<1	$\dfrac{\Sigma p_1 q_1}{\Sigma p_2 q_2}$
IV	$\dfrac{\Sigma p_1 q_1}{\Sigma p_2 q_2}$	>1	$\dfrac{\Sigma p_1 q_1}{\Sigma p_2 q_2}$

and corresponding practical questions, by their very nature, require the application of indices of this specific form. To this class of problem belong, for example, comparisons of the standards of living. Our objections are directed only against the uncritical use of these kinds of composite prices and quantities in certain parts of general theoretical analysis where they are inappropriate. The principal cause of this misplacement seems to be the unwarranted assumption that the nature of these composite commodities is the same, or at least nearly the same, as the nature of the individual goods, that they are subject to the same elementary economic laws as ordinary commodities. We have tried to show that this assumption is utterly misleading; the magnitudes of these composite index commodities are non-measurable, while measurability constitutes the fundamental economic characteristic of ordinary commodities and their prices.

III

5. The question still remains, whether it is possible to establish some other methods of reduction of the number of variables in the analysis of an economic system by lumping together individual goods and building up composites which would still retain the fundamental properties[9] (among them the measurability, of the

[9] All the "tests" applied to the determination of the goodness of different index formulae are nothing else than a reformulation of these fundamental properties of "simple" commodities.

"simple" commodities) and, consequently, fit into the body of general theory.

One answer to this question points to the much debated problem of the measurability of utility. Without discussing the controversial issue whether or not utility can be considered as a measurable magnitude (the opponents of this assumption seem still to have a better case), we may accept for a moment the measurability hypothesis and consider the theoretical implications resulting from the introduction of this new dimension. Such an identification of the concept of a quantity of the composite commodity and a quantity of utility, natural as it seems to be, proves much less useful than would be expected. In terms of such a composite quantity it would be impossible to formulate the fundamental principle of diminishing utility. This principle expresses a certain quantitative relation between the total amount of a commodity and the utility of successively added units. Such an interrelation assumes the existence of two independent scales of measurement, a quantity scale and a utility scale. But a distinction between the utility and the quantity in our composite commodity becomes meaningless if the utility unit itself is used as a yardstick for measurement of quantities. A similar situation arises if an attempt is made to use the quantity of a finished commodity as an index of the total physical amount of cost goods which are applied to its production. Described in terms of such composite cost units, every production process will necessarily appear to be subject to the law of strictly proportional returns.

Moreover, the method of lumping the individual commodities on the basis of their utility (or productivity) is subject to another very serious limitation. Even the most ardent proponents of the theory of measurable utility do not maintain that it should be possible to select at will any group of commodities and assign to them a definite utility index. The index could be applied only, if at all, to the combination of all commodities entering the "budget" of a given consumer. Analogously, the production cost index described above can be calculated only for all the cost elements entering a given production process taken together. There is no sense in speaking of an *independent* total utility of a group of two or three consumers' goods so long as they constitute only a part of the total consumption; it is impossible to evaluate the productivity (it should be understood that it is the total and not the marginal productivity that is meant) of two or three factors of production if more agents concur in the same process.

Whatever the general importance of this kind of index measurement may be, it obviously would not solve our problem. A composite commodity constructed according to these prescriptions, although measurable in its magnitude, is subject to so many general limitations and displays at the same time such peculiar characteristics that it would be impossible to incorporate it in the body of the generally accepted economic theory *at par* (side by side) with all the other, non-composite goods. It seems to be advisable to attack our problem from a somewhat different angle.

6. To make the scope of this discussion more general, we change the previous scheme and, instead of two commodities (A and B) and money (M), start with a system of three commodities A, B, C; one of them may easily be replaced by money at any stage of the argument. The utility interrelations among the three goods can be described in a three-dimensional diagram by a series of indifference surfaces. Analogous to a series of indifference curves, a system of superimposed indifference *surfaces* gives a complete and theoretically precise description of the interrelations among three commodities. Each of the indifference surfaces will indicate all possible equivalent combinations of A, B, and C, that is, as an indifference line represents a certain utility level. The relative positions of successive indifference surfaces will indicate "higher" and "lower" utility levels. Figure 5 gives a schematic representation of such an indifference surface (i-y-e).[10]

In terms of the graph, our index-problem amounts to a translation of the three-dimensional picture into a two-dimensional diagram. This new diagram must have exactly the same general properties as the previously analyzed two-dimensional system of

[10] In the same way as an indifference line may approach the coordinates of a two-dimensional diagram without actually cutting them, an indifference surface may never cut the limiting planes AoB, AoC, and BoC.

144

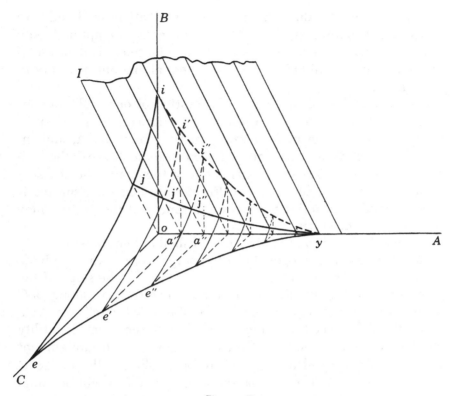

Figure 5

indifference curves. Furthermore, the translation must be accomplished in such a way that while one of the axes will represent the quantities of the new combination of B and C—we will call it I—the other will still measure the original quantities of the third commodity, A.

A solution of this problem is facilitated by the two following considerations:

(a) A simple measurement of the different quantities of the new composite commodity in terms of physical units will be possible only under the condition that its *composition remains constant*. Each unit of the composite good, I, must contain a fixed amount of B and C.

145

(b) In order to reduce the different combinations of B and C to this single denominator, this criterion can readily be applied: Any of this combination can be replaced by a definite equivalent quantity of I, which would mean an exactly equal amount of utility to the consumer.

In terms of the graph (Fig. 5), a solution of our problem consists in putting a plane IoA through the original system of indifference surfaces, the plane footing on the abscissa, oA, and inclined at a certain deliberately selected angle toward the two other coordinates. The cross cuts between this plane and the successive indifference surfaces (on Fig. 5 only one such surface is shown) produce a series of curves and represent the desired new set of indifference lines.

The whole transformation is accomplished in two steps:

(a) The first is the choice of the composition of the synthetic commodity, I. This composition is represented by the slope of the plane IoA. Cutting the system of indifference surfaces along BoC or any other parallel plane, such as i' a' e' or i'' a'' e'', we get a series of indifference lines (Fig. 6) which will represent the utility relation between B and C on the assumption of a constant amount of A (which is equal to o, a', a'', respectively, for the crosscuts mentioned above). The inclination of the plane IoA will be equal to the slope of the line ojI. This slope corresponds to a fixed relation between the quantities of B and C which we choose to combine in each unit of the new composite commodity. This proportion may be, for example, $1B$ to $2C$, $1B$ to $1C$, or any other. Theoretically, the choice of this proportion is absolutely free. Once the composition of the composite commodity is thus established, that is, the slope of ojI is fixed, its quantity can be measured along the line from o toward I in the same manner as the amounts of A, B, and C, are measured along their separate coordinates.

(b) The amount of Oj of I is equivalent in its utility to all the other combinations of B and C which are situated on the indifference line i j e. Similarly, all the points of the indifference curves i' j' e', i'' j'' e'', etc. (Fig. 5), are equivalent to the corresponding amounts of I: a' j', a'' j'', etc. Furthermore, we see that the points j', j, j'', y, being all situated on the same indifference surface,

146

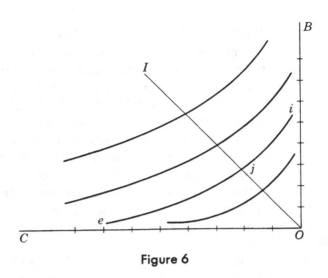

Figure 6

i e y, necessarily represent also an equal utility level. The curve *j j′ j″* y (Fig. 5) represents an indifference line and describes the utility relation between the composite commodity, *I*, and the good, *A*. The three-dimensional utility surface, *j e y*, is reduced to a two-dimensional indifference curve, *j y*. In the same way all the other utility levels of the original three-dimensional system can be represented by corresponding indifference curves on the plane *IoA*.

With the help of a similar transformation, any number of individual commodities can be reduced to a single composite good. Once the substitution is accomplished, this new abstract good can be treated theoretically exactly in the same way as if it were a simple element of the initial uncondensed system.

If the price level of the two commodities must be determined, the problem consists in translating each of the separate points of comparison to the common denominator *I*, the previously selected composite commodity. The price levels are obtained by division of the total expenditures in the particular points by the corresponding amounts of the composite commodity.

An element of *arbitrariness* enters the described procedure with the choice of the "composition" of the index commodity (the slope

147

of the cross cut $o\,J$ on Figs. 5 and 6). As already mentioned, theoretically any slope between $o\,B$ and $o\,C$ will serve the purpose. But it is difficult to see why this circumstance should impair the usefulness of the method. Whatever the choice of the composite commodity, the index will always fulfill the fundamental requirements noted and consequently serve its purpose, which is to the simplification of the system through reduction of the number of variables. The results obtained on the basis of each of the different index commodities will necessarily be compatible with each other and in no case contradictory. Moreover, the transition from one composition of the index commodity to a different one can be accomplished by means of the same technique—translation along the indifference curves.

For index calculations it seems to be advisable to choose the slope of the index cross cut in such a way as to reduce as much as possible the distances between the original combination of the given commodities and the corresponding index points. It would be wrong, however, to use for this purpose a definite formula, to compose, for example, the index commodity according to the average composition of all empirically given original points. A rigid arrangement of this sort would necessitate a revision of the whole system every time a new point was added to the original group of data, which is a complication warranted neither by theoretical nor by practical considerations.

7. The statistical usefulness of this proposed method depends mainly on the possibility of discovering the shape of the indifference curves—an empirical task the difficulty of which can hardly be exaggerated. The previous discussion showed, however, that a given set of indifference curves—although not always explicitly mentioned—is the common basis of many of the rival theoretical approaches to the problem of composite commodities. Because of this, the practical difficulty cited above affects equally all of these theories. Analysis of the usual statistical technique shows that the slightest neglect of this "system of tastes" must in any case lead to faulty results.

As things are, a preliminary practical solution must be sought in deliberate acceptance of some more or less warranted approximations. But, in this respect also, none of the different theoretical approaches could possibly claim a practical advantage.

In connection with this contention it is interesting to see that, with the help of certain "heroic" assumptions, it is even possible to interpret the numerical magnitudes obtained by the "method of limits" in terms of the proposed composite commodities.

Given two points Q_1 and Q_2 (Fig. 2) and the two corresponding price ratios. The latter are represented by the slopes of the two lines, cb and ad. If we now select the proportional combination of the two commodities, A and B, in point Q_1 as our standard combination, the line otQ_1v will represent the direction along which the quantity of the composite commodity has to be measured. According to this set-up, the distance oQ_1 will represent the composite amount in point Q_1. A theoretically correct procedure would require a translation of the point Q_2 along the indifference line $i - i$, and the result obtained would indicate that the combination Q_2 represents exactly the same amount (oQ_1) of the composite commodity as combination Q_1, which means that the quantity index is equal to 1. If the shape of the indifference line is unknown, it is still possible to attempt some kind of approximation. From the fundamental properties of the indifference lines, it follows that the crosspoint between the line otQ_1v and the presumably unknown indifference line on which the point Q_1 is located can in no case be lower than t or higher than v. In other words, the unknown quantity index will certainly not be larger than oQ_1/ot and not smaller than oQ_1/ov. These two ratios may be called the upper and lower limit of the quantity index calculated on the basis of the composite commodity otQ_1v. From the given geometric relations it follows that

$$oQ_1/ot = ko/ao = \Sigma p_2 q_1 / \Sigma p_2 q_2.$$

The latter expression is identical with the "lower limit" of the usual method of limits. The other ratio, oQ_1/ov, has no such well-known counterpart. In order to arrive at the ratio $\Sigma p_1 q_1 / \Sigma p_1 q_2$ (the conventional "upper limit" of the quantity index), it is necessary to *change the composition of the standard commodity* and perform the measurement along orQ_2w instead of otQ_1v. Applying the same reasoning as before, we find that, according to this new scale, the "true" quantity index must lie between ow/oQ_2 and or/oQ_2. And now,

$$or/oQ_2 = oc/om = \Sigma p_1q_1/\Sigma p_1q_2,$$

that is, the "upper limit" of the conventional method is identical with the upper limit calculated along the new scale. The conventional comparison of the two "limits," $\Sigma p_1q_1/\Sigma p_1q_2$ and $\Sigma p_2q_1/\Sigma p_2q_2$, appears to be rather illogical.

13

Introduction to a theory of the internal structure of functional relationships

I

Breaking down an intricate quantitative system with many variables into several simpler relationships—each involving fewer variables—is a standard analytical procedure. Let us consider, for example, the process of steel production. The final output depends here on a very great number of different inputs. If one goes back far enough, these will comprise the quantities of various kinds of labor, machinery, explosives, and other auxiliary materials used in extraction of coal; they will also include a not less heterogeneous collection of cost factors of the iron-mining industry. To be complete this list should contain as well a long array of tools, labor skills, and materials used directly in the operation and maintenance of blast furnaces and open-hearth units.

To avoid an unnecessarily complicated example, let the total number of such separate inputs be limited to eight. In terms of these the "over-all" production function of steel can be written as

(I.1) $$y = F(x_1, x_2, x_3, x_4, x_5, x_6, x_7, x_8).$$

It shows the tonnage y of finished steel as dependent on the amounts $x_1, x_2, \ldots, x_8$ of all the individual inputs—each measured in terms of its own appropriate physical units.

From *Econometrica*, Vol. 15, No. 4, October 1947.

The various material processes covered by this formula are so many and so different from each other that even a verbal description of such a vast technological complex would hardly be possible without reference to intermediate commodities such as coal and ore. The over-all relationships between the set of the independent variables $x_1, x_2, \ldots, x_8$ and the dependent variable, y, can be conveniently thought of as a combination of many separate, intermediate relationships involving not only these original but also some additional, intermediate variables. Let, for example, x_1, x_2, x_3 represent those of the eight factors which are actually used in the production of coal and x_4, x_5, x_6, x_7 those which constitute the cost elements of the iron-mining industry. Let, furthermore, z_1 stand for the amount of coal and z_2 the quantity of ore going into the production of steel and x_8 be the amount of labor used in servicing the blast furnaces. On the basis of appropriate technical information one can establish three intermediate production functions:

$$(I.2) \qquad z_1 = {}_1f(x_1, x_2, x_3),$$

$$(I.3) \qquad z_2 = {}_2f(x_4, x_5, x_6, x_7),$$

$$(I.4) \qquad y = {}_0f(z_1, z_2, x_8).$$

The first describes the output of coal in terms of the original factors—"original" means in this context a factor represented by one of the independent variables in the production function $(I.1)$— actually used in the coal industry; the second gives an analogous description of iron mining. The last is a production function of the steel industry but in contrast to the over-all function $(I.1)$ it does not have among its independent variables any of the original factors used either in the coal or in the iron industry. It describes the output of steel in terms of the two new intermediate variables, coal, z_1, and ore, z_2, combined with one "original" factor, x_8 which does not appear in either one of the two other production functions; as stated before, x_8 represents labor employed on the blast-furnace crews.

Given these three partial relationships the over-all production function can be reconstructed by substitution of ${}_1f(x_1, x_2, x_3)$ and ${}_2f(x_4, x_5, x_6, x_7)$ for z_1 and z_2 in $(I.4)$. Indeed the consistency that necessarily must exist between the three intermediate and the one over-all relationship can be stated in the form of the following identity:[1]

$$(I.5) \quad F(x_1, x_2, \ldots, x_8) = {}_0f[{}_1f(x_1, x_2, x_3), {}_2f(x_4, x_5, x_6, x_7), x_8].$$

Both sides of it represent the same functional relationship between the final output and the original inputs.

While the method of deriving an unknown over-all function through combination of the known subsidiary relationships is so simple as to appear trivial, the solution of the obverse problem is much less obvious. Given a quantitative description of the over-all relationship such as (I.1), can one without any additional outside information, that is, solely through examination of the mathematical properties of the function $F(x_1, x_2, \ldots, x_8)$, establish the possible existence of such subsidiary groups of variables as $[x_1, x_2, x_3]$ and $[x_4, x_5, x_6, x_7]$ and describe the properties of the corresponding intermediate functions ${}_1f(x_1, x_2, x_3)$, ${}_2f(x_4, x_5, x_6, x_7)$, and ${}_0f(z_1, z_2, x_8)$?

A general answer to this question is given below.

I I

Let X be a set of n variables $x_1, x_2, \ldots, x_n$, and y a continuous function of these variables, $y = F(x_1, x_2, \ldots, x_n)$, also written as $F(X)$. Throughout the following discussion all the partial derivatives of that function in some neighborhood of a point $x_1 = a_1$, $x_2 = a_2, \ldots, x_n = a_n$ are assumed to be different from zero. Let S be a subset of X and $\overline{S}$ the complement of S in X (that is, a set of all elements of X not included in S).

DEFINITION I.

(a) *A subset S of independent variables* $x_1, x_2, \ldots, x_v$, *is locally functionally separable from the set X in F(X) if there exist some function* ${}_sf(S)$ *with continuous first derivatives in the neighborhood of* $(a_1, a_2, \ldots, a_v)$ *and another function* ${}_0f$ *also with continuous*

---

[1] This as well as all other equations in this article is an identity in the sense that it holds for all admissible values of the independent variables involved.

first derivatives and defined in some neighborhood of $(b, a_{v+1},$
$a_{v+2}, \ldots, a_n)$, *where* $b = {}_sf(a_1, a_2, \ldots, a_v)$, *such that*

(II.1) $$y = F(X) = {}_of[{}_sf(S), \bar{S}].$$

(b) *The function* ${}_sf(S)$ *as defined above is locally separable in* $F(X)$.

The fundamental concepts of functional separability are defined locally, that is, in the neighborhood of a particular point $(a_1\ a_2, \ldots, a_n, b)$, because all propositions describing the properties of separable sets of variables and separable functions as stated below are derived with the help of conventional methods of infinitesimal calculus which deals with relationships "in the small." The limitations imposed on the empirical applications of mathematical theorems thus obtained are the same as those which apply to similarly derived propositions of physics or, say, mathematical economics. Although explicit references to the neighborhood of a specific point and the use of the adjective "locally" in conjunction with the concept of functional separability are omitted from subsequent discussion, they should be understood to apply to all propositions and definitions in this article. "Separability" has also to be interpreted as meaning functional separability in the sense of Definition I above.

The following propositions can be derived from the basic Definition I of separable subsets of variables and separable functions. The proofs of most of them have already been given in another paper. Being in part rather intricate they are not reproduced here again.[2] The theorems, lemmas, and informally stated corollaries derived in the paper quoted in the footnote are combined here in a slightly modified form with a few additional definitions.

The necessary and sufficient conditions of functional separability can best be formulated in terms of the auxiliary functions ${}_{ij}R$ defined by

(II.2) $${}_{ij}R = F'_i / F'_j,$$

[2] See W. Leontief, "A Note on the Interrelation of Subsets of Independent Variables of a Continuous Function with Continuous First Derivatives," *Bulletin of the American Mathematical Society*, Vol. 53, No. 4, pp. 343-50. This paper will be referred to as the *Math. Bull.* article.

where F_i' and F_j' are the partial derivatives of $F(x_1, x_2, \ldots, x_n)$ with respect to x_i *and* x_j; this function will be recognized by an economist as representing the "marginal rate of substitution" between x_i and x_j in $F(X)$. The necessary and sufficient condition for $_{ij}R$ being independent of a third variable, say x_k, is the realization of the identity

(II.3)
$$_{ij}R_k' = \frac{F_{ik}''F_j' - F_{jk}''F_i'}{[F_j']^2} = 0$$

within the predetermined range of variation of $x_1, x_2, \ldots, x_n$. From this it follows that $_{ij}R_k' = 0$ implies $_{ji}R_k' = 0$; a combination of $_{ji}R_k' = 0$ and $_{il}R_k' = 0$ implies $_{jl}R_k' = 0$; if $_{ik}R_j' = 0$ and $_{jk}R_i' = 0$ then $_{ij}R_k' = 0$.

PROPOSITION I.[3] *A subset S is functionally separable from X in $F(X)$ if and only if the following set of equations is satisfied: $_{s_is_j}R_{\bar{s}} = 0$. The first two subscripts to R refer to any two identical or different elements of subset S, while the last subscript indicates any element of the subset $\overline{S}$ which is complementary to S in X.*

PROPOSITION II. (a) *Each individual independent variable x_i constitutes a subset functionally separable from X in $F(X)$; (b) so does the set X itself.*

PROPOSITION III. *Given A, B, C, three mutually exclusive subsets of X. If each of the sets A, B, C is functionally separable from X in $F(X)$; these subsets can also be separated simultaneously from X in $F(X)$; in other words, such functions of, $_Af$, $_Bf$, and cf exist that we can write the identity*

$$y = F(X) = {}_{0}f[{}_{A}f(A) + {}_{B}f(B) + cf(C), G],$$

where G comprises all elements of X not included in A, B, or C.[4]

PROPOSITION IV.
(a) *If two functionally separable subsets S and T of X in $F(X)$ —of which neither is a subset of the other—intersect each other (that is, have some elements in common), then each of the three*

---

[3] This is Theorem I proven in the *Math. Bull.* article.
[4] This is the Lemma proven in the *Math. Bull.* article.

non-overlapping sets—one of which comprises all elements of S which are not elements of T, the second consists of all the elements of T which are not elements of S, and the third contains all elements common to S and T—as well as their sum, $S \smile T$—are also functionally separable subsets of X in $F(X)$.

(b) Furthermore the three nonoverlapping subsets mentioned above are additively separable subsets of X in $F(X)$; that is, some functions of, $_Af$, $_Bf$, and $_Cf$ exist such that

$$y = F(X) = {_0f}[_Af(A) + {_Bf}(B) + {_Cf}(C), G],$$

where G is a complement of $A \smile B \smile C$ in X.[5]

The last proposition leads to:

DEFINITION II. *(a) A set of independent variables X and the function $F(X)$ are additively composite if X can be partitioned into three or more additively separable subsets.*

A sum of any two of these subsets obviously also constitutes an additively separable subset.

(b) The separable subsets of X in $F(X)$ which can not themselves be partitioned into smaller additively separable subsets of X in $F(X)$ will be referred to as primitive additively separable subsets of X in $F(X)$. We will use a long horizontal bar to mark a group of primitive subsets additively separable in a given additively composite function. Thus the formula in the second part of Proposition IV can be written as

$$y = F(X) = {_0f}(\overline{A, B, C, G}).$$

PROPOSITION V. *(a) The class of functions $_sf(S)$ separating S from X in $F(X)$ can be, in general, described by*

$$_af(S) = \phi[F(S, \overline{S}^0)]$$

where the core $F(S, \overline{S}^0)$ is obtained from $F(X)$ by assigning to the $n - v$ variables comprised in subset $\overline{S}$ (which is complementary to S in X) some arbitrary constant values x^0_{v+1}, x^0_{v+2}, ..., $x_n{}^0$, which do not, however, let $F(S, \overline{S}^0)$ vanish identically, while ϕ is

[5] This is Theorem II in the *Math. Bull.* article.

an arbitrary continuous function with nonvanishing first deriva-tives.[6]

(*b*) *If subsets A, B, and C are additively separated from X in F(X), that is, if*

$$F(X) = {}_0f\{{}_A\phi[F(A, \overline{A}^0] + {}_B\phi[F(B, \overline{B}^0)] + {}_C\phi[F(C, \overline{C}^0)], G\},$$

the functions ${}_A\phi$, ${}_B\phi$, ${}_C\phi$ are not arbitrary; they must be obtained through integration of appropriate differential equations.

PROPOSITION VI. *Let S be a subset separable from X in F(X) and ${}_sf(S)$ a corresponding separable function. Let, furthermore, Q be a proper subset of S.*

(*a*) *If Q is separable from X in F(X), it is also separable from S in ${}_sf(S)$.*

(*b*) *If Q is separable from S in ${}_sf(S)$, it also is separable from X in F(X).*[7]

III

Let us now consider the whole system of subsets of independent variables separable from X in a given function $F(X)$.

Any two different members of this system, say A and B, can in general stand in the following four relationships to each other: (1) A and B can be disjointed, that is, have no elements in common; (2) A can be contained in B; (3) B can be contained in A; finally (4) A and B can intersect each other. The subsequent analysis will be considerably simplified if at the outset all subsets intersecting any other subsets are eliminated from our system. Such elimination does not entail any loss of information provided use is made of the long horizontal bar sign (introduced in connection with Definition II above) to indicate the primitive additively separable subsets belonging to one additively separable set. The relationship (4) of "intersection" can thus be replaced by that (4a) of

---

[6] This proposition is demonstrated in the *Math. Bull.* article in connection with the proof of Theorem I.

[7] This proposition was not mentioned in the *Math. Bull.* article. It follows directly from the definition of separable subsets and functions and Proposition I.

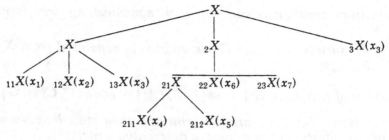

Figure 1

belonging in the same group of primitive additively separable subsets.

The structure of our system of separable subsets can now be described by an "inverted tree" diagram (see Fig. 1).

X is a set of eight independent variables in $F(X)$. $_1X$, $_2X$, and $_3X$ are its separable subsets of the first order, that is, subsets separable from X only and not from any other member of the system. $_{11}X$, $_{12}X$, $_{13}X$, $_{21}X$, $_{22}X$, and $_{23}X$ are subsets of the second order, each separable from X *and* from a subset of the first order.

$_2X$ is an additively composite set and $_{21}X$, $_{22}X$, and $_{23}X$ are the additively primitive subsets separable from it. $_{211}X$ and $_{212}X$ are subsets of the third order, separable from $_{21}X$, $_{21}X \cup {}_{22}X$, $_{21}X \cup {}_{23}X$, $_2X$, and X.

To each separable subset in our system corresponds a separable function. The same "inverted tree" diagram which describes the relationships between X and all other subsets separable from it in $F(X)$ shows also the relationships between function $F(X)$ and all the functions separable from it.

They can also be represented in terms of conventional functional notation. The internal structure of a function on which the system shown in Figure 1 is based can be written down as follows:

(III.1)
$$F(x_1, x_2, x_3, x_4, x_5, x_6, x_7, x_8)$$
$$= {}_0f\{{}_1f(x_1, x_2, x_3), {}_2f[{}_{21}f(x_4, x_5) + {}_{22}f(x_6) + {}_{23}f(x_7)], x_8\}.$$

The individual separable functions have the same subscripts that mark the subsets of variables separable with them. Function signs

158

before non-additive one-member sets containing single variables are omitted.

DEFINITION III. *The order of a separable set within the system of all non-intersecting separable subsets of X in F(X) can, in general, be defined as being equal to the number of the other members of the same system from which it can be separated. The order of a separable function is the same as the order of the subset which it separates.*

The eight subsets such as $_{11}X$, $_{211}X$, $_{23}X$, or $_3X$ that are located at the ends of the respective "branches" of our tree, that is, all subsets that do not include any other separable subsets, are one-element subsets containing each a single independent variable. These variables are entered in Figure 1 in parentheses.

DEFINITION IV. (a) *A set X in F(X) that contains no other separable subsets but itself and those consisting of the individual elements of X can be called simple. The function F(X) of a simple set is also simple.*

(b) *All sets and the corresponding functions that are not simple are composite.*

From these definitions it follows that all functions of one or two independent variables are simple.

In interpreting the meaning of structural formulae such as (III.1) it is necessary to keep in mind that all functions separable from F(X) contain arbitrary constants and—with the exception of the additively separable functions—can be subject to arbitrary nonlinear transformations. Their contents in terms of the sets of the ultimate variables involved and the relative positions of these sets within the internal structure of the given function F(X) are, however, invariant.[8]

Let us analyze, for example, the structure of a particular function

$$\text{(III.2)} \quad \begin{aligned} F(X) &= F(x_1, x_2, x_3, x_4, x_5, x_6, x_7, x_8) \\ &= \{ Ax_1x_2 + Bx_2x_3 + Cx_1x_3 + (x_4 + x_5)x_6x_7 \} x_8. \end{aligned}$$

[8] The remaining portions of this third part of the article may be skipped by readers not concerned with computational details.

To find the subsets separable from the set $[x_1, x_2, x_3, x_4, x_5, x_6, x_7, x_8]$ of all variables in $F(X)$ we compute—according to formula (II.2)—all the $_{ij}R$'s:

$$_{12}R = \frac{Ax_2 + Cx_3}{Ax_1 + Bx_3}, \qquad _{13}R = \frac{Ax_2 + Cx_3}{Bx_2 + Cx_1}$$

and so on. Inspecting the variables upon which each of these $_{ij}R$'s depends, we find that according to Proposition I our function contains the following separable subsets (other than the eight one-member sets containing one variable each):

$$
\begin{array}{llllllll}
[x_1 & x_2 & x_3 & x_4 & x_5 & x_6 & x_7 & x_8], \\
[x_1 & x_2 & x_3], \\
& & & [x_4 & x_5 & x_6 & x_7], \\
& & & [x_4 & x_5], \\
& & & [x_4 & x_5 & x_6], \\
& & & [x_4 & x_5 & & x_7], \\
& & & & & [x_6 & x_7].
\end{array}
$$

The overlapping subsets of $[x_4\ x_5\ x_6\ x_7]$ written out in the four bottom rows can, according to Proposition IV and Definition II, be described as a combination of additively primitive subsets of $[x_4\ x_5\ x_6\ x_7]$. Thus our system of separable subsets is reduced to

$$
\begin{array}{llllllll}
[x_1 & x_2 & x_3 & x_4 & x_5 & x_6 & x_7 & x_8], \\
[x_1 & x_2 & x_3], \\
& & & [x_4 & x_5 & x_6 & x_7], \\
& & & \overline{[x_4} & x_5] & [x_6] & [x_7].
\end{array}
$$

That set structure can easily be recognized as that depicted in Fig. 1.

To arrive at the corresponding functional structure—such as described by (III.1)—one can follow a procedure based on Proposition V. Beginning with functions nearest to the end of the "branches" of the tree we find first that the core of $_1f(x_1, x_2, x_3)$ is $(Ax_1x_2 + Bx_2x_3 + Cx_1x_3 + k_1)k_2$ where k_1 and k_2 are arbitrary constants. Thus

$$_1f(x_1, x_2, x_3) = {}_1\phi\{(Ax_1x_2 + Bx_2x_3 + Cx_1x_3 + k_1)k_2\}.$$

160

To determine the form of the additively composite function $_2f[_{21}f(x_4+x_5)+_{22}f(x_6)+_{23}f(x_7)]$ it is necessary to integrate the two partial differential equations

(III.3)

$$\left(\frac{dx_7}{dx_6}\right)_{_2f\text{const}} = -\frac{Fx_6'}{Fx_7'} = -\frac{x_7}{x_6},$$

$$\left[\frac{dx_7}{d(x_4+x_5)}\right]_{_2f\text{const}} = -\frac{F'(x_4+x_5)}{F'x_7} = -\frac{x_7}{x_4+x_5}.$$

The general integral of this system is

(III.4)

$$_{12}f(x_4, x_5, x_6, x_7) = \psi\left[\ln(x_4+x_5)+\ln(x_6)+\ln(x_7)\right]$$
$$= \psi\{\ln[(x_4+x_5)x_6x_7]\}.$$

Since the core of the left-hand function is $\{k_3+(x_4+x_5)x_6x_7\}\, k_4$ the form of function ψ must be such that

(III.5) $\psi\{\ln[(x_4+x_5)x_6x_7]\} = \{k_3+(x_4+x_5)x_6x_7\}k_4.$

Differentiating both sides with respect to, say, x_6 we have

(III.6) $\psi'\{\ln[(x_4+x_5)x_6x_7]\}\dfrac{1}{x_6} = (x_4+x_5)x_7k_4$

or

(III.7) $\psi'(\ln y) = k_4 y = e^{\ln(k_4 y)},$

where

$$y = (x_4+x_5)x_6x_7.$$

Integrating with respect to y, we have

(III.8) $\psi(\ln y) = k_4 e^{\ln y} + C,$

and putting $C = k_3 k_4$ so as to satisfy the initial condition (III. 5) we have

(III.9)
$\psi(\ln y) = \psi\{\ln[(x_4+x_5)x_6x_7]\} = k_4 e^{\ln(x_4+x_5)+\ln x_6+\ln x_7} + k_3 k_4.$

The last expression is the core of $_2f$ containing a sum of three additively separable functions

$$_{21}f(x_4, x_5) = \ln(x_4 + x_5),$$
$$\text{(III.10)} \qquad _{22}f(x_6) = \ln(x_6),$$
$$_{22}f(x_7) = \ln(x_7).$$

In general

(III.11)

$$_2f[\,_{21}f(x_4, x_5) + {}_{22}f(x_6) + {}_{21}f(x_7)]$$
$$= {}_2\phi(e^{21f(x_4, x_5) + 22f(x_6) + 23f(x_7)} + k_3)k_4 = {}_2\phi(e^{\ln(x_4 + x_5) + \ln x_6 + \ln x_7} + k_3)k_4.$$

The zero-order function of [see (III.1)] must be such as to satisfy equation (III.2) with the two arbitrary functions $_1\phi$ and $_2\phi$ as intermediate first-order variables in it. Thus we arrive at the following description of the given function $F(x_1, x_2, \ldots, x_n)$ in terms of intermediate functions separable from it:

$$\{Ax_1x_2 + Bx_2x_3 + Cx_1x_3 + (x_4 + x_5)x_6x_7\}x_8$$

$$\text{(III.12)} \quad = \Big(_1\phi^{-1}\{_1\phi[(Ax_1x_2 + Bx_2x_3 + Cx_1x_3 + k_1)k_2]\}\frac{1}{k_2} - k_1$$

$$+ {}_2\phi^{-1}\{_2\phi[(e^{\ln(x_4 + x_5) + \ln x_6 + \ln x_7} + k_3)k_4]\}\frac{1}{k_4} - k_3\Big)x_8.$$

$_1\phi^{-1}$ and $_2\phi^{-1}$ are functions inverse to $_1\phi$ and $_2\phi$.

I V

It is not the purpose of these concluding remarks to present a detailed or even systematic discussion of the possible application of the concepts and analytic devices developed above. As a tool of deductive reasoning the general methods of finding separable subsets of independent variables and describing the internal structure of their interrelationships in terms of separable functions might find useful application in many a field of empirical inquiry dealing with quantitative systems involving large numbers of variables. Translation of these basic concepts into the language of stochastic, that is, probability, analysis no doubt should be the first step toward effective statistical application. Professor Hotelling's factor analysis certainly meets the concept of a separable subset of variables halfway. Since, however, nonlinearity of quantitative relationships constitutes the principal basis of nontrivial instances of functional separability (and, incidentally, also of dynamic stability) conventional methods of linear-regression analysis will hardly be able to serve as an instrument of its statistical adaptation.

The recent discussion of the problem of aggregation approached in its theoretical phases some of the question raised and answered in rather more general terms in the first three parts of this article.

The analysis of consumers' choice offers what seems to be a particularly illuminating example of a concrete theoretical issue, the solution of which can be effectively advanced through application of the concept of separable functions. The evolution of theoretical thought on this particular subject followed, as in many other similar instances, a deviously dialectical path of development. It started with the acceptance of conventional and supposedly self-evident notions of the so-called common experience; it went through the antithesis of a rigorous but essentially destructive phase of negative criticism to move finally toward the higher stage of positive synthesis which vindicates again some valuable elements of the original common-sense experience after distilling it in the refining apparatus of exact logical analysis.

The assumption of the existence of general categories of needs, different from demands for particular individual commodities, but still specific enough to be clearly distinguishable from each other, is basic to the man-in-the-street idea of consumers' demand. One speaks of the desire for food as existing behind and separately from the particular demand for bread, apples, or Lobster à la Newburg. This need for food is at the same time spoken of as something clearly distinguishable from the similarly general needs for clothing or, say, for shelter, each of the latter also thought of as existing separately although manifested through the particular demands for one-family houses, apartment flats, or woolen suits and raincoats.

Earlier theorists such as Irving Fisher tried to rationalize this approach through the concept of services of consumers' goods as separate variables distinct from the goods themselves; bread, lobster, and other individual foodstuffs were described as "supplying" the generalized homogeneous service of "feeding" much in the same way as ore and coal serve as means of producing pig iron. Although logically consistent this theory, and rightly so, became a victim of the same wave of criticism that swept away the old-fashioned value theory. If measurable utility proves to be a fictitious concept incapable of operational verification so also will the abstract category of generalized needs.

The third and latest phase of this theoretical development began with the surrender of all the old untenable positions and a complete retreat to the concept of a general indifference variety described in terms of individual consumers' goods. With considerable caution and much methodological circumspection the progress was resumed through careful reconstruction of the technical concepts of substitution and complementarity, dependence and independence of individual commodities defined within a given indifference system. Much ground was gained by painstaking reformulation of the whole theory of consumers' demand[9] undertaken largely in response to the quest for statistical demand curves.

The lack of a precise, operational device for dealing with well-defined groups of individual commodities reduced, however, an important part of the theory of consumers' behavior to hardly more than a collection of isolated, arbitrary definitions.

It is true that practical economists, assisted by practicing statisticians, speak of and deal in food, clothing, or cultural needs in general, even measuring the aggregative quantities of these fictitious entities. This, however, only serves to emphasize the limited usefulness of the conceptual apparatus offered to them by the theoretician. The analysis of the internal structure of functions of many variables, as presented in Parts II and III of this article and the concept of functional separability in particular might help to close that particular gap between pure and applied economics.

The same analytical procedure that made it possible in the previously cited example to establish through examination of the over-all quantitative relationship between the remote inputs of the

[9] Herman Wold, "A Synthesis of Pure Demand Analysis," Parts I and II, *Skandinarisk Akiuarietidskrift*, 1943, pp. 85-118, pp. 220-63; Part III, *ibid.* 1944, pp. 69-120.

many various factors of production on one hand and the final output of finished steel on the other, the existence of the intermediate "ore" and "coal" components, gives operational meaning to general categories of consumers' needs representative of distinguishable subgroups in the class of all consumers' goods. In this as in the other instance the interlocking relationships between such subsets (and the corresponding separable functions) of various orders can be shown to represent the structural interconnection between individual branches and twigs of an intricate but well-defined system.

The only practical difference between the two cases is that in the first instance the results of the deductive, analytical procedure can be easily verified through immediate observation, while in the second such direct approach is impossible, at least for the time being. This only enhances, however, the usefulness of the indirect procedure as applied to the theory of consumption.

While defining certain aspects of the specific shape of the separable functions and establishing the exact contents of the corresponding separable subgroups of independent variables, indirect mathematical analysis allows the introduction of an arbitrary function with every new intermediate variable. Essentially that means that these variables remain dimensionally indeterminate. The only condition imposed on them from the outside is that all the arbitrary dimensional functions placed in their respective positions within the complete system should be consistent with the given dimensional characteristics of the final over-all independent variable.

This condition is significantly missing in the case of the over-all consumption function. The dimensional indeterminateness of the utility concept is demonstrated by the fact—referred to in every elementary treatment of the modern theory of consumers' choice—that every arbitrary continuous function with positive first derivative (the latter being pure convention) of any initially chosen utility measure will fit all observable aspects of this behavior equally well.

This simply means that in application to this particular type of problem the method of separable functions is simplified through removal of a rather bothersome side condition.

14

Delayed adjustment of supply and partial equilibrium

I

For a long time economic theorists have been aware of the fact that a time lag between supply and demand reactions may constitute an important factor in determining the equilibrium state of an economy. Yet, it has been only recently that Professors Ricci and Schultz, and Drs. Tinbergen and Rosenstein-Rodan recognized the vital importance of this problem and laid ground for its analytical treatment.

The following represents an attempt to extend the results of their investigations and to throw some light on the problem of the stability of partial equilibrium.

Given a Marshallian demand and a corresponding supply curve (Figs. 1, 2, 3), the former represents the demand price, p, as a function of the purchased quantity, q:

$$(1) \qquad p = f(q)$$

while the latter describes the quantity demanded as a function of the price[1]

Originally published in German under the title "Verzögerte Angebotsanpassung und Partielles Gleichgewicht," in *Zeitschrift für Nationalökonomie*, Band V, Heft 5, 1934, pp. 670-76. Translation by Charlotte E. Taskier.
[1] For reasons of technical convenience, the positions of the dependent and independent variables in these functions are reversed.

(2) $$q = \phi(p)$$

The two curves are assumed to satisfy the following general conditions:

(a) Both functions are continuous and can be differentiated at all points.

(b) Both functions are monotonic: the demand curve falls steadily to the right

(3) $$f'(q) < 0$$

while the supply curve rises in the opposite direction[2]

(4) $$\phi'(p) > 0.$$

(c) Both curves intersect at point M with the coordinates Q and P. In the following discussion this point will be referred to as the "Marshallian Point."

I I

The problem that we are about to consider arises from the fact that supply adjusts itself to a given market situation at a slower rate than demand. (In the case of a reversed "lag" the following results would have to be written with appropriate changes in negative signs.) This peculiar constellation results in a zigzag or wavy, up-and-down fluctuation of price and quantity. These can be best illustrated by the well-known "cobweb" diagram.

Whenever under the given conditions the quantity q_0 (see Fig. 1) is offered over a certain period of time, then, the instantaneous adjustment of demand will result in price p_0 (point m_0). Thereupon, production will go up and the quantity supplied—lagging behind demand—will be increased in the following period to $\check{q}_1$ (point m_1). Now the price will drop to $\check{p}_1$ (point m_2). Accordingly, supply will be reduced in the next period to $\check{q}_2$. Then, as price increases again, a rise in the supply will follow, and so on. Figure 1 demonstrates a case in which the angular spiral of successive price and quantity fluctuations—as if driven by some

[2] The somewhat less restrictive condition $f'(q) \leq 0$ and $\phi'(p) \geq 0$ suffices for derivation of most of the following results.

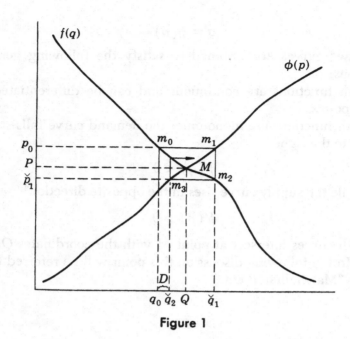

Figure 1

"centripetal" power—approaches the Marshallian intersection point M.

Figure 2 reproduces the supply and demand curves shown in Fig. 1. The process described above, however, starts now at a different point. The result is a fluctuating spiral movement displaying a "centrifugal" tendency.

In Fig. 3, the process starts still in another point: in this case, the open cycle is transformed into a closed rectangle showing a strictly repetitive cycle of up-and-down fluctuation of price and quantities.

The significant properties of the price and quantity fluctuations described above can be formulated as follows:

Let D be the distance between any arbitrarily selected starting quantity q_0 and the quantity $\check{q}_2$ corresponding to the final point m_3 in which the system will find itself at the end of the full swing, m_0, m_1, m_2, m_3:

(5) $$D = \check{q}_2 - q_0$$

168

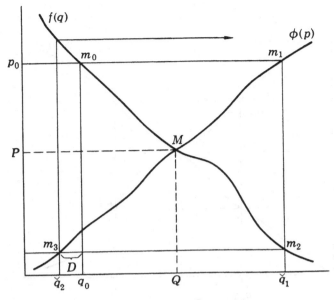

Figure 2

The term D may be called the *cyclical shift* of quantity q_0: $D > 0$ indicates a *shift to the right* (see Fig. 1), $D < 0$ *a shift to the left* (see Fig. 2), and $D = 0$ corresponds to an *equilibrium state* with a closed cycle (see Fig. 3). A closer scrutiny shows that all points where $q_0 < Q$, $D > 0$ signifies a "centripetal" and $D < 0$ a "centrifugal" tendency in the adjustment process. However, when $q_0 > Q$, the opposite is true. In this case, with $D > 0$ the amplitude of the fluctuation increases, while with $D < 0$ it decreases.

The quantity $\check{q}_2$ can be considered to be a function of q_0. The interdependence between two quantities can consequently be derived from the following four equations:

(6)
$$
\begin{aligned}
P_0 &= f(q_0) \\
\check{q}_1 &= \phi(p_0) \\
\check{p}_1 &= f(\check{q}_1) \\
\check{q}_2 &= \phi(\check{p}_1)
\end{aligned}
$$

A chain of substitutions yields:

169

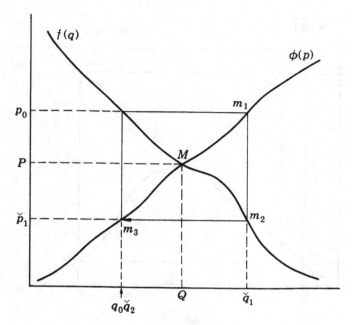

Figure 3

$$(7) \qquad \check{q}_2 = \phi(f\,(\phi\,(f\,(q_0))))$$

Inserting the right hand expression into (5) results in:

$$(8) \qquad D(q_0) = \phi(f\,(\phi\,(f\,(q_0)))) - q_0$$

Since $f(q)$ as well as $\phi(p)$ are continuous and differentiable curves, the function $D(q_0)$ must necessarily be continuous and differentiable too.

III

Equation (8) makes the usual methods of infinitesimal analysis applicable in the analysis of the equilibrium problem. A graph of a $D(q_0)$ function and of its first derivative is presented on Fig. 4. The starting quantity q_0 is measured along the horizontal axis. The vertical distances between that axis and the curve $D(q_0)$ represent the positive or negative values taken on by that function for any given magnitude of q_0.

Every point where $D(q_0)$ intersects the horizontal zero axis

170

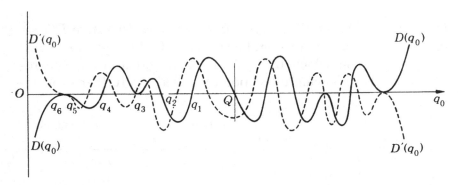

Figure 4

(Q, q_1, q_2, q_3, etc.)—at which therefore, $D(q_0) = 0$—indicates a state of equilibrium. All values of q_0 which lie between two equilibrium points have a tendency to shift. There is a shift to the right at all points where $D(q_0)$ is situated above the horizontal zero axis, and to the left wherever the curve drops below that zero axis.

In the light of the above consideration, all the equilibrium states in which the system can find itself, can be classified in accordance with *stability conditions* that prevail in each of them. Obviously, the latter depend on the shifting tendencies governing the immediate neighborhood of the particular equilibrium point. For example, the equilibrium quantity q_2 in Fig. 4 is stable because the quantities located immediately to the right of it show a tendency to shift to the left, while the quantities adjoining it on the left tend to shift to the right. The stretches adjoining point q_1 are on the contrary characterized by divergent tendencies that make, even after a relatively small chance disturbance, a return to the original equilibrium point impossible. In other words, q_1 is a point of unstable equilibrium.

A simple mathematical criterion of stability is provided by the sign of the first derivative of function $D(q_0)$. Differentiation of (8) yields the following expression:

(9)
$$D'(q_0) = \phi'(f(\phi(f(q_0)))) \cdot f'(\phi(f(q_0))) \cdot \phi'(f(q_0)) \cdot f'(q_0) - 1$$
$$= \phi'(\breve{p}_1) \cdot f'(\breve{q}_1) \cdot \phi'(p_0) \cdot f'(q_0) - 1$$

171

In those cases in which $D'(q_0) = 0$, the second derivative $D''(q_0)$ has to be considered. A general discussion of all the possible equilibrium states in which the system might find itself can be replaced by the following tabulation that needs no further explanation:

| TYPE OF EQUILIBRIUM | CHARACTERISTICS | | | EXAMPLE IN FIG. 4 |
	$D(q_0)$	$D'(q_0)$	$D''(q_0)$	
Stable on both sides	0	<0		Q, q_2
Unstable on both sides	0	>0		q_1, q_4
Stable to the right Unstable to the left	0	0	>0	not occurring
Stable to the left Unstable to the right	0	0	>0	q_3
Neutral	0	0	0	at all points between q_5 & q_6

An examination of the shapes of both curves in Fig. 4 leads to the following two general observations regarding the relative positions of the various equilibrium points:

1. Between two stable equilibrium points there must necessarily be located at least one unstable equilibrium point.
2. Whenever any two freely selected values of q_0 are characterized by tendencies to shift in opposite directions, at least one stable or unstable equilibrium point must be located between them.

A trivial argument demonstrates that the Marshallian intersection point M (see Fig. 2 or 3) must necessarily be an equilibrium point. By definition we obtain:

$$(10) \qquad \begin{aligned} f(Q) &= P \\ \phi(P) &= Q \end{aligned}$$

Repeated substitution in (8) yields

$$(11) \qquad D(Q) = \phi(f(\phi(f(Q)))) - Q = Q - Q = 0$$

In contrast with all other possible positions of equilibrium, each of them representing an infinite chain of consecutive fluctuations of prices and quantities, the Marshallian point constitutes a marginal case in which both price and quantity remain constant.

172

For the Marshallian point equation (9) can be simplified as follows:

(12) $$D'(Q) = [\phi'(P) \cdot f'(Q)]^2 - 1$$

From the above we obtain the following criterion of stability:

(13) $$|\phi'(P)| \cdot |f'(Q)| \begin{cases} > 1 \text{ stable equilibrium} \\ = 1 \text{ neutral equilibrium} \\ < 1 \text{ unstable equilibrium} \end{cases}$$

where $|\phi'(P)|$ and $|f'(Q)|$ represent absolute numerical value of the slopes of respectively the demand and the supply curve at the point of their intersection.[4]

According to Fig. 4, every point on curve $D(q_0)$ situated to the left of Q has its distinct counterpart to the right of Q. The necessary existence of such correspondence becomes obvious when we consider the following equilibrium situation: Fig. 3 shows that a closed cycle necessarily includes two supply quantities, one of them represented by q_0 (identical with $\breve{q}_2!$) situated at the right, the other $\breve{q}_1$, located at the left of quantity Q, which corresponds to the Marshallian equilibrium point M.[5]

Turning again to Fig. 4 and considering any pair of such corresponding equilibrium points, it can be seen that the slope, that is, the first derivative of the curve $D(q_0)$ has to be the same in both points.[6]

[4] It should be noted that tangent $f'(Q)$ is measured on the q axis, while the tangent $\phi'(P)$ is measured on the p axis.

[5] By definition we obtain

(14) $$\breve{q}_1 = \phi \, (f(q_0)).$$

The equilibrium condition is expressed as follows:

(15) $$\phi(f \, (\phi \, (f \, (q_0)))) = q_0.$$

By extending the chain of functions in (14) and substitution from (15) we obtain:

(16) $$\phi(f \, (q_1)) = \phi(f \, (\phi \, (f \, (\breve{q}_0)))) = q_0.$$

A further extension of the chain of functions and substitution from (14) results in:

(17) $$\phi(f \, (\phi \, (f \, (\breve{q}_1)))) = \phi(f \, (q_0)) = \breve{q}_1.$$

The last equation represents the equilibrium conditions for q_1.

[6] Differentiating (17) results in:

(18) $$D'(\breve{q}_1) = \phi'(\breve{p}_1) \cdot f'(q_0) \cdot \phi'(p_0) \cdot f'(\breve{q}_1) - 1.$$

The right side of this equation is identical with the corresponding expression in (9). From this can be derived the identity of the two derivatives, $D'(\breve{q}_1) = D'(q_0).$

The largest possible range of fluctuation of quantity q_0 can be determined as follows: We move the starting point—of the hypothetical price and quantity fluctuations—from the Marshallian point Q to the left. Then, the lower limit of q_0 (denoted by $_{min}q_0$) will be reached at the point where one of the four functions $f(q_0)$, $\phi(p_0)$, $f(q_1)$, $\phi(p_1)$—which depend either directly or indirectly on q_0—acquires the value zero or reaches again its upper or lower limits.

The upper limit of q_0 ($_{max}q_0$) as defined by the equation $_{max}q_0 = \phi\left(f(_{min}q_0)\right)$ will be located to the right of the Marshallian point Q.

Most of the empirical demand and supply curves are—at least at one of their two terminal levels—limited by a positive finite quantity which they approach asymptotically. As an example, it is sufficient to refer to the physical limits which must necessarily restrict the possible expansion of any particular production process.

In a case in which $f(q)$ or $\phi(p)$ processes an upper or a lower limit which that function approaches asymptotically, the corresponding derivatives of $f'(q)$ or $\phi'(p)$ will exceed any finite limit in the proximity of this limiting value. Consequently, the derivative of the determining function $D(q_0)$,

$$D'(q_0) = \phi'(\breve{p}_1) \cdot f'(\breve{q}_1) \cdot \phi'(p_0) \cdot f'(q_0) - 1$$

has to exceed any finite limits as long as the variables $\breve{p}_1$, $\breve{q}_1$, p_0, and q_0 remain larger than zero and, also, none of the four derivatives on the right-hand side of the above equation becomes at the same time infinitely small.

There is good reason to assume that the latter condition is fulfilled in most of the actually observed empirical situations. This signifies that quantity q_0 necessarily has to show a "centripetal" tendency in the immediate proximity of both—its upper and its lower—limit, $D'(_{min}q_0) > 0$, $D'(_{max}q_0) > 0$. "Centrifugal" forces, provided they exist at all within the given system, will be kept in check from outside by a stable equilibrium position (that might be represented either by the Marshallian point or by a closed cycle!).

15

Theoretical note on time-preference, productivity of capital, stagnation, and economic growth

Among the many factors which determine the growth or stagnation—as the case may be—of a national economy, its rate of saving out of current income and the subsequent increase in income resulting from the investment of these savings play an important role. A relatively simple method of graphic presentation and analysis makes it possible to articulate, without explicit recourse to algebra or calculus, the various effects which different configurations of these two determinants can have on the state of the economy and its development over time. Like any other purely theoretical inquiry, this analysis only helps us to draw certain, possibly not immediately obvious, conclusions from alternative sets of hypothetical assumptions.

Figure 1 depicts the preferences of a given national economy between present and future levels of consumption in terms of a conventional set of social indifference curves. It deviates only in one respect from the graph used by Irving Fisher in his classic exposition of his theory of interest. The variables, Y and C, whose magnitudes are measured along the horizontal axis, represent respectively the level of real income and the amount of goods consumed in the present period. The variables Y' and C' measured

From the *American Economic Review*, Vol. 48, No. 1, March 1958.

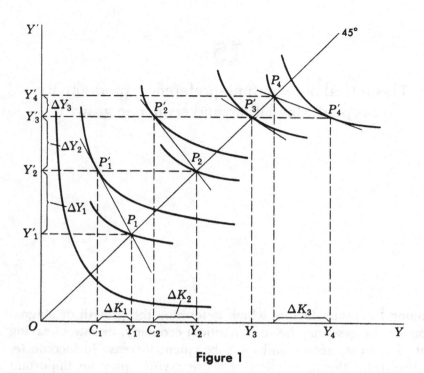

Figure 1

vertically describe future income or consumption; "future," however, not in the sense of a single "second" period—as shown on Fisher's diagram—but in the sense of a steady, even flow which, beginning with the year following the present one, can be maintained in equal annual amounts in perpetuity.

Accordingly, every point between the coordinate axes in Fig. 1 denotes a specific combination of a given present year's income (or consumption) level with a fixed level of annual income (or consumption) flow to be enjoyed in perpetuity from the next year on. Each indifference line represents a set of equally desirable combinations of present consumption levels and future consumption streams, the positions on higher indifference lines being naturally preferable to those on the lower.

The movement, from right to left, along any one of the negatively sloped straight lines, such as P_1P_1' or P_2P_2' accordingly describes an exchange of a batch of present goods for a constant

176

stream of future goods or, in other words, the exchange of a capital sum for a perpetual series of equal annual interest payments. The (absolute) magnitude of the slope of each one of these exchange lines can consequently be interpreted as representing an annual real rate of interest. Given a free choice between alternative positions on a given exchange line, the income receivers would accordingly reach the highest attainable—under the given circumstances—level of welfare at tangency points, such as P_1', P_2' or P_3'.

Any point, such as P_1, P_2 or P_3, situated on the 45° line drawn from the origin, describes a stationary position in which the present (Y) and the future (Y') levels of income and consumption are identical. Actually faced with a choice between the maintenance of such a stationary state and a movement to some other position located along the exchange line which goes through it, income receivers will perpetuate the stationary state only if, as at P_3', it happens also to be the point of tangency between the exchange line and the indifference curve which passes through that point. In other cases, they can improve their welfare by consuming less than their entire present income in order to secure a higher level of future income and consumption streams. Or, on the contrary, they might improve their situation by borrowing against the future, so as to allow the present consumption to exceed the rate of current revenue.

Thus, starting, for example, from the initial position P_1 and facing the exchange line which passes through that point, the representative independent income recipient or the central planning authority—whichever it may be—will move from P_1 to P_1'. It will allocate to immediate direct consumption that part of present income OY_1 which is measured by the distance from O to C_1; the rest of it, C_1Y_1, or ΔK_1, will be saved and exchanged against future income. The rate of the potential income stream to be received in the next, and all later, years will be raised by ΔY_1 from OY_1' to OY_2'. Point P_2, again located on the 45° line thus represents the prospective position of the country in the second year.

Before pursuing further the sequence of given income, saving and increased income, let us turn to Fig. 2 which describes the

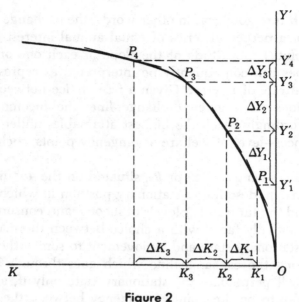

Figure 2

relationship between the total stock of capital invested and the net output (income) which it can produce on the basis of the existing technology in co-operation with the given supply of all other factors. Along the horizontal axis, we measure from right to left (in order to facilitate the subsequent comparison with Fig. 1) the total stock of capital, and along the vertical axis the annual rate of net output, that is, net income. The bending of the curve describes the well-known technical relationship between the stock of productive capital and the flow of output produced with its help. The slope of that curve at any point represents the marginal productivity of the particular amount of capital which corresponds to it.

Point P_1 in Fig. 1 refers to the same state of the economic system as point P_1 in Fig. 2. In this position, the total stock of capital amounts to K_1 and it produces a net income flow of Y_1 units per annum. The potential increase in output, which could be brought about by an increase in the existing stock of capital, can be read off Fig. 2: Specifically, the ratio between the amount of invested

178

savings and the resulting rise in future income flow is represented —at least for changes which are not very large—by the slope of the capital-output curve at point P_1. It is that slope which, when transferred to Fig. 1, describes the real rate of interest, the ratio at which the present consumption can be foregone in favor of additional future income, or, in other words, the slope of the line along which the country moves (see Fig. 1) from P_1 to P_1'. The saving, ΔK_1, when added on Fig. 2 to the original amount of capital, K_1, increases to total stock to K_2 and the corresponding annual rate of income flow—from Y_1' to Y_2'. The same increase is measured on the vertical axis of Fig. 1. The corresponding increase in net annual income flow from Y_1 to Y_2 is measured, on Fig. 1, along the horizontal axis.

The income and consumption, represented by the position of point P_2 in Figs. 1 and 2 could be maintained, as far as the country's productive power is concerned, from now on into the future without any further change. The combination of the marginal productivity of capital and time-preference, as shown at point P_2 in Figs. 1 and 2, is, however, such that instead of consuming all of that increased income our developing economy will move on to point P_2', that is, save and invest again, increase its stock of capital from K_2 to K_3 and its income from Y_2 to Y_3. By the third year, it thus will find itself at P_3'. The slope of the indifference curve passing through that point in Fig. 1 has been drawn so as to be equal to the slope of the capital-output curve at the corresponding point (P_3) in Fig. 2. Hence the marginal productivity of capital is equated to marginal time-preference if the representative consumer, that is, the country as a whole, chooses to consume neither more nor less than its entire current income. It is, in other words, an equilibrium position, a stationary state which can and will be maintained *ad infinitum* as long as no new factors enter the picture. Such a new factor might be a shift of the structural conditions, that is, a change in the form of the production function in Fig. 2 or a variation in the shape of the indifference curves in Fig. 1. Or it might consist in the creation of new "initial conditions": sudden destruction—as the result of war—of some part of the existing stock of capital or, on the contrary, acquisition of additional capital from foreign sources, a developmental grant received from abroad.

On our graphs, the creation of such new initial conditions would be described, for example, as a shift from P_3' to point P_2 or, say, to point P_4. In either case, if left to its own devices, the economy would return at once or by successive steps to its original position at P_3'. The difference between the movement from P_2 to P_3' and from P_4 to P_3' is that, in the latter case, having been pushed beyond the point of stable equilibrium, the system will come back to it through a process of capital consumption, that is, by sacrificing some of the future income stream in order to be able to maintain during the transitory period a "present" level of consumption above its "current" income; while in the former case it would approach the stable equilibrium position, P_3', from below, that is, through a process of capital accumulation.

The economy, of course, does not necessarily find an equilibrium position. It might have none, or more than one, but in the latter case unstable as well as stable equilibria will necessarily be present. We call a state of unstable equilibrium one in which, in the absence of any change in its internal structure and without even the slightest variation in the initial conditions, the system would maintain itself *ad infinitum*, but from which it would tend to depart on the slightest provocation. It is analogous to the position of the proverbial egg, precariously balanced on its narrow end.

To work out in full the implications of the previous analysis, let us now turn to Fig. 3. Along the horizontal axis, we measure the national income, Y. Of the two interlaced curves, MP represents the marginal productivity of capital, that is, the slope of the capital-output line (Fig. 2) as it gradually bends toward the horizontal with the increase in Y. TP measures the marginal time-preference, that is, the slope of the indifference curves as they cross the 45° line in Fig. 1 at various levels of income Y. The third curve below, identified by the letter D, represents the vertical distance (difference) between the first two (that is, the excess of TP over MP); the points, a, b, and c, at which the D-curve crosses the zero axis mark those income levels at which the marginal productivity of capital is equal to the marginal time-preference when the

180

country consumes exactly its entire income. They mark, in other words, the possible equilibrium positions of the system. The D-curve passes below the zero line at those income levels at which the marginal time-preference (or more precisely the slope of the indifference lines at points where they cross the 45° stationary income locus) is smaller than the corresponding marginal productivity of capital. As can be seen from Fig. 1, in all such cases there will be some positive amount of saving. And as a result of it, the income will necessarily grow. Over all those intervals in which the D curve rises above the zero line, current consumption, on the contrary, will exceed net current output, the stock of capital will be diminished and income will consequently fall. The direction of the ensuing upward, or downward, change in income is indicated in Fig. 3 by arrows.

To simplify the explanation of the interplay of the two sets of basic structural relationships represented, respectively, in Figs. 1 and 2, the functioning of the economy has been viewed as if it had proceeded step by step. Such period analysis introduces, however, complications of its own which would be absent if the processes of production, consumption, and investment were described in continuous terms. With due apology to the mathematically interested reader (who, however, should be able to work out all intermediate details himself), we will now interpret the curves in Fig. 3 as if they reflected, as they well might, the properties of a continuous process. (The reader will note that the specific shapes of these curves do not actually correspond to those of the particular set of consumer-preference relationships and the production function depicted in the other graphs. While the combination of the structural relationships shown in Figs. 1 and 2 yield only one equilibrium position (P_s'), Fig. 3 shows the existence of three such positions, a, b, and c.)

Starting with a very small stock of capital and income inferior to that corresponding to the lowest equilibrium point, a, the system would proceed to expand toward a. If in its initial position the economy were located some place between a and b, it would also tend to move toward the former point. In this case, the process is a regressive one characterized by gradual diminution of the

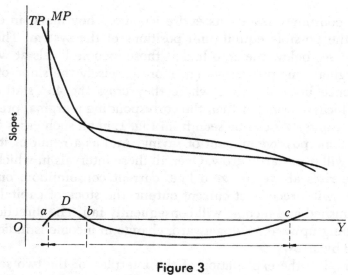

Figure 3

stock of productive capital, reduction in the rate of output (income) and incidentally—as the *MP* curve shows—an increase in the real rate of interest. Once *a* is reached in either way, the system would "stagnate" at that low but stable equilibrium position. When pushed to the left by the action of some outside force, such, for example, as an accidental loss of productive capital, it would move back again toward *a*, but not beyond. If, as beneficiary of a foreign loan or gift, it should find itself in the possession of some additional capital and correspondingly increased income, our country would at once proceed to "live above its means," that is, consume its capital and gradually reduce its output until the stationary state at *a* would again be reached. Even a constant flow of foreign aid could, in such case, do no more than help the system to maintain its income and consumption at some point between *a* and *b*, without, however, releasing any tendency toward further growth.

These latter observations apply, however, only to gifts or loans not large enough to push the rate of output beyond *b*. Once on the other side of that unstable equilibrium position, the economy would begin to save, accumulate, and increase its revenue; in

182

short it would proceed to develop under its own power. According to the graph, a new stable equilibrium would be approached at the much higher income level, c. Had the structural conditions been such as to keep MP above TP, and thus the D-curve below the zero line, throughout its entire stretch to the right of b, the process of economic growth—once that threshold had been passed —would go on indefinitely.

By way of a concluding observation, one might suggest, without detailed explanation, how the three graphs can also be used to trace through the possible effects of changes in the basic structural conditions of the economy. For instance, technological advance, described as an upward shift of the capital-output curve in Fig. 2, might—and most likely actually would—affect the shape of the MP and the D-curve in Fig. 3. The equilibrium positions a, b, and c would shift. Depending on the magnitude and the nature of the change, some of these positions of stationary state might even disappear or new ones might be created.

To the extent to which a rise in the productivity of capital enables the economy to increase its income without any addition to its stock of capital, technological advance will shift the system at once to the right along the horizontal axis in Figure 3 from whatever position it had previously occupied. In fact, however, new technology as a rule requires a new type of equipment and different kinds of skills. That means that its introduction will depend itself on the current rate of saving and accumulation.

Some theorists consider the process of economic growth as being determined over its entire length in one piece, by a grand act of one single choice. To interpret the process of economic growth as if its path were determined by "one" and for all decision, it is necessary to assume the existence of a utility function which shows the level of utility depending simultaneously on the levels of consumption not in two, three, or even twenty years, but in all the years over which the process of economic growth extends. To be consistent they must also assume that their choice is based on a full and a correct knowledge of all relevant conditions from now to the end of time; or perhaps one should say, to the very end of the growth process. If my approach is right a country could most likely profit by revising some of the choices made in the remote past; if that other view is correct, it would not want to change, even in the light of later knowledge, any of the decisions made before. It would persist in acting like a sophisticated dog who follows the shortest, straight intercepting course.[1]

The problem of maximizing utility—by planning the allocation of income between consumption and investment—over long intervals of time is certainly of considerable interest in itself. If it were not, why should Frank Ramsey have brought it up thirty years ago, and why should the operations researchers and dynamic programmers of today be solving it in so many different forms? I would also not deny that a model of economic growth more elaborate than that presented in my note should and could easily be based on a choice-horizon longer than a two-periods interval in time. Let me repeat, however, that the crucial difference between Ramsey's assumptions and those which I preferred to make lies not in the absolute extension of that horizon, but in its length relative to the duration of the entire dynamic sequence that we analyze. If each individual choice is based on a forward view in time which is at least somewhat shorter than the process as a whole, the general properties of economic growth are correctly displayed not by that other model but by mine. The one-shot, pure decision processes which he sets up—if one could visualize it in the context of economic growth—cannot possibly have stable or unstable equilibrium solutions as described in my note; there would be one, the best of all possible solutions, and that is all. As soon however as one choice is assumed to be followed by a second, a third, and so on, the problem of stability of any possible repetitive stationary equilibrium position must arise.

A further pursuit of these speculative arguments must clearly yield diminishing returns. The effort involved in construction and interpretation of more complicated graphs might better be spent on observation and explanation of the real world.

[1] This paragraph and the next are excerpted from my reply to a "comment" on this article by Fred M. T. Westfield, published in the same issue of the *American Economic Review*. (W.L.)

PART THREE

PART THREE

16

Machines and man

Approximately five hundred years ago the study of nature ceased to be solely a servant of philosophy and became a patron of applied arts and a source of practical invention. The economic development of the Western world has since proceeded at an ever increasing pace; waves of technological change, driven by the surge of scientific discoveries, have followed one another in accelerated succession. The developmental lag between pure science and engineering application has progressively shortened. It took nearly one hundred years for the steam engine to establish itself as part and parcel of the industrial scene, but electric power took less than fifty years and the internal combusion engine only thirty. The vacuum tube was in almost every American home within fifteen years of its invention, and the numerous progeny of Dr. Baekeland's synthetic plastics matured before we learned to pronounce "polyisobutylene." At the turn of the twentieth century it was said that "applied science is pure science twenty years later"; today the interval is much shorter—often only five years and sometimes but one or two.

From the engineering standpoint the era of automatic control has begun. Some of the fully automatic "factories of the future"

From *Scientific American,* Vol. 187, No. 3, September 1952.

are already on paper; they can be described and studied. Engineering, however, is only the first step; what automatic technology will mean to our economic system and our society is still decidedly a thing of the future. In judging its probable impact all we have to go by is tenuous analogy with past experience and theoretical deductions from our very limited information on the new techniques. And it is no help that some of the crucial facts and figures are veiled in secrecy.

Important new inventions are traditionally held to presage the dawn of a new era; they also mark the twilight of an old. For some observers they contain promise; for others, fear. James Hargreaves constructed the first practical multiple spindle machine in 1767, and one year later a mob of spinners invaded his mill and destroyed the new equipment. The economists of the time (the golden age of "classical economics" was about to begin) came to the defense of the machines. They explained to labor that the loss of jobs in spinning would be compensated by new employment in machine-building. And for the next hundred years England did indeed prosper. Its labor force expanded both in textiles and in textile machinery, and wage rates by the end of the nineteenth century were at least three times as high as at its beginning.

But the men-v.-machines controversy blazed on. Karl Marx made of "technological unemployment" the cornerstone of his theory of capitalist exploitation. The conscientious John Stuart Mill came to the conclusion that, while the introduction of machinery might—in most cases would—benefit labor, it would not necessarily do so always. The answer depended on the circumstances of the case. And today that is still the only reasonable point of view one can maintain.

We are hardly in a position to reduce to detailed computation the effects that automatic technology will have on employment, production, or our national standard of living. Aside from the paucity of our information on this new development, our understanding of the structural properties of our economic system itself is still incomplete. We must therefore rely on reasonable conjecture.

The economy of a modern industrial nation—not unlike the

188

feedback mechanisms discussed throughout this issue—must be visualized as a complicated system of interrelated processes. Each industry, each type of activity, consumes the products and services of other sectors of the economy and at the same time supplies its own products and services to them. Just as the operating properties of a servo-mechanism are determined by the technical characteristics of the measuring, communicating, and controlling units of which it is composed, so the operating properties of an economy depend upon the structural characteristics of its component parts and on the way in which they are coupled together. It is not by coincidence that in some advanced phases of his work the modern economist resorts to systems of differential equations similar to those used by the designers of self-regulating machinery.

The services of labor constitute one important set of inputs into the national economy. That it is the largest one is reflected in the fact that labor receives in wages some 73 per cent (in 1950) of the nation's annual net product. But labor is not the only type of input that goes into all other sectors. Certain natural resources, machinery, equipment, and other kinds of productive capital feed into almost every branch of agriculture, manufacture, transportation, and distribution. In Chart 1 which depicts the growth of our total national product since 1880, is a breakdown of the share going into salaries and wages on the one hand and into non-labor income (profits, interest, rents, and so on) on the other. The ratio between these two has been generally stable, but labor's share has steadily gained. Behind these figures lie the intricate processes of our economic development, influenced by such factors as population growth, the discovery of new and the exhaustion of old natural resources, the increase in the stock of productive plant and equipment, and last but not least, a steady technological progress.

A better insight into the nature of that progress is given by the Charts 4, 5, 6. The number of man-hours required for an average unit of output has gone down steadily since 1880. In the first thirty years of that period the saving of labor seems to have been accompanied by a corresponding increase in capital investment. Be-

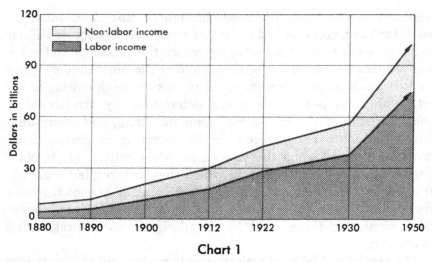

Chart 1

Total national income of the U.S., measured in terms of 1940 prices, has increased from $9.2 billion in 1880 to $160 billion in 1950. The ratio between labor income (the compensation of employees) and non-labor income (profits, interest, rent, and so on) is stable, but the share for labor has increased.

tween 1880 and 1912 the amount of machinery and of other so-called fixed investment per unit of output rose by 34 per cent, while the man-hour input fell 40 per cent. Then the ratio of investment to output began to drop. We introduced more efficient machinery rather than just a greater quantity of it. That it actually was more efficient can be seen from the fact that labor productivity rose apace. In 1938 a unit of output consumed only about half as many man-hours as would have been spent upon its production in 1918.

Such is the stage which the new technology—the technology of automatic control—has now entered. The best index we have of how far automatization has gone is the annual U. S. production of "measuring and controlling instruments." The trend of this production is outlined in Chart 3. After hesitation during the depression and the war years, it now rises rapidly. In part this rise mirrors the recent accelerating pace of industrial investment in

190

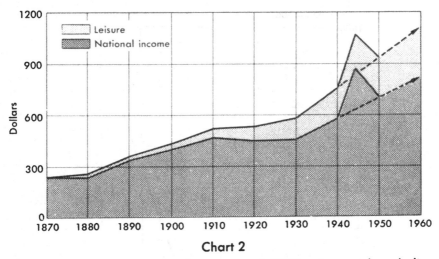

Chart 2

Income per capita, measured in terms of 1940 prices and excluding agriculture, increased from $230.60 in 1870 to $706.70 in 1950 (*bottom curve*). If 1870 hours of work had been maintained, the per capita income would be larger (*top curve*). The difference between the two curves shows increase in leisure.

general, but the chart shows that the instrument production curve is going up more steeply than that of plant investment as a whole. This gain is a measure of the progressive "instrumentation" of the U. S. economy. A breakdown of the relative progress of automatic operation in individual industries appears in Table 1. The chemical and machinery industries lead; next come metal processing (mainly in the smelting department) and ceramics. In interpreting this table one must take into account the fact that instrumental control is less costly for some processes than for others (see *Table 2*).

The estimated cost of complete instrumentation of a new modern plant to automatize it as fully as possible today ranges from 1 to 19 per cent (depending on the industry) of the total investment in process equipment. The average for all industries would be about 6 per cent. On this basis, if all the new plants built in 1950 had been automatized, some $600 million would have been

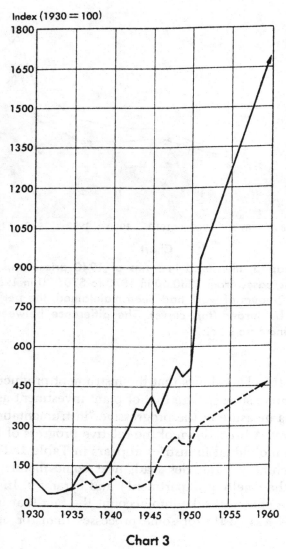

Index (1930 = 100)

Chart 3

Sales of instruments for industrial recording and controlling purposes have increased enormously since 1930 (*solid line*) as compared with the total U. S. expenditure for plant and equipment (*broken line*).

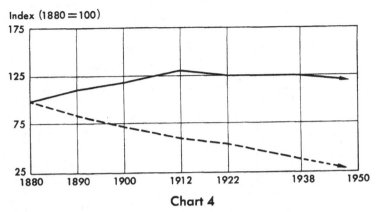

Index (1880 = 100)

Chart 4

U. S. production has increased in efficiency. The solid line plots the decreasing index of plant and equipment required to produce one unit of output; the broken line, the man-hours required to produce one unit.

spent for measuring and control instruments. Actually the production of such instruments in 1950 totaled only $67 million. In other words, to automatize new plants alone, to say nothing of those already built, would require nearly ten times as great an investment in instruments as we are now making.

Yet 6 per cent is far from a formidable figure. Furthermore, the investment in instruments would not necessarily mean a net increase in the total plant investment per unit of output. On the contrary, the smoother and better-balanced operation of self-regulating plants has already shown that they can function with less capitalization than a non-automatic plant of identical capacity. And much existing equipment can readily be converted from manual to automatic control. It therefore seems that the automatization of our industries, at least to the extent made possible by present technology, is likely to advance rapidly. The mechanization of the nineteenth century required heavy capital investment and proceeded slowly; the new technology, unhampered by such vast capital requirements, can be introduced at a much faster pace.

In transportation and agriculture, machines by now have practically eliminated the need for human muscle power. Man has all

193

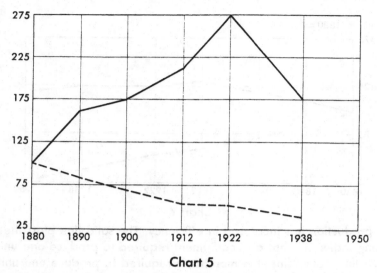

Chart 5

Mining and manufacture similarly increased in productivity. Labor savings have been secured largely by expenditure on plant equipment. Increasing efficiency of plant is now reflected in declining capital cost.

but ceased to be a lifter and mover and become primarily a starter and stopper, a setter and assembler and repairer. With the introduction of self-controlled machinery, his direct participation in the process of production will be narrowed even further. The starter and stopper will disappear first, the setter and assembler will go next. The trouble-shooter and repairman of course will keep their jobs for a long time to come; the need for them will even increase, for the delicate and complicated equipment of automatic control will require constant expert care. We shall continue to need inventors and designers, but perhaps not many even of them: the chief engineer of a large electronic equipment firm recently expressed to me his apparently well founded hope that before long he would have circuits designed by an electronic machine, eliminating human errors.

All this inevitably will change the character of our labor force. The proportion of unskilled labor has already declined greatly in recent decades; it is down to less than 20 per cent. Meanwhile the numbers of the semi-skilled have risen, and they now consti-

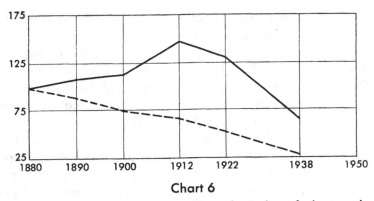

Chart 6

Agriculture shows a similar pattern. Here the index of plant and equipment per unit of output is actually lower in 1938 than in 1880, reflecting the enormous increase in the productivity of agricultural machinery.

tute over 22 per cent of the labor force. This trend has slowed down during the past decade, however. Now we shall probably see an accelerated rise in the proportion of skilled workers, clerks, and professional personnel, who already make up 42 per cent of our working population.

In a country with a less fluid and more differentiated social structure than ours, these rapid changes in the occupational composition of the population might have brought about considerable strain. But the celebrated, and often criticized, uniformity of American living renders the effects of such transition almost imperceptible. For example, recent studies indicate that the family of a typical $3000-a-year clerk spends its money in very much the same way as the family, say, of a machine-press operator with a similar income.

Will the machine-press operator be able to earn his $3000 when an automatic controlling device takes over his job? The answer must depend in part on the speed with which the labor force is able to train and to retrain itself. If such upgrading were to fall behind the demand of the changing technology, semi-skilled and unskilled workers certainly would suffer unemployment or at least sharply reduced earning power. The experience of the last twenty years, however, has underlined the flexibility of U. S. workmen.

195

Under the stimulus of the general American striving toward social and economic betterment, they have been quick to take to vocational training for new jobs. There as been no surplus of unskilled and semi-skilled labor: indeed, wages in these fields have risen even faster than in skilled and professional work.

But if automatic machines largely take over our production, will there be enough jobs, skilled or otherwise, to go around? Admittedly the possibility of eventual unemployment cannot be excluded on a priori grounds. If the capital investment were to increase rapidly while the need for manpower dropped, the resulting rise in capital's share of the national income could cause drastic unemployment. But as we have seen, the amount of capital needed for each unit of output has actually been reduced in recent years, and the installation of automatic machinery will further reduce it. Therefore labor should be able to maintain or improve its relative share of the national income. The danger of technological unemployment should be even smaller in the foreseeable future than it was at the end of the nineteenth century, when capital requirements were rising.

Table 1

INDUSTRY	1946	1947	1948	1949	1950	1951
Ceramics	110	113	106	70	102	131
Chemicals	125	110	101	62	117	208
Foods	125	107	96	66	103	107
Machinery	107	112	119	61	105	168
Metals	113	98	106	81	134	249
Petroleum	80	90	140	86	98	132
Textiles	106	105	112	75	129	128
Utilities	72	96	122	111	147	222
Total	100	104	115	82	122	192

Growth of instrumentation in various industries is shown in this table, which lists the sales of instruments to those industries by years. The index of the table: 1946-1949 average sales of instruments = 100.

While the increase in productivity need not lead to involuntary idleness, it certainly does result in a steady reduction in the number of years and hours that an average American spends at making his living. The average work-week has been shortened from 67.2 hours in 1870 to 42.5 hours in 1950. This reflects a deliberate decision by the American people to enjoy an ever-increasing part of their rising standard of living in the form of leisure. If we had kept to the 67-hour week, we would be turning out a considerably greater amount of goods than we actually are. The difference between this hypothetical per capita output, computed on the basis of the well-known Cobb-Douglas formula, and the actual present output is indicated in Chart 2. This difference represents the amount of commodities and services which the average American has chosen *not* to produce and consequently not to consume in order to enjoy shorter hours and longer vacations. The spread between the two curves has steadily increased: in other words, we have chosen to spend more and more of our ever increasing production potential on leisure. The temporary shift to a high output of material goods during the last war only emphasizes this tendency, for we returned to the long-run trend immediately after the war. In the future, even more than in the past, the increased productivity of the American economy will be enjoyed as additional leisure.

Looking back, one can see that 1910 marked the real turning point in this country's economic and social development. That was the year when the last wave of immigration reached its crest; the year, also, when our rural population began to decline in absolute terms. Between 1890 and 1910 our national input of human labor had shot up from 28.3 million standard man-years to 42.5 million. Then in 1909 the model-T Ford began to roll off the first continuous production line. This great shift to mass production by machine was immediately reflected in shorter hours. In the next decade our manpower input increased by only one million man-years, and after 1920 it leveled off and remained almost constant until the early 1940's. Even at the peak of the recent war effort our total labor input, with an enormously larger population, was only 10 per cent greater than in 1910. Automatization will accelerate the operation of forces which have already shaped the development of this country for nearly half a century.

Table 2

INDUSTRY	PER CENT
Meat packing	19
Pharmaceuticals	15
Textile plants	5-12
Soap	3.2-8.6
Dry ice	6.3
Equipment manufacture for the chemical and oil refining industry	.5-6
Paper mill	5
Rubber	5
Petroleum refining	3-5
Packaged foods	3-5
Mining and processing of ores	2-5
Chlor-alkali electrolytic plants	3.25
Sulfuric acid (*contact method*)	3
Pulp mill	3
Carpets	2-3
Rayon and rayon yarn	1-2

Relative cost of instrumental control in various industries is given by per cent of total equipment cost.

The new technology will probably have a much more revolutionary effect on the so-called underdeveloped countries than on the U. S. or other old industrial nations. Shortage of capital and lack of a properly conditioned and educated labor force have been the two major obstacles to rapid industrialization of such backward areas. Now automatic production, with its relatively low capital and labor requirements per unit of output, radically changes their prospects. Instead of trying to lift the whole economy by the slow, painful methods of the past, an industrially backward country may take the dramatic shortcut of building a few large, up-to-date automatic plants. Towering up in the primitive economy like copses of tall trees on a grassy plain, they would propagate a new economic order. The oil refineries of the Near East, the integrated steel plant built after the war in Brazil, the gigantic fertilizer plant recently put into operation in India—these are examples of the new trend in underdeveloped regions of the world. How formidable the application of modern technology in a backward country may become is demonstrated by the U.S.S.R.'s recent great strides in industrialization.

At the outbreak of the First World War the U. S. suddenly lost its source of many indispensable chemicals in Germany. Domestic production had to be organized practically overnight. The newly created U. S. chemical industry had no force of experienced chemical craftsmen such as Germany had. The problem was solved, however, by the introduction of mechanization and automatization to a degree theretofore unknown. The American plants were run with amazingly small staffs of skilled workers. The same thing is now happening, and possibly will continue on a much larger scale, in backward countries. Advanced design, imported mostly from the U. S., will compensate at least in part for their scarcity of high-quality labor.

Naturally automatization, while solving some problems, will everywhere create new and possibly more difficult ones. In Western civilization the liberation from the burdens of making a living has been going on for some time, and we have been able to adjust to the new situation gradually. In the rising new countries economic efficiency may at least temporarily run far ahead of progress toward social maturity and stability. Much of the stimulus for the educational advancement of the Western nations came from economic necessity. Automatization may weaken that powerful connection. It remains to be seen whether the backward countries will find a driving force to help them develop the social, cultural, and political advances necessary to help them cope with the new economic emancipation.

17

The rates of long-run economic growth and capital transfer from developed to underdeveloped areas

1. The underdeveloped areas, which hold at least two-thirds of the entire population of the world, produce now only about one-seventh of the world's gross output of goods and services; moreover, their rate of economic growth is at the present time much lower—possibly only half as high—as that of the advanced industrialized countries. That means that the contrast between the richer and the poorer areas tends to increase rather than diminish.

A rise in the rate of growth of the underdeveloped areas would demand an increased volume of productive investment. The additional capital could be created through stepped up internal savings, or it might be obtained from abroad, that is, transferred in the form of aid, foreign loans, or direct private investment from the developed countries.

How much additional investment would the underdeveloped parts of the world have to absorb if they were to raise their average growth rate, over the next ten-year period, up to the average growth rate of the economically advanced industrial countries? If capital transferred from developed to underdeveloped areas

From *Proceedings*, Study Week on the Role of Econometric Analysis in Economic Development Plans in Controlling Economic Fluctuations, Pontifical Academy of Sciences, October 1963.

were to constitute the principal source of such additional investment, how large would this transfer have to be?

The simple dynamic system presented below describes in crude aggregative terms the relationships of the magnitude of the capital transfer from developed to underdeveloped areas, and of the levels of saving and investment in both groups of countries to their respective rates of growth. It was designed so as to require not more factual statistical information than is actually available. The over-all capital-output and saving ratios of the more and the less advanced countries as well as the proportion (but not of course the absolute amount) of the gross national product of the developed areas transferred to the underdeveloped countries are assumed to be constant over the ten-year period over which we project their future growth.

Since aggregative capital-output ratios (capital coefficients) and saving ratios can be estimated—particularly for the underdeveloped areas—only within a rather wide margin of error and because our expressed purpose is to assess the possible effect of changes in the amount of outside capital received by underdeveloped areas on their rate of growth, not one, but many alternative projections were made, all computed from the same general formula, but each based on different hypothetical combinations of the magnitudes of the structural parameters enumerated above.

2. The following set of aggregative variables is used to describe the state of the two groups of economies—developed and underdeveloped—at any particular point of time, t:

VARIABLES	DEVELOPED AREAS	UNDERDEVELOPED AREAS
Gross national product (domestically produced)	$Y_1(t)$	$Y_2(t)$
Productive investment (total)	$I_1(t)$	$I_2(t)$
Capital transfer from developed to underdeveloped areas	$H(t)$	
Growth rate of the domestically produced Gross national product, $\dfrac{\dot{Y}(t)}{Y(t)}$	$r_1(t)$	$r_2(t)$

201

The value of these seven variable given (that is, observed or assigned) for the year 1959 constitutes the empirical basis of a series of alternative projections of the economic growth of both groups of countries over the ten-year period ending at 1969.

Developed areas

The following theoretical relationships are used to derive, and to solve, the equations describing the growth of the developed areas:
Saving function:

(1) $$I_1(t) = i_1 Y_1(t)$$

i represents the fraction of the GNP allocated to investment.
Acceleration relationships:

(2) $$\dot{Y}_1(t) = \frac{I_1(t)}{b_1}$$

b_1 is the capital coefficient (capital-output ratio) describing the amount of capital required per additional unit of annual GNP.
Growth rate equation, obtained from (1) and (2):

(3) $$\dot{Y}_1(t) - \frac{i_1}{b_1} Y_1(t) = 0$$

Exponential growth function, obtained by solving (3):

(4) $$Y_1(t) = Y_1(0)e^{\lambda_1 t}, \qquad \lambda_1 = \frac{i_1}{b_1}$$

where $Y_1(0)$ represents the level of the GNP in the base year 0 and λ_1 its growth rate, which remains constant as long as i_1 and b_1 are fixed.

The amount transferred from the developed to the underdeveloped areas is assumed to constitute a fixed fraction, h, of the GNP of the capital-exporting countries. Thus, the following transfer relationship, which is derived from equations (4) above, implies that $H(t)$, the amount transferred, will grow exponentially at the same rate as the developed areas' GNP:
Transfer relationship:

(5) $$H(t) = hY_1(t) = hY_1(0)e^{\lambda_1 t}$$

202

Underdeveloped areas.

The productive investment in the underdeveloped areas is being supported from two sources: The saved fraction, i_2, of their own Gross National Product, $Y_2(t)$, and the capital-imports, $H(t)$:

Investment function:

(6) $\qquad I_2(t) = i_2 Y_2(t) + H(t) = i_2 Y_2(t) + h Y_1(0) e^{\lambda_1 t}$

Acceleration relationship:

(7) $\qquad\qquad\qquad \dot{Y}_2(t) = \dfrac{I_2(t)}{b_2}$

b_2 is the capital coefficient describing the amount of capital required per additional unit of annual GNP.

Growth rate equation derived from (6) and (7):

(8) $\quad \dot{Y}_2(t) - \dfrac{i_2}{b_2} Y_2(t) - \dfrac{h}{b_2} Y_1(0) e^{\lambda_1 t} = 0 \quad , if \ \dfrac{i_2}{b_2} \neq \lambda_1 = \dfrac{i_1}{b_1}$

Growth function, obtained by solving the differential equation (8):

(9) $\quad Y_2(t) = \left[Y_2(0) + \dfrac{H(0)}{b_2(\lambda_1 - \lambda_2)} \right] e^{\lambda_2 t} - \dfrac{H(0)}{b_2(\lambda_1 - \lambda_2)} e^{\lambda_1 t} \quad , \lambda_2 = \dfrac{i_2}{b_2}$

To verify the last equation one can substitute it and its derivative in (8); the expression on the left-hand side will identically equal zero.

The growth of the underdeveloped areas turns out to be described by a combination of two exponential terms. The first reflects the effects of internal savings, the second the contribution of investment financed through capital imports. Accordingly the growth rate, λ_2, of the first component depends on the magnitude of the domestic savings and capital-output ratios while the second term grown at the same rate as the GNP of the developed areas.*

* If the ratio of the saving to the capital coefficient in the developed and underdeveloped regions happens to be equal, the solution of the differential equation (8) is reduced to:

(9-a) $\qquad\qquad Y_2(t) = Y_2(0) e^{\lambda t} + \dfrac{H(0)}{b_2} t e^{\lambda t} \qquad\qquad \lambda = \dfrac{i_1}{b_1} = \dfrac{i_2}{b_2}$

that is, the growth rates of both groups of countries would in this case be equal.

Equations (4) and (9) permit us to project forward the growth of both groups of countries provided their base-year levels of their respective GNP's, savings, growth rates, as well as the initial magnitude of the interregional capital transfer is given. The corresponding values of the constants entering into the two growth functions can be computed from the following formulae:

$$(10) \quad b_1 = \frac{I_1(0)}{\dot{Y}_1(0)} = \frac{I_1(0)}{Y_1(0)r_1(0)} \qquad b_2 = \frac{I_2(0)}{\dot{Y}_2(0)} = \frac{I_2(0)}{Y_2(0)r_2(0)}$$

$$\lambda_1 = \frac{i_1}{b_1} = \frac{\dot{Y}_1(0)}{Y_1(0)} = r_1(0) \qquad \lambda_2 = \frac{[I_2(0) - H(0)]\,\dot{Y}_2(0)}{Y_2(0)I_2(0)} =$$

$$= \left[1 - \frac{H(0)}{I_2(0)}\right] r_2(0)$$

These relations are obtained by inserting the given base-year values of the variables in the appropriate investment functions, accelerations relationships, and growth functions.

3. The base-year values of the variables used for projection, presented in the following tables, are summarized below. The base year is 1959.

	DEVELOPED AREAS	UNDERDEVELOPED AREAS
Gross national product (domestic)	$2,105 billion	$195 billion
Productive investment (total)	$228 billion	$15-$22 billion
Capital transfer from developed to underdeveloped areas		$4 billion
Growth rate of the domestically produced gross national product	4%-6%	2%-3%

The developed areas comprise Western Europe (excluding Spain, Portugal, Greece, and Turkey), the United States, Canada, Japan, Soviet Russia, and other socialist countries; the underdeveloped areas comprise all other countries. Since these estimates, compiled from United Nations and other statistical sources, are supposed to cover all countries, they obviously are subject to

204

a very substantial margin of error. The estimates of the annual rate of gross productive investment in the underdeveloped areas, which is particularly uncertain, is presented not as a single figure but in terms of two figures—a high and a low—which does not mean of course that the true magnitude still might not lie outside of that range.

For similar reasons the base-year estimate of the long-run growth rates of the GNP's is also presented for each area in the form of two percentage figures—a higher and a lower one.

4. The calculations, the results of which are summarized in Tables 1 to 6, show how the future economic growth of the developed and underdeveloped areas might be affected by changes in the fraction of the gross national product of the first transferred for investment purposes into the second area and also changes in the distribution of the GNP—in both groups of countries—between current consumption and productive investment.

The growth functions (4) and (9) are used to project the GNP of the developed and the underdeveloped areas over a ten-year period, 1959-69.

The structural coefficients entering into these equations depend—see (10)—on the base-year magnitude of the GNP's, of the productive investments in both areas and also on their respective long-run growth rates in the base year.

Each table is based on a different combination of the estimated 1959 growth rates of both countries and of the estimated amount of domestically financed investment absorbed by the underdeveloped areas in that year. The estimates of the 1959 GNP's of both areas and of the amount of gross investment absorbed in that year by the developed countries remain the same through all the computation.

The first column of figures in each table presents one particular estimate of the base-year state of both groups of countries and also the levels of their respective GNP's "ten years later," projected from 1959 to 1969. This projection is made on the assumption that the domestic saving ratios in both areas retain their base-year magnitudes and that the economically more advanced countries continue, throughout the ten-year period in question, to transfer to the less advanced the same percentage (h) of their annual GNP as they did in 1959.

The three other columns show how hypothetically postulated changes in original allocation of the GNP's of both areas—if introduced in the base year and then maintained over the ten years covered by our projections—would have affected the levels of their respective GNP's "ten years later," that is, in 1969. The corresponding average annual growth rates over the period 1959-69 are entered below.

The allocations of the GNP of the developed areas is described by the constants i_1 and h, that is, the percentage of the GNP invested domestically and the fraction of that product transferred to the underdeveloped areas and invested there. In the underdeveloped areas it is described simply by i_2—the proportion of it saved and invested; the rest of the investment being equal to the amount received from the developed countries.

In the second column of Table 1, the proportion of the GNP of the developed areas transferred to the underdeveloped areas is assumed to remain—over the ten-year period covered by the projection—the same (0.3 per cent) as it was in 1959. However, the domestic investment ratio is assumed to have been raised in the developed countries from 18.9 per cent to 19.9 per cent and in the underdeveloped countries from 9.2 per cent to 10.8 per cent. As a result of that the average growth rate of the two areas —over the ten-year period, 1959-69—would go up, respectively from 5 per cent to 5.3 per cent and from 3.2 per cent to 3.5 per cent.

In the third column the transfer coefficient, h, is stepped up to 1.2 per cent and in the fourth column to 2.1 per cent. That implies a transfer of $15 billion and respectively, $25 billion in 1959, and of correspondingly larger amounts with the growth of the GNP of the developed areas in subsequent years.

Comparing the projected average annual growth rates shown in columns 3 and 4 we find that even with the capital transfer stepped up to $15 billion already in 1959, the underdeveloped countries would still continue to grow slower than the developed; with $25 billion they would begin to catch up. The "break-even point" at which the two growth rates become equal would be reached with a base-year capital transfer of somewhere between $15 and $25—probably around $20—billion.

The other five tables are organized on the same pattern as the first. The difference between any two tables lies in the assessment of the actual position of the two areas in the base year 1959.

Thus, so far as the original 1959 growth rates are concerned the projections shown on Table 2 are based on the same 5 per cent and respectively 3 per cent figure as the projections presented on Table 1. The actual domestically financed 1959 investment of the underdeveloped countries is estimated in Table 1 at $18 billion, while in Table 2 at only $11 billion. Accordingly, the implicit estimate of the capital-output ratio, b_2, falls from 3.76 on Table 1 to 2.56 on Table 2.

With any given absolute amount of investment, the lower is the capital-output ratio, the higher must be the rate of growth. This explains why in the third projection on Table 2 with a base-year transfer of $15 billion, the underdeveloped countries attained—over the ten-year period, 1959-69—an average annual growth rate of 5.4 per cent, which is higher than the corresponding growth rate of the developed areas, shown to be 5.2 per cent.

A comparison of the implicit capital-output ratios of the two areas throws light on the plausibility of some of the base-year estimates from which the different sets of projections have been derived. For example, in Table 6, $b_1 = 3.15$ and $b_2 = 5.64$. It seems to be quite unlikely that the average capital intensity of production would be so much higher in the less advanced than in the more advanced areas. A combination of a high growth rate for the developed, with a low growth rate and a high investment figure for the less developed areas must be rejected as implausible. This throws considerable doubt also on the validity of all the four alternative projections of future economic growth presented on Table 6.

For reasons similar to those described above, or for some other reasons, a critical examination of the alternative factual assessments of the state in which both groups of countries actually found themselves in 1959 might lead some experts to reject, out-of-hand, some other of the twenty-four different projections presented in these tables.

The examination of all the alternative projections of the prospective growth of the two groups of countries over the ten-year period, 1959-69, enables us in any case to answer the two questions posed in the opening paragraph of this paper. Whichever set of factual assumptions concerning the base-year situation one choses to accept, one reaches the same conclusion that the "break-even point" between the rates of the conomic expansion of the two groups of countries could not be reached before the underdeveloped areas would raise their average annual growth rate to about 5 per cent. To accelerate their present much slower pace, they would have to double the actual 1959 rate of investment in the very first year and then raise it progressively from year to year.

To make this possible the annual transfer of (productively invested) capital from developed to underdeveloped areas would have to increase from $4 to around $15 or even $20 billion in the first year and then go up annually reaching the level of between $28 and $35 billion in the tenth year.

An assessment of the feasibility of such an ambitious investment program for the underdeveloped countries supported by a massive capital inflow from the developed countries lies outside the scope of this paper.

The factual conclusion drawn from the numerical results of our computations has to be accepted, or rejected, in the light of the plausibility of the analytical approach and the reliability of the factual information on which they are based. Being fully conscious of the uncertain and even controversial nature of the statistical estimates, which have to be used in such aggregative analysis, I purposefully presented not one or two but a very large number of alternative projections reflecting a wide range of possible initial conditions. The simple analytical system developed for that purpose is constructed in such a way that with a minimum of computational efforts the spectrum of alternative projections can be expanded further through insertion in the appropriate computational formula of still other, different figures purporting to give a more correct assessment of the base-year situation. Thus, for example, the estimate of the amount of capital transferred in the year 1959 from the developed to underdeveloped areas might possibly be increased from $4 to, say, $5 or even $6 billion. Projections based on such revised descriptions of the base-year situation would incidentally show that a larger amount of additional investment in underdeveloped areas and a correspondingly greater increase in the level of capital imports from the developed areas, than those that were mentioned above, would be required to bring about an equilization in the growth rates of these two groups of countries.

Table 1—Economic growth and capital transfer from developed to underdeveloped areas

DEVELOPED COUNTRIES
(growth rate in base year: 5%, implicit $b_1 = 3.78$)

	ORIGINAL ALLOCATION	ALTERNATIVE ALLOCATIONS		
	1	2	3	4
Base Year (1959)				
Gross National Product	$1205.0 bil.	$1205.0 bil.	$1205.0 bil.	$1205.0 bil.
Capital transfers to underdeveloped areas (h)	$4.0 bil.	$4.0 bil.	$15.0 bil.	$25.0 bil.
as per cent of national product (h)	0.3%	0.3%	1.2%	2.1%
Domestic investment	$228.0 bil.	$240.0 bil.	$237.6 bil.	$235.6 bil.
as per cent of national product (i_1)	18.9%	19.9%	19.8%	19.5%
Total consumption	$973.0 bil.	$961.0 bil.	$952.4 bil.	$944.4 bil.
as per cent of national product	80.8%	79.8%	79.0%	78.4%
Ten Years Later (1969)				
Gross National Product	$1986.7 bil.	$2039.0 bil.	$2029.2 bil.	$2019.9 bil.
Average annual growth rate over the ten-year period	5.0%	5.3%	5.2%	5.2%

UNDERDEVELOPED COUNTRIES
(growth rate in base year: 3%, implicit $b_2 = 3.76$)

	1	2	3	4
Base Year (1959)				
Gross National Product	$195.0 bil.	$190.0 bil.	$195.0 bil.	$195.0 bil.
Domestically financed investment	$18.0 bil.	$21.0 bil.	$21.0 bil.	$21.0 bil.
as per cent of national product (i_2)	9.2%	10.8%	10.8%	10.8%
Total investment	$22.0 bil.	$25.0 bil.	$36.0 bil.	$46.0 bil.
Total consumption	$177.0 bil.	$174.0 bil.	$174.0 bil.	$174.0 bil.
as per cent of national product	90.8%	89.2%	89.2%	89.2%
Ten years Later (1969)				
Gross National Product	$264.7 bil.	$275.7 bil.	$319.6 bil.	$358.3 bil.
Average annual growth rate over the ten-year period	3.2%	3.5%	4.9%	6.1%

Table 2—Economic growth and capital transfer from developed to underdeveloped areas

	ORIGINAL ALLOCATION	ALTERNATIVE ALLOCATIONS		
	1	2	3	4
DEVELOPED COUNTRIES (growth rate in base year: 5%, implicit $b_1 = 3.78$)				
Base Year (1959)				
Gross National Product .	$1205.0 bil.	$1205.0 bil.	$1205.0 bil.	$1205.0 bil.
Capital transfers to underdeveloped areas .	$4.0 bil.	$4.0 bil.	$15.0 bil.	$25.0 bil.
as per cent of national product (h) .	0.3%	0.3%	1.2%	2.1%
Domestic investment .	$228.0 bil.	$238.4 bil.	$236.1 bil.	$234.0 bil.
as per cent of national product (i_1) .	18.9%	19.8%	19.6%	19.4%
Total consumption .	$973.0 bil.	$962.6 bil.	$953.9 bil.	$946.0 bil.
as per cent of national product .	80.8%	79.9%	79.2%	78.5%
Ten Years Later (1969)				
Gross National Product .	$1988.3 bil.	$2036.4 bil.	$2026.8 bil.	$2018.4 bil.
Average annual growth rate over the ten-year period .	5.0%	5.3%	5.2%	5.1%
UNDERDEVELOPED COUNTRIES (growth rate in base year: 3%, implicit $b_2 = 2.56$)				
Base Year (1959)				
Gross National Product .	$195.0 bil.	$195.0 bil.	$195.0 bil.	$195.0 bil.
Domestically financed investment (i_2) .	$11.0 bil.	$11.6 bil.	$11.6 bil.	$11.6 bil.
as per cent of national product .	5.6%	5.9%	5.9%	5.9%
Total investment .	$15.0 bil.	$15.6 bil.	$26.6 bil.	$36.6 bil.
Total consumption .	$184.0 bil.	$183.4 bil.	$183.4 bil.	$183.4 bil.
as per cent of national product .	94.4%	94.1%	94.1%	94.1%
Ten years Later (1969)				
Gross National Product .	$266.6 bil.	$268.4 bil.	$331.3 bil.	$387.8 bil.
Average annual growth rate over the ten-year period	3.1%	3.2%	5.4%	7.1%

Table 3—Economic growth and capital transfer from developed to underdeveloped areas

	ORIGINAL ALLOCATION	ALTERNATIVE ALLOCATIONS		
	1	2	3	4
DEVELOPED COUNTRIES (growth rate in base year: 4%, implicit $b_1 = 4.73$)				
Base Year (1959)				
Gross National Product	$1205.0 bil.	$1205.0 bil.	$1205.0 bil.	$1205.0 bil.
Capital transfers to underdeveloped areas (h)	$4.0 bil.	$4.0 bil.	$15.0 bil.	$25.0 bil.
as per cent of national product	0.3%	0.3%	1.2%	2.1%
Domestic investment (i_1)	$228.0 bil.	$239.0 bil.	$236.0 bil.	$234.0 bil.
as per cent of national product	18.9%	19.8%	19.6%	19.4%
Total consumption	$973.0 bil.	$962.0 bil.	$954.0 bil.	$946.0 bil.
as per cent of national product	80.8%	79.9%	79.2%	78.5%
Ten Years Later (1969)				
Gross National Product	$1784.0 bil.	$1818.0 bil.	$1818.0 bil.	$1801.0 bil.
Average annual growth rate over the ten-year period	4.0%	4.2%	4.2%	4.1%
UNDERDEVELOPED COUNTRIES (growth rate in base year: 2%, implicit $b_2 = 3.85$)				
Base Year (1959)				
Gross National Product	$195.0 bil.	$195.0 bil.	$195.0 bil.	$195.0 bil.
Domestically financed investment (i_2)	$11.0 bil.	$11.6 bil.	$11.6 bil.	$11.6 bil.
as per cent of national product	5.6%	5.9%	5.9%	5.9%
Total investment	$15.0 bil.	$15.6 bil.	$26.6 bil.	$36.6 bil.
Total consumption	$184.0 bil.	$183.4 bil.	$183.4 bil.	$183.4 bil.
as per cent of national product	94.4%	94.1%	94.1%	94.1%
Ten years Later (1969)				
Gross National Product	$240.0 bil.	$240.0 bil.	$275.0 bil.	$309.0 bil.
Average annual growth rate over the ten-year period	2.1%	2.1%	3.5%	4.7%

Table 4—Economic growth and capital transfer from developed to underdeveloped areas

	ORIGINAL ALLOCATION	ALTERNATIVE ALLOCATIONS		
	1	2	3	4
DEVELOPED COUNTRIES (growth rate in base year: 4%, implicit $b_1 = 4.73$)				
Base Year (1959)				
Gross National Product	$1205.0 bil.	$1205.0 bil.	$1205.0 bil.	$1205.0 bil.
Capital transfers to underdeveloped areas (h)	$4.0 bil.	$4.0 mil.	$15.0 bil.	$25.0 bil.
as per cent of national product	0.3%	0.3%	1.2%	2.1%
Domestic investment (i_1)	$228.0 bil.	$239.0 bil.	$236.0 bil.	$234.0 bil.
as per cent of national product	18.9%	19.8%	19.6%	19.4%
Total consumption	$973.0 bil.	$962.0 bil.	$954.0 bil.	$946.0 bil.
as per cent of national product	80.8%	79.9%	79.2%	78.5%
Ten Years Later (1969)				
Gross National Product	$1784.0 bil.	$1818.0 bil.	$1818.0 bil.	$1801.0 bil.
Average annual growth rate over the ten-year period	4.0%	4.2%	4.2%	4.1%
UNDERDEVELOPED COUNTRIES (growth rate in base year: 2%, implicit $b_2 = 5.64$)				
Base Year (1959)				
Gross National Product	$195.0 bil.	$195.0 bil.	$195.0 bil.	$195.0 bil.
Domestically financed investment (i_2)	$18.0 bil.	$19.0 bil.	$19.0 bil.	$19.0 bil.
as per cent of national product	9.2%	9.7%	9.7%	9.7%
Total investment	$22.0 bil.	$23.0 bil.	$34.0 bil.	$44.0 bil.
Total consumption	$177.0 bil.	$176.0 bil.	$176.0 bil.	$176.0 bil.
as per cent of national product	90.8%	90.3%	90.3%	90.3%
Ten years Later (1969)				
Gross National Product	$238.0 bil.	$242.0 bil.	$267.0 bil.	$291.0 bil.
Average annual growth rate over the ten-year period	2.0%	2.2%	3.2%	4.1%

Table 5—Economic growth and capital transfer from developed to underdeveloped areas

	ORIGINAL ALLOCATION	ALTERNATIVE ALLOCATIONS		
	1	2	3	4
DEVELOPED COUNTRIES (growth rate in base year: 6%, implicit $b_1 = 3.15$)				
Base Year (1959)				
Gross National Product	$1205.0 bil.	$1205.0 bil.	$1205.0 bil.	$1205.0 bil.
Capital transfers to underdeveloped areas .	$4.0 bil.	$4.0 bil.	$15.0 bil.	$25.0 bil.
as per cent of national product (h) . .	0.3%	0.3%	1.2%	2.1%
Domestic investment	$228.0 bil.	$239.0 bil.	$236.0 bil.	$234.0 bil.
as per cent of national product (i_1) . .	18.9%	19.8%	19.6%	19.4%
Total consumption	$973.0 bil.	$962.0 bil.	$954.0 bil.	$946.0 bil.
as per cent of national product . . .	80.8%	79.9%	79.2%	78.5%
Ten Years Later (1969)				
Gross National Product	$2158.0 bil.	$2220.0 bil.	$2220.0 bil.	$2199.0 bil.
Average annual growth rate over the ten-year period	6.0%	6.3%	6.3%	6.2%
UNDERDEVELOPED COUNTRIES (growth rate in base year: 2%, implicit $b_2 = 3.85$)				
Base Year (1959)				
Gross National Product	$195.0 bil.	$195.0 bil.	$195.0 bil.	$195.0 bil.
Domestically financed investment	$11.0 bil.	$12.0 bil.	$12.0 bil.	$12.0 bil.
as per cent of national product (i_2) . .	5.6%	6.2%	6.2%	6.2%
Total investment	$15.0 bil.	$16.0 bil.	$27.0 bil.	$37.0 bil.
Total consumption	$184.0 bil.	$183.0 bil.	$183.0 bil.	$183.0 bil.
as per cent of national product . . .	94.4%	93.8%	93.8%	93.8%
Ten years Later (1969)				
Gross National Product	$242.0 bil.	$242.0 bil.	$286.0 bil.	$324.0 bil.
Average annual growth rate over the ten-year period	2.2%	2.2%	3.9%	5.2%

Table 6—Economic growth and capital transfer from developed to underdeveloped areas

	ORIGINAL ALLOCATION	ALTERNATIVE ALLOCATIONS		
	1	2	3	4
DEVELOPED COUNTRIES (growth rate in base year: 6%, implicit b_1 = 3.15)				
Base Year (1959)				
Gross National Product	$1205.0 bil.	$1205.0 bil.	$1205.0 bil.	$1205.0 bil.
Capital transfers to underdeveloped areas	$4.0 bil.	$4.0 bil.	$15.0 bil.	$25.0 bil.
as per cent of national product (h)	0.3%	0.3%	1.2%	2.1%
Domestic investment	$228.0 bil.	$239.0 bil.	$236.0 bil.	$234.0 bil.
as per cent of national product (i_1)	18.9%	19.8%	19.6%	19.4%
Total consumption	$973.0 bil.	$962.0 bil.	$954.0 bil.	$946.0 bil.
as per cent of national product	80.8%	79.9%	79.2%	78.5%
Ten Years Later (1969)				
Gross National Product	$2158.0 bil.	$2220.0 bil.	$2220.0 bil.	$2199.0 bil.
Average annual growth rate over the ten-year period	6.0%	6.3%	6.3%	6.2%
UNDERDEVELOPED COUNTRIES (growth rate in base year: 2%, implicit b_2 = 5.64)				
Base Year (1959)				
Gross National Product	$195.0 bil.	$195.0 bil.	$195.0 bil.	$195.0 bil.
Domestically financed investment (i_2)	$18.0 bil.	$19.0 bil.	$19.0 bil.	$19.0 bil.
as per cent of national product	9.2%	9.7%	9.7%	9.7%
Total investment	$22.0 bil.	$23.0 bil.	$34.0 bil.	$44.0 bil.
Total consumption	$177.0 bil.	$176.0 bil.	$176.0 bil.	$176.0 bil.
as per cent of national product	90.8%	90.3%	90.3%	90.3%
Ten years Later (1969)				
Gross National Product	$240.0 bil.	$242.0 bil.	$272.0 bil.	$297.0 bil.
Average annual growth rate over the ten-year period	2.1%	2.2%	3.4%	4.3%

18

On assignment of patent rights on inventions made under government research contracts

Of the fifteen billion dollars spent throughout the United States economy in fiscal 1962 on research and development, less than one-third was supplied by private business and more than two-thirds by the federal government. If Congress continues to support the present ambitious space program, the federal share of total research and development expenditures will make up an even larger proportion in years to come. Approximately two-thirds of publicly financed research is done through contracts with private industry, about 10 per cent through grants and contracts with universities and other non-profit institutions, and the remainder within various governmental departments.[1] Approximately 60 per cent of the funds spent on research and development in industrial laboratories in that year were supplied by the Government, and that governmental share is steadily increasing.[2]

With public money playing an already dominant and steadily increasing role in financing scientific and technical research the question of who should hold the patents on inventions arising

From *Harvard Law Review*, Vol. 77, No. 3, January 1964.
[1] *The Budget of the United States Government for the Fiscal Year Ending June 30, 1964*, at 391 (1963).
[2] U.S. Bureau of the Census, Dep't. of Commerce, *Statistical Abstract of the United States 543* (84th ann. ed. 1963) (preliminary figure).

from work done by private business under government contracts acquires more than purely academic interest. Several congressional committees have been looking into this problem for some time without arriving, however, at any definite conclusion.[3] Thus, it is not surprising that governmental practice exhibits no uniformity in this particular respect. The Atomic Energy Commission, for example, has tended in the past to acquire the patents developed under its research contracts and to encourage through free licensing the widest possible application of new technical ideas produced at public expense. The Defense Department, on the other hand, is in most instances satisfied if it obtains a license allowing direct governmental use of the patented procedure; it lets the contractor retain ownership of the patent and all control over its use by any third party. An economic analysis of the basic purposes and actual effect of the patent system leads to the conclusion that the public interest would be served best if patents resulting from work done under government contracts became the property of the Government.

What role does the ancient institution of patents play, what function does it perform in our competitive free enterprise economy? And why? So far as the general conditions of production are concerned, organized research is not different from any other industry. One builds a laboratory or a pilot plant, installs the necessary equipment, hires qualified personnel, and waits for the results. These, as in the case of any other product, either can be used directly by the same business in which they were made or can be sold to others, for a price—or, as often happens, both. In one respect, however, the product of industrial research, which is new scientific knowledge or technical know-how, differs from most other goods: It can be useful, it might turn out to be useless, but it cannot be used up. Not only can the same person make use of an idea, of some specific piece of technical information, over and over again without the slightest danger of exhausting it

[3] These include the Subcommittee on Patents, Trademarks, and Copyrights of the Senate Committee on the Judiciary, 87th Congress, and the Subcommittee on Monopoly of the Senate Select Committee on Small Business, 86th, 87th, and 88th Congresses.

through wear, but the same idea can serve many users simultaneously, and as the number of customers increases, no one need be getting less of it because the others are getting more.

This unlimited, universal availability of knowledge and ideas produced by research is certainly a very desirable property for society and for mankind as a whole. But it creates a serious problem for anyone who would like to engage in research, that is, in the production of knowledge as a business enterprise (that is, for profits). To justify investment in research, a corporation must be able to sell its results directly—or indirectly, as a component part of some other product—for a price. But who would pay for a good which, once it has been produced, becomes available to everyone in an unlimited amount? Why not wait until someone else pays for it or invests in its production and then have a free ride? Who would want to enter the bakery business if seven loaves of bread—baked by anyone—could still the hunger not only of a multitude of four thousand men, and women and children besides, as is told in the New Testament, but also of anyone else who cares to partake of it?

The patent, the copyright, and the licensing laws take care of this. They provide the quantity dimensions for objects which intrinsically have none and thus make it possible for private enterprise to engage in the production of ideas and new knowledge and to sell or to use them profitably as one can use or sell steel or bread. This is an ingenious and, as far as it goes, a very effective solution of the problem; unfortunately it is not effective enough. Under the patent and licensing system, the range of practical applications of new ideas is necessarily narrower than it otherwise could have been, and the total volume of human and material resources devoted to production of useful knowledge is necessarily smaller than it should be. This is because the patent holder, in his search for profit, sets a license fee high enough to be prohibitively expensive for many people who could make good use of the patented item were it made available to them at a lower price.

This becomes clear as soon as we ask what would happen if the producer of a new technical idea, after having, through the sale of licenses, recovered his expenses plus a reasonable return on capital investment, proceeded to issue additional licenses at progressively reduced prices. All potential customers who before could not afford to buy the new idea would now, of course, acquire it and put it to good use. Since selling the same item over and over does not increase the costs of making it, all the additional receipts of the producer of the new idea will be added to his net return on the invested capital. Not only would there be gain all around at once, but, in the long run, the higher rate of profit would most likely increase the total amount of capital invested in research.

What is described above is, of course, nothing else but price discrimination—a device often used to secure the largest possible market for a good or service. Railroads practice price discrimination, for example, when they show themselves prepared to haul bulky goods at reduced per-ton-mile charges in order to attract additional traffic. In principle, a system of graduated licensing fees could be designed in every case in such a way that it would safeguard and even increase the monopolistic revenue of the owner of the patent and at the same time would encourage the use of the invention covered by patent, extending it to the very limits of its economic effectiveness. In practice, however, such perfect discrimination, even if legal, would inevitably break down under the burden of administrative red tape. It is difficult even to imagine how one would go about constructing a list of differentiated license fees so as to collect not too little, but also not too much, for each of the possible uses of the newly invented principle of, say, a "transistor" or a "laser."

The brief excursion into the unreal world of perfectly discriminatory monopoly, however, confirms our previous conclusion: In principle the economic benefits of scientific and industrial research can be exploited fully only if no one, no one at all, is prevented from using its fruits—once they have been obtained—by the price which he has to pay to do so. Though practical and legal obstacles prevent discriminatory pricing and would probably stand in the way of the Government's buying all patent rights arising out of privately financed research, no such problems exist when the Government pays for research under contract. The Government can simply make the knowledge it has bought freely available to the public. A telling example of productivity increase that can, in the long run, be brought about by absolutely free access to a steady flow of advanced technical ideas is offered by American agriculture. Traditionally the bulk of agricultural research in this country has been financed by federal funds, and its results have been brought to the attention of potential users and put at their disposal free of charge. In consequence, agricultural productivity continues to increase by leaps and bounds.

To expect private enterprise to provide all the necessary investment for scientific research and development is no more reasonable than to expect that it could be induced to build, at its own expense, all our highways and roads if the investors were offered the opportunity to secure compensation for the capital investment (and the risk incurred) through collection of universal tolls. The need for large-scale public investment in research, as well as in highways and roads, has by now been fully recognized; so has the desirability of attracting additional private capital to both through the grant of patent rights and the right of collecting tolls. However, to give the business enterprise, or the non-profit institution, the right to retain the patent rights on inventions resulting from work performed under contract for the Government is quite another matter. It is no more reasonable or economically sound than to bestow on contractors who build a road—and are paid for it from public funds—the right to collect tolls from cars that will eventually use it.

The analogy can be pursued still further: Even if, in anticipation of a lucrative toll booth business, the contractors agreed to charge the Government a lower price for the construction work, a road system financed and operated in this way would be very inefficient. It would reduce the traffic on most of our roads far below the level that they can actually support. Drivers who could not afford the tolls would be prevented from using the roads even though allowing them to drive on the toll roads would add nothing to the costs of building and maintaining the highway. Fortunately, the federal interstate highway program secures the fullest possible utilization of our roads system by making the

American people pay for it not through tolls, but through taxes. What is true for roads is even more true for production and utilization of scientific and technical ideas. A road can be crowded to capacity. The "capacity" of an invention is, by its very nature, unlimited.

Having committed, for general reasons of national and international policies, many billions of dollars of public money to the support of large-scale scientific and technical research, the federal government now has an unprecedented opportunity to correct, to some extent, a basic defect of the patent system without initiating any change in the present patent law itself. It has only to follow the practice established by private businesses when they negotiate research contracts among themselves: The patents are usually assigned to the corporation that lets out the contract and pays —to another corporation—the costs of the work performed under it.

As is well known, a new technical idea cannot, as a rule, be applied directly in manufacture of a marketable product without substantial expenditure on additional developmental work. Occasionally, it has been said that contractors working for the Government retain control of the patent as a means of protecting their own subsidiary investment in the development of such practical know-how. Those who advance this argument overlook the fact that, in contrast to a patentable idea itself, most supplementary know-how can be acquired only through practical experience, which is a learning process. To acquire somebody else's know-how, without incurring the necessary expenditures, is as difficult as it is to imitate another person's knowledge of a foreign language. Far from needing special protection for his investment in practical know-how, the contractor, even if he does not control the patent, enjoys considerable competitive advantage over all other potential users of the patented invention. Having developed the new idea himself, he acquires a firsthand familiarity with it which, initially at least, nobody else can possess.

It has also been argued that by depriving a private contractor of patent rights, the Government would deprive him of compensation for general research carried on in his private capacity, which does not directly yield patentable results, but which is reflected in the final product. However, the problem here is no greater than in the many cases where a private company keeps the patent rights covering the results of research which it has commissioned from other private firms. Further, inequities could be eliminated from any such situation by the Government's paying a higher price for the research it requests. The practical difficulties involved do not appear substantial enough to warrant the sacrifice of the evident economic benefits to the nation which result when the Government retains patent rights arising from its research contracts with private industry.

19

The decline and rise of Soviet economic science

I

One of the notable aspects of Soviet reality is the paradoxical co-
existence of the old and the new, of the modern side by side with
the old-fashioned. A visitor to Moscow cannot but be struck by
the contrast between the twenty-nine-story skyscraper of the
Hotel Ukraina and the pre-revolutionary log cabin with intri-
cately carved window frames nestling practically within its long
shadow. Contemporary Russian literature and art present a strik-
ing example of revolutionary, socialist content poured into Vic-
torian forms. One of the most notable paradoxes of this kind was
—until recently—the contract between the Soviet economy and Soviet economics.

The Soviet economy, directed with determined ruthless skill,
has been advancing for years at such a fast and steady pace that
in total—if not per capita—national income, Russia is now second
only to the United States; the output of certain of its key industries, such as machine tool building, for example, has even ex-
ceeded that of ours. By contrast, Soviet economics, that is, Soviet economic science, has remained static and essentially sterile
over a period of more than thirty years—a huge, impassive, and
immovable monument to Marx—with scores of caretakers engaged

From *Foreign Affairs*, Vol. 38, No. 2, January 1960.

in its upkeep, fresh flowers placed in slightly different arrangements at its feet from time to time, and lines of dutiful visitors guided past in never-ending streams.

The decline of economics in Soviet Russia dates back to the late 1920's, to the time of the inauguration of the original five-year plan. The first decade of the Communist regime—the years of civil war and famine and then of economic rehabilitation and "primitive accumulation" assisted by the partial restoration of private enterprise—was marked by lively economic discussion. It ranged from immediate issues of economic policy to the most general problems of economic theory. This was the time when the Communist Basarov expounded his mathematical theory of economic growth and Professor Kondratieff, director of the Moscow Business Cycle Institute, developed the statistical analysis of long and short waves of economic growth which has exerted considerable influence on Western theory of business cycles. (A few years later both of these men vanished without a trace.)

Looking back it is not difficult to explain the decline of economic science in the first planned socialist economy. Marx was a prophet of socialism, but he was a student of capitalism; to be more exact, he was a student of the first hundred years—vital and incredibly creative, but also ruthless and destructive—of modern, mechanized large-scale industry. Marxism, as an economic theory, is a theory of rampant private enterprise, not of the centrally guided economy. Whatever references Marx made to the economy of the socialist order were brief, quite general, and extremely vague. Some of his most poisonous verbal darts were reserved for Lassalle, Proudhon, and other contemporary social reformers who took delight in minute descriptions of production, distribution, and consumption in ideal socialist or anarchist commune. He considered these men naïve and impractical, and dubbed them "Utopists."

The Soviet economists of the Stalin era were no "Utopists" in any possible sense of that word; for sound practical reasons they devoted their undivided attention to paraphrasing and interpreting Marx and Lenin. The fact that capitalism—the subject of all these labors—had been by this time abolished in Russia in a sense

224

simplified their assignment job. Meanwhile, the Communist leaders were engaged in the unprecedented task of transforming literally at breakneck speed a technologically backward, predominantly peasant country into an industrialized military power dedicated to the pursuit of further economic growth. They were their own economists.

The fundamental proposition which explains the high rate of Soviet economic development is simple enough. Nearly two hundred years ago it had already been clearly stated by Adam Smith and in more homely language by Ben Franklin. To expand one's income fast, one must channel as large a part of it as possible—and then more—into productive capital investment. This means that consumption must be restricted; while thus holding down the living standard of the masses, one must at the same time keep them working hard. Marx, in his theory of capitalist accumulation, describes exactly such a process, except that he refers to it in pejorative terms: the owners of the means of production use their monopolistic position vis-à-vis the working classes to keep wage rates down and profits up. Low wages mean a low level of consumption. High profits—the high "rate of exploitation"—mean a high rate of accumulation, since the capitalists forever strive to increase their capital so as to be able to compete better with each other and also to employ more workers to exploit. This prescription was followed by Communists in Russia steadily over a period of thirty years. However, the unmistakable success of that ruthless experiment bears testimony not so much to the economic sophistication of the Soviet rulers as to their political perspicacity and determination.

So far as the Russian technique of economic planning is concerned, one can apply to it in paraphrase what was said about a talking horse: the remarkable thing about it is not what it says, but that it speaks at all. Western economists have often tried to discover "the principle" of the Soviet technique of planning. They never succeeded, since, up to now, there has been no such thing. The "Method of Balances," to which the Soviet writers themselves invariably refer, hardly deserves its high-sounding name. It simply requires that the over-all national ecoonmic plan be constructed in such a way that the total output of each kind of goods be equal to the quantity which all its users are supposed to receive. The method does not, however, say what information and what computational procedure can be used to achieve the simultaneous balancing of many thousands of different goods and services covered by a comprehensive blueprint of a national economy.

The immense scope of the problem becomes clear if one considers the fact that each item requires for its production several other items directly, and many more—as a matter of fact, all others —indirectly. Thus whenever the planner attempts to balance the supply and demand of any one particular item, by expanding its output or by reducing its consumption, he is bound to disturb the balance of many, and ultimately of all other, goods and services. Moreover, an efficient planner must compute more than a single over-all balance. Land can be tilled with horses or with tractors; electric energy can be generated by burning coal, oil, or natural gas as well as by harnessing water power. All such alternatives can be used in innumerable combinations and each combination will require a different kind of over-all economic balance. However, some of these will serve the national objectives—whatever they may be—more effectively than others.

Soviet planning procedures, in practice, do not—or at least did not up to now—differ very much from those that were used during the war by our War Production Board, by the English Supply Ministries, and by their counterpart in Germany. The larger decisions are first made by balancing the requirements for selected high-priority objectives with the available amounts of the strategic resources, that is, the most important scarce ones. Next, the details of the plan are worked out through application of standard ratios based on past experience. Final adjustments are left to informal trial-and-error procedures of the actual month-by-month and week-by-week operations.

Soviet press reports over the years abound in examples of obvious miscalculations. For instance, too much ore is mined and not enough coke is made to produce the planned amount of steel; or insufficient quantities of spare parts are turned out to keep in good repair machinery installed in new plants. More difficult to detect, because it does not show up in a glaring imbalance between the supply and the demand of some specific item, but probably not less deleterious in its effect on the over-all efficiency of the system, is the failure to make correct choices among several possible alternatives. The failure to substitute gas for coal on the supply side of the national fuel balance, or too hurried a substitution, might mean an even larger potential loss of national income than that which is brought about by the more obvious kinds of miscalculations mentioned above.

To solve all these problems in a systematic way, the planning technician must be able to compute not only one balanced plan, but many, and then he must be able to compare the efficiency of all these alternative plans in attaining whatever the specific, over-all objective of the national economic policy might be. This is an assignment easy enough to envisage, but most difficult to accomplish; it is, moreover, a highly technical task which even a very shrewd politician and powerful dictator cannot perform by himself, any more than he can, by himself, build an atomic bomb or send a rocket to the moon. He can, however, decide that the solution of this problem is worth the cost involved in solving it; he can set the experts to work on it and give them all possible support. This is what actually happened in Russia two or three years ago in respect to the important problems of economic planning discussed above. The top leadership, with Khrushchev probably taking a hand in it, apparently decided that with the rapid increase in the size and complexity of the Soviet economy, rule-of-thumb planning procedures would do no longer and must be replaced as soon as possible by more efficient, scientific methods.

The high price the Russian rulers have shown themselves willing to pay is, in this instance, not so much material as, one might say, moral: as in the case of atomic power, the scientific basis of the new techniques is being borrowed wholesale from the West—to be more specific, from the United States. This time it is "bourgeois economics" rather than physics that is about to be used to serve Soviet aims. For Communists and Marxists to concede the superiority of Western science in this particular field must be especially painful from both the ideological and the propaganda points of view; but just because of this, the significance of the move must be considered to be particularly great. To avoid any possible misunderstanding, let it be emphasized that what the Soviets are about to adopt is Western economic science, not Western economic institutions. There is good reason to believe that this can actually be done. Those Western observers who say that this cannot be done and who believe that the use of interest on capital in planning calculations presages at least a partial restoration of the system of private enterprise misunderstand, I think, the internal logic of Soviet evolution.

I I

The early mid-nineteenth century successors of Adam Smith—and Marx was one of them—were concerned mainly with problems of economic growth, that is, of increasing wealth and income and of the distribution of that increasing income among labor, capital, and the landowning groups. Later, the focal point of theoretical inquiry shifted to problems of economic efficiency and has remained centered on these problems ever since. It is true that the catastrophe of the Great Depression dramatically raised the question of full employment, and the recurring smaller ups and downs in business conditions continue to keep it on the map. However, looking back at the Keynesian Revolution, with its paradoxical advocacy of spending for spending's sake and the implied fear of a rapid rise in the productivity of labor, one must recognize it for what it was: a long detour rather than a basic change in the general orientation of Western economics. The question of efficiency and of rational allocation of scarce resources dominates the field of advanced scientific inquiry again. It was restored to that central position, however, with a new and different emphasis.

The traditional approach to these problems was broad, abstract and purely deductive; the new post-Keynesian, postwar inquiry is concise, specific, factual, and eminently practical. The so-called "neoclassical" school, which carried on the classical theoretical tradition between the two world wars, mainly expounded and elaborated the liberal free-trade theme of the "invisible hand." It demonstrated in great detail, occasionally even making use of mathematical language, the automatic efficiency of competitive pricing. It classified and reclassified various theoretically possible situations, particularly those in which free competition breaks down or in any case does not bring about the most efficient allocation of economic resources. The "neoclassical" economists made it very clear that efficiency is a relative concept, that an allocation most efficient for the achievement of one economic end might be quite inefficient from the point of view of another. Incidentally, they have also shown that in a free competitive economy the overall economic goal is determined by a kind of universal suffrage in which everyone has a multiple vote proportional to his dollar income.

The postwar generation of American economists takes up where the neoclassical analysts left off. Discussion of general principles is extended into the solution of specific problems, hypothetical assumptions are replaced by actual observation, and purely symbolic mathematics are carried down to numerical computations. The entire national economy is viewed by the modern theorist as a gigantic, automatic computing machine, the price system being interpreted as an ingenious computing aid. To test and to extend his understanding of the operation of this machine, the economist now often identifies the specific problem it is supposed to solve, determines through detailed, direct observation the basic numerical data which are supposed to go into the solution, performs the necessary computation, and then compares the final answer obtained from it with the answer to the same question arrived at in real life by operation of the impersonal forces of free competition.

To give a simple example: coal is produced in several parts of the United States, the cost of production and the maximum possible annual output varying from place to place mainly because of differing geological conditions. It moves then by either rail, water, or truck to consuming areas. The actual total output can be allocated in many different ways among the producing regions and the proper amounts can be carried to the consuming regions by many means along various routes. However, some of the possible arrangements must obviously be more economical than others in terms of total combined production and transportation costs. Traditional economic theory explains why—under certain simplifying assumptions—the free competitive pricing mechanism can be expected in this case, as in many others, to bring about the establishment of the cheapest possible production and transportation pattern. The modern analyst goes further. He collects detailed information on the actual cost of production in all the different coal mining regions and on the actual rail, water, and truck rates from these regions to places of consumption; and then he determines by himself—using, if necessary, a modern high-speed computer—the most efficient, that is, the cheapest, of all the possible alternative production and transportation patterns.

The computational procedure the economist uses might be designed in imitation of the process of trial-and-error approximation that is supposed to operate in a free-exchange economy. Or he might decide to use one of the advanced textbook methods of numerical analysis. A comparison of this answer with the observed production and the transportation pattern of coal might show that the economist has, indeed, reached a satisfactory scientific explanation of the actual process. On the other hand, he might turn up a discrepancy which will indicate the direction of necessary improvement in the theoretical formulation of the problem, the computational routine, or the nature of the factual data used. Since these elements are mutually interdependent, the modification in any one of them will usually require a corresponding adjustment in the other two. On the second or the third try, the result usually turns out to be more satisfactory. If nothing helps, the very assumption that costs are minimized in the economy might itself be questioned.

Such relatively simple questions as that of minimizing the combined production and transportation costs are ordinarily formulated as so-called linear programming problems and are solved through application of a computational procedure known as the Simplex method. Conceptually akin to linear programming is the so-called input-output analysis which, for example, has been effectively used in quantitative empirical analysis of the balance or the imbalance, as the case may be, between several hundreds of individual sectors of the United States economy. The application of this method requires a comprehensive statistical mapping of the structural relationship determining the flows of goods and services between all the sectors and a solution of large systems of mathematical equations based on the hundreds or thousands of figures contained in a typical input-output table. The Russians expect this method to be particularly helpful in the solution of their larger planning problems.

Under such names as "operations research," "logistics analysis," or "management science," the new techniques are now being successfully used by most large American corporations in the solution of production scheduling, inventory control, investment planning, and many other of their internal problems which hitherto were met by routine application of conventional and mostly rather wasteful rules of thumb. But certain business circles in the United States have viewed with unconcealed alarm the application of these methods to the traditional problems of the economic system as a whole—the very purpose for which some of the more powerful of the new analytical devices were designed in the first place. No doubt this attitude reflects the fear that too close and too detailed an understanding of the structure of the economic machine and of its operation might encourage undesirable attempts to regulate its course.

III

The first cursory references in Russia to new developments in the West appeared some years ago in the typical polemical forays against "bourgeois economics" published from time to time in *Economic Problems* and similar Soviet journals. Gradually the polemical part of these surveys became less virulent and shorter while the factual description of the new methods became more systematic and longer. Oskar Lange, former professor at the University of Chicago and now a prominent public figure and the leading economist in Poland, has apparently been instrumental in arousing a positive interest in linear programming and input-output economics among his high-placed Russian colleagues. The last edition of the *Textbook of Political Economy* published late in 1958 mentions a bourgeois science called Econometrics, some methods of which—it is significantly stated—might prove to be of interest to socialist economists and planners. Early in 1959 the *Studies on the Structure of the American Economy,* a rather technical volume published six years ago in the United States by the author of this article and several collaborators, appeared in a Russian translation (which incidentally was edited by Professor A. A. Konüs, the last surviving mathematical economist of the pre-revolutionary generation). Another straw in the wind was a popular pamphlet on problems of economic planning written by a prominent member of the research staff of the *Gosplan*—the central planning commission—and printed in several hundred thousand copies. It describes in great detail the use of the mathematical input-output method for balancing planned production and requirements. At the last two meetings of the International Statistical Institute, the official Soviet delegation made input-output analysis the subject of its principal scientific papers. Its leader used this opportunity to declare this to be a topic singularly well suited for scientific exchange between East and West.

As soon as the baby was adopted, the question of its intellectual parentage was investigated with great diligence and it was found to be, after all, of respectable Soviet Russian ancestry. A search through old economic journals revealed that in 1925 a short article on the then newly compiled balance of the Russian national economy was published in one of these periodicals over my signature. (Actually, I wrote this paper when still a student at the University of Berlin; it was first published in Germany and then translated and published in Russia.) Another Soviet priority claim seems to be more substantial. In 1939 a young Leningrad mathematician, L. V. Kantorovich, published two papers in which he presented a general mathematical formulation of certain problems of production planning and transportation scheduling, which in fact did anticipate the conceptual framework of the linear programming theory developed a few years later by Koopmans and Dantzig in the United States. Kantorovich did not, however, devise an efficient computational solution of these problems; Dantzig did, thus opening the door to the practical, large-scale application of the linear programming approach. In any case, Kantorovich's original contribution found no response and recognition till the time when information about new developments in the West reached Moscow and the top decision was made to put them into the service of socialist planning. Professor Kantorovich is now a member of the Academy of Sciences and, according to recent newspaper reports, he even can allow himself, at its public sessions, to make disparaging remarks about "the meaningless discourse" of stalwart Marxist theorists.

Once the crucial decision was made, scientific resources were rapidly mobilized to conquer the field. The details of what actually goes on are shrouded by a veil of secrecy, but it is known that many American articles and books on the subject have been translated into Russian and circulated "privately" among the specialists assigned the task of mastering the new methods. For example, though the Russian edition of *Studies on the Structure of the American Economy* was published in 1959, the translation of that book was actually completed and widely circulated as early as 1955 or 1956.

Among the scores of young economists and mathematicians whom I had an opportunity to meet during a brief visit to Moscow and Leningrad early in 1959, many showed through questions they asked and remarks they made that they had a good acquaintance, both theoretical and practical, with input-output research. Some of these belonged to the selected group of "aspirants" (corresponding to our young post-doctoral scholars) who at the time were completing a course of intensive training in methods of modern quantitative economics under the personal direction of Academicians Kantorovich and Nemchinov. (The latter, an economist and statistician, headed until recently the Section of Social and Philosophical Sciences of the Academy of Sciences and was also a member of the Academy's all-powerful Executive Board; a few months ago he was appointed chairman of the Academy's Commission on the Study of the Productive Resources of the U.S.S.R.) This fall, they are being transferred from Moscow and Leningrad to the new Science City in Novosibirsk, the seat of the rapidly expanding Siberian branch of the Academy of Sciences. Equipped with large-scale computational facilities, this will apparently become the new center of advanced economic research.

It was interesting to note that young men with mathematical or engineering backgrounds and some of the older practical planners and economic administrators took easily to the new discipline, while those who as students had concentrated on regular economic courses were still prone to be beset by doubts. The use —in so-called dynamic allocation theory—of a positive rate of interest on invested capital, for instance, is accepted by the former as a logical necessity, while the latter ask questions which indicate considerable resistance to such un-Marxist thought. As a result of this, the manipulative aspects of the new methodology seem at the present time more advanced in the Soviet Union than the understanding and the exploration of its deeper fundamental levels. This aspect of the problem, however, is also being taken care of: mathematics has been made an obligatory subject in the economics departments of the Universities of Moscow and Leningrad and, in both, new chairs of Econometrics were recently established—but not yet filled, apparently because of lack of suitable candidates.

The massive support which the Soviet Government has given to the development of the natural sciences is widely known. The fact that it is now prepared to discard some of the central themes of traditional Communist lore in order to gain command of the promising new intellectual tools of modern social science indicates that it expects to receive an equally high return from their use.

It will take some time before the Soviet planners will be able to apply in practice the new techniques their economists are now acquiring in theory. Not only must the vast training program, launched only a few years ago, be advanced much further, but the activities of the huge and clumsy Central Statistical Office will have to be reorganized from top to bottom. The new methods of economic analysis can make effective use of a much larger volume of much more detailed statistical and other factual information than was considered practicable heretofore. But first the information must be made available. Lenin's slogan, "Socialism is electrification plus statistics," will once again be often quoted in the Soviet press.

There can be little doubt that in the years to come the introduction of scientific planning techniques will increase the over-all productivity of the Soviet economy, just as the adoption of new methods of scientific management by our own large corporations has raised the efficiency of their internal operations. A centrally planned economy depends on the efficiency—or the inefficiency— of managerial decision to a much greater extent than does the free-market economy, which benefits from the economizing functions of competitive pricing. So, the advantage that the Russians will derive from any improvement in such decision-making procedures is bound to be particularly great. Whether the increased productivity will be used to accelerate still further the high rate of their economic growth, to step up military preparations or, as the free world should hope, to raise their standard of living, one cannot predict.

I V

In the present world-wide contest between the United States and the Soviet Union for the friendship of underdeveloped countries, the reorientation of Soviet economics will probably have an even more immediate effect. For better or worse, these have-not countries are not content to allow their fervently desired economic growth to take care of itself. They regulate their exports and imports, they encourage new industries, their governments finance and build not only dams and roads, but also steel, chemical, and other kinds of plants. In short, most undeveloped countries plan; they also ask for help. Financial support and engineering advice they get both from the Russians and from us. But so far as help on methods of economic planning is concerned, neither side has thus far been able to offer them much. Our advice is long on general wisdom, but short on teachable and learnable techniques. It is the latter, however, that they want; wisdom is not easily transmitted and furthermore no self-respecting politician has even been known to admit the lack of it. The Russians could have been expected to teach how to plan, but for reasons explained above they were able only to refer to the "method of balances," which raises an important question but does not answer it. Until now, as technical advisers on development economics, the Russians have not done any better than we have.

Having adopted modern analytical and programming techniques for large-scale domestic application, the Russians are bound to offer them for export too, and the demand is great. Since the new approach to economics originated in the United States, one would think that in this line of intellectual competition we could hold our own. But as things stand now, this is not the case.

The scientific treatment of management and business problems is expanding rapidly in the United States. But, for reasons noted before, large-scale basic research aimed at the application of these newer methods to the analysis of the structure and the operation of the economic system as a whole has slowed down in recent years. As a matter of fact, in its crucial empirical phase, this fundamental work has now come to a complete standstill because of lack of financial and organizational support. Over twenty countries—not counting the Soviet Union and its satellites—are ahead of us in this field.

20

Modern techniques for economic
planning and projection

Recent advances in the application of quantitative methods in economic theory and economic statistics have had a profound effect in all fields of applied economics. Modern Operations Research, which in the United States and Western Europe is rapidly transforming the management practices of private business, is a direct descendant of the mathematical theories of the profit-maximizing behavior of an individual firm. If twenty years ago one still could question whether detailed rational computations do in fact guide the behavior of an individual firm, today the number of instances in which this actually is the case is rapidly increasing.

The new approach to fundamental problems of economic planning was also born of pure theory—the theory of general equilibrium, or rather general interdependence—which aims at a concise description of the structure and the operation, not of a single firm, but of the national economy as a whole.

In terms of this theory the economic system can be viewed as a gigantic computing machine which tirelessly grinds out the solutions of an unending stream of quantitative problems: the problems of the optimal allocation of labor, capital, and natural

English translation of "Tecniche moderne per la pianificazione e la previsione economica," *La Scuola in Azione*, Ente Nazionale Idrocarburi—ENI Scuola Enrico Mattei, Anno di Studi 1963-64, No. 23.

resources, the proper balance between the rates of production and consumption of thousands of individual goods, the problems of a proper division of the stream of current output between consumption and investment, and many others.

Each of these problems can—in principle at least—be thought of as being represented by a system of equations. Under conditions of perfect competition an impersonal automatic computer—to which we usually refer as the economic system—has been solving these equations year after year, day after day, before the mathematical economists even thought of constructing their systems.

To explain the structure and the operations of this miraculous computer has been the principal task of the neo-classical general equilibrium theory. Pursuing the analogy still further, one can say that—according to the modern version of the general equilibrium theory—the competitive mechanism solves the equations fed into it through application of the so-called iterative methods, that is, the method of successive approximation. To verify, or at least to test, this interpretation of the operation of the competitive economic system one actually could construct a simple model of that system and then insert the system of equations describing it into an electronic computer. The machine can be programmed to work out the numerical solution without any outside interference, through a sequence of successive approximations. This program can incidentally be set up in such a way that at each stage of the iterative process a set of accounting prices would be computed, which in its turn would serve as a basis for the determination of corresponding levels of physical outputs and inputs; this would be followed by the computation of a new set of prices, and so on.

Many other kinds of computational procedures could, of course, yield the same numerical solution of our small system of general equilibrium equations. The method of successive approximation, involving both quantities and prices, seems to depict quite closely one actual operation of the competitive market economy when it performs its function—that of a gigantic automatic calculating machine.

Anyone who has worked with automatic computers knows that

far from being infallible, they are prone to make mistakes. Occasionally the iterative procedure leads at some stages of the computation away from, rather than toward, the correct solution of the given problem. Under certain conditions the sequence of the successive approximation begins to wobble—not unlike a bicycle on a slippery road—first deviating to the one and then to the other side of the correct path. Most of the modern theories of business cycles explain in these terms the fluctuations in production and consumption of various goods and services, and the available empirical evidence seems to indicate that this interpretation might indeed be correct.

When a machine does not perform as expected, one naturally is tempted to interfere. Such interference may consist simply of oiling a bearing or tightening a screw; occasionally we find it necessary to take the computation out of the machine and perform at least some part of it by hand.

Any kind of active economic policy or economic planning represents a purposeful interference with the operation of the competitive machine. If in the pursuit of their particular aims the policymakers rely on such instruments as tariffs, subsidies, or taxes, most of the economic computations still continue to be performed by the market mechanism, the corrective action adds new components to the computer, but does not really interfere with its automatic operation. In designing counter-cyclical fiscal policies, one might introduce, for instance, compensatory taxes which rise automatically during prosperity and fall when depression tends to set in.

Like any other complicated apparatus, a competitive economy tends to malfunction under stress and such stress appears whenever it is confronted with problems which differ greatly from those it has been solving before. It is not surprising, for example, that in transition from peace to war or from war to peace, in transition from long stagnation to rapid growth, or in facing the problems of fast and discontinuous technological change, a certain amount of guiding assistance, that is of planning, might facilitate the solution of general equilibrium problems facing the economic computing machine.

Such is the general context in which one can best understand the developments of the new techniques of economic planning.

An economic plan can be visualized as a numerical solution of a specific system of general equilibrium equations. The unknowns are the outputs and the inputs of goods and services produced and respectively absorbed by each sector of the economy. In a sketchy, very aggregative plan the number of such sectors might be as low as three or four; a detailed plan might be elaborated in terms of twenty, fifty, or even several hundred distinct sectors. Most plans trace the changes in the magnitude of each one of these variables over several successive periods of time extending from the present into the future. This means that a plan is essentially a projection or a conditional prediction.

The equations of which such an analytical system is composed are of two kinds—the balance and the so-called structural equations. The balance equations simply state that in each period of time for every good, the total production and the total consumption, in other words, the total available supply and the total required amount must be equal. Exports and imports as well as additions to and subtractions from stocks existing at the beginning of the year are, of course, entered in the corresponding balance equations.

Most of the basic factual information used in the construction of a plan is contained, however, in the structural equations. They describe quantitative relationships between the inputs absorbed and the outputs supplied by each sector. Housewives would call these structural relationships cooking recipes, economists refer to them as production or transformation functions. Considerable progress has been made in recent years both in private enterprise —and in socialist economies, in the collection and systematic presentation of this kind of data. For purposes of detailed Operations Research type of analysis such information is as a rule obtained from special technical sources; in the construction of systems of more aggregative kinds intended to depict the functioning of an entire national economy, data collected by governmental statistical organizations constitute the principal source of basic quantitative information.

240

One of the most convenient systematic methods of organizing the masses of primary data to be used in structural equations consists of compilations of tables of intersectoral flows of goods and services, which sometimes are also called input-output tables. The first compilations of this kind were prepared for the American economy in the middle 1930's. By now over forty countries—developed and underdeveloped, in the West and in the East—possess them.

An input-output table describes the flow of goods and services between the different sectors of a given national economy. The number of sectors into which the economy is being broken down depends on the amount of detailed information which the table is intended to convey. The figures are presented in a chessboard fashion. Each row shows the distribution of the output of one particular sector among all other sectors and each column, the inputs received by a sector from all the other sectors. Thus, for example, in the column describing the flows of goods and services absorbed by the automotive industry, one entry represents the quantity of steel received from the steel industry, another the amount of electric energy received from a power generating sector, still another the amount of labor services supplied by the household sector. Dividing each of these entries by the total annual output of automobiles we get a set of input coefficients representing the "input requirements per unit of output" of the automotive industry. Similar sets of technical coefficients can be derived from the other columns of the input-output table for each sector of the national economy. Taken together these coefficients make up the hard frame of the system of general equilibrium equations which can be used to translate a global forecast of the gross national income into a detailed estimate of the corresponding quantities of goods and services that will have to be produced and respectively absorbed by each sector if the total output is to be kept in perfect balance with the aggregate demand for each good.

First, the principal aggregative components of the gross national income such as the total consumers' purchases, investment outlays, and government expenditures, have to be broken down into subtotals, each representing the demand by the respective final user for specific goods and services supplied to it by each one of the different producing sectors. The input coefficients of the household serve as a basis for determining the composition of personal consumption; the inputs of schools, hospitals, or the defense establishment and of all other public institutions as well as all types of private and public investment expenditures are similarly classified by their industrial origin. These separate compilations can be next combined into a single shopping list, which shows how much of its respective output each of the productive sectors of the economy will be expected to deliver to the final users, whose total outlays make up the gross national income of our forecast.

Direct deliveries to final users absorb, however, only one part of the annual output of each industry. The rest is destined to be taken by other industries. The basic metals and heavy chemicals producers deliver, for example, their entire output to other producing sectors rather than to the final consumers whose purchases make up the gross national product. In advanced economies even agriculture supplies most of its product not to households but to various food industries. Only some 38 per cent of the combined gross output of the forty-five productive sectors entered in the United States input-output table is absorbed by households, government, and other final users. The rest represents flows of commodities and services between the different industries. In case of a more detailed industrial breakdown the corresponding percentage figure would be even smaller.

The set of general equilibrium equations incorporating the structural information described above permits the planner and the forecaster to determine what the output and the inputs of each one of the many sectors of a given economy would have to be in order to enable it to yield a hypothetical gross national income of a specified composition and size. That gross national product can be visualized as a planning target or it can represent the result of a global economic forecast.

In either case the solution of a system of linear general equilibrium equations leads to construction of an internally consistent

242

input-output table describing the state of the economy at which it would be capable of producing a gross national income of the specified size and composition. The projected levels of itemized deliveries to final users and the sets of the input coefficients of each and every sector enter in the appropriate equations as empirical constants. The numerical solution of so large a system of equations can actually be performed only with the help of an electronic computer.

The results of these calculations often indicate the necessity for revising the original projection of the gross national product from which they start. Comparing the present with the computed future outputs of specific goods and services, we can determine the magnitude of capacity expansions and changes in the size and composition of the labor force and in the availability of various primary resources, which would have been required to realize the projected change. If either one of these changes appears to be unrealizable or at least implausible the original projection of the gross national income has to be rejected or at least revised in some respects. The new projection must of course, in its turn, be developed and tested in the same way.

Empirical experience has shown that the use of structural coefficients derived from an input-output table for a given year in predicting the structural outputs of a later year leads to less and less accurate results as the time interval between the base year and the target year increases. That is not at all surprising: the introduction of new methods of production is bound to bring about a gradual change in the input-output structure of all industries. Because of the interdependent nature of the system, a change in the magnitude of a single input coefficient is bound to affect the magnitude of all intersectoral flows.

The conventional statistical procedure of extrapolating forward trends observed in the past proves to be reasonably effective in anticipating slow but steady technological advances, such, for example, as the gradual year-by-year reduction in the amount of coal absorbed by thermal generating stations per kilowatt-hour of the electric energy that they produce.

In those instances in which new technology might replace

rapidly, not to say suddenly, the old, the substitution of one input structure for another, in principle at least, can be more effectively described and explained in terms of an output maximizing or input minimizing choice between the two.

Even in a most simple case in which such choice has to be made only in respect to a single industry, two separate general equilibrium computations would have to be performed; one in which the structural equations incorporate the first and another in which they contain the second set of structural coefficients describing respectively the two alternative techniques.

If many technologies are competing with each other in several industries, the number of alternative general equilibrium systems which the planner or forecaster has to solve before making the final choice is very great indeed. That an answer to this type of problem can, nevertheless, be found is due to the recent development of "linear programming," a mathematical procedure on the basis of which an automatic computing machine can be instructed to solve a large number of distinct, but closely interrelated, systems of linear equations seriatim without ever stopping in between.

The very simple, not to say simple-minded, application of the static general equilibrium theory to planning and detailed forecasting, as we have described above, is being gradually supplemented—and eventually may be supplanted entirely—by potentially more powerful, but also much more complicated procedures based on the dynamic general equilibrium theory. The principal obstacles to rapid adoption of such advanced methods lie not so much in the complexity of analytical design, but in the continuing inability of governmental and private statistical organizations to provide the large amount of detailed factual information that their practical application requires.

Creation of new productive capacities is the principal material link through which the input-output flows of goods and services characterizing the state of the economy in two or more successive years are causally connected with each other. Capacity expansion means investment—construction of new plants, installation of additional machinery, increase in working capital, that is, in inventories of raw materials, intermediate, and finished goods. In an expanding economy a substantial part of the annual output of many industries serves investment needs and directly or indirectly all industries participate in satisfying them.

In the static general equilibrium system, described above, deliveries on capital accounts are treated as components of the projected gross national product. In a dynamic system, they appear among the unknowns of the problem. At the same time, the set of basic structural equations is augmented by additional relationships. These depict the dependence of the amounts of specific goods and services absorbed for investment purposes by each sector of the economy in a given year on the expected—or planned—increases in that sector's output from that year to the next.

The empirical constants included in these investment equations are called "capital coefficients." The capital coefficients of a particular sector of the economy reflect its physical investment structure in the same way as the input coefficient describes its current input structure. While the input coefficients of the automobile industry tell us, for example, how much steel, chemicals, electrical power, or labor are absorbed by the production of, say one thousand or one million dollars' worth of automobiles, the corresponding set of capital coefficients lists the amounts of metalworking machinery, of the products of the building—and of all other industries—that would have to be added to the existing capital stock of the automobile industry in order to enable it to increase its annual capacity output by a thousand or a million dollars' worth of cars.

A complete dynamic general equilibrium system, as applied in forecasting or planning, traces the development of a given national economy step by step over a period of several years. The actual state of the economy in the base year, that is, the year preceding the first year of the proposed projection, is supposed to be known in sufficient detail to be described in a comprehensive input-output table. A complete array of the investment coefficients of all sectors must also be given as well as other factual information that might be helpful in preparing concrete itemized estimates of capital requirements generated by a hypothetical capacity expansion in any sector.

The gross national product attainable in the first year of the projection can be shown to depend on the proportion into which the base-year gross national product is divided between current consumption and investment; investment in this context means allocation of additional plant machinery and of all other kinds of productive stocks to specified sectors. The gross national product attainable in the second year depends in the same way on the consumption and investment allocation realized in the first year, and so on down to the gross national product of the last year covered by the projection.

All these relationships make up a large, but essentially simple, set of linear equations. Through a step-by-step solution, that is, a successive elimination of variables and equations, the system can be reduced to a concise numerical description of the unique relationship between the itemized gross national product attainable in the last year and the amounts of goods and services allocated to private or public consumption in each one of the intermediate years lying within the time horizon of the particular projection. Such a reduced system contains more variables than equations; hence it does not prescribe a unique developmental path for the economy in question, but rather delineates in specific quantitative terms the limits of the choices open to the planner. He finds himself in a position of a person living on a fixed budget. By reducing consumption expenditures in one month, he can increase them in some other month. The equations of the reduced dynamic system will show not only that a lowering of the consumption level in any given year would permit a rise in the consumption allocations of the later years, but also that the potential increase in the additional amounts of specific goods and services devoted to consumption in later stages of the developmental process would as a rule be larger than the corresponding sacrifices incurred in any of the earlier years. Such gains associated with postponed consumption reflect the same structural properties of the economic system which under condition of quasi-automatic operations of a free capital market find their expression in establishment of a positive real rate of interest.

By fixing—within the limits imposed by the reduced dynamic general equilibrium equations—the level and the composition of a gross national product attained in the last year, and the amount of goods and services to be allocated to consumption in each one of the intermediate years of the projection, the policymaker, in fact, implicitly determines all other aspects of the developmental plan thus chosen by him in preference to all other realizable plans. Once the consumption pattern has been established, the complete picture of the annual flows, investment allocations, and capacity expansions can be elaborated in full detail on the basis of previously established balance equations and structural relationships. The lower are the levels of consumption established for the intermediate years, the higher will be of course the gross national product attainable at the end—in other words, the higher will be the average rate of growth of the economy in question over the entire period of time covered by the plan.

The choice between the alternative development patterns, within the limits imposed by the structural characteristics of the particular economy, essentially determines the distribution of the benefits of the productive activities of a nation between the present and the future generations. The modern methods of economic analysis puts this choice within the reach of an informed and deliberate political decision. Systematic application of these techniques to developmental planning is still in its beginnings. Even in those countries in which the need for some kind of economic planning is fully recognized, the procedures actually used in charting the future course of national economy are of a simpler kind described in the first part of this lecture. The steady advance in collection and systematic organization of basic statistical information will soon permit a practical application of more effective methods based on dynamic general equilibrium analysis, outlined above.

PART FOUR

PART FOUR

21

The balance of the economy of the USSR

A METHODOLOGICAL ANALYSIS OF THE WORK OF
THE CENTRAL STATISTICAL ADMINISTRATION

Among various problems which must be solved by contemporary
Russian statistics, that of representing in numbers the total turnover
of economic life is perhaps the most interesting as well as the most
complex. As a result of many years' work by the Central Statistical
Administration, the "Balance of the Economy of the USSR in 1923/
24" has appeared.[1] The principal feature of this balance, in comparison with such economic-statistical investigations as the American and
the English censuses, is the attempt to represent in numbers not only
the production but also the distribution of the social product, so as to
obtain a general picture of the entire process of reproduction in the
form of a *tableau économique* (economic table).

On the income side of the balance is presented the value of the total
amount of goods at the disposal of the whole economy during the year
under consideration.

All these goods are divided three ways into separate groups. First,
the three large-scale branches of the economy—industry, agriculture, and construction—are separated from one another. Second, all
the goods created are divided into four groups in accordance with, so
to speak, their functional relationships to the process of production:
(1) goods intended for individual consumption (production factor:

Originally published in Russian under the title "Balans narodnogo khoziaistva SSSR"
in *Planovoe khoziaistvo*, No. 12, 1925. English translation from N. Spulber (ed.),
*Foundations of Soviet Strategy for Economic Growth—Selected Short Soviet Essays
1924–1930* (Bloomington: Indiana University Press, 1964), pp. 88–94.
[1] *Ekonomicheskaia zhizn'*, No. 72 of the current year [1925]. Report by P. I. Popov in
the Council for Labor and Defense (STO).

labor); (2) raw and other materials; (3) fuels; and (4) tools of production. Finally, all values are broken down, in accordance with the formation of prices, into their component parts, which jointly add up to consumer prices—namely, local production prices, transportation expenditures, and trade markups.

On the expenditure side, the table shows how the values representing the national economy's income are distributed and used. The distribution of expenditures follows in general the subdivisions of income. The values are divided, according to their origin, into three main groups: products of industry, products of agriculture, and products of construction. The relationship to the process of production is again denoted by subdivisions into (1) consumer goods; (2) raw and other materials; (3) fuels; and (4) tools of production. All goods, whether used in production (namely, in its three main branches), in the process of distribution (transport and trade), or in consumption, are divided into three main groups according to their economic rather than their production and technical functions. They thus find their expression in the income data, which distinguish among expenditures for production, transportation, and trade.

Clearly, this balance scheme is based on the methodological principle of exclusively material accounting. Only material goods are accounted for. The income side of the economic turnover is considered only insofar as it consists of "objectivized" material goods. From this point of view it is fully consistent that the public administration, whose budget has reached almost 1.5 billion rubles, should be represented in the balance by only 475.7 million rubles. The state does not create any material goods; its income is "derived" and as such does not have any counterpart in the income of the economic balance. But neither do its expenditures, for example, the payments without material counterpart to second parties such as officials; these are also treated as "secondary" (derived) income. Inasmuch as state establishments act as immediate consumers, the corresponding expenditures are reflected in the category of collective consumption. The same device is applied to transportation. Its services are taken into consideration only to the extent that they enter as costs in the prices of goods; consequently, passenger traffic has been omitted.

Although this methodological peculiarity limits the attempt to make the balance represent a complete picture of the turnover of the economy, it nevertheless leaves the internal organic structure of the balance scheme untouched. The same thing cannot be said with regard to the concept and the method of calculation of the total income of the economy. This problem has great importance for the methodology of the entire statistics of production, and in the case of generalizations about the balance, its role becomes decisive. For example, in the accounting of "value added"—whose purpose is to calculate the net income of the economy—if total product constitutes only an intermediate item, then the "dualistic" concept of the total product represents the model as well as the basic element of the entire balance system.

Let us, therefore, briefly touch upon the general formulation of this problem, since only in this way can we critically evaluate the method which has been used in this scheme.

The total product is the result of the process of production, which, in addition to newly created values, also contains the value of the goods expended and worn out in its creation.

This latter value is usually called costs. In statistical methodology, the definite distinction between these two value sums means that the first of these sums—the net product—can appear no more than once in the process of production. Cost expenditures, on the contrary, can endlessly pass from one stage of production to another and reappear at each stage in the same form. Thus the net product of several branches of production is always equal to the sum of the individual net products; costs, on the contrary, amount to less than the sum of the individual total products, since they constitute only a part of the total value of production and since the same values are accounted again and again in various technically related processes of production. This reasoning, which appears somewhat complicated in abstract form, will become clearer in a numerical example. Let us imagine a complex branch of industry with three production stages. On the first—the lowest stage—a value (net product) of one unit is added to the value of expended raw materials and other expenditures equaling 2 units.

In this way, total product consists in $2 + 1 = 3$. Further processing occurs at the second stage. To the 3 units, which occur here as expenditures, 4 new ones are added. Consequently, total product comprises $3 + 4 = 7$. In its turn, the second production stage is included in the third and last stage, where to these 7 units 5 more

Table 1—Growth of value in the total product

STAGES	COSTS	NET PRODUCT	TOTAL PRODUCT
I	2	+ 1	= 3
II	3	+ 4	= 7
III	7	+ 5	= 12
Total	12	+ 10	= 22

are added. The values of costs, of the net product, and of the total product of all three stages are summed up in Table 1.

But if we imagine the same process of production as a single phenomenon, then the corresponding formula will appear as $2 + 10 = 12$, where the first figure represents costs; the second, the net product; and their total, the total product. A comparison with the first conclusion shows that the sum of the net product remains the same in both cases (10); the costs, on the contrary, which were expressed by 12 value units in the first method, are expressed by 2 units in the second method thanks to the exclusion of all double counting. In accordance with this, the sum of the total product amounts to 22 units in the first case and 12 in the second. Each of these two magnitudes of the total product—the real one, i.e., that found after excluding any double counting (equal to 12 in our example), as well as the second, designated by us as the "total turnover" (equal to 22 in our example)—has a scientific meaning. The total turnover is more suitable for balance accounting than the real sum, for the same reason that the real gross product is much more suitable than the net product: the more deeply and widely individual relationships are included, the more clearly the organic structure of the economic whole appears. On the other hand, however, it is much more difficult to obtain a total turnover which can be applied in a scientific way than to obtain a corresponding real magnitude.

Every statistical sum should be constituted in such a way that the relationship among the values of its component parts fully corresponds to the actual relationships of individual data included in the subject of statistical investigation. Both component parts of the real sum of the gross product—the net product as well as the original

254

costs, i.e., those computed without any double counting—are accurate and indisputable. For this reason the requirement mentioned above is automatically fulfilled to a certain degree.

The matter of the total turnover is completely different. We have seen above that double calculation consists in considering the same value of costs repeatedly in several parts of a connected process of production. The larger the number of these partial stages, the greater the extent of such double counting, and the greater the corresponding total turnover. If the total turnovers of several branches of industry are to be compared with one another, the dissection of all these processes of production, which is necessary for such a calculation, should be performed in a uniform manner. Such dissection can be undertaken from two points of view. The first is the technical point of view. In this case the various stages of production which are technically analogous are looked upon as separate subjects of calculation. If, for instance, the individual branches of production of the textile industry are to be compared with one another, the production of yarn and fabrics of each branch—cotton, silk, and wool—should be computed and totaled. We thus obtain several total turnovers, computed in an identical manner, whose comparison is methodologically possible; but such a method can lead us to our goal only in the case where a statistical investigation is limited to a narrow circle of related areas of production.

If branches of industry which do not have anything in common technically are included in the investigation, this method will be completely inapplicable; there can be, for instance, no question of analogous stages of production in machine construction and paper production. In an economic balance, however, not just some but all the areas of the economy are compared, and the above method is, as a result, inapplicable. But even in this case various objects of investigation can be reduced to a common denominator, if the necessary dissection is performed from an *economic* point of view. The calculation is based not on any technically separate stages of production, but on economic unity. The total turnover will be the sum of the values of goods which are sold on the free market by the individual enterprises active in the given process of production. It is thus equal to the sum of goods produced by the corresponding enterprises.

Such a method provides a possibility of comparing the economic weight of all the areas of production with one another, leaving aside their technical peculiarities. But even this method is not always applicable; its limitations are greater than those of the method mentioned earlier. Economic dissection of the process of production is possible only when the latter is organized as in a barter economy, while the total amount of goods can be computed only with reference to a commodity economy. Like the ideal socialist economy, a large number of isolated natural economies do not know any intermediate economic division of labor and, consequently, any double economic calculation of costs. Since, for a balanced statistical comparison, subdivisions performed from a technical point of view are insufficient, it follows that the total turnover should be renounced and the real gross product be considered instead. But if the economy is organized partly as a barter economy and partly as a natural economy, a coherent picture of the whole can be obtained only through the computation of the real total income, since this is applicable to all economic systems, whereas the method of the total turnover—as we have seen—is not applicable to the branches of production with a natural economy (at least not to the extent necessary for balanced accounting). The following circumstance must also be taken into consideration: inasmuch as individual branches of production interpenetrate one another to a greater or lesser extent by means of exchange, a certain double counting will take place in totaling their real gross product. Thus the total national gross product will constitute the sum of the turnovers. But a methodological danger will appear only in the case where a comparison with another total national gross product is undertaken.

Let us now turn to the main published table of the balance of production and distribution. The size of the shares marketed by each branch shows that the economy of our Union is still organized, in the main, as a natural economy. Agriculture sells a comparatively small part of its products; the largest part is used by the farm households. Nevertheless, the method of total turnover was applied here. Furthermore, the subdivision of agricultural production shows that the calculation of the total turnover was based on technical dissection: cultivation of the soil and of meadows, animal husbandry, forestry, fishing, and hunting. This method should be recognized as wholly wrong. As we have seen, such a method inevitably leads to a series of discrepancies, since there is no principle on the basis of which an objective calculation can be made of the total amounts of the total product of individual branches of production. Hence it is completely meaningless to compare the shares of the total products obtained in the various branches of production "per worker engaged in production" or "per capita" of the population (as shown in the balance table).

The balance does not give any references to the sources which served as foundations of its construction. Four categories of data can be assumed: (1) current statistics; (2) censuses, namely, the general population and industrial census of 1920 and the urban census of 1923; (3) statistics of the budget; and (4) other sources as, for instance, the data of state and trade organizations, of the cooperatives, etc.

As the first attempt of our statistics, the balance needs further methodological discussion. And such discussion will acquire a firm foundation only with the publication of all materials and with the indication of the methods used for their processing.

22

The theory and statistical description of concentration

I

Any purposeful statistical investigation of a phenomenon requires a special conceptual apparatus, a theory, that will enable the investigator to select from among the numberless multitude of facts those that prospectively fit into some pattern and hence are susceptible to systematization. Even such a relatively simple event as a shift in population must first be placed within a rather complicated conceptual framework before it can be dealt with directly in a statistical investigation. The more complicated the object of inquiry, the more important its theoretical "preparation," so to speak. Accordingly, we too are obliged to erect the requisite theoretical framework before we proceed to the purely statistical aspect of our topic.

Production and industry are comprised of a number of particular processes taking place both in parallel to one another and at different levels. Economic development entails not only the accession of new units and the elimination of many old ones, but also a continuous process of structural change in what is retained; there are two basic aspects to such change that evolve side by side: differentiation and integration.[1]

This qualitative change is accompanied by another, quantitative change: the size of the individual economic units (cells) changes, just

Originally published in German under the title "Über die Theorie und Statistik der Konzentration," in *Jahrbücher für Nationalökonomie und Statistik*, Vol. 126, March 1927. Translation by Michel Vale.
[1] Schulze-Gävernitz, *Der Grossbetrieb* (Leipzig, 1892), p. 88.

as do the overall proportions of the economic system as a whole. These two processes are quite different and totally independent of each other; this is clear from the fact that they can proceed in different directions at the same time. Let us look more closely at the latter of these two processes.

The question may be formulated as follows: What are the effective factors that give rise to quantitative changes in individual production units? (We shall forego a more precise definition of these terms for the time being.)

II

Every production process brings together into a unified, coordinated whole various factors of production. By this we mean simply all types of outlays, such as, for example, those that are enumerated as individual items in the most detailed accounting ledger of an industrial enterprise; by productive factors we do not mean, then, any basic unit or primary factor that cannot be broken down further.

Individual productive factors come together in definite proportions, not in any random quantities. For example, a woodcutter works with one axe. Two workers, however, are needed to use a two-handed saw; three would already be too many, and one not enough—that is, in the first case the workers, and in the second the saw, would not be adequately utilized. Without adducing further examples, we may formulate the following proposition: for every production process there exist some ideal proportions in which all the factors of production involved in that process must be brought together.

Cassel calls this relationship the "technical coefficient."[2] It should be borne in mind, however, that the choice among different factors of production serving the same end depends on their prices; hence, to speak of a specific technical coefficient has meaning only if a specific price level is assumed beforehand.

There is yet another consideration of decisive importance for our discussion: individual factors of production can be used only in quite specific quantities, not in just any arbitrary ones. With the right number of workers, one, two, three, and more saws may be used,

2 *Theoretische Sozialökonomie* (Leipzig, 1921), p. 119.

but never ½, 1½, or 2½ saws. There exists some basic, indivisible quantum.

Thus, a production process will have attained its optimal form only if it is large enough in scope so that the proportions in which the factors of production are present permit the fullest utilization of all basic units. Of course, in this case the crucial factors are those for which the smallest number of indivisible basic units is required in order for them to participate in the production process. For example, if three types of productive factors—such as power-generating equipment, machinery for the actual fabrication, and labor—are involved in the production of an item in the proportions 1:10:200, a factory must employ at least 1 power unit (such as an electric motor), 10 productive machines, and 200 men. If, then, a technological invention made it possible to manufacture electric motors that were half as big as those in our initial example, yet performed just as efficiently, the optimal proportions, and hence peak performance, could be achieved with a (small) power motor and only 5 fabricating machines and 100 men (the proportions in this case would be 1:5:100). On the other hand, the introduction of fabricating machines that were half as big would have no relevance with regard to determining the minimal size of our factory, since the "power-source" factor is an indivisible unit, while the amounts of the other factors could not be reduced without destroying the proportionality. The indicated minimum limit is also a maximum limit, that is, it is an optimum point; no special demonstration of this should be necessary. After the minimum size has been reached, production can be expanded efficiently only by constructing new production units of the same kind, not by expanding the old, if the correct proportionality is to be maintained. Any attempt to expand on existing plant would cause a shift in the proportionality.[3] There is no need to demonstrate at length that all the propositions we have explained on the basis of our "technical" example are equally valid with regard to organizational expenses and other "management costs."[4]

[3] We shall not make the usual distinction between constant and variable costs (e.g., K. Bücher, "Das Gesetz der Massenproduktion," in *Entstehung der Volkswirtschaft*, collection II [Tübingen, 1918]) in our discussion, since such a distinction is not at all absolute, only relative. See J. M. Clark, *Economics of Overhead Costs* (1923).

[4] "The costs of intellectual equipment, then, are one of the big sources of economy in large scale production" (Clark, op. cit., p. 120).

It should be borne in mind, however, that the two magnitudes necessary for determining optimal size—that is, the efficient proportions among the individual factors of production and the size of their elementary units—are by no means constant; they are variables, and any change in them brings about a corresponding change in the optimal size of the particular production unit.

Therein lies the answer to our question. The quantitative change in the size at individual production and trading units is caused by the tendency toward optimization. If the optimum lies beyond the actual size, the tendency will be toward "concentration"; if it is below the actual size, there will be a tendency toward "decentralization."[5] The former is dominant today, but it is just this current state of things that we wish to explore statistically; here we are dealing with what is possible, not with what is.

For the time being, we should like to avoid, if we may, a time-consuming discussion of the wide array of definitions of the concept of "concentration"; most are merely descriptive and do not differ in substance from ours.[6] We should like only to call attention to a few outwardly very similar but in reality fundamentally different phenomena that often are not distinguished clearly enough from those we have just analyzed.

First, the tendency to conglomerate into monopolies. At issue here is not the absolute size of an individual industrial unit, but its size relative to the magnitude of the particular branch of production. This overall magnitude, however, exhibits completely different patterns of development from those seen in the internal tendency toward concentration.

[5] "The most recent development [of the English textile industry] shows an increase in the number of factories and a decrease in the number of workers. From 1890 to 1903 the number of cotton mills in Great Britain increased from 2,363 to 2,476, while according to the census figures the number of workers decreased from 565,000 in 1891 to 546,000 in 1901" (G. Brodnitz, "Betriebskonzentration und Kleinbetrieb in der englischen Industrie," *Jahrbücher für Nationalökonomie und Statistik*, Series III, Vol. 35(1908), 188).

[6] Lexical definition: "The most usual distinction between a large concern and a small concern is based on the amount of capital invested in an enterprise (!)" (*Handwörterbuch d. Staatswiss.*," 3rd ed., Vol. V, p. 67). Further on, the advantages of the large concern are enumerated (just as at one time the advantages of the division of labor were listed): (1) division of labor; (2) more favorable market conditions; (3) better cost structure; (4) cheaper credit. Actually these "advantages" can all be brought under point 3.

Second, there is "locational" concentration. This phenomenon also differs fundamentally from real centralization because it represents a purely mechanical agglomeration in the number of independent industrial units—independent, in any case, from the standpoint of the production process.

Of course, one could object that the statistician is interested in the phenomena themselves, not their causes, and hence is quite right to lump together phenomena that are outwardly similar yet may be quite different in their essential properties. This objection would indeed be valid if a statistical description could limit itself to a mere counting operation. Its tasks, however, are much deeper than that: like abstract theoretical science, it too looks for regularities. The methods are different, but the goal is always the same. It would therefore be quite inappropriate to neglect the findings of theoretical analysis in making a statistical investigation.

III

The definition of this tendency toward concentration (unfortunately we do not have a single term that would include both concentration and decentralization) delimits the domain of inquiry of concentration statistics. The next problem we shall take up is that of the measuring unit to be used. We shall approach this problem by means of theoretical analysis as well.

So far, we have regarded the production process as if the individual forces of production were inseparably linked, and hence all had to participate together in the production process. Graphically, this interaction might be described by a number of arrows pointing toward a single point; the final product would be an arrow emerging from the other side of the point (Fig. 1). However, a complex production process may often be broken down into a large number of stages: the various productive factors do not all act together simultaneously; first one and then another is operative.

This is a vertical breakdown; a horizontal breakdown is also possible since the elementary units of many productive factors allow some breakdown of their functions although they themselves are not divisible. For example, half of a generator cannot be used, but its function, in the form of the electric current it produces, can be divided up into

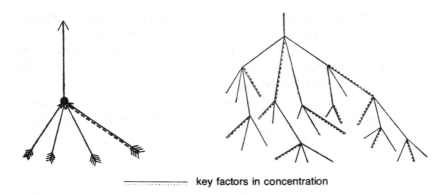

------------- key factors in concentration

Figure 1   Figure 2

any number of small portions. Thus, the complex and indivisible marketing organization of a modern large enterprise, or a retail sales chain, can be used by many discrete, independent production units. This fact is of central importance in determining the optimal size of production units. The correct—that is, the most efficient— proportions for the individual factors of production often cannot be brought into line with one another directly. For example, let us suppose that in the above example there is another, fourth factor in addition to the "power unit" factor, the 10 fabrication machines, and the 200 workers, namely a factory building, and that for technical efficiency the entire production process has to be carried out in two large areas. Now, however, let us suppose that the power unit can only be used when everything is located in one area. The coefficient of proportionality of the building factor would thus be 2 and would stand in a 1:1 ratio to the "power unit" productive factor. There are three possibilities: build a larger, that is, less efficient, work space; install two power sources of appropriate design in two separate buildings (in that case, however, only half of their capacity would be used); or, finally, use two smaller power sources of less efficient design. The final choice of one of these three compromises will depend on the prices of the competing individual factors of production; but whichever is ultimately chosen, some reduction in efficiency will be the price that must be paid.

If, on the other hand, an electric power source of the same capacity is used, the other three factors of production could be arranged into

263

two secondary, subsidiary optimal subgroups organized on the basis of the elementary unit of the productive factor "buildings."

Interpreted from this point of view, modern economic organization represents a composite system of concentration units, each wholly contained in the next larger unit and varying in size from a small workshop to an international commercial enterprise. The relationships existing among them may be represented graphically as a multibranched system of groups of arrows (Fig. 2).

IV

Each of these concentration units may be regarded as a census unit or counting unit for statistical purposes. This does not mean, however, that all units may be lumped together. Any statistical study requires that every system be composed of equivalent units. In our case, the type of unit is determined by the extent of the concentration possibilities, which in turn are dependent on the nature of the productive factors involved, the size of their elementary units, and their coefficients of proportionality.

In regard to the first criterion, there is almost no limit as to what productive factors may be considered as being of the same kind; one need only expand the category to include more items (for example, drills, machine tools, productive machines, machinery in general, technical aids, in ascending order). But much of what might be gained by this method would be lost when the other two elements—size of basic units and coefficients of proportionality—are brought into the picture.

Strictly speaking, the technical coefficient is an invariable quantity; that is, even given the entire range of specificity and diversity of the raw materials, special machines, and so on, used in any particular manufacturing process, there really is still only one efficient proportion that exists for them. In this case, the size of the elementary units is also specifically fixed in just the same way. However, as more and more different productive factors are lumped together into one broader, all-embracing category, the particular case loses its specificity, the corresponding coefficient of proportionality becomes less precise, and the resultant statistical aggregate becomes less homogeneous.

264

It may also happen that concentration units which in reality are of different kinds and different rank—with one actually a constituent part of the other—may be subsumed under the same general term and regarded as equivalent, and thus may be counted as two separate units for census purposes. It would be wrong, however, to try to eliminate this double counting by excluding one of the two. A partial correction here is more dangerous than a systematic error.

V

Now that we have presented the most basic guidelines in at least rough form, let us attempt to assess the actual procedure followed in 1926 in compiling German industrial statistics in the industrial questionnaire and its various appendices. We are quite aware that a criticism of this nature will be quite one-sided, and that the diversity of the tasks involved in a major industrial census—quite apart from the practical difficulties it entails—can be coped with effectively only through a compromise procedure. It is all the more important on that account, however, to be sure that the data obtained in each particular case are usable.

The first problem is the difference between technical and economic units. The technological bias of German industrial statistics has come under sharp criticism for quite some time, but especially since the publication of the final 1907 census report, and the call has been made for a move toward a more economically oriented procedure.[7] This demand was finally met. The results of the 1925 census of industry and trade are classified in terms of "economic units" into eight tables arranged under the letter C.

Normally the particular advantage of these economic units is seen to lie in the fact that, in contrast to specific technical units, they bring together all branches of industry under one common denominator, and hence are especially suited for describing general economic trends. This is not true with regard to the tendency toward concentration, however, as will be clear from a brief reflection on that matter.

---

[7] Conrad, "Die Zählungseinheit der gewerblichen Betriebsstatistik," *Allg. Stat. Arch.*, Vol. 12 (1920); Passow, "Kritische Bemerkungen über den Aufbau unserer gewerblichen Statistik," *Zeitschr. f. Sozialwiss.*, 1911 (also published as an appendix in *Betrieb, Unternehmung, Konzern* [Jena, 1925]).

In question 12 of the industrial questionnaire, independent businesses are all regarded as being of the same type economically. The question now arises: What special place does this type of unit have in the broad hierarchy of concentration units? As we have shown in detail, this position is determined by the special nature of the production and cost factors that come together under this point, of which one plays a decisive role.

To determine this specific cost factor for the economic unit, let us compare two production processes differing only in the fact that one is operated as an independent business while the other is part of a larger economic unit (subsidiary firm). All costs of raw materials, depreciation, internal organization, and administration will be the same; sales and purchasing costs, that is, commercial expenses—the first and last items on the accounting ledger of any independent enterprise—will not exist for the second (subsidiary firm), however. But this is precisely the cost (or productive factor) that might determine the optimal size of the concentrated unit enterprise.

It is quite incomprehensible why such decisive importance should be ascribed to this relatively negligible factor. True, it is encountered in all branches of industry, but this does not mean that it is a decisive concentration factor in every case. The productive factor "power source" is also encountered in almost all branches of industry, yet it would be quite erroneous to say that it has the same significance in a chemical factory as in a machine-building factory.

In quite a large number of cases, technological concentration takes place over the head, as it were, of any breakdown in economic terms. Indeed, this is precisely what makes the social division of labor so unique.[8] On the other hand, in all the analogous cases of conflict analyzed in the foregoing, it is the entrepreneurial—that is, the commercial cost—factor that is sacrificed because of its relatively

---

[8] An interesting example of this kind of concentration is provided by tenement factories in the English metal products industry: "The tenement factory is a factory building in which accommodations with motor power or even fully equipped small factories, i.e., premises with the requisite machinery and power sources, are hired out to small entrepreneurs" (Brodnitz, op. cit., pp. 188–189).

In German industrial statistics such a factory, with its 300 to 400 "independent" workers, would be broken down into just as many "economic" units and ranked together with the other "independent businesses."

minor importance. Most of the common interest groups, mergers, and trusts typical of today's economic development have come into existence because of a striving for a technological, not an economic, optimum. Of course, economic consolidation is a factor, but it would be just as wrong to consider this economic factor as decisive with regard to concentration as it would be to consider one cause of concentration in the aforementioned example to be the fact that the entire production process was brought under one roof—in itself an inexpedient measure—to accommodate the use of an efficient power source.

We do not wish to deny the possibility that an enterprise, while serving as an economic unit, in many cases can also really represent a concentration unit; but we believe we may validly maintain that, from a purely theoretical viewpoint, no particular arguments can be adduced that would warrant preferring this unit over "technological" units as more advantageous to use as a basic concentration unit for census statistics. In particular, it is wrong to think that it represents any universal standard with which the concentration tendencies present in diverse branches of industry could be reduced to one common denominator.[9]

The technological (i.e., not economic) census units of the industrial census are the following:

1. Local units—local establishments
   a. Independent enterprises
   b. Head offices of independent enterprises
   c. Branch offices geographically separated from the main office
2. Technological (industrial) units in the strict sense; subsidiary factories

As is evident from the definition, all these categories are related in some manner to the enterprise unit—specifically, in such a way that these technological units appear as subordinate to the economic

---

[9] We should expressly stress that these assertions do not imply a disregard or outright dismissal of the methodological rule that the technological factor must be rigorously kept distinct from the economic factor. In our view, the concentration problem, on the whole, is basically a technological problem. Therefore, the significance ascribed to economic units in the present case is quite different from their role in statistics on national income (see our "Methodologische Untersuchung: Die Bilanz der Russichen Volkswirtschaft," *Weltw. Arch.*, Vol. XXII).

units, as if the latter were the cornerstones of the entire edifice.[10] We have already shown how mistaken it is to approach the matter in this way, since it simply overlooks the bulk of today's trend toward concentration. Indeed, in only two questions of the industrial questionnaire is there anything that could be regarded as even an attempt to pinpoint supraeconomic or intereconomic concentration factors. In question 4 "a cottage worker or tradesman" is asked to give "the name and domicile of the employer—manufacturer, publisher, salesman, etc."—for whom he works. Question 9V asks whether the business (1C) gets its electricity from other sources (electric power plant, long-distance power station, etc.) and (2B) whether electricity is supplied "to other firms or other consumers."

VI

The third and last question, whose answer is just as important for concentration statistics as the first two, is the question of what yardstick should be used to measure the magnitude of various census units.

Although we realize that a "practical" solution to this problem can be obtained only from considerations of a "practical" nature, let us nevertheless pursue our theoretical line of reasoning a little further as we discuss the theoretical foundations of concentration statistics.

There exist two ideal concentration units (ideal in the sense that they satisfy all theoretical principles). The question to be asked is: Assuming an exhaustive knowledge of all productive factors involved and of the production outputs, in what terms may their magnitudes actually be compared?

If all productive factors and technological coefficients of the two units to be compared were equal, then the relative sizes of the two units could be deduced directly from a comparison of any randomly selected individual combination of factors of production. However, we know that the indicated assumptions are valid only for units of the same size; any difference in size is linked directly as a causal factor with differences among either the technical coefficients or the pro-

---

[10] "The economic unit is the most inclusive of all these statistical units," *Volks-, Berufs- und Betriebszählung*, 1925, instructions for filling out the industrial questionnaire, *Statistisches Reichsamt*, August 1925, p. 1.

ductive factors used. If two production units are of different sizes, then either the factors determining concentration in the two units stand in different proportions to the other productive factors involved, or the latter differ in their degree of efficiency. Any attempt to deduce the overall ratio from a comparison of these concentration-determining factors is doomed to failure in the first case. For instance, to take an extreme example, two factories of different sizes, undergoing concentration with respect to the power source factor, both have a steam power plant. One plant is fully utilized, but the other operates at only half-capacity because of an insufficient number of machines and workers. If the two establishments were compared in terms of the number of power sources, both would be considered the same size, which of course would be quite wrong. It would be more correct, if less exact, to make the comparison in terms of the variable factors, for example, the number of machines or the number of workers; the size of the second factory would have been underestimated in our example, however, to the extent that the unused portion, so to speak, of the power unit was left out of account. When the factors determining concentration are given relatively too little weight, on the other hand, use of this comparative method would give an overestimation.[11]

The material output of a production process is related to this magnitude in the same way as the other "variable" productive factors: as the optimal dimension is approached, the proportion shifts in favor of the output volume. That is of course the entire rationale behind the concentration tendency.

This, however, exhausts the series of possible natural criteria. Thus it proves impossible to make an absolutely accurate comparison of two concentration units by any natural standard.

This leaves only the standard of value. With it, all productive factors can be brought directly together and correctly compared. The other advantage of the standard of value, an advantage associated with

[11] Current industrial taxation practices are quite instructive for the industrial statistician. For example, a deliberate bias is given to the technical coefficient measuring the size of an enterprise on the basis of the number of just those productive factors whose share in the production process exceeds the efficient proportion. For example, the size of sugar factories was measured on the basis of the total space occupied by the diffusion equipment in which the sugar sap is extracted from the beets. This led to a more efficient use of space in processing the intermediate products.

its universality, is that it permits a comparison of qualitatively different concentration units.

In practice, industrial units are compared by the following methods:

I. Material standards
   A. Technical equipment
      1. Special equipment—for example, number of spindles in a textile mill
      2. Power capacity of power units
   B. Quantity of products in kind
   C. Number of persons employed
II. Price measures
   A. Value of total productive factors—capital (scarce)
   B. Value of production (American census)[12]

The number of workers is, of course, a generally accepted standard. Its theoretical advantage lies in the fact that, first, it alone of all the "material" standards is universal and, second, the productive factor "labor" can be broken down into relatively small elementary units (in subsidiary factories, even a *part* of human labor power is used) and hence can almost always be regarded as a variable factor of production. It determines concentration only in small businesses and thus should be used as a measure of size only with great caution.[13] Like any indirect method of calculation, comparison with regard to number of workers involves a source of considerable error. Experience has shown that the technical coefficient of the productive factor "labor"

[12] Astonishingly, Passow ("Der Anteil der grossen industriellen Unternehmungen am gewerblichen Leben der Gegenwart," *Zeitschr. f. Sozialwiss*," 1915, p. 491) omits the gross output in his enumeration of the parameters that might be used to measure the "share of large enterprises in industrial life." He considers "net worth" to be the best parameter. "Net proceeds" is not even considered as a measure of concentration, since it is much more difficult to ascertain than gross output, and moreover gives a much less clear picture of the real dimensions. The ratio of net worth to gross worth may be considered an index of the degree of dependence of a concentration unit on the other (higher) concentration units and hence is quite important for an analysis of vertical concentration.

[13] A typical comment is appended to Table 11 (use of motors, broken down by size category, in factories) of Vol. 113 of the *Statistik der Deutschen Reiches*: "The following table covers only principal factories, because for subsidiary factories the personnel and, hence, size categories are disregarded" (p. 396).

has been on a steady decline, while industrial concentration units have been moving upward toward an optimal size. Thus, in 1895 in Germany there were an average of 5.1 employed workers per horsepower of the power units in all factories employing 1 to 5 persons; for factories employing 6 to 20 persons, 31 to 100 persons, and 101 to 1,000 persons, this figure was 3.2, 2.3, and 1.3, respectively, and so on.[14] The true proportion is thus shifted in favor of the smaller units by the remaining classification.

[14] Calculated according to figures given in Table 15 of Vol. 113 of the *Statistik der Deutschen Reiches* (pp. 528–529). The relationship between labor force and output for different size categories is illustrated by the following example from the milling industry:

ANNUAL PRODUCTION OF MILL (IN 100 KG UNITS)	100 KG PER WORKING DAY
up to 3,000	8.77
3,001–6,000	10.57
6,001–12,000	11.55
12,001–18,000	11.50
18,001–30,000	10.45
30,001–60,000	11.28
60,001–90,000	11.06
90,001–120,000	12.48
120,001–150,000	15.68
150,001–180,000	13.27
180,001–240,000	13.10
240,001–300,000	15.92
300,001–450,000	16.78
450,001–600,000	19.92
600,001–750,000	26.68
750,001–900,000	26.03
900,001 and above	23.15

From *Ergebnissen über die Produktionsverhältnisse des Mühlengewerbes*, compiled by the Department of the Interior (Berlin, 1913).

23

Theoretical assumptions and nonobserved facts

Economics today rides the crest of intellectual respectability and popular acclaim. The serious attention with which our pronouncements are received by the general public, hard-bitten politicians, and even skeptical businessmen is second only to that which was given to physicists and space experts a few years ago when the round trip to the moon seemed to be our only truly national goal. The flow of learned articles, monographs, and textbooks is swelling like a tidal wave; *Econometrica*, the leading journal in the field of mathematical economics, has just stepped up its publication schedule from four to six issues per annum.

And yet an uneasy feeling about the present state of our discipline has been growing in some of us who have watched its unprecedented development over the last three decades. This concern seems to be shared even by those who are themselves contributing successfully to the present boom. They play the game with professional skill but have serious doubts about its rules.

Much of current academic teaching and research has been criticized for its lack of relevance, that is, of immediate practical impact. In a nearly instant response to this criticism, research projects, seminars, and undergraduate courses have been set up on poverty, on city and small town slums, on pure water and fresh air. In an almost Pavlovian reflex, whenever a new complaint is raised,

Presidential address delivered at the eighty-third meeting of the American Economic Association, Detroit, Michigan, December 29, 1970; published in *The American Economic Review*, Vol. 61, 1971.

President Nixon appoints a commission and the university announces a new course. Far be it from me to argue that the fire should not be shifted when the target moves. The trouble is caused, however, not by an inadequate selection of targets, but rather by our inability to hit squarely any one of them. The uneasiness of which I spoke before is caused not by the *irrelevance* of the practical problems to which present-day economists address their efforts, but rather by the palpable *inadequacy* of the scientific means with which they try to solve them.

If this simply were a sign of the overly high aspiration level of a fast developing discipline, such a discrepancy between ends and means should cause no worry. But I submit that the consistently indifferent performance in practical applications is in fact a symptom of a fundamental imbalance in the present state of our discipline. The weak and all too slowly growing empirical foundation clearly cannot support the proliferating superstructure of pure, or should I say, speculative economic theory.

Much is being made of the widespread, nearly mandatory use by modern economic theorists of mathematics. To the extent to which the economic phenomena possess observable quantitative dimensions, this is indisputably a major forward step. Unfortunately, anyone capable of learning elementary, or preferably advanced calculus and algebra, and acquiring acquaintance with the specialized terminology of economics can set himself up as a theorist. Uncritical enthusiasm for mathematical formulation tends often to conceal the ephemeral substantive content of the argument behind the formidable front of algebraic signs.

Professional journals have opened wide their pages to papers written in mathematical language; colleges train aspiring young economists to use this language; graduate schools require its knowledge and reward its use. The mathematical-model-building industry has grown into one of the most prestigious, possibly the most prestigious branch of economics. Construction of a typical theoretical model can be handled now as a routine assembly job. All principal components such as production functions, consumption and utility functions come in several standard types; so does the optional equipment as, for example, "factor augmentation"—to take care of technological change. This particular device is, incidentally, available in a simple exponential design or with a special automatic regulator known as the "Kennedy function." Any model can be modernized with the help of special attachments. One popular way to upgrade a simple one-sector model is to bring it out in a two-sector version or even in a still more impressive form of the "n-sector," that is, many-sector class.

In the presentation of a new model, attention nowadays is usually centered on a step-by-step derivation of its formal properties. But if the author—or at least the referee who recommended the manuscript for publication—is technically competent, such mathematical manipulations, however long and intricate, can even without further checking be accepted as correct. Nevertheless, they are usually spelled out at great length. By the time it comes to interpretation of the substantive *conclusions*, the assumptions on which the model has been based are easily forgotten. But it is precisely the empirical validity of these *assumptions* on which the usefulness of the entire exercise depends.

What is really needed, in most cases, is a very difficult and seldom very neat assessment and verification of these assumptions in terms of observed facts. Here mathematics cannot help, and because of this, the interest and enthusiasm of the model builder suddenly begins to flag: "If you do not like my set of assumptions, give me another and I will gladly make you another model; have your pick."

Policy-oriented models, in contrast to purely descriptive ones, are gaining favor, however nonoperational they may be. This, I submit, is in part because the choice of the final policy objectives—the selection and justification of the shape of the so-called objective function—is, and rightly so, considered based on normative judgment, not on factual analysis. Thus, the model builder can secure at least some convenient assumptions without running the risk of being asked to justify them on empirical grounds.

To sum up with the words of a recent president of the Econometric Society, " . . . the achievements of economic theory in the last two decades are both impressive and in many ways beautiful. But it cannot be denied that there is something scandalous in the spectacle of so many people refining the analysis of economic states which they give no reason to suppose will ever, or have ever, come about. . . . It is an unsatisfactory and slightly dishonest state of affairs."

But shouldn't this harsh judgment be suspended in the face of the impressive volume of econometric work? The answer is decidedly no.

This work can be in general characterized as an attempt to compensate for the glaring weakness of the data base available to us by the widest possible use of more and more sophisticated statistical techniques. Alongside the mounting pile of elaborate theoretical models we see a fast-growing stock of equally intricate statistical tools. These are intended to stretch to the limit the meager supply of facts.

Since, as I said before, the publishers' referees do a competent job, most model-testing kits described in professional journals are internally consistent. However, like the economic models they are supposed to implement, the validity of these statistical tools depends itself on the acceptance of certain convenient assumptions pertaining to stochastic properties of the phenomena which the particular models are intended to explain—assumptions that can be seldom verified.

In no other field of empirical inquiry has so massive and sophisticated a statistical machinery been used with such indifferent results. Nevertheless, theorists continue to turn out model after model and mathematical statisticians to devise complicated procedures one after another. Most of these are relegated to the stockpile without any practical application or after only a perfunctory demonstration exercise. Even those used for a while soon fall out of favor, not because the methods that supersede them perform better, but because they are new and different.

Continued preoccupation with imaginary, hypothetical, rather than with observable reality has gradually led to a distortion of the informal valuation scale used in our academic community to assess and to rank the scientific performance of its members. Empirical analysis, according to this scale, gets a lower rating than formal mathematical reasoning. Devising a new statistical procedure, however tenuous, that makes it possible to squeeze out one more unknown parameter from a given set of data, is judged a greater scientific achievement than the successful search for additional information that would permit us to measure the magnitude of the same parameter in a less ingenious, but more reliable way. This despite the fact that in all too many instances sophisticated statistical analysis is performed on a set of data whose exact meaning and validity are unknown to the author or, rather, so well known to him that at the very end he warns the reader not to take the material conclusions of the entire "exercise" seriously.

A natural Darwinian feedback operating through selection of

academic personnel contributes greatly to the perpetuation of this state of affairs. The scoring system that governs the distribution of rewards must naturally affect the makeup of the competing teams. Thus, it is not surprising that the younger economists, particularly those engaged in teaching and in academic research, seem by now quite content with a situation in which they can demonstrate their prowess (and, incidentally, advance their careers) by building more and more complicated mathematical models and devising more and more sophisticated methods of statistical inference without ever engaging in empirical research. Complaints about the lack of indispensable primary data are heard from time to time, but they don't sound very urgent. The feeling of dissatisfaction with the present state of our discipline which prompts me to speak out so bluntly seems, alas, to be shared by relatively few. Yet even those few who do share it feel they can do little to improve the situation. How could they?

In contrast to most physical sciences, we study a system that is not only exceedingly complex but is also in a state of constant flux. I have in mind not the obvious change in the variables, such as outputs, prices, or levels of employment, that our equations are supposed to explain, but the basic structural relationships described by the form and the parameters of these equations. In order to know what the shape of these structural relationships actually is at any given time, we have to keep them under continuous surveillance.

By sinking the foundations of our analytical system deeper and deeper, by reducing, for example, cost functions to production functions and the production functions to some still more basic relationships eventually capable of explaining the technological change itself, we should be able to reduce this drift. It would, nevertheless, be quite unrealistic to expect to reach, in this way, the bedrock of invariant structural relationships (measurable parameters) which, once having been observed and described, could be used year after year, decade after decade, without revisions based on repeated observation.

On the relatively shallow level where the empirically implemented economic analysis now operates even the more invariant of the structural relationships, in terms of which the system is described, change rapidly. Without a constant inflow of new data the existing stock of factual information becomes obsolete very soon. What a contrast with physics, biology, or even psychology, where the magnitude of most parameters is practically constant and where critical experiments and measurements don't have to be repeated every year!

Just to keep up our very modest current capabilities we have to maintain a steady flow of new data. A progressive expansion of these capabilities would be out of the question without a continuous and rapid rise of this flow. Moreover, the new, additional data in many instances will have to be qualitatively different from those provided hitherto.

To deepen the foundation of our analytical system it will be necessary to reach unhesitatingly beyond the limits of the domain of economic phenomena as it has been staked out up to now. The pursuit of a more fundamental understanding of the process of production inevitably leads into the area of engineering sciences. To penetrate below the skin-thin surface of conventional consumption functions, it will be necessary to develop a systematic study of the structural characteristics and of the functioning of households, an area in which description and analysis of social, anthropological, and demographic factors must obviously occupy the center of the stage.

Establishment of systematic cooperative relationships across the traditional frontiers now separating economics from these adjoining fields is hampered by the sense of self-sufficiency resulting from what I have already characterized as undue reliance on indirect statistical inference as the principal method of empirical research. As theorists, we construct systems in which prices, outputs, rates of saving and investment, etc., are explained in terms of production functions, consumption functions, and other structural relationships whose parameters are assumed, at least for argument's sake, to be known. As econometricians, engaged in what passes for empirical research, we do not try, however, to ascertain the actual shapes of these functions and to measure the magnitudes of these parameters by turning up new factual information. We make an about face and rely on indirect statistical inference to derive the unknown structural relationships from the observed magnitudes of prices, outputs, and other variables that, in our role as theoreticians, we treated as unknowns.

Formally, nothing is, of course, wrong with such an apparently circular procedure. Moreover, the model builder, in erecting his hypothetical structures, is free to take into account all possible kinds of factual knowledge and the econometrician, in principle, at least, can introduce in the estimating procedure any amount of what is usually referred to as "exogenous" information before he feeds his programmed tape into the computer. Such options are exercised rarely and, when they are, usually in a casual way.

The same well-known sets of figures are used again and again in all possible combinations to pit different theoretical models against each other in formal statistical combat. For obvious reasons a decision is reached in most cases not by a knock-out, but by a few points. The orderly and systematic nature of the entire procedure generates a feeling of comfortable self-sufficiency.

This complacent feeling, as I said before, discourages venturesome attempts to widen and to deepen the empirical foundations of economic analysis, particularly those attempts that would involve crossing the conventional lines separating ours from the adjoining fields.

True advance can be achieved only through an iterative process in which improved theoretical formulation raises new empirical questions and the answers to these questions, in their turn, lead to new theoretical insights. The "givens" of today become the "unknowns" that will have to be explained tomorrow. This, incidentally, makes untenable the admittedly convenient methodological position according to which a theorist does not need to verify directly the factual assumptions on which he chooses to base his deductive arguments, provided his empirical conclusions seem to be correct. The prevalence of such a point of view is, to a large extent, responsible for the state of splendid isolation in which our discipline nowadays finds itself.

An exceptional example of a healthy balance between theoretical and empirical analysis and of the readiness of professional economists to cooperate with experts in the neighboring disciplines is offered by agricultural economics as it developed in this country over the last fifty years. A unique combination of social and political forces has secured for this area unusually strong organizational and generous financial support. Official agricultural statistics are more complete, reliable, and systematic than those pertaining to any other major sector of our economy. Close collaboration with agronomists provides agricultural economists with direct access to information of a technological kind. When they speak of crop rotation, fertilizers, or alternative harvesting techniques, they usually know, sometimes from personal experience, what they are talking about. Preoccupation with the standard of living of the rural population has led agricultural economists into collaboration with home economists and sociologists, that is, with social scientists of the "softer" kind. While centering their interest on only one part of the economic system, agricultural economists demonstrated the effectiveness of a systematic combination of theoretical approach with detailed factual analysis. They also were the first among economists to make use of the advanced methods of mathematical statistics. However, in their hands, statistical inference became a complement to, not a substitute for, empirical research.

The shift from casual empiricism that dominates much of today's econometric work to systematic large-scale factual analysis will not be easy. To start with, it will require a sharp increase in the annual appropriation for federal statistical agencies. The quality of government statistics has, of course, been steadily improving. The coverage, however, does not keep up with the growing complexity of our social and economic system and our capability of handling larger and larger data flows.

The spectacular advances in computer technology increased the economists' potential ability to make effective analytical use of large sets of detailed data. The time is past when the best that could be done with large sets of variables was to reduce their number by averaging them out or, what is essentially the same, combining them into broad aggregates; now we can manipulate complicated analytical systems without suppressing the identity of their individual elements. There is a certain irony in the fact that, next to the fast-growing service industries, the areas whose coverage by the Census is particularly deficient are the operations of government agencies, both federal and local.

To place all or even the major responsibility for the collection of economic data in the hands of one central organization would be a mistake. The prevailing decentralized approach that permits and encourages a great number of government agencies, nonprofit institutions, and private businesses engaged in data-gathering activities acquitted itself very well. Better information means more detailed information, and detailed specialized information can be best collected by those immediately concerned with a particular field. What is urgently needed, however, is the establishment, maintenance, and enforcement of coordinated uniform classification systems by all agencies, private as well as public, involved in this work. Incompatible data are useless data. How far from a tolerable, not to say ideal, state our present economic statistics are in in this respect can be judged by the fact that, because of differences in classification, domestic output data cannot be compared, for many goods, with the corresponding export and import figures. Neither can the official employment statistics be related without laborious adjustments to output data, industry by industry. An unreasonably high proportion of material and intellectual resources devoted to statistical work is now spent not on the collection of primary information but on a frustrating and wasteful struggle with incongruous definitions and irreconcilable classifications.

Without invoking a misplaced methodological analogy, the task of securing a massive flow of primary economic data can be compared to that of providing the high-energy physicists with a gigantic accelerator. The scientists have their machines while the economists are still waiting for their data. In our case not only must the society be willing to provide year after year the millions of dollars required for maintenance of a vast statistical machine, but a large number of citizens must be prepared to play, at least, a passive and occasionally even an active part in actual fact-finding operations. It is as if the electrons and protons had to be persuaded to cooperate with the physicist.

The average American does not seem to object to being interviewed, polled, and surveyed. Curiosity, the desire to find out how the economic system (in which most of us are small gears, and some, big wheels) works might in many instances provide sufficient inducement for cooperation of this kind.

One runs up occasionally, of course, against the attitude that "what you don't know can't hurt you" and that knowledge might be dangerous: it may generate a desire to tinker with the system. The experience of these years seems, however, to have convinced not only most economists—with a few notable exceptions—but also the public at large that a lack of economic knowledge can hurt badly. Our free

280

enterprise system has rightly been compared to a gigantic computing machine capable of solving its own problems automatically. But anyone who has had some practical experience with large computers knows that they do break down and can't operate unattended. To keep the automatic, or rather the semiautomatic, engine of our economy in good working order we must not only understand the general principles on which it operates, but also be acquainted with the details of its actual design.

A new element has entered the picture in recent years—the adoption of methods of modern economic analysis by private business. Corporate support of economic research goes as far back as the early 1920s when Wesley Mitchell founded the National Bureau. However, it is not this concern for broad issues of public policies or even the general interest in economic growth and business fluctuations that I have in mind, but rather the fast-spreading use of advanced methods of operations research and of so-called systems analysis. Some of the standard concepts and analytical devices of economic theory first found their way into the curricula of our business schools and soon after that, sophisticated management began to put them into practice. While academic theorists are content with the formulation of general principles, corporate operations researchers and practical systems analysts have to answer questions pertaining to specific real situations. Demand for economic data to be used in practical business planning is growing at an accelerated pace. It is a high-quality demand: business users in most instances possess first-hand technical knowledge of the area to which the data they ask for refer. Moreover, this demand is usually "effective." Profit-making business is willing and able to pay the costs of gathering the information it wants to have. This raises the thorny question of public access to privately collected data and of the proper division of labor and cooperation between government and business in that fast-expanding field. Under the inexorable pressure of rising practical demand, these problems will be solved in one way or another. Our economy will be surveyed and mapped in all its many dimensions on a larger and larger scale.

Economists should be prepared to take a leading role in shaping this major social enterprise not as someone else's spokesmen and advisers, but on their own behalf. They have failed to do this up to now. The Conference of Federal Statistics Users organized several years ago had business, labor, and many other groups represented among its members, but not economists as such. How can we expect our needs to be satisfied if our voices are not heard?

We, I mean the academic economists, are ready to expound, to anyone ready to lend an ear, our views on problems of public policy: give advice on the best ways to maintain full employment, to fight inflation, to foster economic growth. We should be equally prepared to share with the wider public the hopes and disappointments which accompany the advance of our own often desperately difficult, but always exciting intellectual enterprise. This public has amply demonstrated its readiness to back the pursuit of knowledge. It will lend its generous support to our venture too, if we take the trouble to explain what it is all about.

Reference

F. H. Hahn, "Some Adjustment Problems," *Econometrica*, Jan. 1970, *38*, 1–2.

24

An alternative to aggregation in input-output analysis and national accounts

I

The schematic uniformity of standard input-output computations accounts for certain practical advantages of that approach as well as for some of its peculiar limitations. One of the principal advantages of such uniformity is the opportunity it offers for using the matrix of technical coefficients, A, as a central storage bin for the basic factual information used again and again in various computations.

A comparison of the structural properties of two economies—or of the structural characteristics of the same economy at two different points of time—is reduced in this context to a comparison of two A matrices. The only (and admittedly very serious) difficulty arising in any attempt to ascertain the differences and similarities between the magnitudes of individual technical coefficients—or of the whole rows, or entire columns of such coefficients—in two matrices is often caused by the incomparability of the sectoral breakdown in terms of which the two tables were originally compiled.

These differences might turn out to be of a merely terminological or classificatory kind. This means that, in principle, at least, with full access to all the basic facts and figures, new matrices could be constructed that would describe the two essentially comparable

From *The Review of Economics and Statistics*, Vol. 49, No. 3, August 1967.
I want to express my thanks to the staff of the Harvard Economic Research Project and particularly to Mrs. Brookes Byrd for the indispensable assistance in the preparation of the material presented in this paper. Frankly, the responsibility for the minor errors that might have crept into it rests with them.

economic structures in appropriately comparable terms.

The lack of perfect correspondence between the sectoral headings of two input-output tables might, however, frequently reflect the presence in one of the two economies of some goods or services that are neither produced nor consumed in the other. In this instance, reclassification will not help. In the extreme, albeit most unlikely, case in which the two economies have no goods or services in common, the very thought of structural comparison would have to be given up.

More often, when all the justifiable preliminary realignments of the original classifications have been made, the two matrices will turn out to have some reasonably comparable sectors, while some of the other sectors contained in one of them will have no matching counterparts in the other. Even when such incomparability is known to be due only to differences in the commodity and industry classifications used, the figures entered in those rows and columns must be treated as describing structures of incomparable kinds.

In current statistical practice, the solution of the difficulties described above is sought in aggregation. The difference between copper and nickel vanishes as soon as both are treated as "nonferrous metals" and both become indistinguishable from steel as soon as the qualifying specification "nonferrous" has been dropped too. The fact that comparability through aggregation is secured at the cost of analytical sharpness in the description of the underlying structural relationships is too well known to require explanation.

The method of double inversion described below permits us to reduce to a common denominator two input-output matrices that contain some comparable and also some incomparable sectors. In contrast to conventional aggregation, such analytical reduction is achieved without distortion of any of the basic structural relationships. The comparability of input-output tables attained through double inversion is limited in the sense that their respective structures are described only in terms of input-output relationships between goods and services of directly comparable kinds. It is, nevertheless, an overall comparability to the extent that all the structural characteristics of each of the two systems, including the magnitudes of the technical coefficients located in the "incomparable" rows and columns, are taken into account fully without omission or distortion.

II

To facilitate the intuitive understanding of the transformation that leads to the construction of what might be called a reduced input-output matrix of a national economy, we will ask the reader to visualize a situation in which—for trading purposes—all industries of a country have been divided into two groups. The industries belonging to group I are identified as the "contracting," those in group II as the "subcontracting," industries.

Each contracting, i.e., group I industry covers its direct input requirements for the products of other group I industries by direct purchases, and each group II industry makes direct purchases from other group II industries. However, the products of group II industries delivered to group I industries are manufactured on the basis of special work contracts. Under such a contract, the group I industry placing an order with a group II industry provides the latter with the products of all group I industries (including its own), in amounts required to fill that particular order. To be able to do so, it purchases all these goods—from the group I industries that make them—on its own account. The relationship between a contracting (group I) and a subcontracting (group II) industry is thus analogous to the relationship between a customer who buys the cloth himself and the tailor who makes it up for him into a suit.

In determining the amounts of goods and services that he will have to purchase from his own and all the other group I industries, the procurement officer of each group I industry will have to add to the immediate input requirements of his own sector the amounts to be processed for it—under contract—by various group II industries. For all practical purposes, such augmented shopping lists now constitute the effective input vectors of all the group I industries.

The square array of n_1 such column vectors—each containing n_1 elements (some of which may of course be zero)—represents the reduced table of input coefficients that we seek. It describes the same system as the original table; however, it describes it only in terms of goods and services produced by the selected contracting industries included in group I.

The relationship between the two tables is similar to the relationship of an abbreviated timetable that lists only selected large stations to the complete detailed timetable that also shows all the intermediate stops. The subdivision of all the sectors of an economy into groups I and II must, of course, depend on the specific purpose that the consolidated system is intended to serve.

Using a reduced table for planning purposes, we can be sure that if the input-output flows among the group I industries shown in it are properly balanced, the balance between the outputs and inputs of all the group II industries omitted from it will be secured, too.

In the process of consolidation, the allocation of so-called primary inputs will change, as well. The new labor and capital coefficients of each group I industry must now reflect not only its own immediate labor and capital requirements, but also the labor and capital requirements of all the group II industries from which it draws some of its supplies. It is as if, under the imaginary contractual arrangements described above, each group I industry had to provide the group II industries working for it, not only with the goods and services produced by any of the group I sectors, but also with all the capital and labor required by these group II industries to fulfill these contracts. Thus, the output levels of all the group I industries, as projected on the basis of a reduced input-output table (multiplied with the appropriate consolidated capital and labor coefficients), will account not only for the capital and labor requirements of these group I industries, but also for those of all the group II industries without whose support these output levels could not have been attained.

III

Not unlike conventional aggregation, the analytical procedure described below is aimed at a reduction of the number of sectors in terms of which the particular economic structure was originally described. It is, however, a "clean"—not an index number—operation. It does not involve introduction of weights or any other arbitrary constants.

Equation (1) describes—in conventional matrix notation—the relationships between the total output vector, X, of all the sectors of a particular economy, and the corresponding final bill of goods, Y.

$$(1) \qquad\qquad (I - A)\, X = Y.$$

In equation (2), both vectors are split into two parts: the column vectors X_1 and Y_1 represent the total outputs and the final deliveries of group I industries that produce the n_1 goods that will be retained in the reduced matrix, while X_2 and Y_2 represent the outputs and the final deliveries of all the other, i.e., the n_2, goods produced by the group II industries that have to be eliminated.

$$(2) \qquad \left[\begin{array}{c|c} (I - A_{11}) & -A_{12} \\ \hline -A_{21} & (I - A_{22}) \end{array} \right] \left[\frac{X_1}{X_2} \right] = \left[\frac{Y_1}{Y_2} \right].$$

The matrix $(I - A)$ on the left-hand side is partitioned, in conformity with the output vector into which it is multiplied. A_{11} and A_{22} are square matrices whose elements are technical coefficients that govern the internal flows between the sectors of the first and of the second groups, respectively, while A_{12} and A_{21} are rectangular (not necessarily square) matrices describing the direct requirements of industries of the second group for outputs of the first group and vice versa.

Equation (3) is the solution of (2) for X in terms of Y.

$$(3) \qquad \left[\frac{X_1}{X_2} \right] = \left[\begin{array}{c|c} B_{11} & B_{12} \\ \hline B_{21} & B_{22} \end{array} \right] \left[\frac{Y_1}{Y_2} \right].$$

Matrix B is the *inverse* of $(I - A)$. It is partitioned in conformity with the partitioning of $(I - A)$ in equation (2). After the multiplication has been carried out on its right-hand side, equation (3) can be split in two:

$$(4) \qquad X_1 = B_{11}Y_1 + B_{12}Y_2$$

$$(5) \qquad X_2 = B_{21}Y_1 + B_{22}Y_2.$$

Premultiplying both sides of (4) by B_{11}^{-1}, we have:

$$(6) \qquad B_{11}^{-1}X_1 = Y_1 + B_{11}^{-1}B_{12}Y_2.$$

This equation can be interpreted as a reduced version of the original system (2). It describes the same structural relationships; however, it represents them only in terms of the goods and services produced by the n_1 industries assigned to group I. The variables contained in vector X_2—that is, the outputs of the n_2 industries assigned to group II—have been eliminated by means of two successive matrix inversions that led from (2) to (6).

Let a new structural matrix and a new final demand vector be defined by:

(7) $$A_{11}{}^* = I - B_{11}{}^{-1}$$

(8) $$Y_1{}^* = Y_1 + B_{11}{}^{-1}B_{12}Y_2.$$

In this notation (6) can be rewritten as:

(9) $$(I - A_{11}{}^*)X_1 = Y_1{}^*.$$

In perfect analogy with the original system (1) this equation describes the input-output relationships between the redefined vector of final deliveries, $Y_1{}^*$, and the corresponding vector of total outputs X_1.[1] Solved for X_1 in terms of $Y_1{}^*$, it yields:

(10) $$X_1 = (I - A_{11}{}^*)^{-1}Y_1{}^*.$$

This equation is, of course, formally equivalent to (4). $A_{11}{}^*$ is the structural matrix of the economy that was originally described by A. However, the same structure is now described in terms of the n_1 group I industries alone. The first column of $A_{11}{}^*$ consists, for example, of n_1 technical coefficients, $a_{11}{}^*$, $a_{21}{}^*$, . . . , $a_{n1}{}^*$, showing the number of units of each of these n_1 industries of group I required per unit of the total output, x_1, of the first. Although not referring to them explicitly, implicitly these coefficients reflect the input requirements also of the other n_2 industries eliminated in the reduction process.

Let, for example, industry 1 produce "steel" and industry 2, "electric energy," both assigned to group I. In the reduced matrix $A_{11}{}^*$, the coefficient $a_{21}{}^*$ thus represents the number of kilowatt-hours (or a dollar's worth) of electricity required to produce a ton (or a dollar's worth) of steel. This requirement is computed to cover not only the direct deliveries of electricity from generating stations to steel plants, but also the indirect deliveries channeled through industries assigned to group II. If "iron mining" were, for instance, considered as belonging to group II, the electricity used in extraction and preparation of the iron ore that went into the production of one ton (or a dollar's worth) of steel would also be included in the input coefficient $a_{21}{}^*$, and so would electric power absorbed by the steel industry via all other sectors assigned to group II.

[1] The symbol $X_1{}^*$ is not used because the reduced system has been derived in such a way that $X_1 \equiv X_1{}^*$.

288

In other words, the array of the input coefficients (with asterisks) that make up the first column of matrix $A_{11}*$ describes the combination of the products of industries included in group I with which the economy in question would be capable of turning out a ton (or a dollar's worth) of steel. Some of these inputs reach the steel industry indirectly through industries assigned to group II.

The reduced structural matrix $A_{11}*$ describes explicitly only the input structure of the group I industries and this only in terms of their own products. Implicitly, it reflects, nevertheless, the technological characteristics of all the other industries as well. The relationship between elements of the reduced and the original matrix is displayed clearly if $A_{11}*$ is expressed directly in terms of the elements of the partitioned matrix A:[2]

(11) $$A_{11}* = A_{11} + A_{12}(I - A_{22})^{-1}A_{21}.$$

The well-known sufficient conditions for the ability of the given input-output system to maintain—without drawing on outside help—a positive level of final consumption, i.e., to possess a positive inverse $(I - A)^{-1}$, requires that none of the column (or row) totals of the technical coefficients in A_{11} exceed one, and at least one of these sum totals be less than one. This implies that the inverse $(I - A)^{-1}$ is nonnegative. All the components of the second term on the right-hand side of (11) being either zero or positive, each element $a_{ij}*$ of the consolidated structural matrix has to be either equal to, or larger than, the corresponding originally given input coefficient, a_{ij}.

The final deliveries on the right-hand side of the reduced system (6) are composed of two parts. Vector Y_1 is the demand for the products of the group I industries as it appears in the original system (2). Vector $B_{11}^{-1} B_{12}Y_2$ $(\equiv A_{12}(I - A_{22})^{-1}Y_2)$ represents the final demand for the products of the second group of goods translated into the requirements for inputs of goods belonging to the first. In the special case in

---

[2] Since $B = (I - A)^{-1}$,
$$B(I - A) = I.$$
In particular:
$$B_{11}(I - A_{11}) - B_{12} A_{21} = I$$
$$-B_{11} A_{12} + B_{12}(I - A_{22}) = 0.$$
Eliminating B_{12} and rearranging yields:
$$A_{11}* = I - B_{11}^{-1} = A_{11} + A_{12}(I - A_{22})^{-1}A_{21}.$$

which the final users happen to demand directly only commodities and services of group I, while group II consists exclusively of intermediate goods, Y_2 vanishes and, save for the omission of its zero components, the final deliveries vector of the original system would enter without any change into the smaller, reduced system, too.

IV

A primary input, such as labor, a natural resource, or—in a static system—a stock of some kind of capital goods, can be treated in the process of reduction as if it were a product of a separate industry included in group I.

The row assigned to each primary factor in the original matrix A will contain the appropriate technical input coefficients: labor coefficients, capital coefficients, and so on. The columns corresponding to these rows will consist of zeros, since, in contrast to other goods and services, the output of a primary factor is not considered to be formally dependent on inputs originating in other industries.[3]

The labor, capital, and other primary factor coefficients appearing in the appropriate rows of matrix A^* will never be smaller—and in most instances they will be larger—than the corresponding elements of the original matrix A. As all the other input coefficients in the reduced system, they cover not only the immediate requirements of each group I industry, but also the labor and capital employed by group II industries (eliminated in the process of analytical reduction) from which that industry receives all its group II supplies.

V

Any static input-output system implies the existence of linear relationships between the prices of all products and the "value added" in all the sectors per unit of their respective outputs.[4] While a reduction of a structural matrix eliminates some of the prices from the picture, it

[3] The matrix $(I - A)$ is nevertheless not singular: its main diagonal contains positive elements throughout.
[4] The "value added" in any industry can, in its turn, be described as a sum of the input coefficients of all factors multiplied by their respective prices augmented by the amount of positive or negative net surplus earned per unit of its output.

leaves the relationship between the remaining prices and the values added essentially intact.

Let P be the price vector of the original system and V the vector of values added per unit of output in its n different sectors. The basic relationships between the two vectors,

(12) $$(I - A') P = V$$

can be solved for the unknown prices in terms of given values added:

(13) $$\begin{bmatrix} P_1 \\ P_2 \end{bmatrix} = \begin{bmatrix} B_{11}' & -B_{21}' \\ B_{12}' & -B_{22}' \end{bmatrix} \begin{bmatrix} V_1 \\ V_2 \end{bmatrix}.$$

The "primes" above the B's indicate transposition, i.e., permutation of rows and columns. The partitioning of the two vectors and of the structural matrix corresponds to a similar partitioning in (3) above. Solving for P_1 we have:

(14) $$P_1 = B_{11}'V_1^*, \text{ where}$$

(15) $$V_1^* = V_1 + (B_{11}')^{-1}B_{21}'V_2.$$

The last equation shows that, analogous to the reduced final bill of goods, Y_1^*, in (8), V_1^* represents the augmented values added vector of the group I industries. Each element of that augmented vector contains not only the value added—shown for each one of them in the original table—but also the value added in group II industries imputed through all the goods and services which the particular group I sector receives from them. In view of (7), (14) can be rewritten as:

(16) $$P_1 = (I - A^{*'})^{-1}V_1^*.$$

Inserting on the right-hand side the augmented values added in group I industries, we obtain on the left-hand side a set of prices identical with those that would have been derived from group I outputs from the original (unreduced) set of price equations (13–15).

VI

A recently completed study of metalworking industries called for analysis of interdependence among the several branches of production belonging to this group, and for an assessment of its position within the United States national economy as a whole. Of the 73 producing sectors in the 1958 input-output table,[5] 23 are making or transforming metals; 5 of them supply intermediate ferrous or non-ferrous products, while the other 18 are engaged in the manufacture of basic materials and finished metal goods.

The immediate technical interdependence among the 23 metal-working sectors is reflected in the magnitude of the input coefficients located on the intersections of the 23 rows and the corresponding 23 columns in the large 73-sector table mentioned above.

The production of the nonmetal inputs absorbed by metalworking industries often requires the use of various metal products in its turn. The dependence of each metalworking sector upon all the others (taking into account such indirect requirements) is described by the augmented input coefficients entered in the 23 rows and columns of the reduced matrix that was obtained through analytical elimination of all the 50 nonmetalworking sectors from the original table. The full interdependence between the 18 metalworking industries engaged in the manufacture of raw and finished metal products can be brought out through further reduction that eliminates from the large table also the five intermediate metalworking industries.

A row of labor coefficients, and another of (total) capital coefficients, was added at the outset to the original 73-sector matrix. After reduction, appropriately augmented labor and capital coefficients appeared in the last two rows of both reduced matrices as well.

In Table 1, the technical coefficients describing the inputs of various metal products required by the "motor vehicles and equipment" industry, as they appear in the original 73-sector matrix, are shown in column (1). The second column contains the corresponding augmented coefficients, as they appear in the reduced matrix composed of the 23 metalworking sectors. The third column shows the 18 still more augmented coefficients as they appear in the motor vehicles and equipment column of a reduced matrix, from which the five basic metalworking industries were eliminated too. Appropriate labor and capital coefficients are entered at the bottom of all three columns.

[5] U.S. Department of Commerce, *Survey of Current Business*, 44, No. 11 (Nov. 1964); and Anne P. Carter, "Changes in the Structure of the American Economy, 1947 to 1958 and 1962," *Review of Economics and Statistics*, XLIX (May 1967).

Table ? Input coefficients describing the requirements of the motor vehicle and equipment ? for products from other United States metalworking industries[a] in 1958

SECTOR NUMBER THE 73-SECTOR MATRIX	INDUSTRY	INPUT COEFFICIENTS IN THE		
		ORIGINAL 73-SECTOR MATRIX[b]	REDUCED 23-SECTOR MATRIX[c]	REDUCED 18-SECTOR MATRIX
59	Motor vehicles and equipment	0.29757	0.29817	0.29991
37	Primary iron and steel manufacturing	0.08780	0.08874	0.10714
42	Other fabricated metal products	0.03603	0.03713	
41	Screw machine products, bolts, nuts, etc., metal stamping	0.03103	0.03137	
47	General industrial and metalworking machinery, and equipment	0.02364	0.02456	
58	Miscellaneous electrical machinery equipment and supplies	0.01543	0.01557	0.01564
38	Primary nonferrous metals manufacturing	0.01144	0.01205	0.01871
56	Radio, television, and communication equipment	0.00523	0.00557	0.00576
62	Professional, scientific, and control instruments and supplies	0.00438	0.00460	0.00498
55	Electric lighting and wiring equipment	0.00420	0.00441	0.00475
43	Engines and turbines	0.00379	0.00402	0.00437
53	Electrical industrial equipment	0.00217	0.00236	
52	Service industrial machinery, household appliances	0.00129	0.00157	0.00208
44	Farm machinery and equipment	0.00105	0.00129	0.00144
40	Heating, plumbing, and structural metal products	0.00102	0.00147	
64	Miscellaneous manufacturing	0.00092	0.00201	0.00245
61	Transportation equipment, miscellaneous	0.00089	0.00123	0.00143
57	Electronic components and accessories	0.00079	0.00090	0.00111
45	Construction, mining, oil field machinery and equipment	0.00044	0.00062	0.00094
60	Aircraft and parts	0.00039	0.00086	0.00123
46	Materials handling machinery and equipment	0.00022	0.00027	0.00046
63	Optical, ophthalmic, photographic equipment	0.00005	0.00045	0.00053
51	Office, computing and accounting machines	0.00000	0.00069	0.00079
	Labor	0.02645	0.04729	0.05614
	Capital stock	0.24313	0.47495	0.55890

[a] Units of measurement: for labor coefficients, man-years per $1,000 of output; for all other coefficients, 1958 dollars per dollar of output.
[b] This matrix is based on the 1958 input-output table published by the Office of Business Economics, Department of Commerce. See Anne Carter, "Changes in the Structure of the American Economy, 1947–1958, 1962," *Review of Economics and Statistics*, XLIX (May 1967). The labor coefficients are based on Jack Alterman, "Interindustry Employment Requirements," *Monthly Labor Review*, 88, No. 7 (July 1965). The capital coefficients for manufacturing sectors were obtained from Waddell, Ritz, Norton, De Witt, and Marshall K. Wood, "Capital Expansion Planning Factors, Manufacturing Industries, *National Planning Association* (Washington, D.C., April 1966). For nonmanufacturing sectors, the capital coefficients were compiled at the Harvard Economic Research Project.
[c] The sectors eliminated through the reduction procedure are those included in the 73-sector input-output table, but not represented in this column of augmented coefficients.

VII

Table 2 is an example of a reduced national input-output table. This complete, but compact, flow chart was derived from the official 1958 United States table[6] in two successive steps.

First, 34 of the 83 productive sectors of the original table were combined into eight groups. The resulting smaller 57-sector table contained these eight aggregated industries, the 49 sectors carried over from the original 83-order table, a corresponding column of final demand and a value added row.

This 57-sector table was reduced, in a second step, through elimination of all the 49 nonaggregated industries, to a compact 8-sector table. It should be noted that the figures shown in Table 2 are total flows, not input coefficients. They were obtained through multiplication of all elements of each column of the corresponding reduced coefficient matrix by the given total output figure of the industry, the input structure of which that particular column describes.

Table 2 thus depicts the structure of the American economy in terms of flows of commodities and services among eight industrial sectors, a value added row, and a column of final demand, both reduced in conformity with the rest of the table (see equation 8). Wages and salaries paid out by various sectors are, of course, included in the value added row. In addition, a separate row of labor inputs, measured in man-years, was carried along through all computations. This row is reproduced separately at the bottom of the table.

In each cell of the table, below the number describing the appropriately augmented intersectoral transaction is entered, enclosed in parentheses, another figure. This number represents the magnitude of the input—from the sector named on the left to the sector identified at the head of the column—as it appeared in the unreduced 57-sector table obtained at the end of the first step, i.e., before the 49 unaggregated sectors were eliminated from the table in the second step.

In the final demand column, the larger entries represent the augmented deliveries to households, government, and other final users, while the entries in parentheses show the corresponding figures, as

[6] U.S. Department of Commerce, *Survey of Current Business*, 45, No. 9 (Sept. 1965).

Table 2 —Input-output table of the United States economy for the year 1958 reduced to 8 from 57 producing sectors[a]

COLUMN ROW	INDUSTRY	FOOD AND DRUGS (1)	HOUSE-WARES (2)	MACHINERY (3)	TRANS. EQUIP. & CONSUM. APPL. (4)	CONSTRUC-TION (5)	METALS (6)	ENERGY (7)	CHEMICALS (8)	FINAL DEMAND	GROSS DOMESTIC OUTPUT
1	Food and Drugs	15,202 (12,468)	547 (96)	161 (11)	353 (49)	513 (17)	165 (53)	218 (62)	386 (288)	58,728 (55,320)	76,272
2	Textiles, clothing and furnishings	347 (155)	12,815 (12,692)	92 (37)	821 (636)	761 (524)	171 (47)	63 (8)	61 (38)	21,369 (20,033)	36,500
3	Machinery	430 (28)	215 (105)	2,321 (2,186)	2,061 (1,644)	1,397 (748)	819 (545)	406 (141)	200 (150)	13,385 (11,293)	21,233
4	Transportation equipment and consumer appliances	363 (29)	158 (55)	816 (691)	11,791 (11,196)	1,372 (753)	485 (101)	183 (29)	53 (5)	38,691 (32,670)	53,912
5	Construction	1,158 (235)	218 (18)	115 (26)	308 (109)	48 (8)	284 (131)	1,541 (579)	70 (6)	65,117 (56,836)	69,291
6	Metals	1,033 (46)	475 (277)	3,073 (2,631)	6,038 (4,618)	6,468 (3,650)	7,959 (7,335)	388 (110)	479 (389)	2,244 (−45)	28,158
7	Energy	2,158 (783)	652 (293)	371 (226)	805 (404)	2,774 (1,536)	1,704 (1,391)	6,888 (6,236)	1,127 (1,007)	23,851 (17,702)	40,330
8	Chemicals	1,956 (1,056)	1,030 (218)	201 (117)	475 (115)	1,218 (437)	459 (283)	713 (576)	2,500 (2,351)	3,218 (1,510)	11,770
	Value added	53,625 (22,252)	20,390 (12,844)	14,083 (10,254)	31,260 (20,677)	54,308 (28,937)	16,112 (10,509)	29,930 (15,127)	6,894 (4,674)	178,912	405,515
TOTAL		76,272	36,500	21,233	53,912	69,291	28,158	40,330	11,770	405,515	
	Labor	8,182 (2,202)	3,929 (2,808)	1,820 (1,307)	3,891 (2,467)	8,581 (4,847)	1,867 (1,155)	1,775 (1,003)	671 (403)	26,430	57,146

[a] Derived from the 83-sector table published in "Transaction Table of the 1958 Input-Output Study and Revised Direct Requirements Data," *Survey of Current Business,* 45, No. 9 (Sept. 1965). Each of the 8 sectors of the intermediate 57-sector table retained in this reduced table represents an aggregate of the following industries identified by the numbers they carry in the original 83-sector table:
(1) Food and drugs: 14,15,29; (2) textiles, clothing, furnishings: 16, 17, 18, 19, 34, 22, 23; (3) machinery (only final): 51, 44, 45, 46, 47, 48, 49, 50, 63; (4) transportation equipment and consumer appliances: 52, 54, 56, 59, 60, 61, 62; (5) construction: 11, 12; (6) metals: 37, 38; (7) energy: 31, 68; (8) chemicals: 27.
Corresponding entries in the unreduced 57-sector table appear in parentheses. The units are man-years in the labor row and millions of dollars in all other rows.

295

they appeared in the 57-sector table. The first entry exceeds, in each instance, the figure in parentheses below by the amount of the particular type of goods that was absorbed in the production of those final deliveries which were eliminated from the original table. Value added in general—and labor inputs in particular—that were absorbed in this way appear now in the final demand.

VIII

The idea that, in the description of an economic system, some processes and outputs can be reduced, that is, expressed in terms of others, goes quite far back into the history of economic thought. Adam Smith discussed at length the question of whether corn should be measured in labor units required to grow it, or, on the contrary, labor measured in terms of corn that a worker needs to live. Quesnay insisted that various branches of manufacturing should be represented in his tableau only by the amounts of rough materials that they transformed into finished products.

The notion of unproductive—as contrasted with productive—labor, whose product does not deserve to be included in the grand total of national product, was still propounded by Stuart Mill. The Marxian doctrine caused the Soviet official statistician, up until recently, to exclude transportation of persons and products of many service industries from national accounts, and, in the West, the output of governmental and other public services is still often treated in the same way.

In the latter case, the elimination of the output—as contrasted with the input—of the public sector from national accounts is justified, not so much by the distinction between productive and unproductive activities, but rather by the difficulty of measuring the output of "public administration," of "education," or of "national defense."

The number of goods and services that more and more detailed observation of various processes of production and consumption would permit us to distinguish is much greater than even an input-output matrix containing many thousands of rows and columns can possibly hold. For many purposes, that number might also be larger than we would need to carry from the first stage of the analytical procedure to the last. Aggregation, i.e., summation of essentially heterogeneous quantities, is one of the two devices that the economist uses to limit the number of variables and functional relationships in terms of which he describes what he observes. The other is reduction, that is, elimination of certain goods and processes. In this paper, a systematic procedure has been presented that permits us to reduce the size of an input-output table through analytical elimination of any of its rows and columns. A less systematic, intuitive elimination of a much larger number of variables—considered to be secondary or intermediate—occurs, however, already during the collection of the primary statistical information. Thus, even a most detailed input-output table, as well as the national accounts constructed around it, can be said to present the actual economic system, not only in an aggregated, but also in a reduced form.

25

The dynamic inverse

I

The purpose of this paper is to introduce the notion of the dynamic inverse that could play a role in the empirical study of economic change analogous to the role played in static input-output analysis by the inverse of the flow coefficient matrix.

First I shall describe the open dynamic input-output system in terms of a simple set of linear equations. Next, I shall present a general solution of that system, that is, the inverse of its structural matrix. Each element of this inverse represents the combined direct and indirect inputs required from the row industry to permit an additional output of $1 million by the column industry. While in a static inverse such effects can be described by a single number, within the framework of dynamic analysis they have to be presented in a time series: as soon as capacity expansion and the corresponding investment processes are introduced explicitly into the system, the inputs contributing directly or indirectly to the delivery of a certain final output in a given year must be dated too. These come out of the computer as a sequence of numbers stretched back in time. The last sections of this paper are devoted to a brief discussion of the corresponding dynamic price system.[1]

From A. P. Carter and A. Brody (eds.), *Contributions to Input-Output Analysis* (Amsterdam: North-Holland Publishing Company, 1970), pp. 17–46.

In preparation of this paper the author was assisted by Brookes Byrd, Richard Berner, and Peter Petri.
[1] Basic concepts, the industry classification system, and the sources of data used in the study are presented in appendices II, III, and IV.

II

Let the column vector x represent the n sectoral outputs, $_tX_1$, $_tx_2$, $\ldots$, $_tx_n$, produced in year t, and c the corresponding column vector, $_tc_1$, $_tc_2$, $\ldots$, $_tc_n$, of deliveries to final demand. This final demand does *not* include the annual additions to the stock of fixed and working capital (inventories) used by the n productive sectors mentioned above. The structural characteristics of the economy are described by A_t, the square $(n \times n)$ matrix of technical flow coefficients that specifies the direct current input requirements of all industries, and B_t, the corresponding square matrix of capital coefficients. Capital goods produced in year t are assumed to be installed and put into operation in the next year, $t + 1$.

The direct interdependence between the outputs of all the sectors of a given national economy in two successive years can be described by the following familiar balance equation:

$$(1) \qquad x_t - A_t x_t - B_{t+1}(x_{t+1} - x_t) = c_t.$$

The second term on the left-hand side represents the current input requirements of all n industries in year t; the third, the investment requirements, i.e., additions to productive stock that would permit all industries to expand their capacity outputs from the year t to the next year, $t + 1$, from x_t to x_{t+1}. The time subscripts attached to both structural matrices provide the possibility of using different sets of flow and capital coefficients for different years, thus incorporating technological change into the dynamic system. It should be noted that the time subscript attached to matrix B_{t+1} identifies not the year in which the particular capital goods are produced, but rather the year in which they are first put to use. Equation (1) can be rewritten as:

$$(2) \qquad G_t x_t - B_{t+1} x_{t+1} = c_t$$

where $G_t = (1 - A_t + B_{t+1})$. A set of interlocked balance equations of this type describing the development of the given economy over a period of $m + 1$ years can be combined to form a system of $m + 1$ linear equations:

$$
(3) \quad
\begin{bmatrix}
G_{-m} & -B_{-m+1} & & & & \\
 & G_{-m+1} & -B_{-m+2} & & & \\
 & & \ddots & \ddots & & \\
 & & & G_{-2} & -B_{-1} & \\
 & & & & G_{-1} & -B_0 \\
 & & & & & G_0
\end{bmatrix}
\begin{bmatrix}
x_{-m} \\ x_{-m+1} \\ \vdots \\ x_{-2} \\ x_{-1} \\ x_0
\end{bmatrix}
=
\begin{bmatrix}
c_{-m} \\ c_{-m+1} \\ \vdots \\ c_{-2} \\ c_{-1} \\ c_0
\end{bmatrix}
$$

III

The solution of this system determines the sequence of annual total sectoral outputs that would enable the economy to yield the sequence of final annual deliveries described by the array of column vectors entered on the right-hand side. Starting with the last equation, substituting its solution into the equation next to the last and thus proceeding stepwise to the first, we arrive at the following solution of system (3) for the unknown x's in terms of a given set of the c's.

$$
(4) \quad
\begin{bmatrix}
x_{-m} \\ \vdots \\ x_{-2} \\ x_{-1} \\ x_0
\end{bmatrix}
=
\begin{bmatrix}
G_{-m}^{-1}\ldots R_{-m}\ldots R_{-3}R_{-2}G_{-1}^{-1} & R_{-m}\ldots R_{-3}R_{-2}R_{-1}G_0^{-1} \\
\vdots & \vdots \\
R_{-2}G_{-1}^{-1} & R_{-2}R_{-1}G_0^{-1} \\
G_{-1}^{-1} & R_{-1}G_0^{-1} \\
 & G_0^{-1}
\end{bmatrix}
\begin{bmatrix}
c_{-m} \\ \vdots \\ c_{-2} \\ c_{-1} \\ c_0
\end{bmatrix}
$$

where $R_t = G_t^{-1}B_{t+1} = (1 - A_t + B_{t+1})^{-1}B_{t+1}$.

The square matrix on the right-hand side of equation (4) is the inverse of the structural matrix that appears on the left-hand side of equation (3). Every element of this inverse is itself a square matrix.

The wedge-shaped column on the right describes the direct and indirect input requirements generated by the delivery to final demand of one unit (or one million dollars' worth) of the products of any one of the n industries in the year 0. These requirements are distributed backward over time. Matrix G_0^{-1} shows the input requirements that must be filled in year 0, i.e., the same year in which the final deliveries are made; as in a static inverse each column of G_0^{-1} identifies the industry making the delivery to final demand, each row, the industry supplying the specific input. The preceding term, $R_{-1}G_0^{-1}$, specifies the requirements that have to be filled in the preceding year -1, $R_{-2}R_{-1}G_0^{-1}$ specifies those to be filled in the year -2, and so on.

300

The longest term, $R_{-m} \ldots R_{-2}R_{-1}G_0^{-1}$, describes the increments in the outputs of all industries in the year $-m$, i.e., the inputs that have to be provided m years before an additional batch of goods can be delivered to final users. Each term of equation (4) located above the diagonal can be computed by multiplying the term located below it by an appropriate transformation matrix, R_{-t}.

IV

In the absence of any technical change the time subscript can be eliminated from all the structural constants. The elements of each column can in this case be described in receding order by the same simple geometric series,

$$(5) \qquad G^{-1}, RG^{-1}, R^2G^{-1}, \ldots, R^tG^{-1}, \ldots, R^mG^{-1}.$$

It is well known that as the exponent, t, becomes sufficiently large, the ratio between the magnitude of all the similarly located elements of R^t and R^{t+1} asymptotically approaches the same constant, equal to the real part of the dominant characteristic root of R. If μ is the dominant root, then $R^{t+1} \rightarrow \mathbf{R}(\mu)\, R^t$ as $t \rightarrow \infty$, where $\mathbf{R}(\mu)$ denotes the real part of the root μ. If μ is real, positive, and less than 1, the increments to outputs required to deliver any given combination of additional goods to final demand in the final year 0—traced back a sufficiently large number of years—will become smaller and smaller, and will finally become infinitely small.[2]

Thus, for all practical purposes, the chains of inputs stretching backwards from the year in which the delivery to final users is actually made, can, in case of such convergence, be treated as if they were of finite length. The same will be true even if the technical structure of the economy changes from year to year, i.e., when the R matrices retain their time subscripts. The series of required inputs converges backward in this case too, although not necessarily as smoothly as it does without technological change.

The distribution of such required inputs over time, however, varies greatly among industries. Some of the input series even dip below the

---

[2] A mathematical analysis of the convergence properties of the dynamic inverse is presented in appendix I.

zero line at their forward ends. This is the well-known effect of the so-called acceleration principle. As soon as the additional goods demanded directly or indirectly by the final users have been produced, the stocks of capital goods employed in making them will be released. The balance equation (1) is set up in such a way as to indicate negative investment, that is disinvestment, in case $x_{t+1} < x_t$. In fact such potentially idle capacity will usually be absorbed by the direct or indirect input requirements generated by increases in final deliveries scheduled for the next and subsequent years. As will be shown below these must be entered into dynamic input-output accounting in the form of separate but overlapping chains. So long as, in a given year, the sum total of positive incremental output requirements exceeds the sum total of the negative, the output of that sector will increase.

One of the analytically and operationally most useful properties of open input-output systems is the linear additivity of their solutions with respect to any changes in final demand. Each element of the final bill of goods generates a separate chain of direct and indirect input requirements. The total requirements generated by any given vector of final demand are thus represented by the sum of such chains, each corresponding to one particular component of that vector.

This remains true even if some of the separable sets have negative elements, provided the others contain corresponding positive elements large enough to yield a positive or, at least, a nonnegative sum total. In static input-output computations, competitive imports are treated, for example, as generating negative (direct and indirect) input requirements which are subtracted from the corresponding input requirements generated by the positive vector of domestic final demand, thus yielding a smaller, but still positive (or at least nonnegative) sum total. Strictly speaking, this already constitutes a departure from true separability: If that total turns out, for some particular output, to be negative, the entire result is invalidated. A new computation has to be undertaken with the imports previously treated as competitive now shifted over into the noncompetitive category. The treatment of the direct and indirect effects of one part of the final bill of goods turns out, in this case, to be dependent on the magnitude of the—admittedly separately computed—requirements generated by all the other components of that vector. This introduces into the analytical picture cross-dependencies typical of nonlinear systems.

The use of the dynamic inverse brings the obvious advantages of separability and additivity into the empirical analysis of economic change. The presence of negative elements in many of the separate input chains (describing the time sequence of the direct—but mostly indirect—input requirements generated by each individual element of a given time-phased final bill of goods) imposes obvious limits on the strict use of the additivity assumption. Consistent, i.e., feasible sequences of total input requirements can be determined on the basis of a given dynamic inverse only for those time-phased bills of goods that generate larger positive than negative output requirements for the products of each industry in each period of time.

A time-phased vector of final demand—premultiplied by a given dynamic inverse—may arithmetically yield negative total direct and indirect output requirements for some goods in some periods of time. If so, at least some of the balance equations in system (3) do not represent the real world. As everyone who has dealt with this kind of system knows, the problem arises because equation (3) assumes full capacity utilization in all the sectors all the time. By applying, for example, the simplex method routine of linear programming we could find a number of feasible production programs capable of delivering such a time-phased bill of goods. Each one of them would involve a precisely phased switching in and switching out of productive capacities and possibly the planned stockpiling of current outputs.

The operation of an economic process of such a discontinuous kind would be much more difficult to understand and to explain than that of a system whose change can be described in terms of continuous and additive components. In other words, a system with a diverging dynamic inverse that contains negative elements, whose magnitude grows as one goes back in time, could be programmed; however, the actual existence of such an economy would be very difficult to imagine. The explanation of the convergence of the actually observed dynamic inverse of the American economy which I will now describe should possibly be sought in the gradual substitution of new for the old columns of A and B coefficients, characterizing long-run technological change.

V

An open dynamic input-output system was constructed and its inverse computed on the basis of two sets of A and B matrices, one describing the structural properties of the American economy in the year 1947, the other in the year 1958. A third system was formed and inverted on the assumption that the shift from the 1947 to the 1958 technology occurred gradually over the intervening years. In all three instances the dynamic inverse turned out to be well behaved: All time series of which it consists converged backward toward zero.

The same sectoral breakdown is used for both years. It contains 52 endogenous industries and a final bill of goods subdivided into household consumption (durables and nondurables) and government consumption. An alternative treatment of private consumption separates final deliveries to households into deliveries of nondurables and of the

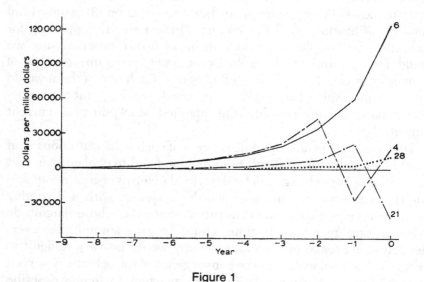

Figure 1

Elements of the dynamic inverse showing the direct and indirect effects of a million dollars' increase in the final demand for the products of industry 3, machinery products, in year 0 on the outputs of industries 4, 6, 21, 28 in this and the preceding years. —·——·—: transportation equipment and consumer appliances (4); —————: metals (6); ·—·—·—·—: lumber and products, excluding containers (21); ·······: rubber and plastic products (28).

304

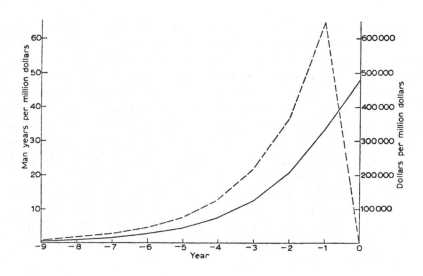

Figure 2

Time series of total direct and indirect labor and capital inputs required to deliver one million dollars' worth of the products of industry 3, machinery products, to final demand in year 0 (the left scale refers to labor, the right scale to capital). ——————: labor; ------------: capital.

estimated replacement requirements for consumers' durables. The rest of the latter is charged to a special household investment account, controlled by an appropriate vector of capital coefficients.

Labor requirements were computed on the basis of sectoral labor input coefficients, and total capital requirements for each sector were determined through summation of all elements of the appropriate column of the B matrix.

All inputs and outputs were measured both for 1947 and 1958 in 1958 prices. In other words, the units in terms of which the numerical computations were performed and their results presented should be interpreted as amounts of the respective commodities and services purchasable for one dollar at 1958 prices.

The entire computation absorbed about an hour's time on the IBM 7094 computer. The program included automatic plotting of the resulting time series by the machine. A selection of such plots is presented in the eight figures that I will now discuss.

Figure 1 illustrates the typical variety of shapes encountered among the time series, each of which constitutes a single element of

305

the dynamic inverse. Each of the four curves represents the time-phased amount of the product of one of the four different industries that were contributing directly or indirectly to supplying (in year 0) final users with one additional unit of the output of the machinery industry. Two of the inputs—"metals," and "rubber and plastic products"—are primary materials; their input curves ascend gradually but steadily from the beginning to the end. The demand for primary metals is much larger and anticipates the final delivery in significant amounts by some eight years. The first significant demand for rubber and plastic products is registered in the year −3.

The corresponding input requirements for transportation equipment and lumber, on the other hand, show a dip below the zero line in the years preceding the delivery of the final product. As explained above, this is typical of goods playing an important part in the process of capital accumulation.

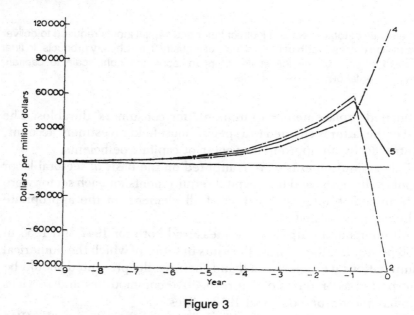

Figure 3

Elements of the dynamic inverse showing the alternative direct and indirect effects on the output of industry 6, metals, of a million dollars' worth of deliveries to final demand for the products of industries 2,4,5 in year 0. · — · —: transportation equipment and consumer appliances (4); — · — · —: textiles, clothing, furnishings (2); ————: construction (5).

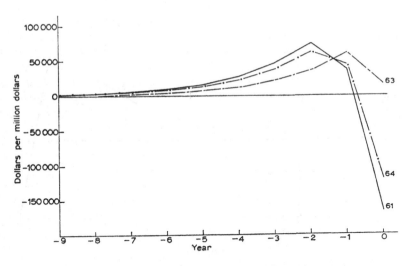

Figure 4

Elements of the dynamic inverse showing the alternative direct and indirect effects on the output of industry 6, metals, of a million dollars' worth of increases in the household, government, and total final demand in year 0. ————: household final demand (61); — · — · —: government final demand (63); · — · — · —: total final demand (64).

Figure 2 supplements Figure 1 by showing the amounts of labor and of capital, i.e., of investment goods, absorbed by *all industries* in the process of filling the direct and indirect input requirements for the delivery to final users (in year 0) of one million dollars' worth of the product of the machinery industry. The smoothness of the gradual rise is, of course, in both instances due to the mutual cancellation of irregularities in the employment and investment requirements of the many different individual industries combined in each of these two totals. The one year time-lag between the installation of new capacities and the delivery of additional outputs explains the last year's drop in the investment curve.

The differences among the reactions of the same industry to various kinds of final deliveries are shown in Figure 3. Metals behave as a typical raw material in their contribution to the production of transportation equipment—that is, mainly automobiles—delivered to final users; they react, however, as a typical investment good, in

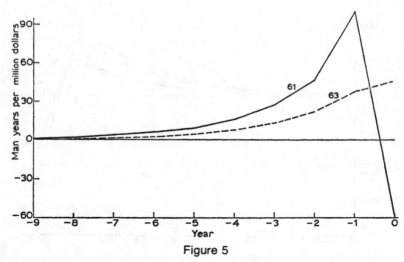

Figure 5

Time series of alternative direct and indirect labor inputs required to deliver a million dollars' worth of increases in the government and household final demand vectors in year 0. ————: household final demand (61); ------------: government final demand (63).

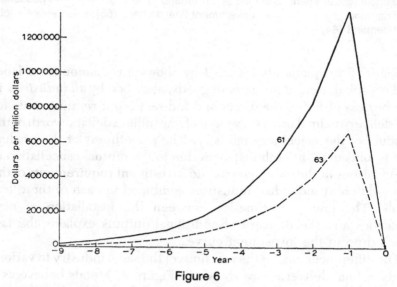

Figure 6

Time series of alternative direct and indirect capital inputs required to deliver a million dollars' worth of increases in the government and household final demand vectors in year 0.————: household final demand (61); ------------: governmental final demand (63).

308

response to an increase in the final demand for textiles. An inter-mediate pattern of behavior marks the contribution of the metals sector to the satisfaction of the final demand for the output of the construction industry.

A similar difference can be seen in Figure 4 between the shapes of two time series, both tracing the requirements for products of the metal sector, one reflecting an additional million dollars' worth of government demand, the other anticipating a delivery of one million dollars' worth of goods and services demanded by households. The first curve reaches its crest one year before the final delivery can actually be made and stays above the zero line in the last; the second starts to fall off a year earlier and plunges below the zero line at the end. As should have been expected, the intermediate product mix-ture of the combined total demand yields an intermediate time profile weighted in favor of households.

The time series of total labor inputs contributing to the two princi-pal components of final demand, as shown in Figure 5, are similar in shape to those shown in Figure 4. The same is true of the correspond-ing total capital requirements shown in Figure 6.

The three sets of curves in Figure 7 demonstrate how the dynamic inverse can reveal the effects of specified technical change on the dynamic properties of a given economic system. Each part of the chart presents the same element of the dynamic inverse in three alternative versions.

All three curves at the top represent the time-phased increase in the output of chemicals contributing directly and indirectly to the delivery of one additional million dollars' worth of food and drug products to final demand in the year 0. The first is computed on the basis of A_{1947} and B_{1947}, i.e., of the flow and capital coefficients charac-terizing the input structures of the 52 producing sectors of the American economy of the year 1947, the second on the basis of A_{1958} and B_{1958}, i.e., of 1958 technology. The third inverse was computed—in accordance with equation (4)—from a sequence of eleven different pairs of dated A and B matrices tracing the gradual shift from the 1947 to the 1958 technology. On the left this curve coincides with the first, but in the terminal year it catches up with the second.

The three sets of curves demonstrate how differently the same overall change can affect various elements of the same dynamic

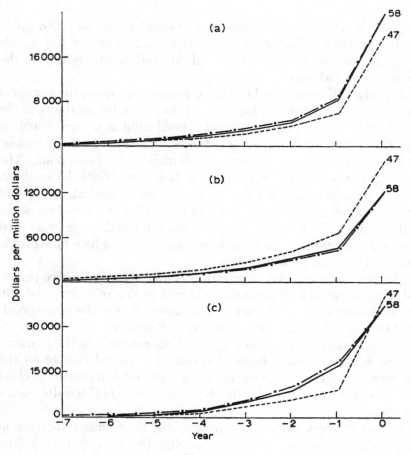

Figure 7

Effects of technological change on the elements of the dynamic inverse. (a) Time series of direct and indirect requirements for chemicals (8) to deliver a million dollars' worth of food and drugs (1) in year 0, computed on the basis of flow and capital coefficients representing the technologies of: ------------: 1947; · — · —: 1958; ————: shifting, year by year, from 1947 to 1958. (b) Time series of direct and indirect requirements for metals (6) to deliver a million dollars' worth of transportation equipment (4) in year 0, computed on the basis of flow and capital coefficients representing the technologies of: ----------: 1947; · — · —: 1958; ————: shifting, year by year, from 1947 to 1958. (c) Time series of direct and indirect requirements for chemicals (8) to deliver a million dollars' worth of nonferrous mining products (16) in year 0, computed on the basis of flow and capital coefficients representing the technologies of: ------------: 1947; · — · —: 1958; ————: shifting, year by year, from 1947 to 1958.

310

inverse. The combined effects of the many technical shifts reflected in the difference between the magnitude of the flow and the capital coefficients describing the input structures of the 52 sectors of the American economy in 1947 and 1958 led to an upward shift in the time series of chemical inputs required for delivery to final users of one million dollars' worth of food and drugs. The three curves in the middle part of the chart indicate that the same combination of structural changes reduced the inputs of metals contributing to the final delivery of consumers' appliances.

The contribution of chemicals to nonferrous metals mining shown on the bottom was affected by the same structural shifts in a more complicated way: The input requirements dropped in the last year of the series, i.e., the year of the final delivery, but they rose in all the previous years.

VI

The dynamic input-output system described above—not unlike the static input-output system—can be of little help in derivation of the golden rules of economic growth or in formulation of any other purely theoretical generalizations. It is too loosely jointed, too flexible for serving such an ambitious purpose. The dynamic inverse is primarily a storehouse of systematically organized factual information. This information is presented in a form particularly suitable for analytical description of intertemporal relations. The individual elements of the inverse can be spun into longer strands, each attached to a given time sequence of final deliveries. These strands can be woven into a broad fabric of intersectoral and intertemporal relationships which make up the analytical picture of economic growth.

Figure 8 illustrates graphically the structure of one such simple strand describing—or explaining, if you will—the increase in the level of output of primary metals called for by a delivery to final users of one million dollars' worth of nondurable consumers' goods (and of proportionally increased services of durable consumers' goods) per year over a period of 17 years. The first delivery to final users is made in the year 0, the last in the year +16.

Each of the partly superimposed curves represents the sequence of

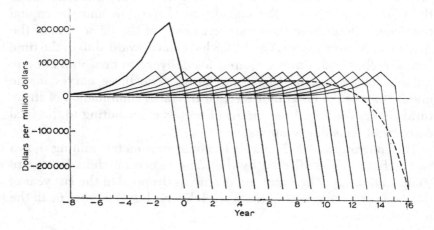

Figure 8

Direct and indirect effects on the output of industry 6, metals, of annual increases of
a million dollars, continued over a 17-year period (years 0 through +16), in the
household final demand vector (61).--------: effects of an increase in demand for a
single year; ————: combined effects of all increases in annual demands.

inputs required for delivery of an additional million dollars' worth of
consumers' goods to households. The year of final delivery is indicated by the position of the forward end of the curve. While the first
delivery is due in the year 0, the first incremental input of nonnegligi-
ble size must be made in year −8. From then on, a new input
sequence has to be started every year over a period of 17 years; the
entire series of required total annual inputs—traced by the heavy
black line on the chart—spans an interval of 25 years. The typical
hump at the beginning reflects the buildup of the required additional
capital stocks; the falling off at the end indicates, on the other hand, a
reduction of these stocks, a gradual liquidation that sets in many years
before the last delivery to households of an additional million dollars'
worth of consumers' goods.

The flat portion of the curve marks what might be called the period
of stationary reproduction, during which only current annual input
requirements, including capital replacements, have to be covered.
With the A and B matrices invariant and the vector of final deliveries,
c, constant over a sufficiently long period of time, the corresponding

312

time-phased output vector, x, can—according to (5)—be determined as follows:

(6) $$x = (1 + R + R^2 + \cdots + R^m)\, G^{-1}c$$

If the series on the right-hand side converges,

$$x \to (1-R)^{-1}G^{-1}c = [G(1 - G^{-1}B)]^{-1}c = (G-B)^{-1}c = (1-A)^{-1}c$$

as $m \to \infty$.

Under stationary conditions governing the flat portion of the cumulative curve in Figure 8, the dependence of sectoral outputs on final demand is controlled by the static inverse, $(1-A)^{-1}$.

Information anticipating the level of final demand eight years hence would, in this particular case, suffice for a reasonably accurate assessment of direct and indirect input needs. The degree of foresight required depends, of course, on the profile of the elements of the inverse from which the total input curve has to be built up. So long as the total final demand continues to rise from year to year, no liquidation of productive stock is likely to be called for. In the summation of the overlapping series of direct and indirect effects of successive changes in final deliveries, the positive elements of the dynamic inverse will tend to dominate its few negative components.

In recent contributions to the pure theory of economic growth the problem of so-called terminal conditions has attracted much attention. According to the evidence presented above, the time horizon on which we could base our plans or make our projections should vary from sector to sector. The time shape of the elements of the dynamic inverse that governs direct and indirect requirements for the products of one particular industry might be such that its output in a given year depends primarily on the composition and the level of the final demand vector of the same year. For another industry that shape might be such that the level of its output in a given year reflects final deliveries, say, four or five years later.

VII

The balance equation (1), and consequently also the formulas describing the dynamic inverse derived from it, are based on the assumption of a uniform one-period ("one year") time lag between the installation of additional stocks of capital goods and the increase in the flow of output resulting from their first use. The same time unit enters into the definition of all the elements of the capital coefficient matrix B ("stocks per unit of *annual* output"). In fact, the time lags between the installation and initial full utilization of incremental capacities in various productive sectors of the U.S. economy—defined in terms of the degree of aggregation used in this study—seem to be around one year or somewhat shorter.

A change in the absolute magnitude of the time unit used in describing an actual economic system in terms of equations (1) would signify a corresponding real change in the length of all the lags. If, despite that change, the real capital requirements of all the sectors remain the same, the capital coefficients described by matrix B have to be "translated" into the new time unit. Thus, if the time lag is reduced from one year to half a year, all elements of B have to be multiplied by 2.

The effects of such a shift on the dominant characteristic root of the system and, consequently, on its convergence are analyzed in appendix I; changes in the time lags and in the magnitudes of the B coefficients tend to offset each other. The three curves entered in Figure 9 show how the time sequence of labor inputs required to increase total deliveries to final demand by one million dollars is affected if the basic structural investment lag is cut from one year to six or to four months. The horizontal axis of the graph is in natural years.

VIII

In static input-output analysis, the inverse of the structural matrix of a particular economy postmultiplied by a given column vector of final demand yields the vector of corresponding total sectoral outputs. The transpose of the same inverse when postmultiplied by a given vector of values added (wage, profit, tax, and other final payments disbursed by each industry per unit of its total physical output) yields the corresponding vector of equilibrium prices, i.e., of prices at which the total outlay (including the values added) of each sector would equal its aggregate receipts. In dynamic input-output analysis the transpose of the dynamic inverse determines the relationship between the time-phased vectors of values added in each of the producing sectors and the set of equilibrium prices that would balance the total outlays and the total receipts of each producing sector over time.

Let p_t represent a column vector, $_tp_1, _tp_2, \ldots, _tp_n$, of the prices of goods and services sold and purchased by various sectors in year t and v_t a column vector, $_tv_1, _tv_2, \ldots, _tv_n$, of the values added in each sector per unit of its output in year t. Value added can be best defined residually as all current outlays of a producing sector other than payments for inputs purchased from the same or from other industries.

Equation (7) below states that in any year t the prices of all goods represented by the vector on the left-hand side must equal their unit costs as represented by the terms appearing on the right-hand side. The product of the transpose of the flow coefficient matrix A' and the price vector p_t represents the costs of current inputs purchased by each productive sector from itself and from other industries. The elements of the value added (column) vector v_t comprise wages, rents, taxes, and profits paid out or charged per unit of its output by the respective industries in year t.

The two terms enclosed in the square brackets describe the unit

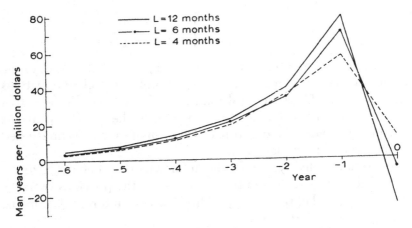

Figure 9

Direct and indirect labor inputs required to deliver an additional one million dollars' worth of goods to total final demand in year 0, assuming investment lags of 12 months, 6 months, and 4 months.

315

cost or gains conventionally booked through the capital account. For purposes of proper cost accounting, the stocks of capital goods are assumed to be acquired by each sector, in accordance with technological requirements, one year before the delivery of the output they produce and then sold off together with that output; in fact the sale will, in most cases, be purely nominal since the sector disposing of the capital goods will repurchase them again and again. Both transactions, of course, are supposed to be made at prices prevailing in the time period during which they take place. The value of capital stock purchased in the year $t-1$ is multiplied by $1 + r_{t-1}$; r_{t-1} represents the annual money rate of interest prevailing in that year. As has been observed before, the stocks of capital released from production of outputs delivered in year t are employed at once to produce goods that will be delivered in the following year $t+1$. The A and B matrices on the right-hand side are dated to reflect the process of technical change.

$$(7) \qquad P_t = A'_t p_t + [(1 + r_{t-1}) B'_t p_{t-1} - B'_{t+1} p_t] + v_t.$$

Equation (7) can be rewritten as

$$(8) \qquad G'_t p_t - \alpha_{t-1} B'_t p_{t-1} = v_t$$

where

$$G'_t = (1 - A'_t + B'_{t+1}) \text{ and } \alpha_t = 1 + r_t$$

Assigning the values $-m, -m+1, -m+2, \ldots, -2, -1, 0$, to the time subscript t, we can construct a system of interlocked equations analogous to (3). The structural matrix on the left-hand side of that new system would resemble the transpose of the structural matrix appearing in (3) with the difference that each of the B_t's is multiplied by a corresponding scalar, α_{t-1}.

The solution of that system for the unknown price vector p_0 in terms of the value added vectors of the same and all the previous years v_0, $v_{-1}, v_{-2}, \ldots$, and of the corresponding "force of interest" factors α_0, $\alpha_{-1}, \alpha_{-2}, \ldots$, has the form:

$$
\begin{aligned}
(9) \qquad p_0 = & (G_0^{-1})' v_0 + (R_{-1} G_0^{-1})' \alpha_{-1} v_{-1} + (R_{-2} R_{-1} G_0^{-1})' \alpha_{-2} \alpha_{-1} v_{-2} \\
& +, \ldots, + (R_{-m} \ldots R_{-2} R_{-1} G_0^{-1})' \alpha_{-m} \ldots \alpha_{-2} \alpha_{-1} v_{-m} \\
& + (R_{-m} \ldots R_{-2} R_{-1} G_0^{-1})' \alpha_{-m} \ldots \alpha_{-2} \alpha_{-1} B'_{-m} p_{-(m+1)}
\end{aligned}
$$

316

The bracketed matrix products on the right-hand side of the first line are identical with the elements of the last column of the dynamic inverse appearing on the right-hand side of (4). These coefficients, however, enter into (9) in their transposed form. Since the series R_{-1}, $R_{-2}R_{-1}$, $R_{-3}R_{-2}R_{-1}$, . . . , converges toward 0, the last term on the right-hand side—containing the price vector $p_{-(m+1)}$—can be disregarded provided that the sequence is extended back over a sufficient number of years.

The price vector of any given year has thus been shown to depend on the value added vectors of that and of all preceding years. This dependence is governed by the transpose of the same dynamic inverse that determines the dated sequence of input requirements generated in the corresponding physical system by a given time-phased bill of goods. For example, in the absence of technical change and on the assumption that both the rate of interest and the value added vectors remain constant over time, equation (9) is reduced to

$$(10) \quad p_0 \to [G^{-1}]' [I + R'\alpha + (R')^2\alpha^2 + (R')^3 \alpha^3 \cdot \cdot \cdot (R')^t\alpha^t]v$$

as $t \to \infty$.

After t becomes sufficiently large, the ratio between two successive terms of the exponential series on the right-hand side tends to equal $\mu_1\alpha$, where μ_1 is the dominant characteristic root of R'. The series will converge and thus yield a finite price vector p only if $\mu_1\alpha < 1$ or, since $\alpha = 1 + r$, if

$$r < \frac{1 - \mu_1}{\mu_1}.$$

The conclusion that, under certain conditions, the characteristic root of the matrix of an open dynamic input-output system imposes an upper limit on the rate of interest has been presented many years ago by Michio Morishima.[3]

Figure 10 shows how the price of the bundle[4] of consumers' goods delivered to final users in 1958 depends on the annual values added per unit of the metal industry's output. The solid curve, based on the

[3]Michio Morishima, *Equilibrium, Stability, and Growth* (London: Oxford University Press, 1964).
[4]A "final demand bundle" consists of goods, weighted according to 1958 consumption patterns, costing $1 in 1958 prices.

unrealistic assumption that the rate of interest through the entire 11-year period was equal to 0 (i.e., $\alpha = 1$), is identical with the corresponding solid curve in Figure 4. The dip below the zero line in the last year reflects negative costs, i.e., the revenue that would have been secured from the liquidation of capital stock purchased in the previous year. The positive expenditure on capital goods reflected in the other points of the same curve will, in most cases, offset this negative amount.

The other two curves were drawn on the assumption that interest rates of 10 and 25 percent respectively prevailed over the entire interval. They show how a rise in the interest rate increases the dependence of present prices on past values added (and, consequently, also on past prices).

Much of what I have said should have a familiar ring. The "productive advances" of Francois Quesnay, the process of expanded reproduction of Karl Marx, and the "roundabout production" of Böhm-Bawerk all contain the basic theoretical notions incorporated in the

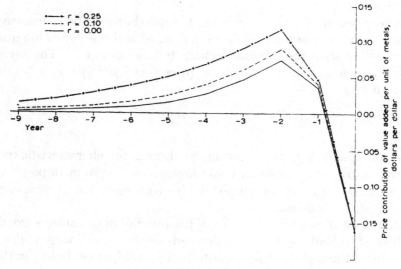

Figure 10

Portion of the price of a 1958 final demand bundle, directly and indirectly attributable to value added paid by the metal industry in year *t*.

derivation of the dynamic inverse. But while these great economists had to content themselves with verbal description and deductive reasoning, we can measure and we can compute. Therein lies the real difference between the past and the present state of economics.

Appendix I

To analyze the convergence properties of the series

(A1)
$$R_{-1}, R_{-2}R_{-1}, R_{-3}R_{-2}R_{-1}, \ldots, R_{-t} \ldots R_{-3}R_{-2}R_{-1}$$
$$R_t = (1 - A_t + B_{t+1})^{-1} B_{t+1}$$

we can first consider the case in which,

$A_t = A$ and $B_t = B$, for all t's and consequently,
$R_t = R$ for all t's.

In this case, series (1) is transformed into the geometric series,

(A2) $\qquad\qquad R, R^2, R^3, \ldots, R^t$

(A3) $\qquad\qquad R = (1 - A + B)^{-1}B$

(A4) $\qquad\quad (1 - A + B) = (1 - A)[1 + (1 - A)^{-1}B]$

(A5) $\quad (1 - A + B)^{-1}B = [1 + (1 - A)^{-1}B]^{-1}(1 - A)^{-1}B = (1 + U)^{-1}U$

where $U = (1 - A)^{-1}B$.
Since $(1 - A)^{-1} > 0$, and $B \geq 0$ and is irreducible, therefore $U > 0$.

(A6) $\qquad\qquad [(1 + U)^{-1}U]^{-1} = U^{-1}(1 + U) = (1 + U^{-1});$

consequently

(A7) $\qquad\qquad R = (1 + U^{-1})^{-1}.$

Let λ_i ($i = 1, 2, 3, \ldots, n$) represent the n roots of the square, nonsingular and indecomposable matrix U. Since $U > 0$, it has—according to the well-known theorem of Frobenius—a positive dominant simple root. Moreover, this root, and only this root, has associated with it a positive eigenvector. Let λ_1 be this root.

For real λ_i the corresponding roots of U^{-1} and of $1 + U^{-1}$ are, $1/\lambda_i$ and $1 + (1/\lambda_i)$, respectively. Thus according to equation (A7), the roots of R are

(A8) $\qquad\qquad \mu_i = \dfrac{\lambda_i}{1 + \lambda_i}$ and in particular, $\mu_1 = \dfrac{\lambda_1}{1 + \lambda_1}.$

From $\lambda_1 > 0$, it follows that $0 < \mu_1 < 1$, which means that R always has a simple positive root μ_1 smaller than 1, associated with a positive eigenvector.

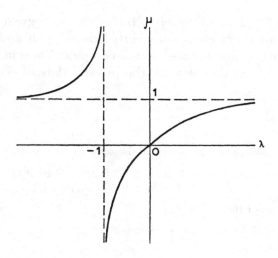

Figure A1

Schematic graph of relationship between μ and λ.

Figure A1 depicts the relationship between μ_i and λ_i for all real λ_i. If some of these subdominant roots are smaller than -0.5, the corresponding μ_i will be greater than 1 in absolute value. The eigenvectors associated with them will have elements of different signs.[5]

This implies that series R^1, R^2, R^3, . . . , could be divergent. Depending on whether the dominant root is real or complex and whether its real part is positive or negative, the elements of the corresponding dynamic inverse would, in this case, diverge—as one moves back in time—expanding without limit either monotonically in the positive or negative direction, or fluctuating with increasing amplitude between the positive and negative domain.

If R_t changes with t, but does so with infinite lower and upper limits, say, $\underline{R}$ and $\overline{R}$, its higher terms will lie between the corresponding higher terms of the series $\underline{R}^1$, $\underline{R}^2$, . . . , and $\overline{R}^1$, $\overline{R}^2$.

The convergence properties of the dynamic inverse depend on the time unit in terms of which the capital coefficients that enter into matrix B are defined. In the basic balance equation (1) that unit also represents the lag, i.e., the difference

[5]The analysis holds for complex roots with the following modification: Let $\lambda_i = a + b_i$.

Then, the real part of the corresponding μ_i becomes $\mathbf{R}(\mu_i) = \dfrac{a(a+1)+b^2}{(a+1)^2+b^2}$.

To guarantee convergence, we must have $(a^2+1.5a) > -(b^2+0.5)$. If $b = 0$, these formulas reduce to the simpler form stated in the text.

320

between the time when additional stocks of capital goods, or inventories of current inputs, are accumulated and the time when they can be put to use.

Let t be a given time interval described in original units and t^* the same time interval measured in different units. If α is the ratio of the length of the first to that of the second unit,

(A9)
$$t^* = \alpha t$$

If, for example, t describes a given stretch of time in years and t^* measures it in months, then, $\alpha = 12$.

The technical flow coefficients have no time dimensions; hence the elements of matrix A will remain the same after the time unit—and consequently the lag built into equation (A1)—has been changed from a year to, say, a month. But all the capital coefficients, that is, the elements of matrix B, will become 12 times larger. Continuing to use an asterisk to mark the values of matrices and their roots after the change of the time unit, we have

$$B^* = B\alpha$$

(A10)
$$U^* = U\alpha \text{ and } 1 + U^{*-1} = 1 + U^{-1}/\alpha$$

It follows that,

$$\lambda_i^* = \lambda_i \alpha$$

and, in accordance with (A8)

(A11)
$$\mu_i^* = \frac{\lambda_i/\alpha}{1 + \lambda_i/\alpha}$$

The relationship between μ_i^* and λ_i/α is thus the same as that between μ_i and λ_i explained above. Inspecting it we find that, if root μ_1 happens to be dominant, its dominance will not be affected by any change in the time unit and the lag. If, on the other hand, some other root μ_i were dominant and, consequently, the system were divergent, an increase in α, i.e., a shortening of the lag, if sufficiently large, could shift any negative magnitude λ_i/α into the interval between -0.5 and 0 and thus make μ_i^* dominant. A lengthening of the lag could, of course, have the opposite effect.

Appendix II

Concepts

I. A matrix
    The A matrix includes current flow coefficients and replacement coefficients. It is on a domestic output base.

II. *B* matrix

The *B* matrix is made up of the capital stock coefficients for all industries. Residential construction is included in the real estate and rental industry. The capital coefficients are capacity based.

III. Labor row

The labor row consists of "man-years" per thousand dollars of output.

IV. Total capital row

This row is simply the column sums of the *B* matrix.

V. Alternative bills of goods

A. Household nondurable goods including replacement of durable

This vector of final demand includes current purchases of nondurable goods and replacement of durable goods by households. It also contains a capital coefficient column, consisting of the stock of consumer durables (the stock of residential construction is in the real estate and rental column). The labor entry into this vector is domestic help.

B. Household goods, durable and nondurable

This vector of final demand contains current purchases of durable and nondurable goods by households.

C. Government

The government vector of final demand consists of purchases by the federal, state, and local governments.

D. Total final demand

Final demand includes expenditures by households (durable and nondurable goods), federal, state, and local governments, exports, and competitive imports. It excludes the gross private capital formation and net inventory change vectors.

All items are in 1958 prices.

1947 through 1958 data

Information regarding capital and technical coefficients is usually unavailable on a year-by-year basis. Since the dynamic model with technological change requires such data for, say, a dozen consecutive years, and since data may exist for no more than three years in this interval, most of the information has to be derived through interpolation. For most coefficients exponential interpolation is used to approximate a constant rate of growth. When one of the terminal year coefficients is zero, the exponential method becomes impractical, and the program approximates with a linear technique.

Suppose $a(47)$ and $a(58)$ represent corresponding elements of two terminal year matrices. Then,

if $a(47) > 0$ and $a(58) > 0$ exponential interpolation is used,
if $a(47) = 0$ and $a(58) > 0$ linear interpolation is used,
if $a(47) > 0$ and $a(58) = 0$ linear interpolation is used, and
if $a(47) = 0$ and $a(58) = 0$ linear interpolation is used.

Appendix III

Table A1—"59-order" classification

NUMBER	NAME	CORRESPONDING 83-ORDER SECTORS
1	Food and drugs	14, 15, 29
2	Textiles, clothing, furnishings	16, 17, 18, 19, 34, 22, 23
3	Machinery (just final)	51, 44, 45, 46, 47, 48, 49, 50, 63
4	Transportation equipment and consumer appliances	52, 54, 56, 59, 60, 61, 62
5	Construction	11, 12
6	Metals	37, 38
7	Energy	7, 31, 68
8	Chemicals	27
9	——	—
10	——	—
11	Livestock	1
12	Crops	2
13	Forestry	3
14	Agricultural services	4
15	Iron ore mining	5
16	Nonferrous ore mining	6
17	Petroleum mining	8
18	Stone and clay mining	9
19	Chemical mining	10
20	——	—
21	Lumber and products, excluding containers	20
22	Wooden containers	21
23	Paper products and containers	24, 25
24	——	—
25	Printing and publishing	26
26	Plastics and synthetics	28
27	Paint and allied products	30
28	Rubber and plastic products	32
29	Leather tanning	33
30	Glass and glass products	35
31	Stone and clay products	36
32	Metal containers	39
33	Heating, plumbing, structural metals	40
34	Stampings, screw machine products	41
35	Hardware, plating, valves, wire products	42
36	Engines and turbines	43
37	Electric apparatus and motors	53
38	Electric lighting and wiring equipment	55

Table A1—"59-order" classification (cont.)

NUMBER	NAME	CORRESPONDING 83-ORDER SECTORS
39	Electronic components	57
40	Batteries, X-ray and engine electrical equipment	58
41	Miscellaneous manufacturing	64
42	Transportation and warehousing	65
43	Communications, excluding radio and TV	66
44	Radio and TV broadcasting	67
45	Trade	69
46	Finance and insurance	70
47	Real estate and rental	71
48	Hotels, personal and repair services	72
49	Business services	73
50	Research and development	74
51	Automobile repair services	75
52	Amusements and recreation	76
53	Medical and educational institutions	77
54	——	—
55	——	—
56	Noncompetitive imports	80
57	Entertainment and business travel	81
58	——	—
59	Scrap and by-products	83
60	Total labor row	
61	Household nondurables including replacement of durables column	
62	Household durables and nondurables column	
63	Government final demand column	
64	Total final demand, excluding gross private capital formation and net inventory change, column	
65	Total capital row	

Alternative bills of goods: 61, 62, 63, 64

Appendix IV

Sources of data

1958 A matrix, current flow coefficients

This matrix is based on the 1958 input-output table published by the Office of Business Economics, Department of Commerce. See A.P. Carter, "Changes in the Structure of the American Economy, 1947 to 1958 and 1962," *Review of Economics and Statistics*, XLIX (May 1967).

1958 A matrix, replacement coefficients

This matrix was developed at the Harvard Economic Research Project based on 1958 capital coefficients and U.S. Treasury Department, Internal Revenue

324

Service, *Depreciation Guidelines and Rules*, Publication No. 456, U.S. Government Printing Office, Washington, D.C. (1964).

1958 *B* matrix, capital coefficients

The capital coefficients for manufacturing sectors were obtained from Waddell, Ritz, Norton, DeWitt, and Wood, *Capital Expansion Planning Factors, Manufacturing Industries*, National Planning Association, Washington, D.C. (April 1966). For nonmanufacturing sectors, the capital coefficients were compiled at the Harvard Economic Research Project by Samuel A. Rea, Jr., and others in 1966–1967.

1958 Labor coefficients

The labor coefficients are based on Jack Alterman, "Interindustry Employment Requirements," *Monthly Labor Review*, 88, No. 7 (July 1965).

1958 Final demand vectors

The final demand vectors are based on the 1958 input-output table published by the Office of Business Economics, Department of Commerce and on Raymond W. Goldsmith, *The National Wealth of the United States in the Postwar Period*, National Bureau of Economic Research, Princeton (1962).

1947 *A* matrix, current flow coefficients

This matrix is based on the Bureau of Labor Statistics 450-order input-output table for 1947, which was obtained by the Harvard Economic Research Project some years ago on cards (Deck A) from the Bureau of Labor Statistics along with mimeographed documentation for individual sectors. It is published at a 50-order level and is described in W. D. Evans and M. Hoffenberg, "The Interindustry Relations Study for 1947," *Review of Economics and Statistics*, XXXIV (May 1952). Adjustments have been made to the 1947 matrix in order to make it comparable with the 1958 matrix. See A. P. Carter, op. cit. Further work in this area is currently being done by Beatrice Vaccara and others at the Office of Business Economics and by the Harvard Economic Research Project.

1947 *A* matrix, replacement coefficients

This matrix was developed at the Harvard Economic Research Project, based on the 1947 capital coefficients and U.S. Treasury Department, op. cit.

1947 *B* matrix, capital coefficients

The 1947 capital coefficients are based on James M. Henderson and others, "Estimates of the Capital Structure of American Industries, 1947," mimeographed, Harvard Economic Research Project (June 1953), and Robert N. Grosse, *Capital Requirements for the Expansion of Industrial Capacity*, Vol. 1, Part 1, Executive Office of the President, Bureau of the Budget, Office of Statistical Standards (November 1953). Further revisions were made to the coefficients by Alan Strout and others in 1958–1962. Additional adjustments to make the 1947 capital coefficients comparable with the 1947 were made by Samuel A. Rea, Jr., and others (1966–1967) at the Harvard Economic Research Project.

1947 Labor coefficients

Same source as 1958 labor coefficients

1947 Final demand vectors

The final demand vectors are based on the Bureau of Labor Statistics 450-order input-output table and on Raymond W. Goldsmith, op. cit.

26

Environmental repercussions and the economic structure: an input-output approach

I

Pollution is a by-product of regular economic activities. In each of its many forms it is related in a measurable way to some particular consumption or production process: The quantity of carbon monoxide released in the air bears, for example, a definite relationship to the amount of fuel burned by various types of automotive engines; the discharge of polluted water into our streams and lakes is linked directly to the level of output of the steel, the paper, the textile, and all the other water-using industries, and its amount depends, in each instance, on the technological characteristics of the particular industry.

Input-output analysis describes and explains the level of output of each sector of a given national economy in terms of its relationships to the corresponding levels of activities in all the other sectors. In its more complicated multiregional and dynamic versions the input-output approach permits us to explain the spatial distribution of output and consumption of various goods and services and of their growth or decline—as the case may be—over time.

This paper was presented in Tokyo, Japan, March 1970 at the International Symposium on Environmental Disruption in the Modern World held under the auspices of the International Social Science Council, Standing Committee on Environmental Disruption; published in *The Review of Economics and Statistics*, Vol. 52, No. 3, August 1970.

Peter Petri and Ed Wolff, both members of the research staff of the Harvard Economic Research Project, have programmed and carried out the computations described in this paper. For their invaluable assistance I owe my sincerest thanks.

Frequently unnoticed and too often disregarded, undesirable by-products (as well as certain valuable, but unpaid-for natural inputs) are linked directly to the network of physical relationships that govern the day-to-day operations of our economic system. The technical interdependence between the levels of desirable and undesirable outputs can be described in terms of structural coefficients similar to those used to trace the structural interdependence between all the regular branches of production and consumption. As a matter of fact, it can be described and analyzed as an integral part of that network.

It is the purpose of this report first to explain how such "externalities" can be incorporated into the conventional input-output picture of a national economy and, second, to demonstrate that—once this has been done—conventional input-output computations can yield concrete replies to some of the fundamental factual questions that should be asked and answered before a practical solution can be found to problems raised by the undesirable environmental effects of modern technology and uncontrolled economic growth.

II

Proceeding on the assumption that the basic conceptual framework of a static input-output analysis is familiar to the reader, I will link up the following exposition to the numerical examples and elementary equations presented in chapter 7 of my book entitled *Input-Output Economics* (New York: Oxford University Press, 1966).

Consider a simple economy consisting of two producing sectors, say, Agriculture and Manufacture, and Households. Each one of the two industries absorbs some of its annual output itself, supplies some to the other industry, and delivers the rest to final consumers—in this case represented by the Households. These intersectoral flows can be conveniently entered in an input-output table. See Table 1, for example. The magnitude of the total outputs of the two industries and of the two different kinds of inputs absorbed in each of them depends on, (1) the amounts of agricultural and manufactured goods that had to be delivered to the final consumers, i.e., the Households and, (2) the input requirements of the two industries determined by their specific technological structures. In this particular instance Agriculture is assumed to require 0.25 (= 25/100) units of agricultural and 0.14 (=

327

Table 1—Input-output table of a national
economy (in physical units)

INTO FROM	SECTOR 1 AGRICULTURE	SECTOR 2 MANUFACTURE	FINAL DEMAND HOUSEHOLDS	TOTAL OUTPUT
Sector 1 Agriculture	25	20	55	100 bushels of wheat
Sector 2 Manufacture	14	6	30	50 yards of cloth

14/100) units of manufactured inputs to produce a bushel of wheat, while the manufacturing sector needs 0.40 (= 20/50) units of agricultural and 0.12 (= 6/50) units of manufactured product to make a yard of cloth.

The "cooking recipes" of the two producing sectors can also be presented in a compact tabular form (see Table 2). This is the "structural matrix" of the economy. The numbers entered in the first column are the technical input coefficients of the Agriculture sector and those shown in the second are the input coefficients of the Manufacture sector.

III

The technical coefficients determine how large the total annual outputs of agricultural and of manufactured goods must be if they are to satisfy not only the given direct demand (for each of the two kinds of goods) by the final users, i.e., the Households, but also the intermediate demand depending in its turn on the total level of output in each of the two productive sectors.

These somewhat circular relationships are described concisely by the following two equations:

$$X_1 - 0.25X_1 - 0.40X_2 = Y_1$$
$$X_2 - 0.12X_2 - 0.14X_1 = Y_2$$

or in a rearranged form,

(1)
$$0.75X_1 - 0.40X_2 = Y_1$$
$$-0.14X_1 + 0.88X_2 = Y_2$$

X_1 and X_2 represent the unknown total outputs of agricultural and manufactured commodities respectively; Y_1 and Y_2 the given amounts of agricultural and manufactured products to be delivered to the final consumers.

These two linear equations with two unknowns can obviously be solved, for X_1 and X_2 in terms of any given Y_1 and Y_2.

Their "general" solution can be written in the form of the following two equations:

$$(2) \qquad \begin{aligned} X_1 &= 1.457Y_1 + 0.662Y_2 \\ X_2 &= 0.232Y_1 + 1.242Y_2. \end{aligned}$$

By inserting on the right-hand side the given magnitudes of Y_1 and Y_2 we can compute the magnitudes of X_1 and X_2. In the particular case described in Table 1, $Y_1 = 55$ and $Y_2 = 30$. Performing the necessary multiplications and additions one finds the corresponding magnitudes of X_1 and X_2 to be, indeed, equal to the total outputs of agricultural (100 bushels) and manufactured (50 yards) goods, as shown in Table 1.

The matrix, i.e., the square set table of numbers appearing on the right-hand side of (2),

$$(3) \qquad \begin{bmatrix} 1.457 & 0.662 \\ 0.232 & 1.242 \end{bmatrix}$$

is called the "inverse" of matrix,

$$(4) \qquad \begin{bmatrix} 0.75 & -0.40 \\ -0.14 & 0.88 \end{bmatrix}$$

describing the set constants appearing on the left-hand side of the original equations in (1).

Table 2—Input requirements per unit of output

INTO FROM	SECTOR 1 AGRICULTURE	SECTOR 2 MANUFACTURE
Sector 1 Agriculture	0.25	0.40
Sector 2 Manufacture	0.14	0.12

Any change in the technology of either Manufacture or Agriculture, i.e., in any one of the four input coefficients entered in Table 2, would entail a corresponding change in the structural matrix (4) and, consequently, in its inverse (3). Even if the final demand for agricultural (Y_1) and manufactured (Y_2) goods remained the same, their total outputs, X_1 and X_2, would have to change, if the balance between the total outputs and inputs of both kinds of goods were to be maintained. On the other hand, if the level of the final demands Y_1 and Y_2 had changed, but the technology remained the same, the corresponding changes in the total outputs X_1 and X_2 could be determined from the same general solution (2).

In dealing with real economic problems one, of course, takes into account simultaneously the effect both of technological changes and of anticipated shifts in the levels of final deliveries. The structural matrices used in such computations contain not two but several hundred sectors, but the analytical approach remains the same. In order to keep the following verbal argument and the numerical examples illustrating it quite simple, pollution produced directly by Households and other final users is not considered in it. A concise description of the way in which pollution generated by the final demand sectors can be introduced—along with pollution originating in the producing sectors—into the quantitative description and numerical solution of the input-output system is relegated to the Mathematical Appendix.

IV

As has been said before, pollution and other undesirable—or desirable—external effects of productive or consumptive activities should for all practical purposes be considered part of the economic system.

The quantitative dependence of each kind of external output (or input) on the level of one or more conventional economic activities to which it is known to be related must be described by an appropriate technical coefficient and all these coefficients have to be incorporated in the structural matrix of the economy in question.

Let it be assumed, for example, that the technology employed by the Manufacture sector leads to a release into the air of 0.20 grams of a solid pollutant per yard of cloth produced by it, while agricultural

330

technology adds 0.50 grams per unit (i.e., each bushel of wheat) of its total output.

Using $\bar{X}_3$ to represent the yet unknown total quantity of this external output, we can add to the two original equations of output system (1) a third,

(5)
$$
\begin{aligned}
0.75X_1 - 0.40X_2 \quad &= Y_1 \\
-0.14X_1 + 0.88X_2 \quad &= Y_2 \\
0.50X_1 + 0.20X_2 - \bar{X}_3 &= 0
\end{aligned}
$$

In the last equation the first term describes the amount of pollution produced by Agriculture as depending on that sector's total output, X_1, while the second represents, in the same way, the pollution originating in Manufacture as a function of X_2; the equation as a whole simply states that $\bar{X}_3$, i.e., the total amount of that particular type pollution generated by the economic system as a whole, equals the sum total of the amounts produced by all its separate sectors.

Given the final demands Y_1 and Y_2 for agricultural and manufactured products, this set of three equations can be solved not only for their total outputs X_1 and X_2 but also for the unknown total output $\bar{X}_3$ of the undesirable pollutant.

The coefficients of the left-hand side of augmented input-output system (5) form the matrix,

(5a)
$$
\left\{
\begin{array}{ccc}
0.75 & -0.40 & 0 \\
-0.14 & 0.88 & 0 \\
0.50 & 0.20 & -1
\end{array}
\right\}
$$

A "general solution" of system (5) would in its form be similar to the general solution (2) of system (1); only it would consist of three rather than two equations and the "inverse" of the structural matrix (4) appearing on the right-hand side would have three rows and columns.

Instead of inverting the enlarged structural matrix one can obtain the same result in two steps. First, use the inverse (4) of the original smaller matrix to derive, from the two-equation system (2), the outputs of agricultural (X_1) and manufactured (X_2) goods required to satisfy any given combination of final demands Y_1 and Y_2. Second, determine the corresponding "output" of pollutants, i.e., $\bar{X}_3$, by entering the values of X_1 and X_2 thus obtained in the last equation of set (5).

Let $Y_1 = 55$ and $Y_2 = 30$; these are the levels of the final demand for agricultural and manufactured products as shown on the input-output

331

Table 1. Inserting these numbers on the right-hand side of (5), we find—using the general solution (2) of the first two equations—that $X_1 = 100$ and $X_2 = 50$. As should have been expected they are identical with the corresponding total output figures in Table 1. Using the third equation in (5) we find, $X_3 = 60$. This is the total amount of the pollutant generated by both industries.

By performing a similar computation for $Y_1 = 55$ and $Y_2 = 0$ and then for $Y_1 = 0$ and $Y_2 = 30$, we could find out that 42.62 of these 60 grams of pollution are associated with agricultural and manufactured activities contributing directly and indirectly to the delivery to Households of 55 bushels of wheat, while the remaining 17.38 grams can be imputed to productive activities contributing directly and indirectly to final delivery of the 30 yards of cloth.

Had the final demand for cloth fallen from 30 yards to 15, the amount of pollution traceable in it would be reduced from 17.38 to 8.69 grams.

V

Before proceeding with further analytical exploration, it seems to be appropriate to introduce in Table 3 the pollution-flows explicitly in the original Table 1.

The entry at the bottom of the final column in Table 3 indicates that Agriculture produced 50 grams of pollutant and 0.50 grams per bushel of wheat. Multiplying the pollutant-output-coefficient of the manufacturing sector with its total output we find that it has contributed 10 to the grand total of 60 grams of pollution.

Table 3—Input-output table of the national economy with pollutants included (in physical units)

INTO FROM	SECTOR 1 AGRICULTURE	SECTOR 2 MANUFACTURE	HOUSEHOLDS	TOTAL OUTPUT
Sector 1 Agriculture	25	20	55	100 bushels of wheat
Sector 2 Manufacture	14	6	30	50 yards of cloth
Sector 3 Air pollution	50	10		60 grams of pollutant

Table 4—Input-output table with labor inputs included
(in physical and in money units)

FROM \ INTO	SECTOR 1 AGRICULTURE	SECTOR 2 MANUFACTURE	HOUSEHOLDS	TOTAL OUTPUT
Sector 1 Agriculture	25	20	55	100 bushels of wheat
Sector 2 Manufacture	14	6	30	50 yards of cloth
Labor inputs (value added)	80 ($80)	180 ($180)		260 man-years ($260)

Conventional economic statistics concern themselves with production and consumption of goods and services that are supposed to have some positive market value in our competitive private enterprise economy. This explains why the production and consumption of DDT are, for example, entered in conventional input-output tables while the production and consumption of carbon monoxide generated by internal combustion engines are not. Since private and public bookkeeping, which constitutes the ultimate source of the most conventional economic statistics, does not concern itself with such "nonmarket" transactions, their magnitude has to be estimated indirectly through detailed analysis of the underlying technical relationships.

Problems of costing and of pricing are bound to arise, however, as soon as we go beyond explaining and measuring pollution toward doing something about it.

VI

A conventional national or regional input-output table contains a "value-added" row. It shows, in dollar figures, the wages, depreciation charges, profits, taxes, and other costs incurred by each producing sector in addition to payments for inputs purchased from other producing sectors. Most of that "value added" represents the cost of labor, capital, and other so-called primary factors of production, and depends on the physical amounts of such inputs and their prices. The wage bill of an industry equals, for example, the total number of man-years times the wage rate per man-year.

In Table 4 the original national input-output table is extended to include the labor input or total employment row.

Table 5—Input requirements per unit of output
(including labor or value added)

INTO	SECTOR 1	SECTOR 2
FROM	AGRICULTURE	MANUFACTURE
Sector 1 Agriculture	0.25	0.40
Sector 2 Manufacture	0.14	0.12
Primary input-labor in man-hours (at $1 per hour)	0.80 ($0.80)	3.60 ($3.60)

The "cooking recipes" as shown in Table 2 can be accordingly extended to include the labor input coefficients of both industries expressed in man-hours as well as in money units.

In section III it was shown how the general solution of the original input-output system (2) can be used to determine the total outputs of agricultural and manufactured products (X_1 and X_2) required to satisfy any given combination of deliveries of these goods (Y_1 and Y_2) to final Households. The corresponding total labor inputs can be derived by multiplying the appropriate labor coefficients (l_1 and l_2) with each sector's total output. The sum of both products yields the labor input L of the economy as a whole.

$$(6) \qquad L = l_1 X_1 + l_2 X_2.$$

Assuming a wage rate of $1 per hour we find (see Table 5) the payment for primary inputs per unit of the total output to be $0.80 in Agriculture and $3.60 in Manufacture. That implies that the prices of one bushel of wheat (p_1) and of a yard of cloth (p_2) must be just high enough to permit Agriculture to yield a "value added" of v_1 (= 0.80) and Manufacture v_2 (= 3.60) per unit of their respective outputs after having paid for all the other inputs specified by their respective "cooking recipes."

$$p_1 - 0.25p_1 - 0.14p_2 = v_1$$
$$p_2 - 0.12p_2 - 0.40p_1 = v_2$$

or in a rearranged form,

$$(7) \quad \begin{aligned} 0.75p_1 - 0.14p_2 &= v_1 \\ -0.40p_1 + 0.88p_2 &= v_2 \end{aligned}$$

The "general solution" of these two equations permitting one to compute p_1 and p_2 from any given combination of values added, v_1 and v_2 is,

$$(8) \quad \begin{aligned} p_1 &= 1.457v_1 + 0.232v_2 \\ p_2 &= 0.662v_1 + 1.242v_2 \end{aligned}$$

With v_1 = \$0.80 and v_2 = \$3.60 we have, p_1 = \$2.00 and p_2 = \$5.00. Multiplying the physical quantities of wheat and cloth entered in the first and second rows of Table 4 with appropriate prices, we can transform it into a familiar input-output table in which all transactions are shown in dollars.

VII

Within the framework of the open input-output system described above any reduction or increase in the output level of pollutants can be traced either to changes in the final demand for specific goods and services, changes in the technical structure of one or more sectors of the economy, or some combination of the two.

The economist cannot devise new technology, but, as has been demonstrated above, he can explain or even anticipate the effect of any given technological change on the output of pollutants (as well as of all the other goods and services). He can determine the effects of such a change on sectoral, and, consequently, also the total demand for the "primary factor of production." With given "values-added" coefficients he can, moreover, estimate the effect of such a change on prices of various goods and services.

After the explanations given above, a single example should suffice to show how any of these questions can be formulated and answered in input-output terms.

Consider the simple two-sector economy whose original state and structure were described in Tables 3, 4, 5, and 6. Assume that a process has been introduced permitting elimination (or prevention) of pollution and that the input requirements of that process amount to two man-years of labor (or \$2.00 of value added) and 0.20 yards of

Table 6—Structural matrix of a national economy with pollution output and antipollution input coefficients included

OUTPUT SECTORS INPUTS AND POLLUTANTS' OUTPUT	SECTOR 1 AGRICULTURE	SECTOR 2 MANUFACTURE	ELIMINATION OF POLLUTANT
Sector 1 Agriculture	0.25	0.40	0
Sector 2 Manufacture	0.14	0.12	0.20
Pollutant (output)	0.50	0.20	
Labor (value added)	0.80 ($0.80)	3.60 ($3.60)	2.00 ($2.00)

cloth per gram of pollutant prevented from being discharged—either by Agriculture or Manufacture—into the air.

Combined with the previously introduced sets of technical coefficients this additional information yields the following complex structural matrix of the national economy.

The input-output balance of the entire economy can be described by the following set of four equations:

$$\begin{aligned}
0.75X_1 - 0.40X_2 &= Y_1 \quad \text{(wheat)} \\
-0.14X_1 + 0.88X_2 - 0.20X_3 &= Y_2 \quad \text{(cotton cloth)} \\
0.50X_1 + 0.20X_2 - X_3 &= Y_3 \quad \text{(pollutant)} \\
-0.80X_1 - 3.60X_2 - 2.00X_3 + L &= Y_4 \quad \text{(labor)}
\end{aligned}$$

(9)

Variables:

X_1 : total output of agricultural products
X_2 : total output of manufactured products
X_3 : total amount of eliminated pollutant
L : employment
Y_1 : final demand for agricultural products
Y_2 : final demand for manufactured products
Y_3 : total uneliminated amount of pollutant
Y_4 : total amount of labor employed by Household
and other "final demand" sectors[1]

[1] In all numerical examples presented in this paper Y_4 is assumed to be equal to zero.

336

Instead of describing complete elimination of all pollution, the third equation contains on its right-hand side Y_3, the amount of uneliminated pollutant. Unlike all other elements of the given vector of final deliveries it is not "demanded" but, rather, tolerated.[2]

The general solution of that system for the unknown X's in terms of any given set of Y's is written out in full below

$$
\begin{array}{llll}
X_1 = 1.573Y_1 + 0.749Y_2 - 0.149Y_3 + 0.000Y_4 & \text{Agriculture} \\
X_2 = 0.449Y_1 + 1.404Y_2 - 0.280Y_3 + 0.000Y_4 & \text{Manufacture} \\
X_3 = 0.876Y_1 + 0.655Y_2 - 1.131Y_3 + 0.000Y_4 & \text{Pollutant} \\
L = 4.628Y_1 + 6.965Y_2 - 3.393Y_3 + 1.000Y_4 & \text{Labor}
\end{array}
$$

(10)

The square set of coefficients (each multiplied with the appropriate Y) on the right-hand side of (10) is the inverse of the matrix of constants appearing on the left-hand side of (9). The inversion was, of course, performed on a computer.

The first equation shows that each additional bushel of agricultural product delivered to final consumers (i.e., Households) would require (directly and indirectly) an increase of the total output of the agricultural sector (X_1) by 1.573 bushels, while the final delivery of an additional yard of cloth would imply a rise of total agricultural outputs by 0.749 bushels

The next term in the same equation measures the (direct and indirect) relationship between the total output of agricultural products (X_1) and the "delivery" to final users of Y_3 grams of uneliminated pollutants.

The constant -0.149 associated with it in this final equation indicates that a reduction in the total amount of pollutant delivered to final consumers by one gram would require an increase of agricultural output by 0.149 bushels.

Tracing down the column of coefficients asssociated with Y_3 in the second, third, and fourth equations we can see what effect a reduction in the amount of pollutant delivered to the final users would have on the total output levels of all other industries. Manufacture would have to produce an additional 0.280 yards of cloth. Sector 3, the antipollution industry itself, would be required to eliminate 1.131 grams of pollutant to make possible the reduction of its final delivery by 1

[2] In (6) that describes a system that generates pollution, but does not contain any activity combating it, the variable X_3 stands for the total amount of uneliminated pollution that is in system (8) represented by Y_3.

gram, the reason for this being that economic activities required (directly and indirectly) for elimination of pollution do, in fact, generate some of it themselves.

The coefficients of the first two terms on the right-hand side of the third equation show how the level of operation of the antipollution industry (X_3) would have to vary with changes in the amounts of agricultural and manufactured goods purchased by final consumers, if the amount of uneliminated pollutant (Y_3) were kept constant. The last equation shows that the total, i.e., direct and indirect, labor input required to reduce Y_3 by 1 gram amounts to 3.393 man-years. This can be compared with 4.628 man-years required for delivery to the final users of an additional bushel of wheat and 6.965 man-years needed to let them have one more yard of cloth.

Starting with the assumption that Households, i.e., the final users, consume 55 bushels of wheat and 30 yards of cloth and also are ready to tolerate 30 grams of uneliminated pollution, the general solution (10) was used to determine the physical magnitudes of the intersectoral input-output flows shown in Table 7.

The entries in the third row show that the agricultural and manufactured sectors generate 63.93 (= 52.25 + 11.68) grams of pollution of which 33.93 are eliminated by antipollution industry and the remaining 30 are delivered to Households.

VIII

The dollar figures entered in parentheses are based on prices the derivation of which is explained below.

The original equation, system (7), describing the price-cost relationships within the agricultural and manufacturing sectors has now to be expanded through inclusion of a third equation stating that the price of "eliminating one gram of pollution" (i.e., p_3) should be just high enough to cover—after payment for inputs purchased from other industries has been met—the value added, v_3, i.e., the payments to labor and other primary factors employed directly by the antipollution industry.

$$p_1 - 0.25p_1 - 0.14p_2 = v_1$$
$$p_2 - 0.12p_2 - 0.40p_1 = v_2$$
$$p_3 \qquad\quad - 0.20p_2 = v_3$$

Table 7—Input-output table of the national economy (surplus pollution is eliminated by the antipollution industry)

OUTPUT SECTORS INPUTS AND POLLUTANTS' OUTPUT	SECTOR 1 AGRICULTURE	SECTOR 2 MANUFACTURE	ANTIPOLLUTION	FINAL DELIVERIES TO HOUSEHOLDS	TOTALS
Sector 1 Agriculture (bushels)	26.12 ($52.24)	23.37 ($46.74)	0	55 ($110.00)	104.50 ($208.99)
Sector 2 Manufacture (yards)	14.63 ($73.15)	7.01 ($35.05)	6.79 ($33.94)	30 ($150.00)	58.43 ($292.13)
Pollutant (grams)	52.25	11.68	−33.93	30 ($101.80 paid for elimination of 33.93 grams of pollutant)	
Labor (man-years)	83.60 ($83.60)	210.34 ($210.34)	67.86 ($67.86)	0	361.80 ($361.80)
Column Totals	$208.99	$292.13	$101.80	$361.80	

$p_1 = \$2.00$, $p_2 = \$5.00$, $p_3 = \$3.00$, $p_l = \$1.00$ (wage rate).

or in rearranged form,

$$
\begin{aligned}
0.75p_1 - 0.14p_2 &= v_1 \\
(11) \qquad -0.40p_1 + 0.88p_2 &= v_2 \\
- 0.20p_2 + p_3 &= v_3.
\end{aligned}
$$

The general solution of these equations—analogous to (8)—is

$$
\begin{aligned}
p_1 &= 1.457v_1 + 0.232v_2 \\
(12) \qquad p_2 &= 0.662v_1 + 1.242v_2 \\
p_3 &= 0.132v_1 + 0.248v_2 + v_3.
\end{aligned}
$$

Assuming as before, $v_1 = 0.80$, $v_2 = 3.60$, and $v_3 = 2.00$, we find,

$$
\begin{aligned}
p_1 &= \$2.00 \\
p_2 &= \$5.00 \\
p_3 &= \$3.00
\end{aligned}
$$

The price (= cost per unit) of eliminating pollution turns out to be $3.00 per gram. The prices of agricultural and manufactured products remain the same as they were before.

Putting corresponding dollar values on all the physical transactions shown in the input-output Table 7 we find that the labor employed by the three sectors adds up to $361.80. The wheat and cloth delivered to final consumers cost $260.00. The remaining $101.80 of the value added earned by the Households will just suffice to pay the price, i.e., to defray the costs of eliminating 33.93 of the total of 63.93 grams of pollution generated by the system. These payments could be made directly or they might be collected in the form of taxes imposed on the Households and used by the government to cover the costs of the privately or publicly operated antipollution industry.

The price system would be different, if through voluntary action or to obey a special law, each industry undertook to eliminate, at its own expense, all or at least some specified fraction of the pollution generated by it. The added costs would, of course, be included in the price of its marketable product.

Let, for example, the agricultural and manufacturing sectors bear the costs of eliminating, say, 50 percent of the pollution that, under prevailing technical conditions, would be generated by each one of them. They may either engage in antipollution operations on their own account or pay an appropriately prorated tax.

In either case the first two equations in (11) have to be modified by inclusion of additional terms: the outlay for eliminating 0.25 grams and 0.10 grams of pollutant per unit of agricultural and industrial output respectively.

$$
\begin{aligned}
0.75p_1 - 0.14p_2 - 0.25p_3 &= v_1 \\
-0.40p_1 + 0.88p_2 - 0.10p_3 &= v_2 \\
- 0.20p_2 + \quad p_3 &= v_3.
\end{aligned}
$$

(13)

The "inversion" of the modified matrix of structural coefficients appearing on the left-hand side yields the following general solution of the price system:

(14)
$$
\begin{aligned}
p_1 &= 1.511v_1 + 0.334v_2 + 0.411v_3 \\
p_2 &= 0.703v_1 + 1.318v_2 + 0.308v_3 \\
p_3 &= 0.141v_1 + 0.264v_2 + 1.062v_3.
\end{aligned}
$$

With "values added" in all the three sectors remaining the same as they were before (i.e., $v_1 = \$.80$, $v_2 = \$3.60$, $v_3 = \$2.60$) these new sets of prices are as follows:

$$
\begin{aligned}
p_1 &= \$3.234 \\
p_2 &= \$5.923 \\
p_3 &= \$3.185
\end{aligned}
$$

While purchasing a bushel of wheat or a yard of cloth the purchaser now pays for elimination of some of the pollution generated in production of that good. The prices are now higher than they were before. From the point of view of Households, i.e., of the final consumers, the relationship between real costs and real benefits remains, nevertheless, the same; having paid for some antipollution activities indirectly he will have to spend less on them directly.

IX

The final Table 8 shows the flows of goods and services between all the sectors of the national economy analyzed above. The structural characteristics of the system—presented in the form of a complete set of technical input-output coefficients—were assumed to be given; so was the vector of final demand, i.e., quantities of products of each industry delivered to Households (and other final users) as well as

341

Table 8—Input-output table of a national economy with pollution-related activities presented separately

	AGRICULTURE			MANUFACTURE			FINAL DELIVERIES TO HOUSEHOLDS		NATIONAL TOTALS
	Wheat	Anti-pollution	Total	Cloth	Anti-pollution	Total	ANTI-POLLUTION	HOUSEHOLDS	
Agriculture	26.12 ($84.47)	0	26.12 ($84.47)	23.37 ($75.58)	0	23.37 ($75.58)	0	55 ($177.87)	105.50 ($337.96)
Manufacture	14.63 ($86.65)	5.23 ($30.98)	19.86 ($117.63)	7.01 ($41.52)	1.17 ($6.93)	8.18 ($48.45)	.39 ($2.33)	30 ($177.69)	58.43 ($346.07)
Pollutant	52.25	−26.13	26.12	11.69	−5.85	5.84	−1.97	30 ($6.26 paid for elimination of 1.97 grams of pollutant)	
Labor (value added)	83.60 ($83.60)	52.26 ($52.26)	135.86 ($135.86)	210.34 ($210.34)	11.70 ($11.70)	222.04 ($222.04)	3.93 ($3.93) ($3.93)		361.80 ($361.80)
Total Costs	($254.72)	($83.24)	($337.96)	($327.44)	($18.63)	($346.07)	($6.26)	($361.80)	

$p_1 = \$3.23,\ p_2 = \$5.92,\ p_3 = \$3.19.$
$v_1 = \$0.80,\ v_2 = \$3.60,\ v_3 = \$2.00.$

the uneliminated amount of pollutant that, for one reason or another, they are prepared to "tolerate." Each industry is assumed to be responsible for elimination of 50 percent of the pollution that would have been generated in the absence of such countermeasures. The Households defray—directly or through tax contributions—the cost of reducing the net output of pollution still further to the amount that they do, in fact, accept.

On the basis of this structural information we can compute the outputs and the inputs of all sectors of the economy, including the antipollution industries, corresponding to any given "bill of final demand." With information on "value added," i.e., the income paid out by each sector per unit of its total output, we can, furthermore, determine the prices of all outputs, the total income received by the final consumer and the breakdown of their total expenditures by types of goods consumed.

The 30 grams of pollutant entered in the "bill of final demand" are delivered free of charge. The $6.26 entered in the same box represent the costs of that part of antipollution activities that were covered by Households directly, rather than through payment of higher prices for agricultural and manufactured goods.

The input requirements of antipollution activities paid for by the agricultural and manufacturing sectors and all the other input requirements are shown separately and then combined in the total input columns. The figures entered in the pollution row show accordingly the amount of pollution that would be generated by the principal production process, the amount eliminated (entered with a minus sign), and finally the amount actually released by the industry in question. The amount (1.97) eliminated by antipollution activities not controlled by other sectors is entered in a separate column that shows also the corresponding inputs.

From a purely formal point of view the only difference between Table 8 and Table 7 is that in the latter all input requirements of Agriculture and Manufacture and the amount of pollutant released by each of them are shown in a single column, while in the former the productive and antipollution activities are described also separately. If such subdivision proves to be impossible and if, furthermore, no separate antipollution industry can be identified, we have to rely on the still simpler analytical approach that led up to the construction of Table 3.

X

Once appropriate sets of technical input and output coefficients have been compiled, generation and elimination of all the various kinds of pollutants can be analyzed as what they actually are—integral parts of the economic process.

Studies of regional and multiregional systems, multisectoral projections of economic growth and, in particular, the effects of anticipated technological changes, as well as all other special types of input-output analysis can, thus, be extended so as to cover the production and elimination of pollution as well.

The compilation and organization of additional quantitative information required for such extension could be accelerated by systematic utilization of practical experience gained by public and private research organizations already actively engaged in compilation of various types of input-output tables.

Mathematical appendix

Static-open input-output system with pollution-related activities built in

Notation

Commodities and services

$$1, 2, 3, \ldots i \ldots j \ldots m, m + 1, m + 2, \ldots g \ldots k \ldots n$$
$$\quad \text{useful goods} \qquad\qquad\qquad \text{pollutants}$$

Technical coefficients

a_{ij}—input of good i per unit of output of good j (produced by sector j)
a_{ig}—input of good i per unit of eliminated pollutant g (eliminated by sector g)
a_{gi}—output of pollutant g per unit of output of good i (produced by sector i)
a_{gk}—output of pollutant g per unit of eliminated pollutant k (eliminated by sector k)
r_{gi}, r_{gk}—proportion of pollutant g generated by industry i or k eliminated at the expense of that industry

Variables

x_i—total output of good i
x_g—total amount of pollutant g eliminated
y_i—final delivery of good i (to Households)
y_g—final delivery of pollutant g (to Households)
p_1—price of good
p_g—the "price" of eliminating one unit of pollutant g

344

v_i—"value added" in industry i per unit of good i produced by it

v_g—"value added" in antipollution sector g per unit of pollutant g eliminated by it

Vectors and matrices

$$
\begin{aligned}
A_{11} &= [a_{ij}] & & i, j = 1, 2, 3, \ldots, m \\
A_{21} &= [a_{gi}] & & \left. \begin{array}{l} i = 1, 2, 3, \ldots, m \\ g = m + 1, m + 2, m + 3, \ldots, n \end{array} \right\} \\
A_{12} &= [a_{ig}] & & \\
A_{22} &= [a_{gk}] & & g, k = m + 1, m + 2, m + 3, \ldots, n \\
Q_{21} &= [q_{gi}] & & i = 1, 2, \ldots, m \\
& & & g = m + 1, m + 2, \ldots, n \\
Q_{22} &= [q_{gk}] & & g, k = m + 1, m + 2, \ldots, n
\end{aligned}
$$

where $q_{gi} = r_{gi}a_{gi}$

$\qquad q_{gk} = r_{gk}a_{gk}$

$$
X_1 = \left\{ \begin{array}{c} x_1 \\ x_2 \\ \cdot \\ \cdot \\ \cdot \\ x_m \end{array} \right\} \quad
Y_1 = \left\{ \begin{array}{c} y_1 \\ y_2 \\ \cdot \\ \cdot \\ y_m \end{array} \right\} \quad
V_1 = \left\{ \begin{array}{c} v_1 \\ v_2 \\ \cdot \\ \cdot \\ v_m \end{array} \right\}
$$

$$
X_2 = \left\{ \begin{array}{c} x_{m+1} \\ x_{m+2} \\ \cdot \\ \cdot \\ x_n \end{array} \right\} \quad
Y_2 = \left\{ \begin{array}{c} y_{m+1} \\ y_{m+2} \\ \cdot \\ \cdot \\ y_n \end{array} \right\} \quad
V_2 = \left\{ \begin{array}{c} v_{m+1} \\ v_{m+2} \\ \cdot \\ \cdot \\ v_n \end{array} \right\}
$$

PHYSICAL INPUT-OUTPUT BALANCE

$$
(15) \quad \begin{bmatrix} I - A_{11} & \vdots & -A_{12} \\ \hdotsfor{3} \\ A_{21} & \vdots & -I + A_{22} \end{bmatrix} \begin{bmatrix} X_1 \\ \cdots \\ X_2 \end{bmatrix} = \begin{bmatrix} Y_1 \\ \cdots \\ Y_2 \end{bmatrix}
$$

$$
(16) \quad \begin{bmatrix} X_1 \\ \cdots \\ X_2 \end{bmatrix} = \begin{bmatrix} I - A_{11} & \vdots & -A_{12} \\ \hdotsfor{3} \\ A_{21} & \vdots & -I + A_{22} \end{bmatrix}^{-1} \begin{bmatrix} Y_1 \\ \cdots \\ Y_2 \end{bmatrix}
$$

INPUT-OUTPUT BALANCE BETWEEN PRICES AND VALUES ADDED

$$
(17) \quad \begin{bmatrix} I - A'_{11} & \vdots & -Q'_{21} \\ \hdotsfor{3} \\ -A'_{12} & \vdots & I - Q'_{22} \end{bmatrix} \begin{bmatrix} P_1 \\ \cdots \\ P_2 \end{bmatrix} = \begin{bmatrix} V_1 \\ \cdots \\ V_2 \end{bmatrix}
$$

$$
(18) \quad \begin{bmatrix} P_1 \\ \cdots \\ P_2 \end{bmatrix} = \begin{bmatrix} I - A'_{11} & \vdots & -Q'_{21} \\ \hdotsfor{3} \\ -A'_{12} & \vdots & I - Q'_{22} \end{bmatrix}^{-1} \begin{bmatrix} V_1 \\ \cdots \\ V_2 \end{bmatrix}
$$

Supplementary notation and equations accounting for pollution generated directly by final consumption

Notation

Technical coefficients

$a_{gv,\ (i)}$—output of pollutant generated by consumption of one unit of commodity i delivered to final demand.

Variables

y_g^*—sum total of pollutant g "delivered" from all industries to and generated within the final demand sector,

x_g^*—total gross output of pollutant g generated by all industries and in the final demand sector.

$$A_y = \left\{ \begin{array}{cccc} a_{m+1,\ y(1)} & a_{m+1,\ y(1)} & \cdots & a_{m+1,\ y(m)} \\ a_{m+2,\ y(2)} & a_{m+2,\ y(2)} & \cdots & a_{m+2,\ y(m)} \\ \cdot & \cdot & & \\ \cdot & \cdot & & \\ \cdot & \cdot & & \\ a_n\ y_1 & a_n\ y_2 & \cdots & a_n\ y_m \end{array} \right\}$$

$$Y_2^* = \left\{ \begin{array}{c} y^*_{m+1} \\ y^*_{m+2} \\ \cdot \\ \cdot \\ \cdot \\ y_n^* \end{array} \right\} \qquad x_g^* = \left\{ \begin{array}{c} x^*_{m+1} \\ x^*_{m+2} \\ \cdot \\ \cdot \\ \cdot \\ x_n^* \end{array} \right\}$$

In case some pollution is generated within the final demand sector itself, the vector Y_2 appearing on the right-hand side of (15) and (16) has to be replaced by vector $Y_2 - Y_2^*$, where

$$(19) \qquad\qquad Y_2^* = A_y Y_1.$$

The price-value added equations (17), (18) do not have to be modified.

Total gross output of pollutants generated by all industries and the final demand sector does not enter explicitly in any of the equations presented above; it can, however, be computed on the basis of the following equation,

$$(20) \qquad\qquad X^* = [A_{21} \ \vdots \ A_{22}] \left[\begin{array}{c} X_1 \\ \cdots \\ X_2 \end{array} \right] + Y_2^*.$$

27

National income, economic structure, and environmental externalities

I. National income as a welfare index

The per capita net national income used as a measure of the level of welfare is a typical index number. The computation of an index number involves application of some well-defined but essentially arbitrary conventional procedures to direct or indirect measurements of observed, or at least in principle observable, phenomena.

The conventional interpretation of net national income valued in some constant prices can be conveniently rationalized in terms of the ad hoc assumption that preferences of a representative average consumer can be described by a social utility function or a fixed set of well-behaving social indifference curves.

At this point observed or at least observable facts come in. The bundle of goods actually consumed by a representative individual has been obviously preferred—so goes the argument—to all the other alternative bundles that were accessible to him.

Under the special conditions of a market economy the set of all alternative bundles accessible to a representative consumer is uniquely determined by (a) the amounts of various goods that he has actually consumed and (b) the relative prices of these goods. The relative prices represent the marginal opportunity costs of each good in terms of every other good as seen from the point of their actual or potential consumer.

From M. Moss (ed.), *The Measurement of Economic and Social Performance*, Studies in Income and Wealth, Vol. 38 (New York: National Bureau of Economic Research, 1973), pp. 565–76.

This factual information, combined with the before-mentioned ad hoc assumption concerning the existence of a "well-behaved" set of collective indifference lines, permits us to identify *some* of the bundles of goods that the representative consumer apparently judges to be *less desirable* than the particular bundle that he actually chose to use.

This analytical proposition constitutes the basic, not to say the sole, theoretical justification for interpreting the *differences* in per capita net national income—valued in fixed prices—as an index of changes in the level of average per capita welfare attained by a particular society in different years.

Goods acquired through other means than purchases at given prices on a free market can still be taken into account in computation of the conventional welfare index provided their opportunities costs—as perceived by the representative consumer—can be ascertained in some other way.

Much of the work aimed at inclusion of various nonmarketable components into the measure of national income is centered on devising plausible methods of determining the imputed prices or more generally the opportunity costs of such goods.

In the light of what has been said above, the inclusion of pollutants and other kinds of environmental repercussions of economic activities into the measurement of the per capita national income as a welfare index requires answers to two sets of questions. One concerns the establishment of acceptable conventions pertaining to the inclusion of environmental repercussions into the conceptual framework of an all-embracing social utility function and a corresponding set of representative indifference curves. The other pertains to the actual physical description and measurement of the generation and elimination of pollutants by the economic system and the empirical determination of their opportunity costs in terms of ordinary goods and of each other.

The answer that one can give to these questions is critically influenced by the typically external nature of most environmental repercussions of economic activities and also by the fact that because of that measures aimed at abatement of their undesirable effects must in most instances be promulgated by the government.

Speaking in this context of collective indifference lines or preferences of a representative individual one must interpret such preference—at least so far as the environmental effects of economic activities are concerned—as being revealed not through private but rather through collective choice reflected in specific actions of the government.

Moreover, in case the conjectured opportunity costs reflected in the level of antipollution actions actually observed differ from the true opportunity costs, it is the former rather than the latter that would have to provide the base for proper weighing of pollution components to be included in a revised, more comprehensive, national income index.

Who would pretend to know what opportunity costs (if any) are being taken into account in the design of antipollution measures now actually being carried out in the United States?

Many of the contributors to the present symposium when touching upon problems of social valuation abandon the difficult revealed preference criteria in favor of a strictly axiomatic approach.

That solves the problem of welfare measurement as simply as Columbus solved his problem with the egg. One chooses ad hoc a social utility function which for some ethical or mathematical reason is appealing, inserts into it the levels of consumption of ordinary goods and net output of pollutants as they actually are, and then compares the index of welfare thus attained with the highest number of points that could be reached if the society were to move to the optimal point along the empirically given opportunity costs frontier.

Who can decide, however, what social utility function one should finally choose? Certainly not the economists in their professional capacity!

II. Enlarged input-output table, structural coefficients, and intersectoral dependence

Exhibit 1 presents a schematic outline of an expanded input-output table that traces not only the intersectoral flows of ordinary commodities and services, but also the generation and elimination of pollutants. The conventional classification of economic activities and goods is accordingly expanded to include the names of various pollutants and activities aimed at their elimination.

Notes to Exhibit 1

(1,1) Inputs of (ordinary) goods into industries. Most of these goods are produced by industries listed on the left, but some might originate as the "by-product" in pollution-eliminating activities. See (1,3).

(1,2) Inputs of ordinary goods into various pollution-eliminating activities and outputs of ordinary goods (entered with a negative sign) generated as by-products of pollution-eliminating activities. Reprocessed materials, for example, are entered here.

(1,3A) Goods delivered to the final demand sector are entered along the main diagonal of this square. See (3,3B).

(1,4) These totals do not include amounts of ordinary goods (as their by-products) originating in the pollution-eliminating activities and thus represent the activity levels of ordinary industries.

(2,1) Each row shows the amounts of one particular pollutant generated by industries listed at the heads of different columns. In other words, pollutants are treated here the way by-products are treated in ordinary input-output tables.

(2,2) Along each row are entered—as negative numbers—the amounts of one particular pollutant eliminated by activities named at the heads of different columns. The amounts of a pollutant generated, as is often the case, in the process of elimination of some other pollutants are entered along its appropriate row as positive numbers.

(2,3A), (2,3B) For purely descriptive purposes the total amounts of various pollutants generated in the final demand sector can be presented in a single column. For purposes of structural analyses, however, these totals should be distributed among as many separate columns as there are different inputs, i.e., industrial product inputs and primary factor inputs, absorbed by the final demand sector. In the process of final consumption each of these inputs is liable to generate its own "column" of pollutants. The inputs of ordinary goods into the final demand sector are entered in rows along the main diagonal of the square formed by (1,2) and (2,2) considered together. It sounds rather complicated, but that is the price one has to pay for orderly bookkeeping.

Exhibit 1

Interindustrial flows expanded to include the generation and elimination
of pollutants

	Industries 1	Pollution-eliminating Activities 2	Final Demand Sector 3		Totals 4
Industries 1	(1,1) Inputs of goods into industries (+) $[a_{ij}]$	(1,2) Inputs of goods into pollution eliminating activities (+) Output of goods by pollution eliminating activities (−) $[a_{ig}]$	(1,3A) Delivery of goods to final demand sector (+)	(1,3B) (Empty)	(1,4) Total outputs of goods excluding the amounts generated by the pollution eliminating activities
Pollutants 2	(2,1) Outputs of pollutants by industries (+) $[s_{gj}]$	(2,2) Elimination of pollutants by pollution eliminating activities (−) Output of pollutants by pollution eliminating activities (+) $[a_{gk}]$	(2,3A) Outputs of pollutants by final demand sector (connected with the consumption of goods) (+) $[c_{gi}]$	(2,3B) Outputs of pollutants by the final demand sector (connected with the consumption of primary factors) (+) $[c_{gr}]$	(2,4) *Net* outputs of pollutants (+)
Primary Inputs 3	(3,1) Inputs of primary factors into industries (+) $[v_{fj}]$	(3,2) Inputs of primary factors into pollution eliminating activities (+) $[v_{fg}]$	(3,3A) (Empty)	(3,3B) Delivery of primary factors to final demand sector (+)	(3,4) Total inputs of primary factors (+)

(2,4) Each figure in this column is obtained by subtracting the sum of all negative from the sum of all positive entries appearing to the left along the entire length of the row. These are the undesirable *net* outputs of various pollutants delivered by the economic system to the final users alongside the desirable ordinary goods and primary factors entered in (1,3A) and (3,3B). Together they make up the final results of economic activities upon which the welfare of the society supposedly depends.

(3,1), (3,2), (3,3B), (3,4) These contain a single row of aggregated value-added figures or several rows of physical or dollar figures depending on the amount of detail one wants to present.

The entries are organized in such a way as to have each column contain inputs and outputs controlled by the same autonomous set of structural relationships (i.e., by the same "cooking recipe"). The table is subdivided into rows and corresponding column strips. Each strip can be thought of as containing many rows of figures not shown in this schematic presentation. Each of the rectangular intersections on a row and a column can be conveniently identified by two numbers.

All entries can be interpreted as representing physical quantities measured in appropriate physical units or indices of physical amounts. All dollar figures appearing in the table can be interpreted as such indices (with a defined or undefined base). Hence, the usual *column* sums are pointedly omitted.

III. Structural relationships and opportunity costs

The figures entered in each one of the separate columns of the first three vertical strips of the enlarged flow table can be interpreted as representing the inputs absorbed and outputs generated by one particular process carried on side by side with many other structurally different processes within the framework of the given economic system.

Assuming that the structure of each such process can be described in terms of a linear or at least linearized "cooking recipe," the actual level of each output and each input as entered in the flow table can be interpreted as a product of two numbers: a technical coefficient and a number describing the level at which the process that absorbs that particular input or generates that particular output actually operates.

The levels of operation of ordinary industries are usually measured in terms of their principal output, while the level of operation of a pollution-eliminating activity can be conveniently described by the number of units of the specific pollutant that it eliminates. The levels of consumption activities that might generate pollution are described by the number of units of a particular good or primary factor delivered to the final demand sector.

The structural matrix of the economy—corresponding to the enlarged flow table described above—can be written in the following partitioned form:

	1	2	3 A	B
1	$[a_{ij}]$	$[a_{ig}]$		
2	$[a_{gi}]$	$[a_{gk}]$	$[c_{gi}]$	$[c_{gf}]$
3	$[\nu_{fi}]$	$[\nu_{fg}]$		

The elements of each submatrix are technical input or output coefficients; they are defined concisely in the Mathematical Appendix, below.

While the input coefficients of ordinary goods can usually be derived from the observed flows, information on the magnitude of the structural coefficient describing the generation and elimination of pollutants has in most instances to be obtained directly from technological sources. Combined with appropriate figures of the outputs of all pollution-generating activities, these coefficients provide a basis for estimation of the pollution flows.

In many, not to say in most, instances pollution is being combated not through the operation of separate elimination processes, but rather through the use of less polluting alternative techniques for production of ordinary goods. To incorporate such additional information the structural matrix would have to describe the input structure of some industrial and possibly even of some final demand sectors in terms of several alternative columns of input and output coefficients. The corresponding flow tables would, and actually do already in many instances, show for some sectors two or more columns of input-output flows.

Without explaining in detail the mathematical formulation and solution of the system of input-output equations involved[1] it suffices here to say that on the basis of the information contained in an enlarged structural matrix of a given economy it would be possible to compute (and some such computations have already been made) the total factor inputs (measured in physical amounts or more or less

[1]See Mathematical Appendix; see also essay 6 in this volume; and Wassily Leontief and Daniel Ford, "Air Pollution and the Economic Structure: Empirical Results of Input-Output Computations," *Proceedings*, Fifth International Input-Output Conference (Amsterdam: North-Holland Publishing Co., 1972).

aggregated "value added" dollars) required directly and indirectly: (a) to deliver to final users one additional unit of any particular good while keeping the deliveries of all the other goods and the net outputs of all pollutants constant; (b) to reduce by one unit the *net* output of any particular pollutant while keeping constant the net outputs of all the other pollutants and final deliveries of all goods.

This means that factual information contained in an enlarged structural matrix of a particular economy would permit us to compute in a rough and ready fashion the opportunity costs of an additional unit of any good and of an eliminated unit of the "net output" of each pollutant. The basic matrix of structural coefficients that governs the physical flows presented on the enlarged input-output table determines also a corresponding set of price-cost relationships.

The elimination of pollutants originating in various sectors can be paid for either directly by the final users or by the producing sectors in which they are being generated. In the latter case the cost of doing so will obviously be included in the price of the finished product. I have explained elsewhere[2] how these institutionally determined parameters can be introduced in standard input-output formulation of balanced price-cost equations.

If the prices are expected to reflect the true opportunity costs of various goods (including the "products" of pollution-eliminating activities) to final users, they must cover the costs of eliminating all additional pollution generated in the process of their production. Otherwise in purchasing a useful good the consumer would receive, probably unwittingly, an additional delivery of undesirable pollutants. Hence, the system of prices to be used for purposes of welfare decisions should be computed on the assumption that each industry and each pollution-eliminating process bears the full cost of eliminating all pollutants generated by it. This of course does not imply that the actual institutional arrangement and consequently the actual pricing should necessarily be governed by the same principle, the more so that the distributional effect of such "pure" opportunity cost pricing might turn out to be undesirable.

Once the prices of all outputs (including those of all antipollution

[2]*Ibid.*

354

activities) have been determined, all entries in the expanded tables of interindustrial flows can be valued in dollars. Marginal totals can be entered not only at the end of each row but also at the bottom of each column. The outputs of all pollutants will be represented by negative dollar figures; the amounts of pollutants eliminated by positive dollar figures. In particular the net outputs of pollutants delivered to final users (2,4) will add up to a negative dollar figure. It can be interpreted as representing the upper limit of the amount that would have to be spent (but in fact was not spent) for this particular purpose if the final users decided to eliminate all pollution actually delivered to them.

Mathematical appendix

The numbering of goods, pollutants, and primary factors

$1, 2, \ldots, i, \ldots, j, \ldots, n$
   n goods.
$n + 1, n + 2, \ldots, g, \ldots, k, \ldots, n + m$
   m pollutants.
$n + m + 1, n + m + 2, \ldots, f, \ldots, n + m + h$
   h primary factors.

Technical coefficients

a_{ij}—input of good i per unit of output of good j (produced by industry j).

a_{ig}—if > 0, input of good i per unit of eliminated pollutant g; if < 0, output of good i per unit of eliminated pollutant g.

a_{gi}—if > 0, output of pollutant g per unit of output of good i (produced by industry i); if < 0, input (productive use) of pollutant g per unit of output of good i (produced by industry i).

a_{gk}—output of pollutant g per unit of eliminated pollutant k.

c_{gi}—output of pollutant g generated in the final demand sector in the process of consuming one unit of good i.

c_{gf}—output of pollutant g generated in the final demand sector in the process of consuming one unit of the primary factor f.

v_{fi}—input of factor f per unit output of good i (produced by industry i).

v_{fg}—input of factor f per unit of eliminated pollutant g.

v_i—"value added" paid out by industry i per unit of its output.

v_g—"value added" paid out by the pollution-eliminating sector g per unit of pollution eliminated.

Vectors of technical coefficients

$[a_{ij}]$, $[a_{ig}]$, etc.

Variables

x_i—total output of good i by industry i.
x_g—total amount of pollutant g eliminated by pollutant-eliminating activity g.
x_f—total amount of factor f used in all sectors.
y_i—total amount of good i delivered to final demand.
y_g—*net* output of pollutant (delivered to final demand).
y_f—total amount of factor f delivered to final demand.
p_i—price of one unit of good produced by industry i.
p_g—price of eliminating one unit of pollution g by sector g.

Vectors of variables

$$
X_1 = \begin{bmatrix} x_1 \\ x_2 \\ \cdot \\ \cdot \\ \cdot \\ x_i \\ \cdot \\ \cdot \\ x_j \\ \cdot \\ \cdot \\ \cdot \\ x_n \end{bmatrix}
\qquad
X_2 = \begin{bmatrix} x_{n+1} \\ x_{n+2} \\ \cdot \\ \cdot \\ x_g \\ \cdot \\ \cdot \\ x_k \\ x_{n+m} \end{bmatrix}
\qquad
X_3 = \begin{bmatrix} x_{n+m+1} \\ x_{n+m+2} \\ \cdot \\ \cdot \\ x_f \\ \cdot \\ \cdot \\ x_{n+m+h} \end{bmatrix}
$$

$$
Y_1 = \begin{bmatrix} y_1 \\ y_2 \\ \cdot \\ \cdot \\ y_i \\ \cdot \\ \cdot \\ y_j \\ \cdot \\ \cdot \\ y_n \end{bmatrix}
\qquad
Y_2 = \begin{bmatrix} y_{n+1} \\ y_{n+2} \\ \cdot \\ \cdot \\ y_g \\ \cdot \\ \cdot \\ y_k \\ y_{n+m} \end{bmatrix}
\qquad
Y_3 = \begin{bmatrix} y_{n+m+1} \\ y_{n+m+2} \\ \cdot \\ \cdot \\ y_f \\ \cdot \\ \cdot \\ y_{n+m+h} \end{bmatrix}
$$

356

$$V_1 = \begin{bmatrix} v_1 \\ v_2 \\ \cdot \\ \cdot \\ v_i \\ \cdot \\ \cdot \\ \cdot \\ v_j \\ \cdot \\ \cdot \\ v_n \end{bmatrix} \qquad V_2 = \begin{bmatrix} v_{n+1} \\ v_{n+2} \\ \cdot \\ \cdot \\ v_g \\ \cdot \\ \cdot \\ \cdot \\ v_k \\ \cdot \\ \cdot \\ v_{n+m} \end{bmatrix} \qquad P_1 = \begin{bmatrix} p_1 \\ p_2 \\ \cdot \\ \cdot \\ p_i \\ \cdot \\ \cdot \\ \cdot \\ p_j \\ \cdot \\ \cdot \\ p_n \end{bmatrix} \qquad P_2 = \begin{bmatrix} p_{n+1} \\ p_{n+2} \\ \cdot \\ \cdot \\ p_g \\ \cdot \\ \cdot \\ \cdot \\ p_k \\ \cdot \\ \cdot \\ p_{n+m} \end{bmatrix}$$

Balance equations

Each of the following matrix equations describes the balance between the outputs and the inputs entered in one of the three row strips of the enlarged input-output table.

(1)
$$\begin{aligned} \text{Goods} \quad & [I - a_{ij}] X_1 - [a_{ig}] X_2 && = Y_2 \\ \text{Pollutants} \quad & -[a_{gi}] X_1 + [I - a_{gk}] X_2 = [c_{gi}] Y_1 - Y_2 + [c_{gf}] Y_3 \\ \text{Factors} \quad & -[v_{fi}] X_1 - [v_{fg}] X_2 + X_3 = && Y_3 \end{aligned}$$

The general solution of that system for the unknown x's in terms of given y's is

(2)
$$\begin{bmatrix} X_1 \\ \hline X_2 \\ \hline X_3 \end{bmatrix} = \begin{bmatrix} [I - a_{ij}] & \vdots & -[a_{ig}] & \vdots & 0 \\ \hline -[a_{gi}] & \vdots & [I - a_{gk}] & \vdots & 0 \\ \hline -[v_{fi}] & \vdots & -[v_{fg}] & \vdots & [I] \end{bmatrix}^{-1} \begin{bmatrix} Y_1 \\ \hline [c_{gi}] Y_1 - Y_g + [c_{gf}] Y_3 \\ \hline Y_3 \end{bmatrix}$$

Separating the effects of the three kinds of outputs delivered to the final demand sector and expressing the relationship (2) in incremental terms:

(3)
$$\begin{bmatrix} \Delta X_1 \\ \hline \Delta X_2 \\ \hline \Delta X_3 \end{bmatrix} = M \begin{bmatrix} \Delta Y_1 \\ \hline [c_{gi}] \Delta Y_1 \\ \hline 0 \end{bmatrix}^{-1} + M \begin{bmatrix} 0 \\ \hline -\Delta Y_2 \\ \hline 0 \end{bmatrix}^{-1} + M \begin{bmatrix} 0 \\ \hline [c_{gf}] \Delta Y_3 \\ \hline \Delta Y_3 \end{bmatrix}^{-1}$$

The inverse of the enlarged structural matrix of the economy appearing on the right-hand side is the same that appears in (2) above.

The first and the third terms on the right-hand side describe the effect—on the output of goods (ΔX_1), the level of antipollution activities (ΔX_2), and total factor inputs

357

(ΔX_3)—of a given change in the final demand for goods (ΔY_1) and, respectively, final demand for primary factors (ΔY_2). These effects are computed on the assumption that the level of pollution-eliminating activities will be adjusted in such a way as to leave the net delivery of pollutants to final users unchanged (i.e., $\Delta Y_2 = 0$).

The second right-hand term shows what it would take—in total outputs of goods and total primary factor inputs—to *reduce* the delivery of (uneliminated) pollution to final users by the amount ΔY_2, while holding the deliveries of goods and factor services constant ($\Delta Y_1 = 0$, $\Delta Y_3 = 0$).

For purposes of price-cost computations, all primary factor flows entered along the second row-strip of the expanded input-output table can be valued in dollars and consolidated into a single row of "value added" figures. Accordingly the two coefficient matrices $-[v_{fi}]$ and $[v_{fg}]$ can be reduced to row vectors V_1 and V_2 of value-added coefficients.

If each industry and each antipollution activity were to pay—and include in the price of its product—the costs of eliminating all pollution directly generated by it,[3] the balance between revenues and outlays in all goods-producing and pollution-eliminating sectors could be described by the following matrix equations.

(4) Goods $[I - a'_{ij}]P_1 - [a'_{gi}]P_2 = V_1$
        Pollutant elimination $[a'_{ig}]P_1 + [I - a'_{gk}]P_2 = V_2$

The general solution of that system for unknown p's in terms of given v's is

(5)
$$\begin{bmatrix} P_1 \\ \hline P_2 \end{bmatrix} = \begin{bmatrix} [I - a'_{ij}] & -[a'_{gi}] \\ \hline -[a'_{ig}] & [I - a'_{gk}] \end{bmatrix}^{-1} \begin{bmatrix} V_1 \\ \hline V_2 \end{bmatrix}$$

[3]For price computations based on different assumptions see the article cited in notes 1 and 2.

28

An international comparison of factor costs and factor use

A REVIEW ARTICLE

For over 30 years—to be exact, since 1928—whenever a working economist was called on to describe in numbers or to interpret in analytical terms the relationship between the inputs of capital and labor and the final product of a plant, an industry, or a national economy as a whole, he was more likely than not to reach out for the Cobb-Douglas production function. Theorists questioned the arbitrariness of its form and statisticians the validity of procedures used in fitting it to given sets of data, but despite all criticism the familiar exponential equation was used over and over again, essentially, I think, because of its convenient simplicity. But now this remarkable career is apparently coming to an end. The old formula is being rapidly replaced by a new, improved recipe: the constant elasticity of substitution production function. In quantitative empirical analysis, the CES function can perform essentially the same role that the Cobb-Douglas function played up until now, but, owing to its less restrictive shape, it offers at the same time the indisputable advantage of greater flexibility.

In this monograph,[1] the new tool is used with considerable skill in a statistical inquiry designed to test—and, as it turns out, to disprove—one of the factual assumptions of the much-debated Hecksher-Ohlin interpretation of the classical theory of international

From *The American Economic Review*, Vol. 54, No. 4, June 1964.
[1]Bagicha Singh Minhas, *An International Comparison of Factor Costs and Factor Use*. Contributions to Economic Analysis, No. 31. Amsterdam: North-Holland Publishing Co., 1963.

trade. Mr. Minhas is one of the four joint authors—Professors Arrow, Chenery, and Solow are the others—of the article[2] published three years ago in which the CES function was not only described in some detail, but also, so far as I know, for the first time fitted to actual statistical data. Thus, it is not surprising to encounter in his book formulations and arguments already developed, or at least suggested, in that article.

The principal ideas are developed in four chapters which make up the first half of the book; the three remaining chapters are devoted to systematic statistical description and international comparison of the rates of return on capital in different industries. Presenting the results of what apparently first was conceived as a separate inquiry, the second half of the book bears only a loose, sketchily delineated relationship to the central line of argument developed in the first four chapters.

In a laudable endeavor to bring together theoretical and factual analysis, Minhas continuously shifts his argument from one to the other. For purposes of a critical review it seems to be more appropriate, after restating the substantive issue to which he addresses himself, to examine separately the new tool he chooses to use, the specific method of its application, and the interpretation of the results obtained.

The factual assumption of the modern theory of international trade that Minhas sets out to disprove is that a meaningful distinction can be made between capital- and labor-intensive industries, a distinction that incidentally plays a crucial role in analysis of economic development.

If the amounts of capital and of labor employed per unit of their respective outputs were technologically fixed, the ranking of different industries in accordance with the relative magnitude of the two input coefficients would certainly be valid. It still would be meaningful even if, in response to a given change in relative prices of the two factors, capital were substituted for labor or vice versa, provided the downward or the upward shifts of the capital-labor input ratios were so uniform as not to disturb to any significant extent the relative position of the individual industries on the capital-labor intensity scale. If, on the contrary, some industries responded to a given

[2]"Capital-Labor Substitution and Economic Efficiency," *Review of Economics and Statistics*, Aug. 1961, *43*, 225–50.

change in the relative price of the two factors by a much larger shift in their relative inputs than others, then their comparative position on the capital-labor intensity scale would often be reversed. The distinction between capital- and labor-intensive industries must lose in such a case much of its analytical usefulness. Neither in explanation of the pattern of international trade nor in the study of economic growth would it be permissible to utilize it as a technological datum. Minhas sets out to demonstrate empirically that this is actually the case, and he employs the constant elasticity of substitution production function to do so.

The constant elasticity of substitution—or as Minhas prefers to call it, the homohypallagic—production function can be written in the following form:

$$(1) \qquad V = (AK^{-\beta} + \alpha L^{-\beta})^{-1/\beta}$$

where V represents the output; K and L stand respectively for the inputs of capital and labor. Each one of the three quantities should be thought of as being measured in different physical units or, in the case of aggregative analysis, described by an appropriate index number. A, α, and β are constants which are supposed to reflect the technical characteristics of the particular production process. If K and L on the right-hand side of the formula are multiplied by an arbitrary positive constant, λ, the corresponding total output on the left-hand side will become $V\lambda$: this means that the production function described by equation (1) is homogeneous of the first degree; it obeys the law of constant returns to scale.

The partial derivatives of V in respect to L and K, i.e., the marginal productivities of labor and of capital, are:

$$(2a) \qquad \frac{\partial V}{\partial L} = \alpha \left(\frac{V}{L}\right)^{\beta+1} \qquad (2b) \qquad \frac{\partial V}{\partial K} = A \left(\frac{V}{K}\right)^{\beta+1}$$

and the marginal rate of substitution of capital for labor—let it be called x—is:

$$(3) \qquad x = \frac{\partial V}{\partial L} \Big/ \frac{\partial V}{\partial K} = \frac{\alpha}{A} \left(\frac{K}{L}\right)^{\beta+1}$$

Translated into logarithmic terms, that equation describes a straight line:

(4) $$\log x = \log \frac{\alpha}{A} + (\beta + 1) \log \left(\frac{K}{L}\right).$$

Its constant slope $(\beta+1)$ is the reciprocal of the elasticity of substitution between capital and labor, σ:

(5) $$\sigma = d \log \left(\frac{K}{L}\right) \Big/ d \log x = \frac{1}{\beta+1}.$$

To demonstrate that the Cobb-Douglas production function represents a special case of the CES function in which $\sigma = 1$, i.e., $\beta = 0$, we can rewrite (3) interpreting its left-hand side as a derivative of K in respect to L along a constant output curve:

(6) $$\frac{dK}{dL} = -\frac{\alpha}{A} \frac{K}{L} \text{ or } -A \frac{dK}{K} = \alpha \frac{dL}{L}.$$

Integration of the two sides of the second expression gives:

(7) $$V = K^A L^\alpha$$

where the constant of integration, V, represents the output measured in appropriately defined units. After raising both sides of (1) to the power β, we can see that $A+\alpha=1$, if $\beta=0$, which is indeed the condition satisfied by the two exponents in the homogeneous Cobb-Douglas production function.

Perfect substitutability between capital and labor can also be interpreted as being a special case of the CES function (1): If $\sigma = \infty$ and consequently $\beta=-1$, it acquires the simple linear form,

(8) $$V = AK + \alpha L.$$

On a familiar two-dimensional graph the corresponding isoquants are represented by a set of negatively sloping parallel straight lines.

At the opposite extreme, when the elasticity of substitution tends toward 0 and β tends toward ∞, equation (1) degenerates into an input-output relationship characterized by constant capital and labor coefficients of production. However, for reasons that I will explain later, this rather special interpretation of a strictly complementary relation between capital and labor, though formally correct, is apt to be misleading when applied in statistical analysis of observed facts.

If a profit-maximizing industry considers the price of labor, w, and

362

the price of capital, r, as given, it will employ these two factors of production in such amounts as to equate the price ratio, $\frac{w}{r}$, to the marginal rate of substitution of capital for labor. According to (3) and (4), in the case of a CES function, the dependence of the factor input ratio, $\frac{K}{L}$, on the price ratio, $\frac{w}{r}$, is described by the simple log-linear relation,

$$(9) \qquad \log\left(\frac{w}{r}\right) = \log\frac{\alpha}{A} + (\beta + 1) \log\left(\frac{K}{L}\right).$$

Minhas illustrates his crucial argument concerning the possible effect of changing price ratios on the capital-labor input ratio in different industries by drawing the graph in Figure 1.

The two lines represent the relationship between the capital-labor ratio, $\frac{K}{L}$, and the relative price, $\frac{w}{r}$, in two different industries. The first industry will be more capital-intensive (and less labor-intensive) than

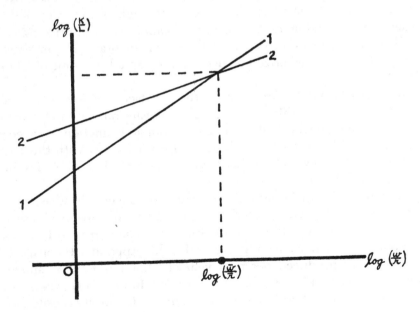

Figure 1

363

the second if the labor-capital price ratio happens to be higher than $\frac{\bar{w}}{\bar{r}}$, but the second will become more capital-intensive (and less labor-intensive) than the first if the labor-capital price ratio is lower than the critical level, $\frac{\bar{w}}{\bar{r}}$. The point A at which the two industries, while confronted with the same relative prices of capital and labor, would combine the two factors in exactly the same proportion is called by Minhas the crossover point. The position of the crossover depends on the slope $(\beta+1)$ and the level $\left(\frac{\alpha}{A}\right)$ of each of the two curves. If the slopes of the two lines—that is, the elasticity of substitution between capital and labor in the two industries—happen to be exactly the same, the capital intensities of both industries will be identical throughout if the levels of both the lines happen to be also equal; otherwise, they will be parallel, which means that the capital-labor ratio in one of the two industries will be higher throughout than in the other. In case the elasticities are unequal, that is, the slopes of the two lines differ, they must necessarily intersect somewhere. The crossover points might, however, be located to the right or to the left of the usual or even possible range of observed capital-labor or price ratios. In this case, one industry can still be, for all practical purposes, unequivocally characterized as using more capital per unit of labor than the other.

Minhas sets out to demonstrate that, in fact, crossovers can be expected to occur within the practically relevant range so often as to vitiate the analytical usefulness of conventional distinctions between capital- and labor-intensive industries. I cannot agree with this and will now try to show that Minhas' own empirical evidence justifies the opposite conclusion.

To demonstrate the importance of the crossovers, Minhas, by a very ingenious procedure, fits CES production functions to 24 industries distributed over 19 different countries. The approach is cross-sectional; the primary data (presented in his Appendix I) consist of "value added produced per man year of labor input" and "annual wage rate payment per worker" compiled from official statistical publications for each industry in each country. Ingenuity is called for

364

because no information on corresponding capital inputs or prices is used in the process. Values added, i.e., the gross revenues minus the costs of materials, are used throughout to represent the outputs, V. All wage rates and values added are converted to U.S. dollars in accordance with the fixed official or free market exchange rate.

On the assumption that the real wage rate paid equals the marginal productivity of labor, w can be substituted for $\frac{\partial V}{\partial L}$ on the left-hand side of (2a). The resulting equation can be written in the form of the following log-linear relationship:

(10) $$\log \left(\frac{V}{L}\right)_{ij} = \log a_i + b_i \log w_{ij}$$

where $\log a_i = -\log \alpha_i \frac{1}{\beta + 1}$ and $b_i = \frac{1}{\beta + 1} \equiv \sigma_i$.

Subscript i identifies the industry and subscript j the country. The constants, $\log a_i$ and b_i, carry only the industry but not the country subscript since the CES production function, the shape of which they are supposed to reflect, is assumed to be the same in all the countries.

The magnitude of parameters, $\log a_i$ and b_i, can thus be estimated by fitting a least-squares regression line through the scatter of $\log \left(\frac{V}{L}\right)_{ij}$ on $\log w_{ij}$, with a fixed i and varying j. The slope b_i of that regression line represents the elasticity of substitution between labor and capital in the ith industry. Among the 24 regression lines fitted by Minhas, the estimated magnitude of σ_i ranges from 0.7211 in Dairy Products to 1.0114 in Primary Nonferrous Metals; in 20 instances it exceeds 0.8, and in 8 of these it lies above 0.9.

To determine the location of potential "crossover" points marking the reversal in the relative capital-labor intensity of any two of the 24 industries, it is necessary to draw up for each one of them a log-linear relationship between $\frac{K}{L}$ and $\frac{w}{r}$ as described in equation (9) and shown in Figure 1. The elasticity of substitution between capital and labor determines, however, only the slope of the straight lines drawn on that graph. Their levels depend on the value of the two other constants, α_i and A_i, entering in the CES function of each industry, i. Equation (10) in addition to β_i (and, consequently, σ_{ij}) yields an estimate of α_i—the constant associated in the CES production function (1) with the labor input, L—but it is incapable of supplying also an estimate of A_i, which is the corresponding constant associated with the capital input, K.

To apply an analogous procedure in estimating the A's, it would be necessary only to replace the ratio $\dfrac{V}{L}$ on the left-hand side of (10) by the corresponding ratio $\dfrac{V}{K}$, and on its right-hand side replace the wage rate, w_{ij}, by r_{ij}, i.e., the rate of profit earned per unit of capital employed by industry i in country j.

Minhas presents the estimates of both the α's and the A's for only six of the many industries covered by his elasticity computations. The magnitudes of the α's and σ's entered in small Table IV correspond exactly to the least-squares estimates of these parameters—based on equation (10)—shown for all the 24 industries in his Tables I and II. No word is said, however, in explanation of the origin of the estimates of the six corresponding A's. This is the more surprising since the examination of the five "crossovers" between the capital-labor intensities of these particular six industries (shown on his Figures 5 and 6) constitutes the sole and only factual evidence that Minhas can cite in support of his sweeping and emphatic rejection of the conventional distinction between capital- and labor-intensive industries.

As I have said above, in Chapters 5 and 6, Minhas presents a rather detailed statistical analysis of the rates of return on capital invested in the same industries in different countries. Table XVII on page 92 summarizes the results of his inquiry; it covers 17 industries and five countries: United States, Canada, United Kingdom, Japan, and India. Most of the industries included in the larger set of data which Minhas actually uses to estimate two of the three parameters of the 24 CES production functions are represented directly or in slightly aggregated form also in Table XVII. The information contained in it can thus be used to estimate the missing third parameter for 17 of the 24 industries covered in his Table I. The two-step procedure I have used is described below.

Parameter A_i enters as denominator in the middle term of equation (9); for the purpose at hand it suffices to estimate for each industry the

366

magnitude of that entire term, rather than of A_i alone. Equation (9) can be rewritten in the following form:

$$(9a) \qquad \log\left(\frac{\alpha_i}{A_i}\right) = \log\left(\frac{w_{ij}}{r_{ij}}\right) - (\beta_i + 1)\log\left(\frac{K_{ij}}{L_{ij}}\right).$$

In estimating the elasticities of substitution, Minhas has already obtained the magnitudes of the corresponding β_i's. He compiled and used in his computations the wage rates, w_{ij}; he also compiled—but apparently did not use for the same purpose—the r_{ij}'s for 17 industries in five countries.

The magnitude of the capital-labor ratio, $\left(\frac{K}{L}\right)_{ij}$, appearing in the second right-hand term of (9a), can be derived by combining the profit-rates data with information on wage rates and value added per worker, $\left(\frac{V}{L}\right)_{ij}$, which, as we have seen above, Minhas uses too. By his own assumption, the value added in any industry is exactly exhausted by payments to capital and labor employed by it: $V_{ij} = L_{ij} w_{ij} + K_{ij} r_{ij}$. Dividing both sides by $L_{ij} r_{ij}$ and rearranging the terms, we arrive at the following relationship:

$$(11) \qquad \left(\frac{K}{L}\right)_{ij} = \left(\frac{V}{L}\right)_{ij}\frac{1}{r_{ij}} - \frac{w_{ij}}{r_{ij}}.$$

With all the magnitudes appearing to the right of the equation sign given, we can compute $\left(\frac{K}{L}\right)_{ij}$. Inserted on the right-hand side of (9a), this completes the information required to determine the magnitude of the constant, $\log\left(\frac{\alpha}{A}\right)_i$.

I have performed these additional computations for 21 of the 24 industries covered in Minhas' study, all those industries for which his Table XVII supplies an estimate of the rate of return on capital, r_{ij}. The results are shown in Figure 2. The factor price ratios, $\frac{w_{ij}}{r_{ij}}$, inserted in the course of these computations in equation (11) are those recorded for the industry in question in the United States. This means that the magnitude of the constant term, $\log\left(\frac{\alpha}{A}\right)_i$, was determined so as to make each one of the straight lines shown on Figure 2 pass

367

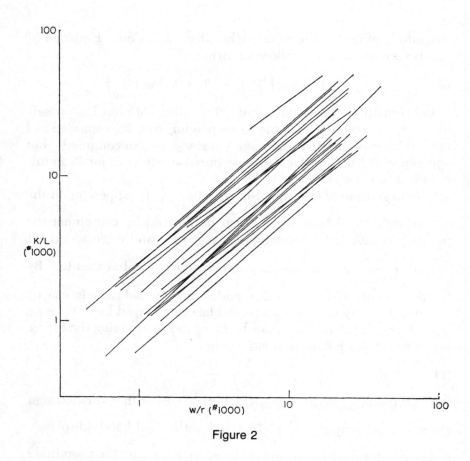

Figure 2

exactly through the point describing the combination of factor prices and factor inputs actually recorded for that particular industry in the United States. As should have been expected, all these points are located at the upper right-hand ends of all the 21 corresponding lines. The lowest of the $\left(\dfrac{K}{L}\right)_{ij}$ ratios observed in any industry i—typically observed in India—determine the cutoff at the lower left-hand end of each line. The corresponding lowest factor price ratios, $\left(\dfrac{w}{r}\right)_i$, would

have been equal to the wage-profit ratio actually observed in India if the theoretical assumption on which these computations are based were faultless and the empirical information error-free. In fact, the actual ratios deviate, of course, from those predicted on the assumption that the U.S. price and input ratios lie exactly on the curve.

The picture emerging from supplemental computations as shown in Figure 2 does not confirm Minhas' emphatically stated conclusion that "the strong factor intensity assumption, the conventional distinction between capital and labor intensive industries is of limited practical validity." On the contrary, it seems to confirm the conventional view. Of the theoretically possible 210 crossover points between the 21 lines entered on the graph, only 17 are found to be located within the wide range of factor price ratios, spanned on the one end by those observed in the United States and on the other by those reported from India. Moreover, most of these crossovers occur between industries whose curves run so close together throughout the entire range that for all practical purposes their capital-labor intensities would be considered identical. With two or three exceptions, each one of the 21 industries represented can be characterized as capital-intensive, labor-intensive, or as belonging to an intermediate group. In the light of this evidence the modern theory of international trade stands vindicated.

To avoid undesirable confusion of related but separable issues, up to this point I have presented Minhas' arguments and examined his conclusions without questioning the general theoretical framework within which they have been set. Interested in demonstrating the practical importance of crossovers, he naturally rejected the Cobb-Douglas function—which excludes crossovers by definition—and reached out for a formula capable of showing their existence. But if this were the principal reason for acquiring one more degree of freedom, the result of my extended computations shown in Figure 2 could easily justify a return to the simpler Cobb-Douglas formula. This suggestion would appear to be even more plausible if in applying the least-squares method to estimate the slopes, b_i, in the log-linear equations (10), Minhas had not proceeded on the assumption that only the variable $\left(\dfrac{V}{L}\right)_i$ is subject to random errors, while the variable w_i is not. Had he instead, in fitting the slopes of these regression lines, allowed also for errors affecting the observed magnitudes of w_i, all estimated elasticities would necessarily turn out to be larger, since in 23 out of the 24 industries examined by him, the magnitudes of the b_i's, i.e., the elasticities of substitution, turn out to be less—although in most instances only slightly less—than 1. This means that their values would be still closer to 1—the constant elasticity of the Cobb-Douglas function.

The inverse proportionality (implied by $b_i = 1$) between the number of workers employed per unit of output of a particular industry and the wage rate paid to them by that industry in different countries can be explained in entirely different terms. The assumption that a man-year of labor in one part of the world is equivalent to a man-year of labor in any other part, i.e., that the typical worker employed, say, in India is equal in productive efficiency to his similarly employed counterpart in the United States, can be questioned. If such equivalence were the rule rather than an exception, why should economists studying problems of economic development be so much concerned with investment—or rather the lack of it—in "human capital"?

Let it be assumed, for argument's sake, that an average man-year of labor employed by a given industry in one country is twice as efficient as a man-year employed by the same industry in another country. The production function in both instances can still appear to be, and actually will be, essentially the same, provided that, in measuring labor inputs for purposes of comparison, we multiply the figure describing the amount of labor absorbed by that industry in the first country by 2. At the same time, for comparison of the real unit costs of labor to that industry, the actual annual wage rate paid by it in the first country would have to be divided by 2. Such a procedure would be analogous to that used by Ricardo in his theory of rent. He visualized an agricultural production function allowing for several different grades of land and explained the higher price paid for an acre of better land by its proportionally greater efficiency. A similar argument was used recently by Houthakker when he interpreted the difference in the unit price paid by consumers for grades of nominally the same article as a measure of intrinsic qualitative difference.

The elasticity which Minhas estimates by fitting equation (10) to cross-section data measures—if it is interpreted in this sense—not substitution between capital and labor but rather substitution between different grades of labor, or possibly some combination of both. In the first case, the magnitude of the elasticity constant, b_i, in equation (10), as estimated by him, would necessarily be close to 1.

To determine which interpretation of Minhas' findings is correct, it is necessary to bring information on capital inputs explicitly into the picture. An elaborate comparison of rates of return on capital in different industries and countries can be found in the last two chapters. As I said above, the author nevertheless relies exclusively on the elegant but, even for his own purposes, not sufficiently powerful procedure in the course of which the elasticity of substitution between capital and labor is derived on the basis of information pertaining to labor only.

I have performed the simple numerical manipulations (similar to those described above in connection with the construction of my Figure 2) required to determine the capital-output ratios, $\left(\dfrac{K}{V}\right)_{ij}$, that would match the labor-output ratios, $\left(\dfrac{L}{V}\right)_{ij}$, used in Minhas' own computations. An examination of the resulting scatters shows that, as compared to the corresponding labor intensity, the capital intensity of any given industry varies little from country to country, and only in a few instances could one discern a visible negative relationship between the two. The overall picture is thus quite different from that which emerges from what Minhas calls the straightforward, but which in fact is a rather one-sided, method of estimating the elasticity of substitution between capital and labor.

In the light of closer examination of empirical evidence, fixed capital and labor coefficients (the latter measured in comparable efficiency units) might after all prove to be more appropriate for description of the specific productive relationships than the CES function in its general, or its particular Cobb-Douglas, form.

Judging by the practical implication that Minhas draws from it, the formally correct interpretations of fixed capital and labor coefficients as a special case of the CES function tend to be misleading. Fixed coefficients of production can be interpreted more meaningfully as representing a special case of technological conditions under which the two factors can be substituted for each other, but only within relatively narrow limits: the rate of substitution of capital for labor decreasing sharply and approaching zero whenever the capital-labor input ratio approaches a finite upper limit, but falling and becoming infinitely large when that ratio approaches the—also finite—lower limit. The elasticity-of-substitution concept proves to be a very awkward tool for analyzing this type of situation, and the assumption of constant elasticity of substitution simply breaks down in such a case. If the upper and lower limits of the admissible capital-labor input ratios lie comparatively close together, the average fixed coefficients will give an adequate description of such a technology. A combination of two or more alternative sets of such coefficients would of course do still better.

Except in its degenerate form when $\sigma = 0$, the CES function itself represents, as a matter of fact, a special case of homogeneous production characterized by literally unlimited substitution possibilities between factors, thus implying—when these factors are capital and labor—that any amount of a finished product can be obtained with a practically negligible amount of either capital or labor provided the supply of the other factors is large enough. This might be a good enough assumption in aggregative analysis where all possible products and processes of production are subsumed under a single loosely defined production function describing not so much a substitution of one method of production for another as a changing product mix. It is, however, hardly adequate for description of alternative input structures of sharply defined individual industries.

The length of this review testifies to the amount of stimulation an interested reader can find in this slim volume. The questions which the author asks are so well put that they will advance the understanding of factor use by the various branches of production in an international setting even if some of the answers which he gives cannot be accepted.

29

Explanatory power of the comparative cost theory of international trade and its limits

Old well-established truths need to be from time to time reexamined. On a second or a third inspection some of their implications might turn out different from what one remembers them to be.

The theory of comparative costs[1] is often assumed to be capable— in principle at least and with proper empirical implementation—of explaining the network of interregional trade flows. The magnitude and the direction of these flows is supposed to depend on the specific combinations of capital, labor, and other primary resources possessed by each one of the trading countries, the shapes of the production and consumption functions, i.e., the alternative input-output combinations that can actually be used in each country to transform primary resources and intermediate products (some of which will also be imported or exported) into final goods, and the valuation of alternative combinations of these goods by different groups of potential consumers.

Perusal of empirical studies concerned with the explanation of bilateral trade flow between two or several countries or groups of countries leaves no doubt that behind such specific quantitative explanations lies very often the belief that all such analysis can indeed be firmly rooted in the formal framework of the comparative cost theory referred to above.

From *Economic Structure and Development* (Amsterdam: North-Holland Publishing Co.; and New York: American Elsevier Publishing Co., 1973), pp. 153–60.
[1]An excellent exposition and discussion of several of its most recent versions can be found in Paul Samuelson [1].

Actually this is not so, except in very special instances. Only to the extent to which transportation costs, customs tariffs, or any other differential transfer costs between the individual trading countries can actually be taken into account and happen to be of decisive importance, will the comparative cost theory be capable of explaining the magnitude and the composition of all the observed export-import flows. In case such differential transfer costs do not exist or if they do exist but cannot be accounted for, the magnitude and composition of the flow of goods or services from any one to any other country remain within the framework of such theory entirely indeterminate.

To demonstrate that this is actually so let us visualize the trading countries being represented by players sitting around a table and the goods that they are trading by chips of as many different colors as there are different kinds of such goods.

Given the quantities of primary resources possessed by each country, the set of production technologies among which it actually can choose, as well as conditions determining the structure of each country's final demand for various goods, the comparative cost theory provides a systematic means of determining, i.e., of explaining how many chips of different colors each individual player will be prepared to give away to all the other players in exchange for specified amounts of chips of other colors received from them. How the theory determines these amounts is strictly speaking irrelevant to the present argument; it suffices to know that the answer it provides will satisfy the condition that the aggregate number of chips of a particular color "supplied" by all the players giving them away will be exactly equal to the total number of chips of that particular color "demanded" by those who would want to receive them.

The actual transaction can be visualized as being accomplished in two steps supervised by a croupier. First he collects the chips given away by all the players and sorts them out in piles of different colors. Next he deals from each pile the number of chips of that color which according to the comparative cost solution various players are entitled to receive. At the end of that second round the piles in the middle of the table will be gone and each player will have given away and received as many chips of each color as he wanted to.

Now let us introduce into this procedure an additional step: before handing over to the croupier the chips which he decided to give away each player will write his name on the back of them. In receiving, piling up, and dealing out the chips to the individual players the croupier will handle them so as to keep the reverse sides down. Only after the entire transaction has been completed will each player be asked to turn the chips received by him reverse-side up. On the basis of the additional information thus revealed the croupier will then construct a transaction table showing how many chips of a particular color have been "traded" by any one player to any other player.

Now let us ask whether, if this game were repeated many times without any change in any of the basic factors determining the "comparative costs" position of all the players, the figures entered on the transaction table constructed at the end of each round would remain the same? Certainly they would not. The *total* number of chips of one particular color "exported" and "imported" by each country would of course remain the same, but their *distribution* by countries of destination, or respectively of origin, would change from one round of the game to the next in a random fashion. Translated back into economics' language this means that so long as transportation and other transfer costs are not taken into account, the comparative cost theory cannot explain why a particular amount of this or that good is exported to or imported from this or that particular country. Within the limits set by given aggregate amounts of each type of good exported or imported, as the case may be, by each of the trading countries, the country-to-country flows remain completely indetermined.

If all transfer costs were zero, a great many—strictly speaking infinitely many—different interregional trade patterns could satisfy all the minimization and maximization criteria inherent in the application of the comparative cost principle equally well. Any attempt to explain why West Germany is for example exporting more chinaware to Italy than to France or why the United States buys more oil from Venezuela than from Iran would be futile.

In fact the transfer costs of course hardly ever equal zero and the optimal trading pattern can in principle at least be uniquely determined by minimizing their sum total. However, if such costs represent a relatively small fraction of the total costs of the internationally traded goods the formally unique optimal trading pattern would be as sensitive to small random shock as the position of a billiard ball placed on a flat marble table.

While speaking of transfer costs, I really have in mind *differential* transfer costs since only the differences between the costs of, for example, moving coal, say, from the United States to France, to Japan, to Italy, or to any of the other coal importing countries can affect the regional distribution of the U.S. coal exports. In the game described above, if a special but equal charge were to be paid by the American player for each coal-black chip laid down by him on or scooped up by him from the table the entire comparative cost solution would of course be affected, but the country-to-country flows of the black as well as of all the other chips would remain as indetermined as they were before.

This means that the so-called terminal costs have to be omitted from any comparison of differential transfer costs. Loading costs can for example not affect the differences between shipping a particular good from any given port to one or to another port, neither can the unloading charges affect differences between the cost of importing goods from one or from another country. The same is true of course of import duties subject to the "most favored nations" clause that bars an importing country from varying the height of a levy imposed on a given type of good according to the country of its origin.

Turning from theory to observed facts we find that information contained in the U.S. input-output table for 1963 shows that in that year the combined transportation and insurance margins constituted 7.5 percent and custom duties 7.2 percent of the aggregate value of imports (at domestic ports).

Since the great bulk of trade was covered by the most favored nations clause, the duties however did not constitute part of differential transfer costs. A very large proportion of internationally traded goods is moved over the water. Closer examination of the transportation margins shows (see the appendix) that terminal charges, which affect all incoming cargoes irrespective of their origin and outgoing cargoes irrespective of their destination, constitute as much as 85 percent (for conventional ships) and not less that 50 percent (for container ships) of the total transportation costs in trans-Atlantic and in trans-Pacific trade of the United States; insurance costs also depend to a large extent on conditions prevailing at points of origin and destination points rather than time or distance that separates them from each other.

All in all differential transfer costs constitute but a small fraction of the total value of most internationally traded goods. Hence while the assumption of zero differential transfer cost is strictly speaking invalid, so far as the applicability or rather the nonapplicability of the comparative cost theory in explanation of the actually observed international trade pattern is concerned the theoretical implications of this assumption can be expected to be practically true. Such an explanation has to be consequently sought in quotas, discriminatory duties, and other preferential arrangements of a formal or informal kind.

In a special case in which either the total international supply of or the entire demand for a particular good is concentrated in a single country the origin as well as the destination of all its shipments will obviously be uniquely determined. The question does not even arise in the simple textbook example (usually illustrated by a graph) in which the world is assumed to consist of only two countries.

In connection with what has been said above, it might be worthwhile to remember that the explanatory power of comparative cost theory turns out to be even more restricted in the actually hardly ever existing, but theoretically much discussed, case of international factor price equalization. The well-known Samuelson-Stolper theorem states that under certain conditions the free, unimpeded international exchange would equalize not only the price of goods and services actually sold and purchased across national borders, but also of the so-called primary factors of production such as labor, capital, and natural resources.

Without entering into the detail of the theoretical argument it suffices to observe that such international factor price equalization could occur if the total number of goods were larger than the number of primary factors and if all countries had free access to the same production techniques. Under such conditions one can visualize a state in which each good is being produced throughout the entire world with the same input combination of primary factors (per unit of output) and at the same time different industries are distributed between the different countries in such a way as to make full use of the particular combinations of primary resources available in each one of them. The national surpluses and deficits of goods would be of course balanced out—as in the game described above—through trade. No reason would exist in such a state for pricing any factor in one country higher or lower than in any other country.

In the discussion of the factor price equalization theorem however it is not often enough emphasized that under the (obviously quite unrealistic) set of conditions described above, not only one, but many alternative distributions of industrial activities between different countries could yield the same combination of aggregate world outputs of all goods while satisfying at the same time the requirement of full utilization of all primary resources that happen to be available in each country. This means that under such conditions and in the absence of international transfer costs not only the network of country-to-country commodity flow, but even the level and the composition of each country's total exports and imports (in our example—the total number of chips of different colors offered and received by each player) could not be uniquely determined.

In case the interregional transfer costs are known, their minimization, combined with the comparative costs conditions mentioned above, can lead to determination of a unique optimal output pattern for each country as well as of its total export or total import of each type of goods. In case transfer costs consisted only of terminal charges and thus had not depended on the length and direction of various transportation routes, the bilateral intercountry trading pattern would still of course be indetermined.

The theorists who formulate and reformulate the theory of comparative costs are certainly aware of what it can and what it cannot be expected to explain; they often fail however to emphasize its limitations to those who might want to use it in empirical research or in defense of particular specific policy decisions.

Appendix

1. The breakdown of international transfer costs of goods imported by the United States in the year 1963 as derived from the official U.S. input-output data for that year is presented in Table 1.

Those figures cover some 90 percent of total U.S. merchandise imports. The remaining 10 percent consist of so-called noncompetitive imports such as coffee, tin, and other agricultural and mineral products not produced in the United States. The margins on these products are about the same as those on imports included in the table.

2. Available shipping data strongly support the contention that international freight costs are largely invariate with route length. Estimates in Table 2 attribute

378

Table 1—1963 United States merchandise imports by industrial sector:
domestic port values and tariff, freight and insurance margins
(percentage of domestic port value)

SECTOR	DOMESTIC PORT VALUE ($1,000)	TARIFF MARGIN (%)	FREIGHT MARGIN (%)	INSURANCE MARGIN (%)
Agriculture	1224.3	7.0	9.9	0.5
Iron ore	533.2	1.6	19.0	0.1
Nonferrous ores	425.5	1.6	3.0	0.2
Coal	2.2	0.0	0.0	0.0
Oil	1340.3	3.2	18.2	0.6
Mining	233.3	2.0	13.8	0.3
Food	2569.7	7.7	5.0	0.3
Tobacco	4.5	16.3	3.7	0.3
Textiles	970.5	13.5	4.5	0.7
Apparel	507.9	20.6	4.5	0.5
Wood	502.9	1.5	9.6	0.8
Lumber	307.2	11.6	10.4	0.9
Furniture	40.3	11.3	8.0	0.3
Paper	1168.9	1.2	3.3	1.0
Printing	71.4	4.1	6.5	0.3
Chemical products	401.5	8.2	5.9	0.6
Plastics	71.3	13.5	3.8	0.3
Heavy chemicals	78.8	12.0	2.5	0.5
Paint	0.7	0.0	14.3	0.0
Petroleum products	935.2	2.3	9.7	0.7
Rubber	182.3	11.3	4.2	0.7
Leather	225.2	12.4	4.9	0.4
Glass	202.0	20.5	6.4	0.4
Stone products	130.0	8.3	8.0	0.9
Steel	825.2	5.8	6.9	0.7
Nonferrous metals	1168.8	3.2	1.8	0.4
Structural metals	5.5	14.5	5.5	3.6
Metal products	276.3	10.4	3.7	0.6
Engines	29.2	7.9	1.9	0.7
Machines, specialized	357.2	4.8	3.1	0.7
Metalworking machines	72.7	13.1	1.8	0.3
Machines, general purpose	62.5	11.4	2.5	0.7
Machines, office	115.7	6.9	2.6	0.6
Heavy electric machines	48.5	9.7	5.0	0.4
Heavy appliances	214.2	9.7	3.8	0.9
Electronics	350.8	9.4	4.2	0.9
Motor vehicles	645.3	6.6	5.3	0.4
Aircraft	101.1	2.1	2.1	1.0
Transport equipment	111.9	10.4	5.0	0.6
Precision instruments	142.7	25.0	2.4	0.5
Photo optical	149.1	13.3	3.3	0.6
Miscellaneous manufactures	934.0	16.8	4.4	0.6
Total	17319.5	7.2	6.9	0.6

Source: The table was compiled by Peter Petri from information supplied by the Office of Business Economics, U.S. Department of Commerce.

379

Table 2—Terminal charges as a percentage of total U.S. freight revenue,
by carrier type, 1964 and 1965

CARRIER TYPE	1964	1965
Tramp service	88	72
Liner service	74	70
Tanker service	56	60
Total	74	69

Source: James R. Barker and Robert Brandwein [2].

Table 3—Itemized freight cost breakdown for typical conventional and container ships, in percent

COST ITEM	CONVENTIONAL SHIP	CONTAINER SHIP
Costs variable with route length		
Crew	6.3	3.8
Fuel	2.2	5.5
Costs not variable with route length		
Capital costs	8.5	22.8
Maintenance	1.5	4.2
Port charges	2.0	1.5
Administrative	2.1	7.5
Cargo-handling	77.3	54.7
Total	100.0	100.0

Source: United Nations [3].

nearly three-fourths of U.S. freight revenues to terminal charges—mainly port dues and stevedore services.

An itemized freight cost breakdown for conventional and container ships appears in Table 3. These estimates are based upon typical values of vessel capacity, performance, and construction cost.

References

1. P. Samuelson, "Ohlin Was Right," *Swedish Journal of Economics* 73, No. 4 (Dec. 1971) pp. 365–384.
2. J. R. Barker and R. Brandwein, *The United States Merchant Marine in National Perspective* (D.C. Heath and Co., Lexington, Mass., 1970) p. 226.
3. Unitization of cargo, United Nations Conference on Trade and Development (U.N., New York, 1970).

30

Structure of the world economy

OUTLINE OF A SIMPLE INPUT-OUTPUT FORMULATION

I

The world economy, like the economy of a single country, can be
visualized as a system of interdependent processes. Each process, be
it the manufacture of steel, the education of youth, or the running of a
family household, generates certain outputs and absorbs a specific
combination of inputs. Direct interdependence between two processes arises whenever the output of one becomes an input of the
other: coal, the output of the coal mining industry, is an input of the
electric power generating sector. The chemical industry uses coal not
only directly as a raw material but also indirectly in the form of
electrical power. A network of such links constitutes a system of
elements which depend upon each other directly, indirectly, or both.

The state of a particular economic system can be conveniently
described in the form of a two-way input-output table showing the
flows of goods and services among its different sectors, and to and
from processes or entities ("value added" and "final demand") viewed
as falling outside the conventional borders of an input-output system.
As the scope of the inquiry expands, new rows and columns are added
to the table and some of the external inflows and outflows become
internalized. Increasing the number of rows and columns that de-

Nobel Memorial Lecture. © The Nobel Foundation, 1974; published in *The Swedish
Journal of Economics*, Vol. 76, 1974.
   The author is indebted to Peter Petri for setting up and performing all the
computations, the results of which are presented in this lecture, and to D. Terry
Jenkins for preparing the graphs and editorial assistance.

scribe an economic system also permits a more detailed description of economic activities commonly described in highly aggregative terms.

Major efforts are presently underway to construct a data base for a systematic input-output study not of a single national economy but of the world economy viewed as a system composed of many interrelated parts. This global study, as described in the official document, is aimed at

> helping Member States of the United Nations make their 1975 review of world progress in accelerating development and attacking mass poverty and unemployment. First, by studying the results that prospective environmental issues and policies would probably have for world development in the absence of changes in national and international development policies, and secondly, by studying the effects of possible alternative policies to promote development while at the same time preserving and improving the environment. By thus indicating alternative future paths which the world economy might follow, the study would help the world community to make decisions regarding future development and environmental policies in as rational a manner as possible.[1]

Preliminary plans provide for a description of the world economy in terms of 28 groups of countries, with about 45 productive sectors for each group. Environmental conditions will be described in terms of 30 principal pollutants; the use of nonagricultural natural resources in terms of some 40 different minerals and fuels.

II

The subject of this lecture is the elucidation of a particular input-output view of the world economy. This formulation should provide a framework for assembling and organizing the mass of factual data needed to describe the world economy. Such a system is essential for a concrete understanding of the structure of the world economy as well as for a systematic mapping of the alternative paths along which it could move in the future.

Let us consider a world economy consisting of (1) a Developed and

[1] Quoted from: "Brief Outline of the United Nations Study on the Impact of Prospective Environmental Issues and Policies on the International Development Strategy," April 1973.

Table 1—World economy in 1970 (billions of 1970 dollars)

Developed Countries

	Extraction Industry	Other Production	Abatement Industry	Final Demand		Total Output
				Domestic	Trade	
Extraction Industry	0	76	0	2	−15	63
Other Production	21	1 809	21	2 414	19	4 284
Pollution	5	62	−63	60	0	64
Employ- ment	18	1 372	20	287	0	
Other Value Added	21	996	22	0	0	

Less Developed Countries

	Extraction Industry	Other Production	Abatement Industry	Final Demand		Total Output
				Domestic	Trade	
Extraction Industry	0	8	0	2	15	25
Other Production	7	197	0	388	−19	573
Pollution	2	8	0	11	0	21
Employ- ment	9	149	0	99	0	
Other Value Added	8	220	0	0	0	

(2) a Less Developed region. Let us further divide the economy of each region into three productive sectors: an Extraction Industry producing raw materials; All Other Production, supplying conventional goods and services; and a Pollution Abatement Industry. In addition to these three sectors, there is also a consumption sector specified for each region. The function of the Abatement Industry is to eliminate pollutants generated by the productive sectors, consumers, and the Abatement Industry itself.

The two input-output tables displayed as Table 1 describe the intersectoral flows of goods and services within the Developed and the Less Developed economies. The flow of natural resources from the Less Developed to the Developed Countries, as well as the opposite flow of Other Goods from the Developed to the Less Developed Countries are entered in both tables: positively for the exporting region, and negatively for the importing region.

In each of the two tables the right-most entries in the first and second row represent the total domestic outputs of the Extraction Industry and of Other Production, respectively.

Each positive number along the third (pollution) row shows the physical amount of pollutant generated by the activity named at the head of the column in which that number appears. The negative quantity shown at the intersection of the third column and the third row represents the amount of pollutant eliminated by Abatement activities. Inputs such as power, chemicals, etc., purchased by the Abatement Industry from other sectors, and value added paid out by that industry are entered as positive amounts in the same third column. The difference between the total amount of pollution generated in all sectors and the amount eliminated by the Abatement sector is represented by the *net* emission figure, the right-most entry in the third row. Finally, labor inputs used in each sector and payments made to other income-receiving agents are shown in the bottom two rows.

The numbers in these two tables are, strictly speaking, fictitious. But their general order of magnitude reflects crude, preliminary estimates of intersectoral flows within and between the Developed and Less Developed regions during the past decade.[2]

For analytical purposes, the outputs and inputs of the Extraction Industry and Other Production, as well as the amounts of pollutants generated and abated, can be interpreted as quantities measured in the appropriate physical units (pounds, yards, kilowatts, etc.). The same is true of the services of some of the so-called primary factors: labor inputs, for example, are entered in the second to last row of each table. A similar physical measurement of the other components of value added, even if it were possible in principle, is impossible given the present state of knowledge. In pure or, should I say, speculative economic theory, we can overcome this kind of difficulty by introducing some convenient albeit unrealistic assumptions. But a theoretical formulation designed to permit empirical analysis has to account for the fact that at least some components of value added cannot be interpreted as payments for measurable physical inputs, but must be treated as purely monetary magnitudes.

[2] All quantities are measured in billions of dollars "in current prices"; pollutants are "priced" in terms of average "per unit" abatement costs.

III

The flows described in the two input-output tables are interdependent. They have to satisfy three distinct sets of constraints. First, within each production or consumption process there exists a technological relationship between the level of output and the required quantities of various inputs. For example, if we divide each figure in the first column of the first section of Table 1 (the inputs of the Extraction Industry) by the total output of that sector (the last figure in the first row), we find that to produce one unit of its output this sector absorbed 0.3372 units of the output of Other Production, used 0.2867 units of Labor Services and spent 0.3332 dollars for other value added. Moreover, for each unit of useful output the Extraction Industries generated 0.0859 units of pollution. Other sets of input-output coefficients describe the technical structure of every sector of production and consumption in both groups of countries.

While statistical input-output tables continue to serve as the principal source of information on the input requirements or "cooking recipes" of various industries, increasingly we find economists using engineering data as a supplemental source. Complete structural matrices of the two groups of countries used in our example are shown in Table 2.

Table 2—Technical and consumption coefficients[a]

Developed countries

$$A_1 = \begin{bmatrix} .0 & .0178 & .0 \\ .3372 & .4223 & .3298 \\ .0859 & .0144 & .0118 \end{bmatrix} \quad C_1 = \begin{bmatrix} .0007 \\ .8834 \\ .0218 \end{bmatrix}$$

$$l_1 = [.2867 \quad .3203 \quad .3161] \quad l_1^c = [.1050]$$

$$r_1 = [.3332 \quad .2324 \quad .3482] \quad r_1 = [.0 \quad]$$

Less developed countries

$$A_2 = \begin{bmatrix} .0 & .0141 & .0 \\ .2934 & .3437 & .3298 \\ .0859 & .0144 & .0118 \end{bmatrix} \quad C_2 = \begin{bmatrix} .0037 \\ .7943 \\ .0218 \end{bmatrix}$$

$$l_2 = [.3729 \quad .2597 \quad .3161] \quad l_2^c = [.2020]$$

$$r_2 = [.3337 \quad .3825 \quad .3541] \quad r_2 = [.0 \quad]$$

[a]The coefficients in these tables do not sum to unity because the pollution generated by industry and by final demand is only partially abated in the developed countries and not abated at all in the less developed countries.

The second set of constraints that has to be satisfied by every viable system requires that the total (physical) amounts of outputs and inputs of each type of good must be in balance, i.e., total supply must equal total demand. In the case of a pollutant, *net* emission must equal the total amount generated by all sectors less the amount eliminated by the abatement process.

For example, the balance between the total output and the combined inputs of extracted raw materials can be described by the following equation:

(1)

$$\underbrace{(1-a_{11})x_1}_{} - \underbrace{a_{12}x_2}_{} - \underbrace{a_{13}x_3}_{} - \underbrace{c_1y}_{} - \underbrace{T_1}_{} = 0$$

net output of Extraction Industry	amount delivered to Other Production	amount delivered to the Abatement Industry	amount delivered to Final Users	amount exported

The equation describing the balance between generation, abatement and net emission of pollution reads as follows:

(2)

$$\underbrace{-a_{31}x_1 - a_{32}x_2}_{} + \underbrace{(1-a_{33})x_3}_{} - \underbrace{c_3y}_{} + \underbrace{E}_{} = 0$$

gross amount of pollution generated by sectors 1 and 2	amount abated by abatement activities	gross amount generated by consumers and government	net amount emitted into the environment

x_1 and x_2 represent the total outputs of the Extraction Industry and of Other Production respectively; x_3, the level of activity of the Abatement sector; y, the sum total of values added, i.e., gross national income. The "technical coefficient" a_{ij} represents the number of units of the product of sector i absorbed (or generated in the case of pollution) by sector j in producing one unit of its output; c_j is a "consumption coefficient" describing the number of units of the output of sector j consumed (or generated in the case of pollution) per unit of total value added, i.e., per unit of gross national income.

Table 3

Physical subsystem

Equation number	${}_1X_1$	${}_1X_2$	${}_1X_3$	L_1	Y_1	E_1	${}_2X_1$	${}_2X_2$	${}_2X_3$	L_2	Y_2	E_2	T_1	T_2	B	
1.1													1			
1.2	$I-A_1$													-1		
1.3						1										
1.4	I_1			-1	I^C_1											=[0]
1.5												-1				
1.6							$I-A_2$			$-C_2$				1		
1.7												1				
1.8							I_2			-1	I^C_2					
1.9													P_1	$-P_2$	1	

Price subsystem

Equation number	${}_1p_1$	${}_1p_2$	${}_1p_3$	w_1	${}_1r_1$	${}_1r_2$	${}_1r_3$	${}_2p_1$	${}_2p_2$	${}_2p_3$	w_2	${}_2r_1$	${}_2r_2$	${}_2r_3$	
2.1			$-{}_1q_1\cdot{}_1a_{31}$												
2.2	$I-A'_1$		$-{}_1q_2\cdot{}_1a_{32}$	$-l'_1$	$-I$										
2.3			$1-{}_1q_3\cdot{}_1a_{33}$												
2.4										$-{}_2q_1\cdot{}_2a_{31}$					
2.5								$I-A'_1$		$-{}_2q_2\cdot{}_2a_{32}$	$-l'_2$	$-I$			=[0]
2.6										$1-{}_2q_3\cdot{}_2a_{33}$					
2.7	1							-1							
2.8		-1							1						

Table 3 displays the complete set of linear equations describing the physical balances between outputs and inputs of all sectors in both countries in terms of compact matrix notion. The last of these equations—written below in its explicit form—describes the flows of exports and imports that link the Developed and Less Developed areas into a single world economy.

(3) $$B = T_2 p_2 - T_1 p_1$$

The balance of trade B, i.e., the difference between the monetary value of the two opposite trade flows, depends not only on the quantities T_1 and T_2 of traded goods but also on their prices, p_1 and p_2. The higher the price a country receives for its exports, or the lower the price it pays for imports, the better are its "terms of trade."

The last of the three sets of relationships describes the interdependence of the prices of all goods and services and the values added paid out, per unit of output, by each industry. For example, a typical equation in this set states that the price at which the Extraction sector sells one unit of its output equals the average outlay incurred in producing it. This includes the costs (i.e., quantities $\times$ prices) of inputs purchased from other sectors, wages paid, and all other value added:

$$(4) \quad \underline{p_1} \quad - \underline{a_{11}p_1 - a_{21}p_2} \quad - \underline{q_1 a_{31}p_3} \quad - \underline{l_1 w} \quad - \underline{r_1} \quad = 0$$

| price of output | cost of material inputs | cost of pollution abatement | cost of labor inputs | other value added |

The technical coefficients (a_{ij} and l_i's) appearing in this equation are the same as those appearing in the structural matrices of Table 2. The abatement ratios q_i represent the fraction of the gross pollution emission of industry i that is eliminated (at that industry's expense)[3] by the Abatement Industry.

In this example, the system of physical balances contains 9 equations with 15 variables, while the price-values-added system has 8 equations with 14 variables. But these 14 variables are reduced to 12 and the number of equations to 6 if one assumes from the outset that the internationally traded products of the Extraction Industry and Other Production have the same price in the Developed and the Less Developed Countries. Equations 2.7 and 2.8 worked out explicitly read:

$$(5) \qquad {}_1p_1 = {}_2p_1(\equiv p_1) \text{ and } {}_1p_2 = {}_2p_2(\equiv p_2)$$

The combination of both systems viewed as a whole contains 29

---

[3]This formulation is based on the assumption that the pollution generated by a particular sector is being eliminated at its own expense. In case the abatement cost is being paid by the government out of its tax revenues, the price equations have to be modified accordingly. See essays 6 and 7 in this volume.

Table 4—Physical system assumptions

Variables		Developed countries			Less developed countries		
		Case I	Case II	Case III	Case I	Case II	Case III
Extraction output	X_1	Capacity limited to 150% of 1970 levels			Endogenous		
Other production	X_2	Endogenous			Capacity grows 6.4% per annum between 1970 and 2000		
Abatement output	X_3	Endogenous			0	Endogenous	
Employment	L	Increase proportional to population increase			Endogenous		
Final Demand	Y	Endogenous					
Net pollution emission	E	Limited to current levels assuming 1970 standards			Endogenous		Limited to twice 1970 levels
Net trade in Extractive goods	T_1	Endogenous					
Net trade in Other goods	T_2	Endogenous					
Trade balance	B	A deficit for Less Developed Countries amounting to 1% of Developed Countries' income, reflecting capital flows and aid					
Technical Coefficients	A	Unchanged from 1970		Twice 1970 levels for Extraction Industry	Unchanged from 1970		
Labor Coefficients	I	1/3 1970 levels, due to increased productivity		2/3 1970 levels for Extraction Industry	1/3 1970 levels due to increased productivity		
Consumption coefficients	C	Unchanged from 1970					
Extraction goods price	P_1	Obtained from solution of price system					
Other goods price	P_2						

389

unknowns but only 17 equations. Thus, to arrive at a unique solution, we have to fix the values of 12 variables on the basis of some outside information, i.e., their values have to be determined exogenously.

Two types of quantitative information are required for the solution of this system. First, some data are used in the form of appropriate structural coefficients. Other kinds of factual information are introduced by assigning specific numerical values to appropriate "exogenous" variables.

In view of the uneven quality of data that will constitute the empirical basis of the present inquiry, it would be a tactical mistake to pour all the factual information we possess into the rigid mold of a single, all-embracing, inflexible explanatory scheme. The decision of which variables should be treated as dependent and which should be fixed exogenously is essentially a tactical one. The theoretical formulation is a weapon; in deciding how to use it we must take into account the nature of the particular empirical terrain.

To assess the influence of factors considered external to our theoretical description of the world economy, we earmark six physical and five value added variables as "exogenous." Tables 4 and 5 show which variables are endogenous and assign values to all exogenous variables. These assumptions permit us to project changes in our simple world economy from a state representative of the present ("1970") to three alternative hypothetical states about thirty years hence ("2000 (I)," "2000 (II)," and "2000 (III)").

Total labor input in Developed Countries, L_1, is exogenous: under full or nearly full employment, its magnitude depends on demographic and cultural factors not accounted for within our formal theoretical system. Substantial endemic unemployment in the Less Developed Countries makes it advisable to consider the level of total employment as depending on the level of output—that is, to treat L_2 as endogenous.

The output of the Extraction Industry in the Developed Countries is restricted by the limited availability of natural resources. We account for this limitation by making $_1x_1$ exogenous. In the Less Developed Countries, where natural resources are still plentiful, the output of the Extraction Industry, $_2x_1$, depends partly on a small domestic market but primarily on the import requirements of De-

Table 5—Price system assumptions

Variables		Developed countries — Case I	Case II	Case III	Less developed countries — Case I	Case II	Case III
Extraction goods price	P_1	Endogenous					
Other goods price	P_2	Endogenous					
Abatement Price	P_3	Endogenous					
Wage rate	w	Kept at 1970 levels (index=1.0)			Kept at 1970 level (index=1.0)		
	r_1	Kept at 1970 levels (index=1.0)			Endogenous		
Other value added in Other Production	r_2	Kept at 1970 levels (index=1.0)			Endogenous		
Other value added in Abatement	r_3	Kept at 1970 levels (index=1.0)			Kept at 1970 level (index=1.0)		
Technical coefficients	A	Unchanged from 1970		Twice 1970 levels for Extraction Industry	Unchanged from 1970		
Labor coefficients	l_a	1/3 1970 levels, due to increased productivity		2/3 1970 levels for Extraction Industry	1/3 1970 levels, due to increased productivity		
Abatement coefficients	q	$q_1 = q_2 = x_3/(x_3 + El)$, that is, all Abatement coefficients of a given country are set to a value that reduces net pollution to the exogenously specified level E					

veloped Countries. Thus, $_2x_1$ can be treated as a dependent variable.

The situation is reversed in the case of Other Production. In Developed Countries the output of manufactured goods normally adjusts to the level of final demand, making $_1x_2$ a dependent variable. Yet in the Less Developed Countries the output of Other Production, $_1x_2$, is restricted by external factors such as weak infrastructure and limited capital. In this case rising domestic inputs usually stimulate a growing demand for imports. Hence, $_2x_2$ is treated as independent and T_1 and T_2 as dependent variables.

In the price-value-added system of equations, all money wages and other value added payments in the Developed Countries (w, r_1, r_2 and r_3) are exogenously determined. This means that the prices of all three products can be derived endogenously. In Less Developed Countries the situation seems to be different: since the prices of commodities produced by Extraction and Other Production are determined by the cost of their production (including the exogenous valued added) in the Developed Countries, the value added that can be paid out by the two sectors producing these goods in the Less Developed Countries, $_2r_1$ and $_2r_2$, simply reflect the difference between a given price and the production costs.

Raw materials are, as a rule, relatively more abundant and more cheaply extracted in Less Developed Countries; thus the value added earned by Extraction Industries in Less Developed Countries can be expected to be relatively high. Ricardo speaks in this connection of "mining rents." On the other hand, technical input coefficients or, more properly, costs in Other Production of the Less Developed Countries can be expected to be higher than in Developed Countries. Because of this, the value added earned per unit of output in that sector tends to be relatively low.

Since a principal purpose of the aforementioned United Nations project is a "realistic evaluation of the effects of alternative types of environmental policies on the economic prospects of Less Developed Countries," net pollution emissions E_1 and E_2 are treated as exogenously determined in two of our projections.

Assigning specific numerical magnitudes to all exogenously determined variables permits effective use of a variety of external data in arriving at a unique numerical solution of the formal input-output system. As the empirical inquiry advances, exogenous variables can be internalized through introduction of additional equations.

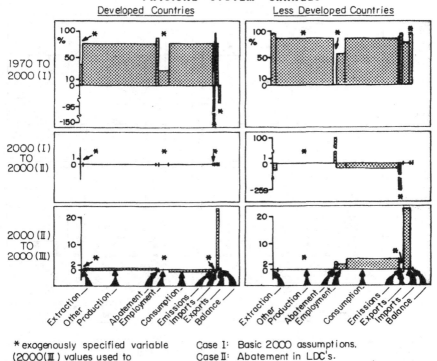

PHYSICAL SYSTEM CHANGES

Developed Countries   Less Developed Countries

1970 TO
2000 (I)

2000 (I)
TO
2000 (II)

2000 (II)
TO
2000 (III)

Extraction, Other, Production, Abatement, Employment, Consumption, Emissions, Exports, Imports, Balance

* exogenously specified variable   Case I: Basic 2000 assumptions.
(2000(III) values used to   Case II: Abatement in LDC's.
compute percentage changes)   Case III: Higher extraction costs in DC's

Figure 1

The most important but also the most demanding step in implementing an empirical input-output system is the determination of values of hundreds or even thousands of structural coefficients. The relevant methodologies are so varied and specialized that I abstain from discussing them in this general context.

IV

As has been explained above, three different sets of factual assumptions provided the basis for the three alternative projections of the state of one simple world economy for the year "1970" to the year "2000." Tables 4 and 5 contain their full specification, while the results of the computations are summarized in three pairs of input-output tables presented in the Appendix.

The bar charts displayed in Figures 1 and 2 facilitate a systematic

PRICE SYSTEM CHANGES

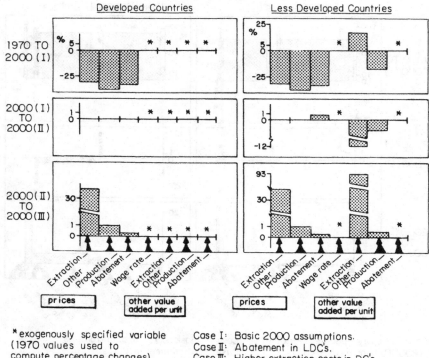

*exogenously specified variable
(1970 values used to
compute percentage changes)

Case I: Basic 2000 assumptions.
Case II: Abatement in LDC's.
Case III: Higher extraction costs in DC's.

Figure 2

examination of these findings. The width of each bar represents the relative size of the corresponding economic activity measured in base-year dollars. The length of each bar indicates the percentage increase or decrease in the level of each activity as the world economy passes from one state to another. Exogenous variables are identified by asterisks.

The long bars in the uppermost rows of these economic profiles indicate an upsurge in output and total consumption and a downward movement of prices: a "great leap forward" from 1970 to 2000. Case I is a projection that critically depends on two assumptions. First, the employed labor force in Developed Countries will increase with population growth. Second, labor productivity in both regions (the

394

reciprocal of the labor coefficient) will be three times as high in 2000 as in 1970, with all other input coefficients remaining the same. Strict enforcement of standards contained in the United States Clean Air Act of 1967 (as amended in 1970) will bring about a sharp drop in unabated emissions in the Developed areas, while in Less Developed Countries the absence of any abatement activity will force the pollution level up. International trade will expand faster than domestic economic activities. Prices (measured in wage units) will decline, while the value added in Less Developed Countries will rise in the Extraction Industry but fall in Other Production.

How would the future economic picture change if strict antipollution standards were also observed in Less Developed Countries? The answer is presented in the second row of bar graphs in Figures 1 and 2. In the Developed Countries there will be practically no change. In Less Developed Countries the inauguration of abatement activities aimed at limiting pollution to twice its 1970 level would bring about expanded employment while requiring some sacrifices in consumption. Value added would fall sharply in the Extraction Industry and somewhat less in Other Production.

How would the situation thus attained be affected by a significant increase in the operating costs of the Extraction Industry in the Developed Countries? The bottom row of profiles in Figures 1 and 2 shows how the conditions in both regions of the world economy would be affected if the productivity of labor in the Extraction Industry of Developed Countries rose only 1.5 rather than 3 times between 1970 and 2000 while the amounts of other Extraction inputs doubled per unit of output. The output of Other Production in the Developed Countries would register a slight increase and the level of consumption a slight decrease. Consumption in the Less Developed Countries would experience a substantial increase. The mechanism responsible for such a redistribution of income between the Developed and Less Developed Countries involves a steep increase in the price of Extraction goods compared to other prices, a corresponding rise in value added (rents yielded by the Extraction Industry of the Less Developed Countries) and, finally, a substantial increase in imports accompanied by slight reduction of exports from these countries, both reflecting a marked improvement in their "terms of trade."

I refrain from drawing any factual conclusion from the economic projections presented above. The computer received fictitious inputs and necessarily issued fictitious outputs. All theories tend to shape the facts they try to explain; any theory may thus turn into a procrustean bed. Our proposed theoretical formulation is designed to protect the investigator from this danger: it does not permit him to draw any special or general conclusions before he or someone else completes the always difficult and seldom glamorous task of ascertaining the necessary facts.

Appendix

Projected world economy in 2000 (Case I) (billions of 1970 dollars)

Developed Countries

	Extraction Industry	Other Production	Abatement Industry	Final Demand Domestic	Final Demand Trade	Total Output
Extraction Industry	0	316	0	8	−226	98
Other Production	33	7 502	160	9 713	357	17 765
Pollution	8	256	−479	240	0	25
Employment	9	1 897	51	379	0	
Other Value Added	33	4 129	169	0	0	

Less Developed Countries

	Extraction Industry	Other Production	Abatement Industry	Final Demand Domestic	Final Demand Trade	Total Output
Extraction Industry	0	52	0	12	226	290
Other Production	85	1 254	36	2 632	−357	3 650
Pollution	25	53	−108	72	0	42
Employment	36	316	12	223	0	
Other Value Added	100	1 118	39	0	0	

Projected world economy in 2000 (Case II) (billions of 1970 dollars)

Developed Countries

	Extraction Industry	Other Production	Abatement Industry	Final Demand		Total Output
				Domestic	Trade	
Extraction Industry	0	316	0	8	−226	98
Other Production	33	7 502	160	9 713	357	17 765
Pollution	8	256	−479	240	0	25
Employment	9	1 897	51	379	0	
Other Value Added	33	4 129	169	0	0	

Less Developed Countries

	Extraction Industry	Other Production	Abatement Industry	Final Demand		Total Output
				Domestic	Trade	
Extraction Industry	0	52	0	12	226	290
Other Production	85	1 255	0	2 668	−357	3 650
Pollution	25	53	0	73	0	151
Employment	36	316	0	226	0	
Other Value Added	112	1 143	0	0	0	

Projected world economy in 2000 (Case III) (billions of 1970 dollars)

Developed Countries

	Extraction Industry	Other Production	Abatement Industry	Final Demand		Total Output
				Domestic	Trade	
Extraction Industry	0	315	0	8	−225	98
Other Production	66	7 472	159	9 678	461	17 836
Pollution	8	255	−477	239	0	25
Employment	19	1 890	51	378	0	
Other Value Added	33	4 112	168	0	0	

Less Developed Countries

	Extraction Industry	Other Production	Abatement Industry	Final Demand		Total Output
				Domestic	Trade	
Extraction Industry	0	51	0	13	225	289
Other Production	85	1 254	37	2 735	−461	3 650
Pollution	25	53	−111	75	0	42
Employment	36	316	12	232	0	
Other Value Added	189	1 125	40	0	0	

31

National economic planning: methods and problems

When I speak of national economic planning, the notion I have in mind is meant to encompass the entire complex of political, legislative, and administrative measures aimed at an explicit formulation and practical realization of a comprehensive national economic plan. Without a comprehensive, internally consistent plan there can be, in this sense, no planning. But the preparation of a script is not enough; the play has to be staged and acted out.

It is incumbent on anyone who favors introduction of national economic planning in this country—and I am one of these—to propose a plan describing how this might be done. Several congressional committees and at least one commission appointed by the President, not to speak of groups outside of the government, are now engaged in this task.

I

In its published form a national economic plan, or rather the statistical appendix to its text, can be visualized as a detailed, systematic annual survey of manufacture and agriculture, of transportation, and of trade and the federal and local budgets. However, it describes the state of the economy not for a given past year—as does the *Statistical Abstract* or the *Census of Manufacture*—but rather for five years in

From *The Economic System in an Age of Discontinuity* (New York: New York University Press, 1976), pp. 29–41.

advance and, in a more summary form, for a much longer interval of time stretching into the future. This does not mean that a plan must be rigidly adhered to over the entire period of, say, four or five years. On the contrary, the plan should be revised each year in the light of past experience and newly acquired information and pushed out as a moving average one year ahead.

A plan is not a forecast. The whole idea of planning assumes the possibility of choice among alternative feasible scenarios. Feasibility is the key word.

A particular national economy can and, in the context of the planning process, has to be visualized as a system consisting of mutually interdependent parts. The trucking industry must be supplied with fuel by the oil refining sector; in order to expand, it must be supplied by the automobile industry with vehicles as well as replacements for worn-out equipment. To provide employment for additional workers, the automobile industry must not only be assured of an outlet for its products, but in the long run it must construct new plants and retool the old. In the process of doing so, it must receive more plant space from the construction industry, and additional equipment from the machine-building industry, not to speak of a greater flow of power, steel, and all its other inputs.

Traditional economic theory not only poses the problem but also explains how its solution is, or at least can be, brought about through the operation of the competitive price mechanism, that is, a trial-and-error procedure that automatically brings about equality between supply and demand in each and every market. In some markets and under certain conditions this actually works. But considering the lack of any reliable information on which to base their expectations, many business leaders have come to recognize that this trial-and-error game, instead of bringing about a desired state of stable equilibrium, results in misallocation of resources, underutilization of productive capacities, and periodic unemployment. This means lost wages, lost profits, and lost taxes—conditions that are bound to engender social unrest and sharpen the political conflict.

Conventional monetary and fiscal policies relying on a rather sketchy aggregative description and analysis of the economic system appear to be no more successful in compensating for the lack of systematic foresight than frantic pushing and pulling of the choke is able to correct the malfunctioning of a motor. Occasionally, it works, but usually it does not.

II

The first input-output tables describing the flow of goods and services among the different sectors of the American economy in census years 1919 and 1929 were published in 1936. They were based on a rather gross segregation of all economic activities into 44 sectors. Because there were no computing facilities available to make analytical calculations, the sectors had to be further grouped into only 10 sectors.

The data base, the computing facilities, and the analytical techniques have advanced much farther than could have been anticipated forty years ago. National input-output tables containing up to 700 distinct sectors are being compiled on a current basis, as are tables for individual, regional, state, and metropolitan areas. Private enterprise has entered the input-output business. For a fee one can now purchase a single row of a table showing the deliveries of a particular product, say, coated laminated fabrics or farming machine tools, not only to different industries, but within each industry to individual plants segregated by zip code areas.

Not that anyone could contemplate including such details in a national economic plan. Such systematic information proves to be most useful in assessing structural—in this particular instance, technological—relationships between the input requirements, on the one hand, and the levels of output of various industries, on the other. In the case of households, these relationships would be between total consumers' outlay and spending on each particular type of goods. Stocks of equipment, buildings, and inventories, their accumulation, their maintenance, and their occasional reduction are described and analyzed in their mutual interdependence with the flows of all kinds of goods and services throughout the entire system.

Detailed, as contrasted with aggregative, description and analysis of economic structures and relationships can, indeed, provide a suitable framework for a concrete rather than purely symbolic description of alternative methods of production and the realistic delineation of alternative paths of technological change.

400

III

Choice among alternative scenarios is the clue to rational national economic planning rather than crystal-ball gazing that, with the rise of general uncertainty, became a marketable product of the economic forecasting industry. Also this is preferable to the equally fashionable, although not as profitable, preoccupation with lofty national goals.

The important practical difference in making a choice between alternative national economic plans and selecting an appropriate set of national goals can best be explained by the following example: A friend invites me for dinner in a first-class restaurant and asks that I supply him with a general description of my tastes so that he can order the food in advance. Unable to describe my—or anyone else's—tastes in general terms, I prefer to see the menu and then select, without hesitation, the combination of dishes that I like.

Confronted with alternative national economic plans—each described in great detail, particularly with respect to items that are likely to affect my own well-being and my personal assessment of equity and fairness of the whole—I would have no difficulty in deciding which of them I would prefer or, at least, consider not inferior to any other. I could do this, despite my inability to describe my preferences, my predilections, and my prejudices in general terms. A philosopher, a social psychologist, or a historian might succeed in arriving at such a generalization by inference based on an interpretation of my utterances or, even better, of specific choices I have actually made before. But this, of course, is an entirely different matter.

This, I submit, is the reason why a planning process should start out not with the formulation of what theoretical economists refer to as the general "objective function," but with elaboration of alternative scenarios each presenting in concrete, nontechnical terms one of the several possible future states of the economy. The volume or a series of volumes containing such alternative scenarios would read not unlike issues of the *United States Statistical Abstract* with sections devoted to Industrial Production, to Agriculture, to Trade and Transportation, to Consumption, to Medical Services, to Education, and so on, not only on a national but also on regional and even local levels.

Karl Marx would have rejected this as a utopian approach and so do the libertarian opponents of national economic planning. Both view the concrete shape of the unknown future as unfolding itself while time marches on. The only difference between these believers in the "invisible hand" is that the latter are ready to accept and approve whatever might come, provided it has not been planned, while the former is convinced that, while unpredictable in all its details, the path inevitably leads to violent collapse of the present social and economic order.

IV

To repeat: Public discussion and democratic choice among the available alternatives will be possible only if each of them is presented in concrete tangible details rather than in such summary terms as the per capita GNP, the average rate of unemployment, or the annual rate of growth of the "implicit price deflator."

The technical apparatus we would require in order to project such detailed realistic images is bound to be quite intricate and very costly, as is the inside of a television set. When it comes to preparation of a national economic plan, no effort should be spared in making use of the most dependable data-gathering and data-handling techniques and of the most advanced economic model-building and computational procedures.

The programs of the principal federal statistical agencies will have to be greatly strengthened and, in some instances, overhauled. Much of the needed additional information can be obtained not through official questionnaires, but by means of more sophisticated methods successfully employed in commercial market research and with the help of specialized private data-gathering organizations.

Most of the economic forecasters develop their projections in such aggregative terms that relevant details pertaining, for example, to anticipated technical change are either disregarded at the outset or become dissipated in the ascent (or should I say descent?) from concrete engineering details to the formation of representative indices or broad statistical aggregates.

The data gatherers and model builders involved in the planning process will have to break down the barrier that separates economists—academic economists, in particular—from experts possessing specialized technical knowledge of various fields of production and consumption, as well as of private and public management.

Alternative scenarios can be expected to differ from each other mainly in the extent to which the available economic resources are apportioned for private and public use and, in the case of the latter, whether more or less of the resources are allocated to the satisfaction of this or that category of pressing needs. The scenarios will incorporate alternative policy proposals concerning energy, environment, or, say, foreign aid and national defense. To the extent that resource availability and even the fundamental consumption patterns of various types of households are not overly affected by a shift from one scenario to another—however different they may be in their political, economic, and social implications—such shift will involve the use of essentially the same analytical formulation and the same data base.

V

The internal setup of the organization responsible for preparation of alternative scenarios as well as elaboration of the national economic plan and its subsequent revisions must be dictated by requirements of its technical, nonpolitical task. One can visualize it as an autonomous public body loosely connected with the executive branch of the federal government. Eventually, it should be linked with its counterparts in the fifty states and possibly some large metropolitan areas.

The final version of the national economic plan will be an end product of the typically American political logrolling and legislative wrangles. The stand-by role of the technical organization referred to above will consist in seeing that, through all its transformation from the first to the last, the overall plan retains its integrity: Do not allocate more than you can produce, but also see to it that nothing is left over (unemployment is labor that is left over!).

VI

However intricate the process of drawing up the blue-print of the building, the task of actual construction poses a still greater challenge.

To try to describe systematically and in full detail the array of measures to be used for the practical implementation of the first national economic plan would be as futile as an attempt to trace in

403

advance the route Lewis and Clark followed on their way to the mouth of the Columbia River. I will take up one by one, however, some questions that have been raised about the practical possibilities of introducing national economic planning in this country.

In abstract, one could imagine a self-fulfilling plan that would be acted out without any prompting on the economic stage, once the script has been explained. Practically, this is an impossibility. However, if the main characters can be induced, in one way or another, to play their parts, the rest of the cast can be expected to join in spontaneously. Once, for example, a decision has been made and necessary capital has been provided, in compliance with the plan, to proceed with construction of a new fertilizer plant, equipment manufacturers, building contractors, and other suppliers will fall over each other to provide the necessary structures, machinery, and all the other inputs. The force propelling them will be, of course, the profit motive operating through the automatic supply-demand mechanism. As a matter of fact, that force and that mechanism can be expected to operate particularly well if, in accordance with provisions of the national plan, the availability of energy, labor, and all other inputs will be secured in required amounts in the right place at the right time. In a planned economy the price mechanism will be an effective but humble servant of the society not, as it frequently is, an overbearing and all too often fumbling master.

In the example given above, the point of direct, as contrasted with indirect, enforcement of a plan was the decision to expand the productive capacities of particular sectors. The specific means used in this case might have been selective control of capital and credit flows, tax exemption, or even direct public investment.

The selection of strategically commanding points in which to apply direct influence or control as well as choice of the method or of a combination of methods to be applied in each point to bring about compliance with the plan has to be based on the concrete study of the specific configuration of economic flow. The analogy with the tasks of a hydraulic engineer charged with regulating a major water system is more than superficial. Dams, dikes, and occasional locks have to be placed so we can take advantage of the natural flow propelled by gravity (the profit motive) but at the same time permit us to eliminate floods and devastating droughts.

404

Considering the great variety of ways and the extent to which the government now affects the operation of the economy of the United States, one of our lesser worries should be the lack of the accelerating, braking, or steering devices that could be used to guide it smoothly and securely along a chosen path. The real trouble is that, at present, not only does the government not know what road it wants to follow, it does not even have a map. To make things worse, one member of the crew in charge presses down the accelerator, another pumps the brakes, a third turns the wheel, and a fourth sounds the horn. Is that the way to reach one's destination safely?

VII

These observations naturally lead to the question of planning within the federal government itself; charity should begin at home. The recent establishment of orderly budgetary procedures is a move in the right direction, but it only scratches the surface of the problem.

Consider, for example, the lack of effective coordination between our environmental and our energy policies. Each is controlled by a different department, not to speak of many smaller, often semiautonomous, agencies. Production of fuel and generation of energy are some of the principal sources of pollution. Any major move in the field of energy can be expected to have far-reaching effects on the environment, and vice versa! The energy-producing industry is immediately and directly affected by antipollution regulations. The obvious practical step to take to solve this problem is for both agencies to combine their data banks (their stocks of factual information) and to agree to base their policy decisions on a common model. This model should be capable of generating scenarios displaying jointly the energy and the environmental repercussions of any move that either of the two agencies might contemplate. Adversary policy debate could and should continue, but adversary fact finding would have become impossible, and policies that tend to cancel out or contradict each other would at least be shown up for what they are.

But why should not the railway industry and air and highway transport be included in the same picture? These sectors, after all, not only use fuel but also move it and discharge pollutants unless precautionary measures have been taken. Indeed, why not? Particularly if that could induce the semi-independent agencies concerned with the regulation of these sectors to coordinate their actions with those of the Energy Research and Development Administration and the Environmental Protection Agency. But this leads directly to national planning; yes, indeed, it does.

While monetary and fiscal measures have for years served as instruments of economic policy planning, the nearly exclusive reliance on these two tools, under the influence of the Keynesian, and perhaps I should add Friedmanian, doctrines can hardly be justified by the results attained. Other means of keeping the economy on the right course must come into their own.

VIII

This has immediate bearing on the problem of inflation. The fact that the labor unions, while concerned with real wages, can bargain only for money wages is a major, possibly *the* major, factor contributing to perpetuation of the inflationary spiral. General wage and price controls, without supporting national planning action, are bound in the long run to bring about cumulative distortions in the allocation and utilization of economic resources. Within the framework of an effectively conceived planning action they would become unnecessary and eventually obsolete. By offering labor leaders the opportunity to take a responsible and effective part in the design and implementation of a national economic plan, the power of organized labor would thus be applied where it counts, instead of being dissipated or absorbed by inflation.

I see no reason to assume that the introduction of national economic planning would require or could bring about a marked shift in the overall national balance of economic and political power. The wealthy with the support of their retainers can be expected to continue to rule the roost. The inner workings of the system would, however, become more transparent. By comparing scenarios prepared in conformity with Mr. Reagan's or President Ford's ideas and those constructed in conformity with Senator Humphrey's or Congressman Udall's or Governor Carter's specifications, the American citizen would find it easier to make a rational choice.

406

Index

Academic economics, xi-xiv

Acceleration principle, 302

Aggregate: demand, 71; demand and supply of paper money, 107; supply and demand functions, 69

Aggregating, 56

Aggregation: in input-output analysis, 283-84, 269-70; problem of, xii, 163

Aggregative: approach, 19; equations, xiii; theory, 39, variables, xi

American Economic Review, xiii

Arrow, K., 360

Assumptions: classical, 105; Keynesian, 87

Automatization, 193, 197, 199

Automatic control, 187; technology of, 190

Balance, method of, 225, 236. *See also* Physical balances system; Prices-value-added system

Balzac, Honoré de, 12

Basarov, 224

Bernoulli, Daniel, 24, 43

Böhm-Bawerk, Eugene von, 76, 77, 318

Cambridge School, 58

Cannan, Edwin, 58

Capital: coefficients, 201, 202, 245, 299; from foreign sources, 180; inputs, time series curves of, 305, 306-7, 308, 309; intensity, 360-64, 366, 369; marginal productivity of, 178; output ratios, 201, 207; productivity of, 175, stock of, 178, 182; transfer of, 200, 203, 210, 215

Capital-labor ratio, 363-64, 367

Cassel, Gustav, 104, 259

Census, German industrial, 265-68

Central Statistical Administration, USSR, 251

Ghenery, H.D., 360

Clapham, Sir John H., 80

Cobweb theorem, 167

Comparison, as a method of scientific inquiry, 19

Competitive mechanisms in economic systems, 238

Comte, Auguste, 10

Concentration: definition of, 261-62; "locational," 262; statistical description of, 265-71; theoretical framework of, 258-61; unit of, 262-67, 268-71

Conglomeration, 261

Consumer: behavior of, 25; choice of, 163

Consumption: levels of, 175; personal, 242; restriction of, in Soviet Union, 225

Costs: in balance table, 253-54; differential transfer, 374, 375-77; freight, 376, 378, 380; terminal, 376, 377, 380; theory of comparative, 373-77

Cournot, Augustin, 24, 29, 43

Dantzig, George B., 232

Darwin, Charles, xi

Definition: implicit, 63; intermediate, 62

Demand: excess-demand functions, 106; excess-demand equations, 107; Marshallian curve, 166

407

Development: possible courses of, 6; theory of, 12; economic, 187, 258
Developing economy, 179, 204. *See also* Growth
Distribution and production, in USSR balance table, 251-57
Dorfman, Robert, 43
Double inversion, method of, 284-91
Douglas, Paul, 37, 44
Duopoly, 29; theory of, 73
Dupuit, E.J., 24
Dynamic: elements in Keynes, 101; stability, 163; theory, 100
Dynamic inverse, 298-325; application of, 304-13; concepts in, 321-22; conversion properties of, 303, 319-21; and investment time lag, 313-14; and price system, 315-18; as solution of open input-output system, 299-303; and technological change, 309-11
Dynamic systems, 12, 15, 32, 201; input-output, 42; stabilities of, 36

Economic units, 265-68, 268n10
Economics: academic, xi-xiv; agricultural, 278-79; critique of, 272-82; as an empirical science, xi, xii, xiii
Edgeworth, Francis Y., 50, 109, 116
Employment: levels of, 102; total, 70
Engels, Friedrich, 75, 79
Ente Nazionale Idrocarburi, 237
Equilibrium: economic, 116; point of, 181; position of a system, 181; stability conditions of, 171; stable/unstable, xiv, 180; state of, 166, 169
Exchange, of present goods for future goods, 176
Expenditures, in USSR balance table, 252
Externalities, environmental. *See* Pollution

Fisher, Erving, 22, 37, 163, 175
Foreign trade, 116
Francis the First, 12
Franklin, Benjamin, 225
Frisch, Ragnar, 43
Functions: internal structure of, 158; separable, 154

Games, theory of, 29, 33
General equilibrium: computations, 244; dynamic system, 245; equations, 29, 240, 242; static system, 245; theory of, xi, 23, 28, 46, 74, 237, 238
Gibbs, J. Willard, 22, 34
Gosplan, 232
Gross National Product. *See* National Product, Gross
Growth, 175, 205, 235; process of economic, 32, 183, 228; projection of economic, 282; rights of long-run economic, 200, 203, 206, 210-15; in Soviet Union, 225

Harberler, G., 136
Hargreaves, James, 188
Harris, Seymour, 93
Hayek, Friedrich A. von, 77
Hecksher-Ohlin, 359-60
Heimann, Eduard, 78
Hicks, J.R., 68, 92
History: as a dynamic process, 12; interpretation of, 4
Homogeneity postulate, in Keynesian system, 88, 91
Hotelling, H., 162
Houthakker, H., 370

Income: national, 18, 39, 180; net, 178; in USSR balance table, 370, 371; as welfare index, 347-48
Index-numbers, 126, 141; commodities, 147
Indices, aggregative, 18
Indifference curves, 116, 128, 177, 179
Inflation, 406
Input coefficients, matrix of. *See* Structural matrix
Input-output analysis, 40, 43, 230, 326; flow tables, 327, 328, 381-82, 400; comparability of flow tables, 283-84; flow tables including pollution, 332, 349-51; reduced flow tables, 285-92; flow tables of U.S. economy, 294-96, 400; flow tables of world economy, 383-85, 396-97; method of aggregation, 283-84, 296-97; method of double inversion, 283-97; as a method for

balancing planned production, 232; notation and concepts, 231-32, 344-46, 355-58; dynamic open system, 299-311; properties of open system, 302-3; inclusion of pollution, 326-46, 349-58; relationships, 25, 35; changes in structure of, 243; substitution of, 244; tables, 231; vectors, 31; of world economy, 381-96. *See also* Capital coefficients; Physical balances system; Prices-value-added system; Structural matrix

Interdisciplinary cooperation, 3-11, 57, 82

Interest, real rate of, 177

International Statistical Institute, 232

International trade, 115, 166; terms of, 117

Investment, 175, 200; expenditures, 242; per unit of output, 190; rate of, 102

Iverson, Kenneth, 42

Kahn, R.F., 67, 68

Kantorovich, L.V., 52, 53, 232, 233

Keynes, John M., 23, 67-71, 79, 87-103, 134, 136; Keynesian revolution, 228

Kondratieff, N.D., 224

Konüs, A.A., 232

Labor: classical supply curve of, 97; comparative efficiency of, 370; inputs, time series curves of, 305, 306-7, 308, 309, 314, 315; intensity, 360-64, 366, 369; requirements per unit of output, 198; skilled and unskilled, 194, 196; supply of, 94; supply curve of, 99; supply function of, 90, 91. *See also* Substitution, capital-labor

Lange, Oskar, 79, 80, 81, 231

LaSalle, Ferdinand, 224

Leisure, 197; utility of, 102

Lenin, V.I., 224, 235

Leontief, Wassily, 44

Linear programming, 25, 33, 54, 230, 244

Liquidify preference, theory of, 99, 100

Malthus, Thomas, R., xi, 73

Marschak, Jacob, 43

Marshall, Aflred, 93, 116

Marx, Carl, 74-83, 103, 188, 223-25, 228, 318, 401-2; on business cycles, 75; Marxian economics, 72; concepts of the "socially necessary labor," 71; labor theory value, 72

Mathematical economics, xii-xiii, 23, 373-74; approach to business cycle analysis, 74

Mattei, Scuola Enrico, 237

Mill, John Stuart, xi, 73, 188, 296

Mitchell, Wesley C., 45, 54, 281

Models, mathematical-economic, xii, xiii, 273-76

Monopoly: discriminatory, 219; theory of, 110-13

Moore, Henry, 37, 44

Morgenstern, Oskar, 43

Morishima, Michio, 317

National accounts, 291, 314-18

National income, 18, 39, 180

National Product, Gross, 201; Growth of, since 1880, 189

Nemchinov, V.S., 233

Neumann, John von, 33

Newton, I., 79

Oligopoly, 29

Opportunity cost, 122, 348, 349, 354

Pareto, Vilfredo, xi, 24, 33, 50, 109, 116, 137

Passow, R., 270n12

Patent rights, 216-22

Patinkin, Don, 104-7

Period analysis, 167-181

Plan, national economic, 398-40, 402-3, 404

Planning, 31, 398-406; allocation of income between consumption and investment, 184; economic, 239; horizon, 184, 246; technique of economic, 225, 237

Physical balance system, 286-88, 299-300, 302, 328-29; 386; including pollution, 331-32; 336-37, 344-45, 349-58, 386-88, 390-92

monetary, 90, 97; technological, 77, 188, 196

United States: input-output system for economy of, 291-96, 304-11; merchandise imports and costs, 376, 379, 380; sector classification table for, 323-24

USSR: balance table for economy of, 251-57; economics in, 223

Utility, 46, 164, 165; dependence of, 164; function, 25; of an independent good, 143; Keynesian function, 96; of leisure, 102; maximizing, 28, 34; measurability of, 143; measure of, 52; theory, 50; under uncertainty, 26

Value added, 291n4, 315, 333. *See also* Prices-value-added system

Variables, 23, 47; breaking down a system within, 151; economic and other, 82; in economic theory, 54; non-priced, 48; separable subsets, 154

Veblen, Thorstein, 45; and Karl Marx, 83

Wages: guaranteed annual, 108-15; money, 90, 94; money in utility function, 96; real, 91, 94, 126, 127; sticky money, 101, theory of, 101; total wage bill, 111

Wald, Abraham, 43, 45

Walras, Léon, xi, 23, 33, 43. Walrasian equilibrium, 33; system, 91. *See also* General equilibrium

Weaver, Warren, 44

Welfare: economics, 113; functions, 27; index of, 347-49

Westfield, Fred M.T., 184

Wilson, Edwin B., 22

Wold, Herman, 164

Work week, shortened, 197

Printed in the United States
by Baker & Taylor Publisher Services